Wiltshire Record Society

(formerly the Records Branch of the Wiltshire
Archaeological and Natural History Society)

VOLUME 76

1864 VISITATION RETURN QUESTIONS

1. What is the name of your parish, and is the benefice a rectory, vicarage or perpetual curacy?
2. State the name and address of the patron or patrons.
3. What is the amount of the population of your parish?
4. What is the name of the incumbent, and the date of his institution and induction.
5. Has he during the last year been resident the time prescribed by law, viz, 275 days?
6. Has he resided in the glebe-house, or where else?
7. If not resident, who is the curate? And is he resident?
8. Does the incumbent possess any other benefice? If so, state in what Diocese or Dioceses?
9. If resident, has he any assistant curate.
10. If he has an assistant curate, when was he licensed?
11. What is his name, is he a priest or deacon.
12. Does the assistant curate perform any other duty as incumbent, curate, lecturer, chaplain, master, or assistant in any school; and where?
13. Does the benefice comprise more than one church or chapel?
14. If so, enumerate them, and give the date of consecration, and the name by which each was called when it was dedicated to God
15. Is your church or chapel in good repair, and duly provided with all things necessary for the decent performance of divine service according to law?
16. Is your churchyard well fenced and well kept?
17. Do your churchwardens regularly discharge their duties?
18. Have any alterations been made in the church or chancel, either as to the fabric or in the manner of fitting up, since my last visitation, and if so, under what authority? Specify what they are.
19. Are baptisms, marriages and burials performed in the chapels (if any) respectively?
20. What is the distance of each chapel from the mother church?
21. What are the sources and amount of the endowments of the benefice?
22. If the benefice is composed of two or more parishes or chapelries, state how much of the annual value, whether from glebe, tithe, rent charge or otherwise arises from each.
23. Is there more than one glebe house of residence on the benefice? If so, where are they respectively situated?
24. What is the Sunday duty in the church and chapels (if any) respectively? Mention the hours appointed for the different services, and whether sermons are preached or lectures given at those services.
25. Do you always say the whole service without omissions?
26. Do you ever catechise publicly in your church? If so, be good enough to state shortly what method you pursue, and what your opinion is as to its advantage.
27. Do you when at home and not otherwise reasonably hindered, say daily the

Morning and Evening Prayers in the parish church or chapel?

28. On what days of the year besides Sundays is there service in the church and chapels (if any) respectively. And what average number of persons attend on those days?

29. Is the Holy Communion administered in your Church and Chapels (if any) on Christmas Day, Easter Day, Ascension Day, Whit Sunday, the Feast of Trinity?

30. On what other days is the Holy Communion administered?

31. Do you keep a list of communicants?

32. What is the number of communicants in your parish?

33. How many of these have not to the best of your knowledge communicated in your church or chapel (if any) during the year ending 31st December 1863?

34. What is the average number of communicants at the great festivals?

35. What is the average number at other seasons?

36. For what number of worshippers at one time is there accommodation in your church or chapels (if any) respectively?

37. What is the average number of your congregation; is it increasing or decreasing?

38. Is there any want of further church accommodation in your parish? If so, in what manner do you think it desirable that this want should be supplied?

39. What number have been baptised, married, buried in the past year?

40. What number of persons have been confirmed in your parish in the years 1861, 1862, 1863.

41. Do you make public for the information of your parishioners any statement of the offerings and collections in your church and chapels (if any)?

42. What has been the amount of the sacramental alms?

43. Is any regular account kept of them in a book set apart for that purpose?

44. What dissenting places of worship are there, and what is the probable number of dissenters in your parish or chapelry, and of what denomination?

45. Is there a daily school in your parish?

46. Have you been able to take advantage of the aid offered by the Committee of Council on Education for the improvement of your school?

47. At what age do the children in your parish ordinarily cease to attend the daily school?

48. Are you able to retain them in your Sunday school after they have ceased to attend the daily school?

49. Have you adopted any other mode of retaining them under instruction by adult or evening schools? And if so, what success have you found to attend such schools?

50. Have you transmitted copies of the parish register for the last year ending the 31st December to the office of the Registrar of the Diocese, at Salisbury?

51. State the different objects for which collections have been made at your church and chapels (if any) during the last year and the sums collected.

52. Can you mention anything which specially impedes your own ministry or the welfare of the church around you? Can you also suggest any remedies?

Signature.

Questions.	Answers.
40. What number of persons have been Confirmed in your parish in the years 1861, 1862, 1863.	My means of knowing are not equal to those of the right rev'd Bishop, who doubtless receives lists.
41. Do you make public for the information of your parishioners any statement of the offerings and collections in your Church and Chapels (if any)?	Yes. orally from the Pulpit, or otherwise
42. What has been the amount of the Sacramental Alms?	An average of Nine shillings each Sacrament.
43. Is any regular account kept of them in a book set apart for that purpose?	Yes — of the amount — and of the distribution.
44. What Dissenting Places of Worship are there, and what is the probable number of Dissenters in your Parish or Chapelry, and of what denomination?	One "Independent" Chapel; rebuilt as Bicentenary. One "Primitive" Do. (The majority of the population attend Church & meeting at their leisure)
45. Is there a Daily School in your Parish?	Yes — and found it work eminently for the advantage of the School — The Revised Code gave our School new life —
46. Have you been able to take advantage of the aid offered by the Committee of Council on Education for the improvement of your School?	
47. At what age do the Children in your Parish ordinarily cease to attend the Daily School?	— About 10 —
48. Are you able to retain them in your Sunday School after they have ceased to attend the Daily School?	In some cases — yes —
49. Have you adopted any other mode of retaining them under instruction by Adult or Evening Schools? And if so, what success have you found to attend such Schools?	I have found night classes for boys, or young men, very useful; almost the only practical instrument of good here, as regards the diffusion of information.
50. Have you transmitted copies of the Parish Register for the last year ending the 31st December to the office of the Registrar of the Diocese, at Salisbury?	— I hope to do so —
51. State the different objects for which collections have been made at your Church and Chapels (if any) during the last year and the sums collected.	— The only object for which I felt inclined to collect was the Infirmary at Salisbury, to which useful charity my Parishioners resort largely.

52. Can you mention anything which specially impedes your own Ministry or the welfare of the Church around you? Can you also suggest any remedies?

Besides the general tendency of English notions to consider extempore prayer and emotional preaching as more proof of "religion" than any Liturgical or organised system, the more "special impediments" to my own ministry, and to the welfare of the Church, have arisen from Episcopal litigation. It would be too stormy, or hardly generous, to describe the whole process as an enforcement of the Theology of hate in the spirit of Titus Oates, it must at least be considered as an introducing the most inappropriate test possible for either literary fact or opinion. It has exhibited a Bishop professing to honour the Bible, yet labouring to close it against this People, pleading "loyalty" to a Protestant Church as an excuse for urging an almost idolatrous materialism as regards the Sacraments; and more than one eminent person, whose fortune was judicial, ...

(Signature) Rowland Williams

Replies by Rowland Williams of Broad Chalke to questions 40-52 of the visitation queries (see pp. 54-5)

RETURNS TO THE BISHOP OF SALISBURY'S VISITATION ENQUIRY

ENQUIRY

1864

edited by

HELEN TAYLOR

CHIPPENHAM

2023

Published on behalf of the Wiltshire Record Society
by The Hobnob Press,
8 Lock Warehouse, Severn Road,
Gloucester GL1 2GA
www.hobnobpress.co.uk

© Wiltshire Record Society, 2023
c/o Wiltshire and Swindon History Centre,
Cocklebury Road, Chippenham SN15 3QN

www.wiltshirerecordsociety.org.uk

ISBN 978–0–901333–53–7

Typeset by John Chandler

CONTENTS

1864 Visitation Return Questions   *ii-iii*
Preface   *ix*

INTRODUCTION   *xi*
   Episcopal Visitation   *xi*
   The Bishop   *xii*
   The Returns   *xiii*
   The Manuscript   *xxvi*
   Editorial Method   *xxvi*
   General Sources and Background Reading   *xxvii*

RETURNS TO THE BISHOP OF SALISBURY'S VISITATION
   ENQUIRY, 1864   I

INDEX OF PERSONS AND PLACES   383

List of officers   395
List of members   395
List of publications   398
1864 Visitation Return Questions   402-3

PREFACE

The Wiltshire Record Society is deeply grateful to the Rt Revd Stephen Lake, Bishop of Salisbury, and the Diocese of Salisbury for their kind permission to publish the documents that form the text of this volume (WSA, D1/56/7). The editor would like to express her grateful thanks for the assistance she has received in the preparation of this volume, particularly regarding the interpretation of the wide range of handwriting in which the returns were completed. In particular, Miss Taylor would like to express her sincere gratitude to Robert Jago, who meticulously checked every transcription and also transcribed some of the more difficult handwriting. Miss Taylor would also like to thank Steven Hobbs and John Chandler, who freely gave their time to assist Robert.

Tom Plant
General Editor

INTRODUCTION

EPISCOPAL VISITATION

The practice of episcopal visitations of English dioceses became widespread in the 13th century, in part to curb monastic abuses, but also to monitor the conduct of the clergy and laity.[1] By the 15th century churchwardens or other laymen were required to report problems of discipline in their parishes,[2] and in the Elizabethan period questionnaires, described as 'articles of inquiry' were issued, and answered by churchwardens' presentments. After the restoration such presentments proliferated, and might be collected into bound volumes, a number of which have been edited and published. In Salisbury diocese presentments for most Wiltshire deaneries survive from 1662, but by 1700 they had become stereotyped and uninformative.[3] They continued until 1885, when they were replaced by printed articles of visitation and enquiry.

   Alongside the presentments submitted by churchwardens developed the practice of questioning the clergy. At his primary visitation in 1783 after his installation as bishop the previous year, Shute Barrington sent a list of twenty queries to the clergy of his diocese, and the Wiltshire returns were edited and published in 1972.[4] Subsequent enquiries, in 1801, 1839 and 1842, have resulted in less detailed and fragmentary returns, but in 1864 and for some later visitations (1867, 1873, 1876, 1879) the responses to a very comprehensive questionnaire have been preserved, and it is the Wiltshire returns of the earliest of these, for 1864, that is transcribed and edited in this volume.[5]

   When Barrington was bishop Salisbury diocese comprised all Wiltshire and Berkshire, and some Dorset parishes which were peculiars.

1   D.M Owen, *Records of the Established Church in England* (1970), 30-5.
2   Records of visitation proceedings of his peculiars by the dean of Salisbury, John Chandler, in 1405, 1408-9 and 1412, have survived, and have been published: T.C.B. Timmins (ed.), *The Register of John Chandler, Dean of Salisbury, 1404-17*, (Wiltshire Record Soc. vol. 39, 1984), 1-50, 72-129.
3   P. Stewart, *Diocese of Salisbury: guide to the records . . .* (1973), 43-9.
4   M. Ransome (ed.), *Wiltshire Returns to the Bishop's Visitation Queries 1783* (Wiltshire Record Soc. vol. 27, 1972).
5   Stewart, *op. cit.*, 49-50.

The published edition of the 1783 visitation returns covered the whole of Wiltshire. In 1837 Cricklade and Malmesbury deaneries, comprising much of north Wiltshire, were transferred to the diocese of Gloucester and Bristol. The 1864 visitation of Salisbury diocese, therefore, does not consider them, and this volume covers only the Wiltshire parishes that remained in Salisbury diocese after 1837. No equivalent visitation returns exist for this period among the records of the Gloucester and Bristol diocese or its successors.

THE BISHOP

Walter Kerr Hamilton was born in 1808, the eldest son of Anthony Hamilton, archdeacon of Taunton and prebendary of Lichfield.[1] His early childhood was spent at Loughton in Essex, where his father was rector. He was educated privately, then at Eton; later he was a private pupil to Dr Thomas Arnold of Rugby. Hamilton was deeply influenced by Arnold but did not share his theological views. He later went to Oxford, where he met Edward Denison, who was to become bishop of Salisbury. Hamilton was ordained in 1833 and his second curacy in 1834 took him to St Peter's-in-the-East, Oxford, where Denison was vicar. He took over as vicar of the parish in 1837 when Denison was promoted to the see of Salisbury. He was an indefatigable parish priest, and an earnest evangelical preacher.

Hamilton's theological beliefs underwent a great change in the 1830s. In 1833 a sermon by John Keble saw the beginning of the Oxford Movement, which sought to restore the High Church ideals of the 17th century, and Hamilton was one of its early followers, labelled Tractarians from the theological tracts that the movement published 1833-41. Hamilton, an evangelical early in his career, came under the influence of John Henry Newman during the late 1830s, while at Oxford, and became, in his own words, a High Churchman. In 1837 he was made examining chaplain to the bishop of Salisbury and in 1841 left Oxford with some reluctance to

---

1 Biographical information from H.P. Liddon, *Walter Kerr Hamilton: Bishop of Salisbury* (Rivingtons, 1869); W. A. Greenhill, revised by H. C. G. Matthew, 'Hamilton, Walter Kerr, *Oxford Dictionary of National Biography*, online edition (accessed 10 Nov. 2023). In the following discussion much information about Hamilton's career and policies as bishop is derived also from *VCH Wilts*, vol. III (1956), 65-71.

become a canon in Salisbury Cathedral.

In 1854 Hamilton succeeded Bishop Denison, who had recommended him as his successor. Hamilton continued all his predecessor's episcopal reforms and improved upon them. He increased the number of confirmations, and raised the standard in his ordinations, both of theological attainments and also of spiritual preparation. The idea of establishing at Salisbury a theological college had been suggested to him by his predecessor in 1841, but it was 20 years later that the plan became a reality.

Constant residence was very important to Hamilton, and he declined the rectory of Loughton when it was offered to him on his father's death. He was never absent from Salisbury except on diocesan business, or for a short holiday in the autumn. He was a hard-working bishop, greatly respected and liked by both clergy and laity, even those who did not share his high church opinions. It is probable that hard work coupled with anxiety shortened his life, and the first signs of heart disease appeared in 1868; Hamilton died the following year. He was married in 1845 and his wife Isabel survived him with eight of their children.

THE RETURNS

The 1864 returns edited here were not therefore the consequence of Hamilton's primary visitation, but fell quite late in his tenure as bishop. In fact he delivered episcopal charges in 1855, 1858, 1861, 1864 and 1867 and these, along with the visitation queries in 1864, give a clear indication as to the subjects that mattered to him.

The printed form of articles of enquiry sent to all incumbents in 1864 comprised no fewer than 52 questions (reproduced at the beginning and end of this volume).[1] They covered many aspects of parish life, including the clergy and their patrons, church buildings, services, dissent, education and charities, concluding with a catch-all opportunity for the parson or his curate to mention anything impeding his ministry or church welfare, and to suggest remedies.

Patronage

Although there was no question in 1783 relating to patronage, the editor's introduction makes a brief reference to the influence of the Earl of Pembroke, who was the most important lay patron in Wiltshire and

1   The 1783 visitation asked only 20 questions, although most were in more than one part.

held 10 livings. In 1867 he was patron of 11 livings.[1] Almost half of the Wiltshire livings were held by the church. There were 41 in the hands of individual clergy, 24 by various deans and 6 by the bishop of Winchester. The bishop of Salisbury held 43, in contrast to the 20 he held in 1783. Bishops in the 19th century were increasing their patronage in order to reward hard-working curates who had neither the means nor the contacts to promote themselves.

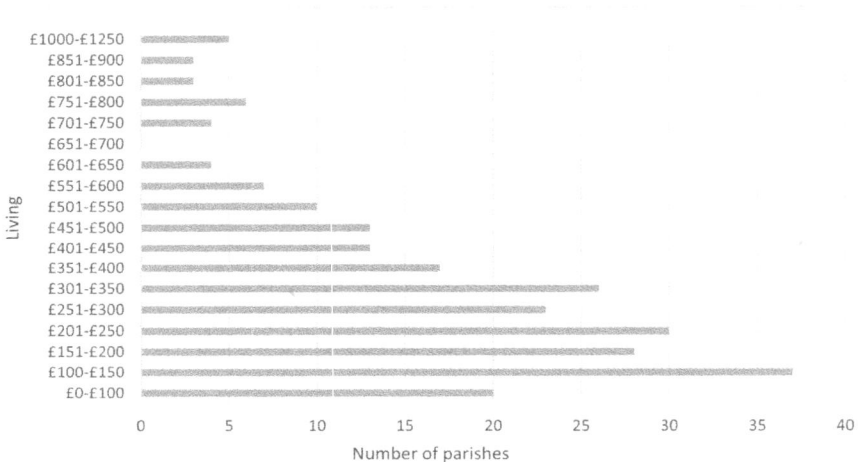

The Clergy

By the 1820s the Church was in crisis. Attacks were mounted on its corruption, nepotism, income from livings to which no spiritual duties were attached and other financial abuses. The most notorious defect of the 18th-century church was pluralism, and the non-residence which resulted from it. Many livings were extremely poor. In Wiltshire at the close of the 17th century the average annual income was £80, not very far above the poverty line figure of £50.[2] Queen Anne's Bounty, a fund created in 1704 to augment the livings of the poorer Anglican clergy, in 1783 assisted a number of very poor livings in Wiltshire; over a hundred were probably worth less than £100. By the early 19th century £150 was considered the lowest salary acceptable for a reasonable standard of living. Clergy income in Salisbury diocese in 1867 ranged from a mere

1   Information derived from *Kelly's Directory of Wiltshire* (1867 edn.).
2   R. Strong, *A Little History of the English Country Church* (2008), 175.

£22 at Ansty to £1,250 at Pewsey, with the majority of clergy earning between £100 and £350.

Another reason for non-residence was accommodation. Some parishes did not have a parsonage house, and in others it was not fit for habitation. Both the 1783 queries and those for 1864 included questions about the incumbent's residence; whether or not he resided on his cure and whether he was in possession of any other benefice. Of the 232 parishes making returns in 1783, only 90 were served by a resident incumbent, but 39 more were served by a resident curate. In 1840, 39 incumbents were non-resident by licence in the Wiltshire parishes in the Salisbury diocese.[1]

In his 1858 charge Bishop Hamilton noted 62 parishes in the Salisbury diocese without a resident incumbent. Of these 27 held other benefices in the diocese, 13 had benefices in other dioceses, 9 parishes had no residence and 6 clergy were suffering from ill-health. The pluralism problem took decades to solve, as once an incumbent was appointed, he was immovable until death. The Pluralities Act of 1838 laid down that no cleric could hold more than two benefices, which should not be more than ten miles apart, and that their joint value was not to exceed £1,000 per year. In 1850 the distance was narrowed down to three miles and the income of one of the benefices was not to exceed £100 per annum.

In a number of benefices the incumbent in 1864 had been appointed before 1838. Benjamin Pope was appointed vicar of Nether Stowey (Somerset) in 1824. Two years later, he was also appointed vicar of Ogbourne St George; both livings were in the gift of the Dean and Canons of Windsor. In 1868 the Somerset living was worth £480 and the Wiltshire living £270; both had houses. Rushall had been held by Sir Erasmus Williams, who was living in St David's, since 1829. In 1868 it was worth £400. William Tomlinson was appointed to two livings in 1837; the rectory of Sherfield English (Hampshire) and the vicarage of neighbouring Whiteparish in Wiltshire. In 1864 the curate in his visitation return declared that the vicar resided at Brighton and Nice! William Raymond presented himself to the rectory of Stockton-on-Teme (Worcs.) in 1834; the following year he also obtained the vicarage of Wilsford cum Manningford Bohune in Wiltshire. By 1868 the livings were worth £250 apiece.

The majority of the clergy were Oxford or Cambridge graduates. The 1867 directory records 134 from Oxford, 84 from Cambridge, one

1   *VCH Wilts*, vol. III (1956), 64.

from Dublin and just 29 without a degree. The Oxford and Cambridge alumni entries, plus the censuses, are a good indication as to individual circumstances. William Swayne at Whiteparish was the son of a Bristol gentleman. The 1871 census shows that he was living in the vicarage with his wife and five children, plus a governess, a nurse and a housemaid. He was content to stay at Whiteparish for 14 years, moving on in 1874 to become vicar at Chitterne. By contrast, Joseph Holden Johnson, son of the vicar at Tilshead, remained a curate all his life. His first three posts were in Lancashire before returning to his home county in 1863. He had three curacies in Wiltshire, at Berwick St Leonard, Winterbourne Stoke and Donhead St Mary. He never married and always lived in lodgings. Joseph died in 1893 at the age of 69 when he was lodging in Berwick St John and apparently retired.

In more recent times it became customary for an incumbent to move on after about ten years. The bishops were anxious for both clergy and laity regularly to have a change. This was not the case in the 19th century, when it was quite possible for a man to spend his entire adult life in one parish. It was very difficult to obtain a living and almost impossible without money and connections. Once instituted, a clergyman was immovable; pensions were non-existent, and the poorer clergy stayed in post long after they were physically capable of working, because they could not afford to retire. Instead, they would hire a curate at a salary of their choice. The Wiltshire clergy in 1864 was a fascinating mix. Some were fortunate to hold one of the better livings in the diocese and led active and successful lives. Others were not so fortunate, but worked quietly in their own parish, grateful to be in a post with a guaranteed income, however small.

Bishop Hamilton, in his 1867 charge, paid tribute to Canon John Guthrie, who had died in 1865. Guthrie was appointed vicar of Calne in 1835 and served his community for 30 years. The tributes to him in the *Devizes & Wiltshire Gazette* described a kind and generous man who was much respected. Calne was one of the most valuable livings in the bishop's patronage and Guthrie gave liberally. St Mary's was rebuilt in 1863 with a generous donation and Holy Trinity was built entirely at his own expense in 1852.

In 1861 Bishop Hamilton had a serious theological disagreement with Rowland Williams, the vicar at Broad Chalke, resulting in the bishop prosecuting Williams for heresy. The previous year Williams had contributed an article dealing with Biblical criticism to *Essays and Reviews*, a collection of essays by seven authors who believed that recent scientific advances rightly encouraged Biblical criticism. Hamilton discussed this subject at length in his 1861 charge. The Court of Arches sentenced Williams to one year's suspension, but this was overturned by the Privy Council in 1864. The bishop was convinced that he had been right to prosecute, albeit with some reluctance. Williams lived the remainder of his life quietly at Broad Chalke. He died in 1870, aged 52 years, following a brief illness. His funeral report said that 'the deceased had endeared himself to his parishioners of all religious denominations by his many acts of liberality and benevolence'.

Richard Chermside was the hard-working rector of Wilton, devoted to his community. He arrived in 1848, but died in 1867 at the age of just 44; according to the death certificate, the causes were diabetes and nervous exhaustion. The report in the *Salisbury Journal* refers to 'our revered and lamented rector'. On the day of the funeral, which was conducted by the bishop, the shops in Wilton were closed and all business was suspended during the funeral. The rector had been the chaplain to the 14th (Wilton) Wilts Rifle Volunteer Corps; a member of the Corporation of Wilton; a member of the Wilton Local Board of Health; and president of the Wilton Literary and Scientific Institution.

Harry Lee was the vicar of North Bradley from 1832 until 1880, when he died at the age of 84. The last marriage at which he was the celebrant was in 1869, after which he left all his parish work in the hands of a steady stream of curates. In 1864 he complained that 'my curate has left very unceremoniously'. At the taking of the 1871 census, Lee was living very comfortably in Winchester with his wife, looked after by nine servants, including a butler, ladies' maid, coachman and footman.

By contrast there were many clergy living on a small income. In 1867 there were still 51 parishes in the Wiltshire part of the Salisbury diocese worth less than £150 (the lowest income considered necessary for a reasonable standard of living). David Llewellyn was the perpetual curate at Easton Royal from 1839 until his death in 1868 at the age of 75. In the 1864 return he said that he had 'no reason to complain' of the salary paid to him by the Marquess of Ailesbury, which according to Crockford's was £120.

William Dyer was perpetual curate at Imber, 1841–1865; this living was worth £124. Marrying later in life he had no children and lived with his wife and two servants in this remote village. Hamilton's predecessor, Bishop Denison, had expressed concern about the remoteness of some of his parishes. Dyer was an Oxford graduate with an M.A. but he had little scope for intellectual stimulation in Imber. Was this an example of a man without money and social connections, who felt he had no choice but to remain at Imber? Many of the more affluent clergy had the time to pursue their interests, in particular history and archaeology. The membership list for the Wiltshire Archaeological and Natural History Society around this time includes 106 clergy, out of a total membership of 387.[1] One example was Alfred Charles Smith, who became rector of Yatesbury in 1852. The following year he helped to inaugurate the Society and shared the role of general secretary with Canon Jackson. He was the author of numerous books, including *The Birds of Wiltshire* which was published in 1887.[2] In the preface he refers to an illness resulting in a six-month absence from his parish, which enabled him to devote more time to his writing. The Yatesbury return was completed by a recently appointed curate and most of the questions are blank.

Lastly, there would have been a sprinkling of 'characters' among the clergy. Francis Hutchinson was instituted as vicar at Tisbury in 1858, where he remained until his retirement in 1915. He and his wife were both wealthy individuals and, having no children, they generously improved the church, built schools and school houses and also a new vicarage. As a young man Hutchinson was a great athlete, and various stories have been passed down the generations. On one occasion he was walking from Salisbury back home to Tisbury. A Tisbury resident passed by on his horse and trap and offered the vicar a lift. Hutchinson politely declined, saying he was in a hurry to get home. He walked and ran, getting home much sooner than the trap![3] There is a description of him regularly running to church, coat-tails flying and always wearing a shovel hat on his head.[4]

Curates

There were approximately 100 curates working in the Wiltshire part of the Salisbury diocese in 1864. Some were running a parish on their own while others were assisting their incumbent. Curates' pay and standard of living were the subject of national debate in the early 19th century. The Curates' Act 1813 laid down a minimum stipend of £80 to be paid to a resident curate, with or without the consent of the incumbent.

The Pluralities Act 1838 set a curate's stipend in a parish where the incumbent was non-resident at approximately £80 to £100 for a small country village, £120 for a population of 500, rising to £150 for

---

1   Appendix to *WAM*, vol. 7 (no. 21), October 1862.
2   M. Darby, 'WANHS and Natural History', in J.H. Thomas (ed.), *WANHS: the First 150 Years* (2003), 209-12.
3   E. Miles, Tisbury Past and Present (2nd ed. 1920), 74.
4   J. and P. Drury, A Tisbury History (1980), 54.

a population of over 1000. Benefices of more than 2000 souls were to be served by two curates. Unfortunately for the curates, this law did not apply to parishes where the incumbent was resident and could pay what he pleased. In 1838, nationally there were 3,078 curates serving non-residents; by 1864 this number had reduced to 955. This competition for curacies resulted in many men accepting salaries of £50 or even less. In contrast, as early as the 1830s a butler could earn £70 and an elementary schoolmaster £150.[1]

This subject was of great concern to Bishop Hamilton who included it in his 1864 Charge: 'there are, I am sorry to say, many cases in my Diocese which urgently require augmentation'. Queen Anne's Bounty had been in existence since 1704, assisted by the Ecclesiastical Commissioners from 1835. Hamilton noted 180 benefices whose average annual gross income was below £119. It was necessary to set up a local fund in order to take advantage of any help provided by the Commissioners and Hamilton set up a Poor Benefice Augmentation Fund in November 1862. He issued a Pastoral Letter in 1863 and the following year his Charge recorded 264 collections across the diocese that raised £745.

The social circumstances of a curate varied greatly, ranging from those with a good background who had private means to men who came from a poor background and often led poverty-stricken lives. The 1864 return makes few mentions of curates' salaries. The curate at Tisbury was paid £40, while at Bower Chalke the income of £100 was 'absorbed by curate and other charges.' At Bulkington, the curate John Tandy was paid £50, but he was able to supplement his income as a master at the grammar school in Devizes.

Services
The 1783 return had four questions relating to services. The bishop asked how many services were held on a Sunday and at what time; how many weekday services; how many communion services and the number of communicants. Hamilton's questions were far more detailed and included the provision of daily prayers, the average number of communicants at festivals and ordinary services, the average size of the congregation and whether or not the church was large enough.

The canons of 1604 decreed that every church should provide two services every Sunday, but only about 40% of the 1783 returns met this requirement. The minimum requirement in terms of Holy Communion

1   Hart, A Tindal, *The Curate's Lot* (1970), 136-7.

was that it should be celebrated at least three times a year, preferably four. About 73% of the returns show at least four, if not more, celebrations a year, which was a good figure for a predominantly rural area.

In 1864 only thirteen returns were from parishes not offering two services every Sunday.[1] The incumbent at Swallowcliffe also looked after Ansty; the residents at Ansty were mostly employed by Lord Arundell of Wardour and were consequently Roman Catholic. The Ansty farmers were all Catholic; no church rates could be levied and there were no churchwardens. The rector at Fifield Bavant (population 33) was also perpetual curate at Ebbesbourne Wake. He had no curate and took three services every Sunday, two at Ebbesbourne and one at Fifield. Berwick St James had a population of 290 and a church that could accommodate 150 people, but its income was only £77. Consequently, it was joined with neighbouring Winterbourne Stoke and was another example of one vicar holding three services. Berwick St Leonard and Great Chalfield were other examples of tiny populations, and were joined with Sedgehill and Atworth respectively. At Pertwood there were just 28 residents, but it had its own rector, who lived at Chicklade. The church was in good repair, held about 50 people and the average congregation was said to be 40. However, the people were all employed by the one farmer and the rector could only hold services on Sundays, Good Friday and Christmas Day. He hoped to persuade the farmer to give time during Lent for more services.

Fewer than 20% of the clergy replied positively to the question about catechising, the majority of the answers being a simple 'no'. This is in great contrast to the 1783 return, where just over 70% of the parishes attempted catechising, mostly in Lent. In 1864, of those that said yes, Lent was still the most popular time. The rector at Berwick St John was not the only one to mention that it was not popular and discouraged some parishioners from attending church on that day. The rector at Chilmark cited the longer service as a particular reason for non-attendance. The incumbent at Dilton Marsh declared that 'with George Herbert I value "Catechising" highly as calculated to infuse a competent knowledge of salvation in every one of my parishioners'. The Chilton Foliat rector's reply was 'it is in my judgement a very important and effective method of instruction' while the vicar at Broad Chalke grudgingly admitted 'probably, it does more good than harm'. At North Tidworth and Studley the complexity of the catechism seems to have been beyond the children.

1   Ansty, Berwick St James, Berwick St Leonard, Blackland, Buttermere, Calstone Wellington, East Grimstead, Fifield Bavant, Great Chalfield, Highway, Pertwood, Rollestone and Swallowcliffe.

There was both difficulty in teaching children who left school very young and in encouraging them to answer questions.

The next question in the return related to daily prayers in church and fewer than 15% offered these. The incumbent at Bulford spoke for most of his colleagues when he replied that because 'men, women and children being all employed in farm labour from sunrise to sunset', they were prevented from attending daily prayers. In contrast, the rector at Chilmark was content to offer daily morning prayer to his family, three or four others and six schoolchildren. The rector at Rushall was genuinely disappointed he could not get a congregation and seemed to think it was his fault, saying 'I am sorry my services have been a failure'.

Hamilton urged his clergy to increase the frequency of Holy Communion. Of the 263 churches mentioned in the returns, 161 were offering a communion service at least once a month. The remaining 102 celebrated between four and eight times a year, the only exception being Heywood, where communion was celebrated at Christmas, Easter and Whit Sunday. Approximately a third of the population here supported the Independent chapel. In terms of numbers attending communion, the pattern in general was very low, often below 10%.

The figures attending morning and evening prayer were more encouraging. Although the figures are not able to take into account the amount of church accommodation, or the inevitable competition from the chapels, a good number of the clergy declared that between 20% and 40% of the population were attending church every Sunday. The vicar at Norton Bavant attributed the rise to the 'novelty of a newly appointed vicar', while at Sutton Mandeville the rector acknowledged that his congregation had increased since the church had been restored. Music was a new attraction. At Rushall the previous incumbent had been forced to abandon his choral service, as he was drawing worshippers away from neighbouring churches. At Upton Lovell, where the church had space for 200 people, the rector was pleased to say that his church was full every Sunday evening; a new organ had been installed and the services were choral using the Salisbury Hymn Book.

The larger towns would expect to draw a large congregation, but Trowbridge, for example, had seven chapels. In terms of population, Salisbury was the largest community. Salisbury St Edmund attracted a congregation of approximately 500 and at St Thomas's it was 900. The largest congregation was at Warminster St Denys. Here, there were 1,100 at the morning service, 500 in the afternoon and 1,400 (a full church) in the evening.

By contrast, the vicar at Westbury was unable to estimate his congregation. Here, a good number of pews were 'appropriated', preventing the poor from using them: 'Much room is lost in my church through the operation of the 'pew system' which works as injuriously here as in any parish that I have known'. The church at Aldbourne had 466 private sittings and only 264 free. The vicar complained about 'illegal claims to seats in the church' and wanted the whole church to be re-seated, to enable all his parishioners to attend. The rector at Pewsey reported that the poor were 'almost excluded from this parish church' as the 'wealthy farmers are not disposed to waive their (imaginary) rights for the convenience of their less prosperous brethren'.

An alternative point of view was that pew rents were a source of much needed income. The incumbent at Road Hill was pleased that the rents had increased fourfold since 1851, 'showing that the church has made great progress'.

Dissent

When asked in the return what challenges they faced, the answer most often given by the clergy was 'dissent'. A large proportion of the towns and villages in Wiltshire offered an alternative form of worship. In some places the chapel congregation greatly outnumbered that of the church; in others, the parishioners divided their loyalty between both. There were a number of reasons why a chapel could attract a large congregation. Nonconformity was deep-rooted in some places, such as Trowbridge, Bratton and North Bradley, where chapels had been established since the 18th century.

At Mere and East Knoyle, the Anglican clergy were unable to compete with the chapels provided by Charles Jupe, a wealthy silk manufacturer who employed between 500 and 600 people. At Mere it was estimated that 1,400 people were nonconformists, a little over half the population, while at East Knoyle the rector complained of the 'enormous sum expended in support of the Independent establishment in the village'.

At Downton, where Richard Payne had been the vicar since 1841, there were six chapels supported by approximately 20% of the population. The Baptist chapel is said to have been founded in 1666 and had the largest support. The Baptist chapel at North Bradley was built in 1779. In 1851 the average Sunday evening congregation was 240, and there were 135 Sunday School pupils. The average congregation at the parish church in 1864 was 150. The vicar chose to ignore completely the question relating to non-conformity when completing his return.

The small parish of Ebbesbourne Wake was in the care of the rector at Fifield Bavant. Here two-thirds of the population supported the Independent chapel while the average church congregation was only 40. The incumbent stated that 'nothing can be done until there is a resident clergyman in the village, the neglect of the church having confirmed the people in dissent'.

Homington was one of many examples of the population supporting both church and chapel. A Primitive Methodist chapel had been founded in 1841. The incumbent stated that 'nearly all who come to the church in the morning go to the chapel in the evening'. Not all churches were offering an evening service and the chapels were able to benefit from this. People were looking for somewhere to go for company on a Sunday evening and the chapel provided this. Occasionally the attraction was simply that the chapel was warmer! At Martin, the incumbent blamed the large non-conformist congregations on the lack of stoves in the church.

Schools

In 1783 Bishop Barrington included a question about schools. He wanted to know if there was a public or charity school, how it was funded, how many children attended, what they were taught and did the lessons include religious instruction, what happened to the children when they left school and was the school generally successful. Education for all children was important to Bishop Hamilton and he made reference to it in his Charges. In 1858 he acknowledged the difficulties caused by children being taken out of school at a very young age to go to work, but that this could be counteracted by making sure the teaching they received was of a good standard. He also emphasised the importance of the Sunday and evening schools to continue children's education. Boys generally left school at the age of about 10, although 8 was not unusual, while at Winterbourne Bassett few boys remained beyond the age of 5. The rector at Newton Tony declared a lack of education to be of great concern and he wished for an Act of Parliament preventing the employment of children under 12.

Hamilton's predecessor Bishop Denison had founded in 1838 a Diocesan Board of Education, in unison with the National Society, to encourage the education of the poor. Two teacher training colleges were established, for men at Winchester and for women at Salisbury. The Salisbury college opened in 1841 and by 1854 had trained 243 pupils and

41 serving teachers at a cost of £8,000.[1] The Board organised a system of diocesan inspectors who visited most schools annually and reported their findings to the bishop.

Most parishes offered a Sunday school, but not all held an evening school. Children would usually stay at the Sunday school until they were confirmed, which was approximately 15 years. After that, the aim of the night school was to keep them at least until their late teens. Most replies to the question about evening schools are very brief, but some give more detail. Most schools were only for the boys; only eight replies mention girls. The school was usually offered three times a week during the winter months; the session lasted 1½ hours which was divided equally between reading, writing and 'summary'. At Rushall the curate declared his night school to be 'the most cheering part of my ministerial labours'. The vicar at Tisbury was not alone in believing that the night school kept the children 'in communication with the clergyman' and helped to promote 'that self respect and carefulness of conduct which keeps them out of scrapes.' The influence he obtained over them was so great that they would do almost anything he asked of them. The night school offered at Warminster St Denys was three nights a week for six months and the average attendance was 96. At Burcombe the incumbent had students in their late 20s, but he needed to provide other inducements to encourage their attendance, music being the most popular. The vicar at Damerham was pleased that eight of his students had presented themselves for examination and all passed. At Barford St Martin the rector believed evening schools to be a 'very efficient means of retaining a hold on lads after the age of 16 and of bringing them forward for confirmation'. He attributed the high number of male catechumens to the success of the evening school, as it enabled him to get to know the young men. In complete contrast, the vicar at Ogbourne St Andrew was unable to hold an evening school, as no one was interested in attending. This was probably because the children left school at 8 years and did not regularly attend Sunday school. The Rev. Hutchinson at Tisbury was convinced that all boys should attend an evening school from the age of 10, 'otherwise they will never take to work.'

Some parishes had both daily and Sunday schools that were run by the nonconformists, as well as those run by the church of England. The incumbent at West Grimstead was very disappointed that the Wesleyan school he thought had closed down, was re-opened. The rector at Heddington reported that too many children were attending the Wesleyan

1   *VCH Wilts*, vol. III (1956), 65.

Sunday school. He countered this by insisting that all children who attended the day school must also attend his Sunday school.

Charitable collections
In 1783 there was one question relating to money collected at communion services, which on average was four times a year. Half of the returns stated that no collections were ever made, the usual reason being that the congregation were too poor. In 1864 there were two questions, as collections were made for specific charitable purposes as well as the sacramental alms. The bishop expressed disappointment in his 1864 Charge as to the number of parishes who did not respond to his pastoral letters. In 1862 he asked for collections to be made for foreign missions and Lancashire distress; in 1863 for the poor benefices fund. He referred to the excuses made by his clergy, none of which he was prepared to accept. To those who did not like to ask for money, the clergy should say to their parishioners that they were only following the bishop's instructions. Others said that they gave priority to their own local charities; the bishop's reply was that supporting diocesan charities would help their own. Lastly, some clergy said that their people were too poor to give, but the bishop replied that every gift, however small, would be gratefully received.

The returns show that a total of 15 different charities were supported. The most frequent were the Poor Benefice Augmentation Fund, Society for the Propagation of the Gospel, Lancashire distress, Church Missionary Society, Diocesan Church Building Society (founded by Denison in 1837), Sarum Church Union Society (founded by Bishop Burgess) and the Jews' Society. Some of the clergy collected for hospitals in Bath and Salisbury, where their parishioners had been treated.

The Final Question, 52
The final question in the return is often the most interesting, as the clergy were here given the opportunity to mention any subject that troubled them, plus an invitation to offer a solution. Apart from dissent, one of the most common causes of complaint related to alcohol. At Chirton 'drunkenness prevails to a lamentable extent, and is, in fact, the crying sin of the parish.' At Marlborough St Peter, the rector hoped that a working man's hall 'may lead to an improvement of the moral and religious habits of the people'. The incumbent at Bishopstone suggested that more frequent holidays might help, also better living conditions for the poor.

Other clergy complained about bad behaviour in general and the lack of parental control. The vicar at North Newnton mentioned 'the over indulgence of parents in allowing the young people to do as they like after the age of 12' while the incumbent at Broad Town talked of 'dreadful laxity of the prevailing opinion and habits as to the relations of the sexes'.

The bishop was no doubt relieved that some of his clergy had something positive to say. The vicar at Figheldean attempted to counteract dissent by making his services more attractive by offering music. He also ran a parish library that was supported by the Society for the Promotion of Christian Knowledge (S.P.C.K.) and was very popular with the poor.

At Pitton and Farley the vicar was generous in his comments about his two hard-working curates. The rector at Orcheston St George, who had been in post since 1830, was fortunate to 'have every encouragement and no impediment whatever!' Finally, the closing comment comes from Samuel Ward, rector at Teffont Evias since 1830: 'I have nothing to complain of. My people attend church regularly and are a well conducted, civil, sober people.'

THE MANUSCRIPT

The bound volume of the 1864 visitation returns is one of the largest books in the Wiltshire and Swindon Archives (WSA, D1/56/7). It measures 44cm x 30cm x 10cm and weighs 10kg. Each parish return consists of three printed pages containing a total of 52 questions. The bishop's letter is printed at the top of page one.

As was the case in 1783, the handwriting varies greatly. Each writer had developed his own individual style; some are clear and easy to read, others are a challenge. Where the handwriting is large, some had difficulty squeezing a particular reply into the space allotted. The amount of content also varies. Some returns contain the bare minimum and would have been of limited value to the bishop. Many clergy took the trouble to answer to the best of their ability and these are the more informative and interesting returns, especially when in answer to question 52 they expressed opinions and suggestions.

EDITORIAL METHOD

This edition attempts to offer a complete and faithful transcript of the returns, with the following exceptions. Questions are often answered in note form, rather than structured sentences, and punctuation has occasionally been added to improve the flow. Some words, in particular the time of day, can be written in various forms and these have been standardised throughout. For question 29, which relates to the days that Holy Communion was celebrated, the convention used in the edition of the 1783 return has been adopted, using lower case letters to indicate each of the five occasions. Excessive capitalisation of words by respondents has not been retained. Where the incumbent has not answered a question, this is indicated as [Blank].

GENERAL SOURCES & BACKGROUND READING

Anon, *Reverend Rowland Williams*

Antrobus, A, *History of the Wilts & East Somerset Congregational Union*, Independent Press Ltd, 1947

Bettey, J H, *Church & Community*, Moonraker Press, 1979

Brown, C.K. Francis, *A History of the English Clergy 1800-1900*, The Faith Press Ltd, 1953

Brown, C.K. Francis, *The Church's part in Education 1833-1941*, National Society & S.P.C.K., 1942

Doel, W, *Twenty Golden Candlesticks*, B. Lansdown & Son, 1890. Reprinted Wiltshire County Council Libraries & Heritage, 2005

Drury, J & P, *A Tisbury History*, Element Books Ltd, 1980

Haig, A, *The Victorian Clergy*, Croom Helm Ltd, 1984

Hart, A Tindal, *The Country Priest in English History,* Phoenix House Ltd, 1959

Hart, A Tindal, *The Curate's Lot*, John Baker Ltd, 1970

Hart, A Tindal, *The Nineteenth Century Country Parson*, Wilding & Son Ltd, 1954

Holden, J, *Wiltshire Nonconformist Chapels & Meeting Houses*, Hobnob Press, 2022

Horn, P, *Labouring Life in the Victorian Countryside*, Alan Sutton, 1976

Knight, F, *The Nineteenth Century Church & English Society*, Cambridge University Press, 1995

Lee. R, *Rural Society & the Anglican Clergy 1815-1915 Encountering & Managing the Poor*, Boydell & Brewer Ltd, 2006

Liddon, H P, *Walter Kerr Hamilton: Bishop of Salisbury*, Rivingtons, 1869

McLeod, H, *Religion & Society in England 1850-1914*, Macmillan Press Ltd, 1996

Strong, R, *A Little History of the English Country Church*, Jonathan Cape, 2007

Tonks, W.C., *Victory in the villages: the history of the Brinkworth circuit*, William Wilcox, 1907

RETURNS TO THE BISHOP OF SALISBURY'S VISITATION ENQUIRY, 1864

1. ALDBOURNE   D. Marlborough

1. Aldbourne – a vicarage.
2. The Lord Bishop of the Diocese – Palace Salisbury.
3. 1539.
4. George Parker Cleather – Nov 5th 1852.
5. Yes.
6. In the glebe house.
7. [Blank]
8. No.
9. He has an assistant curate.
10. March 1st 1863.
11. Edward Burbidge – A priest.
12. No.
13. One church and one chapel.
14. Woodsend school chapel – not consecrated, but licensed.
15. Requires a thorough restoration.
16. Yes.
17. Yes.
18. None.
19. Only baptisms.
20. 3 miles.
21. Tithe rent charge £224.6s.7½d. Glebe £417.10s.0d.
22. Pension from the rectory of Aldbourne £2.0s.0d. Total £643.16s.7½d.
23. No.
24. In the church- morning service at 11.15am – afternoon at 3.00pm – sermons at both services. At the chapel morning and afternoon service alternately – at 10.30 am and 3.00pm with a sermon.
25. Yes.
26. No.
27. No.
28. Every Friday evening with sermon during Advent. Every Wednesday morning during Lent, and evening with sermon – this latter service is continued until the end of May – every day in Holy Week, and on Ascension Day. The average attendance is 30. Every Wednesday evening with sermon during Lent at the chapel – also on Good Friday and Christmas Day.
29. [a] Yes [b] Yes [c] No [d] Yes [e] No.
30. The 1st Sunday in each month at the parish church and the last Sunday in each month at the chapel.
31. No – but I know every individual.
32. 101.
33. All have attended at different times – excepting those who are confined to the house by infirmity to whom I administer the Holy Com at stated times.

34. 50.

35. 35.

36. The following return was made to the Bishop of Sarum July 11th 1842. Free sittings 264. Private sittings 466. This return includes the hideous galleries.

37. 400 – stationary.

38. No.

39. 58 baptisms 7 marriages 39 burials.

40. 47.

41. The churchwardens are always informed of the amount of collections – but not of the amount of the offertory.

42. £23.7s.6½d.

43. Yes. There are two books – in one is entered the amount rec'd at each offertory, in the other the expenditure.

44. Three – namely Wesleyans and Primitive Methodist and Baptists.

45. Yes.

46. Yes.

47. The boys at 8 yrs the girls at 10 yrs. These ages apply to the very poor – others remain somewhat beyond these ages.

48. [Blank]

49. By an evening school, which has been more numerously attended, and with greater success than in any former year.

50. Yes.

51. For the improvement of small benefices in this diocese – collected - £4.8s.3d.

52. The prevalence of dissent. The willow trade, which is increasing, and keeps away many children from the daily school. The illegal claims to seats in the church, whereby many are deterred from attending the services of the church, who would be present if they felt certain of not being disturbed. The church requires to be re-seated, and an entirely new appropriation of the seats. I have every reason to think and believe that the number of worshippers would be increased if this were affected.

G.P. Cleather

2. ALDERBURY   D. Amesbury

1. Alderbury with Pitton and Farley. A vicarage.

2. The Bishop of Salisbury.

3. Alderbury alone 742. Inclusive of Pitton and Farley 1438.

4. Newton Smart. 1843.

5. Yes.

6. Yes.

7. [Blank]

8. No.

9. Yes, three.

10. In 1861 and 1863.

11. Edward B Martin, a priest, curate of Alderbury. J Farnham Messenger, a

priest, senior curate of Pitton and Farley. Henry Barton, a deacon, junior curate of Pitton and Farley.

12. Rev Messenger is Sub Warden of Farley Hospital.[1] Mr Martin and Mr Barton have no charge except their curacies.

13. Yes.

14. Alderbury 1858 St Mary. Pitton St Peter. Farley, date and dedication not known.

15. Yes.

16. Yes.

17. Yes.

18. No.

19. Yes.

20. Pitton 4 miles. Farley 3½.

21. Tithe rent charge, reserved rent, glebe, Queen Anne's Bounty, Ecclesiastical Commissioners £367.4s 8d.

22. From Alderbury £216.10s. From Pitton and Farley £122.18s. Conjointly £27.16s 8d. Total £367.4s 8d.

23. No.

24. Two full services with a sermon at each. Alderbury at 10.30am and 3.00pm. Farley 10.30am and 2.30pm. Pitton 10.30am and 2.30pm. In summer at 6.30pm.

25. Always a whole portion of the service, but on Wednesdays and for early communion the Litany and sometimes the communion service by itself.

26. I did so this year during Passion Week. It gives a more sacred and solemn character to the repetition and explanation of the church catechism than in the school and offers an opportunity for an address suited to the children, the Holy Week and the House of God.

27. No.

28. For the chapels see their returns. At Alderbury generally on Wednesdays with Evening Prayer on Friday morning. Average attendance, morning 10, evening 35. On the Circumcision, Ash Wednesday, in Passion Week, on Ascension Day, ditto.

29. [a] Yes [b] Yes [c] Yes [d] Yes [e] Yes.

30. The 1st Sunday of every month.

31. Yes, by my curates for each place.

32. Alderbury 175. Pitton 70. Farley 75. Total 320.

33. In Alderbury about 35.

34. The number of communicants at the great festivals varies considerably. At the early and midday communion on Easter Day 1863 there were 83; in 1864, 89, and on the 3rd April, 21, for a day [?] within the Octave 110. On Whit Sunday 1863 there were only 32, on Christmas Day 58.

35. It also varies considerably, probable average 30.

36. 450 inclusive of the seats in the chancel and chancel aisle and in the transept set apart for Clarendon.

37. The morning congregation on the 24th April was 217; in the afternoon 188. The one I should consider rather above and the other below the average, which I should set at 200 for the morning but above it for the afternoon and has greatly

increased since the new church was built.

38. No.

39. 15 baptisms 0 marriages 16 burials.

40. 27 in 1861; 23 in 1862; 18 in 1863.

41. The receipts for collections which have been transmitted to any Society or Public Body are affixed to the board for notices at the church.

42. In 1863 £23.5s.4d.

43. Yes.

44. There is a Wesleyan chapel at Alderbury; number of united members stated by themselves to be 80 at Alderbury and 20 at Whaddon where some Primitive Methodists hold meetings in a private house.

45. Yes.

46. Yes.

47. The boys from aged 10 to 11, the girls from 12 to 13. There are now 25 boys above 10 in the school.

48. Yes to a considerable extent.

49. By evening schools. The great difficulty is to obtain the services of a competent master. Mr. Martin has devoted much time to the evening classes with good success.

50. Yes.

51. For the chapels see the returns for them. At Alderbury church, February 15th for Church Missionary Society £4 9s 2d. At the spring and autumn Chapters [?] at the Offertory for the additional curates fund £2 14s. On October 18th for home and foreign missions, the S.P.G. and the additional curates fund £8 11s 6d. November 29th for the poor benefice augmentation fund £3 4s 2d.

52. Dissent necessarily impedes the church's work where she can provide her ministrations for the whole population; but it is not here aggressive, and my system, as the best remedy, is for myself and curates to ignore as far as possible its existence, and to visit all who will receive visits. The church in this parish seems under the Divine Blessing to be steadily extending her influence and increasing her usefulness as shown by the following results:- Persons confirmed in the last four years inclusive of the present 107; number of communicants on the list 175; communicated within the Octave of last Easter day 110, of whom 100 were different persons; average congregations above 200; alms and offering in 1863 £23.5s.4d ; subscribed and collected for other religious objects beyond the parish £36; the number of scholars on the books of the day school 166, and of the Sunday 90 some of whom remain after confirmation; the cost of maintaining the day school for the past year was £104.14s.10½d.

Newton Smart

---

[1]Founded in 1681 by Sir Stephen Fox. The Hospital (which survives) consisted of 12 almshouses and a central wardenry.

3. ALL CANNINGS D. Avebury

1. All Cannings, a rectory.
2. The Lord Ashburton. The Grange, Alresford, Hants.
3. 1000 including the hamlets of Etchilhampton and Allington. The population of All Cannings alone, <u>exclusive</u> of the said hamlets of Etchilhampton and Allington is <u>under</u> 600 – about 550.
4. Thomas Anthony Methuen. Instituted in 1809.
5. Yes.
6. Yes.
7. [Blank]
8. Garsdon (rectory) near Malmesbury in the diocese of Gloucester.
9. Yes.
10. In 1861.
11. Francis Paul Methuen[1]. He is a priest.
12. No.
13. Yes; it comprises the chapelry of Etchilhampton
14. St Anne's – of Norman origin.
15. Yes.
16. Yes.
17. Taking the word 'duties' in its most <u>extended</u> sense, I can make but a qualified reply.
18. No.
19. No chapel at All Cannings.
20. Etchilhampton chapel is about 2 miles from the church at All Cannings.
21. Tithes.
22. But one benefice with the chapelry at Etchilhampton (see the sheet relating to it).
23. No.
24. Two, with sermon on every Sunday at 11.00am and 5.00pm – after Michaelmas at 11.00am and 3.00pm.
25. Yes.
26. No.
27. No.
28. On festivals – also on Good Friday – from 100 to 200 persons at least present.
29. [a] Yes. [b] Yes. [c] No. [d] No. [e] Yes.
30. On the 1st Sunday of every month.
31. No – too small to be necessary.
32. From 25 to 35.
33. No <u>such absentees</u> that I am aware of.
34. From 25 to 35.
35. The same.
36. For 350 to 400.
37. About 140 in the morning and about 300 in the afternoon. The number is increasing.
38. No.

39. 21 baptisms 11 marriages 19 burials.

40. 18.

41. No.

42. [Sum not entered]

43. Yes.

44. There is a chapel connected with the Particular Baptists in the hamlet of Allington about one mile and a half from All Cannings. The greater part of the Allington people attend it in the winter times, as the pathway to All Cannings is almost impassable but very few of them are regular <u>members.</u>

45. Yes.

46. Yes.

47. 10 to 12.

48. A few of them.

49. No.

50. Yes.

51. [Blank]

52. [Blank]

I am, my Dear Lord, your Lordship's faithful & obedient Thomas Anthony
Methuen, Rector
March 29th 1864

[1] The rector's son.

4. **ALLINGTON**   D. Amesbury

1. Allington. The benefice is a rectory.

2. The Earl of Craven. Ashdown Park, Lambourne & Coombe Abbey.

3. About 100.

4. Fulwar William Fowle, instituted 1816.

5. [Blank]

6. [Blank]

7. Alfred Child, assistant curate, resident.

8. Prebend of Chesenbury and Chute, rural dean and perpetual curate of Amesbury, all in the diocese of Sarum.

9. [Blank]

10. Assistant curate licensed May 31st 1863.

11. Alfred Child, a deacon.

12. Assistant curate of Amesbury.

13. [Blank]

14. There is one parish church in Allington called St John the Baptist, consecrated Tuesday 7th January 1851.

15. The church is in good repair and provided with things necessary for divine service.

16. The churchyard is fairly kept.

17. As far as I know.

18. No alteration.

19. No chapels.

20. [Blank]

21. Gross value of benefice £270.

22. The benefice is one parish.

23. One glebe house.

24. Morning at 10.30am, evening at 2.30pm, sermon at Evensong.

25. Yes.

26. No.

27. No.

28. Since Trinity 1863. Special services have been held on September 23rd (Harvest Festival), Christmas Day, Ash Wednesday, every Wednesday in Lent and on Good Friday. This has been customary before.

29. [a]Yes [b] Yes [c] No [d] Yes [e] Yes.

30. About five times in the year.

31. [Blank]

32. About 14. E.F¹. (late curate).

33. They have all communicated E.F.

34. 9.

35. 9.

36. [Blank]

37. I am unable to give the average. The numbers of the congregations for the last three Sundays were respectively: – Easter Sunday 12 in the morning and 30 in the evening; Low Sunday 10 in the morning and 37 in the evening; 2nd Sunday after Easter 16 in the morning and 23 in the evening; 3rd Sunday after Easter 16 in the morning and 29 in the evening.

38. The church accommodation is ample for the population.

39. 4 baptisms 0 marriages 1 burial.

40. 7.

41. I place a statement of the amount on the church door after a collection with a receipt of its payment if any.

42. The Holy Communion has been administered four times since I have been here. The alms have been 6s 3d, 4s 2d, 5s (the last I have not yet received from the officiating priest).

43. Yes.

44. A Primitive Methodist meeting house. Nearly all the parish at times go to the meeting house, at times to church. There is also a Baptist or two in the place.

45. No.

46. [Blank]

47. [Blank]

48. [Blank]

49. A night school during the winter months, fairly attended for the population.

50. Yes.

51. I am unable to state the amounts, but collections have been made for the Society for the Propagation of the Gospel and for the Augmentation of Small

Benefices.

52. The Primitive Methodist meeting house.

Alfred Child

> [1] Edmund Fowle, son of Fulwar Fowle.

5. **ALTON BARNES**   D. Avebury

1. Alton Berners or Barnes, a rectory.
2. The Warden and Fellows of New College Oxford.
3. 177 by the last census.
4. David Williams 1835.
5. The Rector is non resident by licence.
6. He resides at Pewsey.
7. Edward Henry Mainwaring Sladen, resident curate.
8. No.
9. [Blank]
10. In 1856.
11. Priest.
12. No.
13. No.
14. The parish church is dedicated to St Mary the Virgin.
15. Yes.
16. Yes, fairly so.
17. Yes.
18. The praying desk and pulpit have been arranged more conveniently with the sanction of the rector and churchwarden. At the same time the interior of the church was repaired and the walls fresh washed.
19. [Blank]
20. [Blank]
21. The tithe, glebe and rent of a farm – attached to the living by the Warden and Fellows of New College Oxford.
22. [Blank]
23. No.
24. Two full services at 11.00am and 2.30 or 3.00pm according to the season. This year I have omitted the afternoon sermon once a month and given the time to the Sunday school, divine service then commencing half an hour later.
25. Yes, always on Sunday during the Holy Week, when (except on Good Friday) divine service a.m. concludes with the prayer for the church militant, etc. I omit the prayers on several occasions; proceeding at once from the prayer for the clergy and people to that of St Chrysostom. This shortens the service for the school children and enables them to go home to dinner in good time and takes them only half an hour from school.
26. Not in this church.
27. There is not daily prayer in this church.
28. Christmas Day, Ash Wednesday, Holy Week and Ascension. Two services

on each, with the exception of Monday or Tuesday before Easter when there is only one. As a general rule the church is less attended on such days than on Sunday. The church is also open during Lent in the morning of Wednesday with a sermon, and on Friday morning for prayers. Except on Xmas Day and Good Friday scarcely any attend am, but the service pm is fairly attended. In the Lenten evening services this year (excepting Good Friday) the largest congregation was 38, the least 21, the general attendance about 30.

29. [a] Yes [b] Yes [c] No [d] Yes [e] No.

30. On Quinquagessima Sunday and in all six or seven times a year according to the time from Whit S[unday] to Advent.

31. Yes.

32-33. 23 besides myself, all having communicated in this church with one exception in 1863.

34-35. There is no perceptible difference.

36. 85 adults and 50 school children.

37. The average adult congregation on Sunday morning and afternoon last year (taking one season with another) was 54 at each service, with the addition of an average of 22 school children. As to increase or decrease I can hardly judge at present; of course there is a large falling off in the number in consequence of the people of Great Alton not frequenting this church as they used when I was their curate. But I hope that a greater proportion of the people of this parish attend one or other of the Sunday services.

38. No.

39. 8 baptisms 0 marriages 0 burials.

40. None.

41. The receipt is affixed to the church door after every collection.

42. The amount in 1863 at the seven communions was £6. 8s. 9d.

43. Yes.

44. There is no dissenting place of worship in this parish. There are three families, and one or two individuals besides, who never come to church, being dissenters (Wesleyans). There are others who at times frequent conventicles; it is difficult to state how many.

45. Yes.

46. No.

47. Boys seldom remain after 7 years of age. Girls seldom after 11 or 12.

48. Yes, the boys generally until about 14 and the girls until they are 15 and perhaps confirmed.

49. Yes, we have tried evening schools for the elder secondary boys, and likewise for young men, but not with much lasting success. The number is not sufficient without regular attendance (which cannot be secured) to pay the necessary expense of carrying on the school. Still, no doubt some two or three have derived real benefit.

50. The copy of the register of baptisms for 1863 will be transmitted as soon as I have the parchment sheet for the purpose.

51. Distress in manufacturing districts collected in 1863 £18. 13s. 6d. Bath

Hospital £1. 14s. 6d. Foreign Missions (moieties to S.P.G and C.M.S) £1. 15s. 10d. Augmentation of Poor Benefices £11. 2s. 10d. Total £33. 6s. 8d. (The sum of £12. 10s. 8d. entered at first as collected for the distress of the manufacturers was raised in the year 1862 for that purpose).
52. There is nothing new.

Edward H. M. Sladen

6. ALVEDISTON D. Chalke

1. Alvediston, a perpetual curacy.
2. Dr Rowland Williams, Broad Chalke.
3. 260.
4. Philip S. Desprez. 23rd December 1862.
5. Yes.
6. Yes.
7. [Blank]
8. No.
9. [Blank]
10. [Blank]
11. [Blank]
12. [Blank]
13. One church.
14. [Blank]
15. The church is in a dilapidated state and so also the churchyard fence. It is in contemplation to restore them.
16. [See 15]
17. Yes.
18. None.
19. In the parish church.
20. [Blank]
21. Vicarial tithes £80 per annum.
22. [Blank]
23. [Blank]
24. Morning service at 10.30am, afternoon at 3.00pm, in the summer at 6.00pm. Sermons at both.
25. Yes.
26. On Sunday mornings, generally.
27. No.
28. Morning prayers on Wednesdays during Lent. Four or five persons.
29. [a] No [b] Yes [c] No [d] Yes [e] Yes.
30. On the 1st Sunday in the month generally.
31. I know who they are.
32. 18.
33. They have all communicated at various times during the year.
34. The same as at other times.

35. 15.

36. About 100 (including children).

37. I cannot say; I have never counted them. The congregation appears stationary.

38. The church accommodation is deplorable.

39. 7 baptisms 2 marriages 6 burials.

40. None have been confirmed in 1863.

41. Occasionally – not as a general rule.

42. £3 12s 3½d.

43. In a book for my own private guidance.

44. None. A few (possibly 20) belonging to the denomination of the Primitive Methodists.

45. Yes.

46. No.

47. 8 or 9.

48. In a few cases.

49. There is an evening school during the winter months. The greatest attendance about 20.

50. Not yet.

51. Harvest sermon for the school £1 14s. Poor benefice augmentation fund £3 17s 6d.

52. [Blank]

Philip Desprez

7. AMESBURY D. Amesbury

1. Amesbury, a perpetual curacy.

2. The Chapter of Windsor.

3. 1172.

4. Fulwar William Fowle, 1817.

5. Yes.

6. Yes.

7. [Blank]

8. Allington in Salisbury.

9. He has an assistant curate.

10. Licensed June 1863.

11. Alfred Child, a deacon.

12. He performs the duty of Allington as curate and no other.

13. No.

14. [Blank]

15. Yes.

16. Yes.

17. Yes.

18. None.

19. No chapels.

20. [Blank]

21. £40 per annum from Sir Edmund Antrobus. £20 per annum from Windsor. Interest of £500 in New 3 per cents. £14 per annum land in parish of Hungerford. Queen Anne's Bounty £42. The whole amounts to about £133 8s.

22. [Blank]

23. No.

24. Morning service at 10.30am, without a sermon. Afternoon service at 3.00pm, with a sermon.

25. Always.

26. I do not.

27. I do not.

28. Christmas Day and Good Friday, the same as on Sunday with a like large congregation. Morning service on Wednesdays Fridays and Saints' days, on which occasions there are, excepting during Lent, not ten persons on an average besides schoolchildren.

29. [a] Yes [b] Yes [c] No [d] Yes [e] No.

30. On the 1st Sunday in every month.

31. I do not; it would be most difficult, if not impossible.

32. I cannot say; but the average during the last 12 months has been 70.

33. There is a large number of parishioners who never communicate in the church. Dissenters never do. I should say all have communicated, who ever do.

34. About 80.

35. About 70.

36. I think the church is calculated to hold perhaps 650.

37. My church, with its chancel, nave, two transepts and side aisle is very inconvenient for numbers. Strangers − clergy or laity − commonly remark that the congregation is unusually large. Among the lower orders it is increasing, rather than otherwise. Among some of the higher there is great laxity.

38. There is no further accommodation required.

39. 17* baptisms 7 marriages 19 burials. * An unusually small number. In the present year up to this date, (April 19) there have been 12 baptised.

40. In 1861 were confirmed about 60. I have mislaid the particulars of that confirmation. None have been confirmed in either 1862 or 1863.

41. Not in reference to alms collected at the Holy Communion. Collections in the church are immediately placed in the hands of the parish churchwarden, and by him remitted to their destination.

42. The amount in 1863 was £24 14s 6¾d.

43. A regular account is kept of receipts and expenditure in two books set apart for that purpose.

44. There is a proselytizing body of Wesleyans, very active. I cannot at all state their number.

45. Yes; wholly supported by Sir Edmund Antrobus and managed by his Lady. There are also two endowed schools.

46. Yes; to a considerable extent.

47. Boys at 8 or 9, girls at 11 or 12.

48. More or less, generally, until they have been confirmed.

49. There has been for some few years past an adult evening school, attended with much success.

50. Yes.

51. There were two collections in church – one for the Augmentation of Small Benefices in the Diocese of Salisbury - £9 18s 9½d. Another for the Indian Mission £9 4s ½d. I would mention that my parishioners contribute to the Society for the Promotion of the Gospel and to the Society for the Promotion of Knowledge about £28 or £29 per annum: and that on some special occasions they subscribe largely – for instance Lancashire distress more than £140. But collections in church are sadly unpopular, and made in such a grudging spirit that I shrink from them.

52. This question has given rise to many, many hours of anxious thoughts, which the present state of my mind and health make me almost unfit to commit to writing. I fear I could only tell the evils, without suggesting the remedies. However, I have written something and if I can complete it one day next week, I will send it, to be either laid aside, or appended to my report, at your Lordship's discretion.

F.W. Fowle

8. ANSTY   D. Chalke

1. Ansty, a perpetual curacy.
2. Bishop of Salisbury, Palace, Salisbury.
3. At the last census 298.
4. John Harman Samler, never regularly inducted but came in April 19th, 1846.
5. He has performed the duties of the parish from his residence in parish adjoining, during the time prescribed by law.
6. He has resided in the glebe house at Swallowcliffe.
7. No curate.
8. The perpetual curacy of Swallowcliffe in same diocese.
9. No.
10. [Blank]
11. [Blank]
12. [Blank]
13. No.
14. [Blank]
15. The church is not in poor repair. The south wall is very damp, and the chancel requires repair in roof. No church rates can be levied. Things necessary for decent performance of divine service in pretty good order.
16. Churchyard fence wants repairing.
17. No regular churchwardens.
18. No alterations have been made.
19. [Blank]
20. [Blank]
21. A payment is annually made by Lord Arundell of Wardour (the lay rector) of

about £22 5s 4d less income tax.

22. [Blank]

23. [Blank]

24. There is duty in the morning or afternoon with sermon every Sunday at 10.30am, or in afternoon at 2.30pm or 3.00pm according to time of year.

25. Yes, omitting however in the morning service the church militant prayer, as I never, except on the Sundays when Holy Communion is administered, return after sermon to the altar.

26. Yes, during the Sunday afternoons of Lent, when I take some portion of the church catechism for examination.

27. No, I have tried for years prayers on the Friday morning, but we have been unable often to get a congregation. These I have therefore discontinued. During Lent I serve them church prayers twice in the week and in the Holy Week daily. About I should think three or four persons attend during Lent in the morning because my school children in the evening perhaps about 10.

28. Christmas Day, Ash Wednesday, Good Friday and Ascension Day, when with the exception of Ascension Day, I get congregations almost equal to Sundays.

29. On Christmas Day, Easter Day, Whit Sunday and Trinity Sunday if service in morning. Holy Communion is administered, if not, on following Sunday. No communion on Ascension Day.

30. About every 6 or 7 weeks.

31. Yes, of the number who attend but not of the names. I always however keep a list of the names of the confirmed who first attend the holy table.

32. On average my communicants have been through the past year about 10 out of about 20 who are communicants.

33. I think there are none who have not communicated either publicly in church or privately with the sick, or are sick themselves.

34. About the same number at the festivals and other times.

35. [See 34]

36. For, I should think, about 130.

37. Remains I think about the same (about 80) or perhaps it has a little lessened owing to one or two church families having left the parish.

38. No.

39. 8 Baptisms 2 Marriages 3 Burials.

40. In the year 1861 there were eight persons confirmed. None in the years 1862-3.

41. No, but I keep a private account of the account of sacramental alms and collections in church.

42. The amount last year was £2 19s 11d.

43. Yes, of what is collected each Sunday when Holy Communion administered.

44. There is no dissenting place of worship. Those who do not attend church are Romanists, and comprise about half of the parish.

45. The school is in Swallowcliffe, to which the children of Ansty are admitted both on working days and Sundays. As the master is not certificated I receive no benefit from the Committee of Council.

46. [See 45]

47. At about 12 or earlier, as soon as they can get work.

48. Yes, some of them on the Sundays. I make it a rule that they attend on Sundays until confirmation.

49. Yes, I have kept on for the last two years a night school from the end of October to the beginning of March at which I attend three nights a week with my schoolmaster and the attendance we have deemed satisfactory.

50. Yes, I have transmitted my registers for the last year to the registrar of the diocese.

51. Collections have been made during the past year in church for small livings 19s 9d and S.P.G 12s 6d for parochial association.

52. The prevalence of Romanism and the encouragement which is given to those who attend the Romish worship. I have now no farmer who is not of the Romish persuasion.

John Samler

9. ATWORTH D. Potterne

1. Atworth with S Wraxall a perpetual curacy.

2. The Dean and Chapter of Bristol.

3. Population of Atworth 608.

4. William Laxton 1848.

5. Yes.

6. There being no glebe house he has resided at Holt.

7. [Blank]

8. No.

9. Yes.

10. In June 1863.

11. Geo. Lax. Farthing a deacon.

12. Yes he is also Curate of Chalfield Magna.

13. Yes.

14. The church of Atworth is called after St Michael. Date of original consecration unknown. Body of church rebuilt.

15. Yes. Enlarged in 1832.

16. Yes.

17. Yes.

18. No.

19. Vide S Wrax in A.

20. Ditto.

21. Tithe rent charge, rent charge and glebe.

22. Tithe rent charge of Atworth £105 2s 6d. Rent charge on Cottles estate £10. Glebe let at £5.

23. There is none.

24. There is service in the morning and aft[ernoon] of one Sunday at Atworth and aft duty on the following Sunday. A sermon after each service.

25. Yes.

26. No.

27. I consider that I am reasonably hindered.

28. Ash Wednesday, Good Friday, Ascension Day and Christmas Day.

29. The Sunday after Christmas Day, the Sunday after Easter Day and the Sunday after Whit Sunday.

30. Thrice besides during the year.

31. No.

32. The number being lamentably small.

33. One I believe at <u>my</u> church, but she may frequently attend another.

34. About 15 or 16.

35. Ditto.

36. 428.

37. About 100: about stationary.

38. No.

39. 21 baptisms 6 marriages 6 burials.

40. Seven at Atworth in 1861.

41. Yes.

42. £1 13s 5d.

43. Yes.

44. Three; viz one belonging to the Independents, one Baptist, one Primitive Methodist.

45. Yes.

46. No.

47. 10 or 11.

48. Rarely.

49. No.

50. Yes.

51. Small benefices augmentation fund <u>about</u> 18s. The precise amount I do not remember and the report (acknowledging it) I cannot on the moment put my hand on.

52. The non- residence of any influential inhabitant attached to the Church of England and the fact that the Squire (who however does not proselytize) is a member of the Church of Rome. His influence is not on our side.

W. Laxton

10. AVEBURY   D. Avebury

1. Avebury, a vicarage.

2. Lord Chancellor, House of Lords.

3. 725.

4. Bryan King Nov 1863.

5. Resident since his induction.

6. In the glebe house.

7. [Blank]

8. United benefice of Winterbourne Monkton Di: Sarum.
9. No.
10. [Blank]
11. [Blank]
12. [Blank]
13. Two churches.
14. S James Avebury – S [blank] Winterbourne Monkton.
15. Yes.
16. Yes.
17. Yes.
18. No.
19. [Blank]
20. [Blank]
21. Tithe rent charge, pension, glebe land, Easter dues, surplice fees = £250 p.a.
22. Avebury £142 W Monkton £108 = £250.
23. No.
24. Occasional early celebrations of Ho: Euch at Avebury. Morning and afternoon at Avebury and Monkton alternately – evening at Avebury, sermons at all.
25. Yes.
26. On saints' days – on the commemoration of the day - I trust with considerable advantage.
27. Only occasionally.
28. Saints' days, Wednesday and Friday weekly; about 12 adults and school children.
29. [a] Yes [b] Yes [c] Yes [d] Yes [e] Yes.
30. On 1st Sundays of month, (and occasionally upon other Sundays at 8.00am).
31. [Blank]
32. There are now only about 30 communicants.
33. [Blank]
34. 20 or 22.
35. 16.
36. About 310.
37. About 200 – I trust increasing.
38. Better and more convenient accommodation is required by the rearrangement of the church.
39. 16 baptisms 0 marriages 15 burials.
40. I have no record.
41. I propose to do so annually.
42. About 12s per month.
43. I keep such an account.
44. Two – I am unable to give any approximate estimate of the number.
45. Yes.
46. No.
47. About 8 or 9.
48. Very generally.

49. By evening school in the winter with fair success.

50. I am now doing so.

51. I have no record of such collections.

52. Traditions of dissenting teaching and influence tending to the depreciation in general estimation of the importance of the sacrament and of the sacramental character of the church of Christ.

Bryan King

11. BARFORD ST. MARTIN   D. Chalke

1. Barford St. Martin, a rectory.

2. Warden and Fellows of All Souls College Oxford.

3. 530 at the last census.

4. Charles Hinxman[1] M.A. Balliol College Oxford. Instituted February 5th 1861, inducted March 30th 1861.

5. Resident the whole time prescribed.

6. In the glebe house.

7. [Blank]

8. No other benefice.

9. None.

10. [Blank]

11. [Blank]

12. [Blank]

13. One only – the parish church.

14. [Blank]

15. In substantial repair and provided with all things necessary.

16. It is.

17. They do.

18. None whatever.

19. No chapels.

20. No chapels.

21. Rent charge commuted at £560. Rent of glebe £105.

22. One parish only.

23. One glebe house only.

24. Morning service in the parish church at 10.30am. Evening service at 6.00pm. Sermons at both. Service at 3.00pm on the second Sunday in the month for baptisms when required. Lecture usually given on such occasions.

25. The whole service said.

26. No catechising in the <u>church,</u> but in the school every Sunday at 2.00pm. Inhabitants attend. The object of this catechising is in some measure to neutralise the effect of the dissenting worship in the afternoon, when there is no service in church. Adults are encouraged to come. There is a good deal of psalmody and missionary information, and other statements of general interest are occasionally imparted.

The children are prepared for the catechising by means of books with which the teachers are furnished and out of which, in part, the children are questioned. The point which strikes me as disadvantageous, is the <u>collective</u> nature of the catechising. To make it useful to the youngest classes, is to do little good to the elder, and if the latter are addressed, the younger learn but little. <u>With a curate</u> I should divide the school into senior and junior catechisms.

27. Not said. I have found by experience that without the help of a curate the exertion would be too great.

28. Evening service on each Wednesday throughout the year, consisting of Litany and sermon – full service during Lent and Advent. Morning Prayer through Holy Week, average number attending 40.

29. [a] Yes [b] Yes [c] Yes [d] Yes [e] No.

30. On the last Sunday in each month.

31. Yes.

32. 48.

33. No more than four.

34. 40.

35. About the same. The attendance at the Lord's Table does not vary in this place, as in most
others. Those who do attend are seldom absent. I attribute this to the view of the Holy Eucharist so long inculcated: as of <u>a special privilege of the elect.</u> The attendance of any but those who could speak strongly of spiritual experience and held Calvinistic views, was greatly discouraged, and in some instances, forbidden. The number then became small, but those who attended were very anxious to be present on all occasions. I hope the number will soon be largely increased and a somewhat different view be taken. It has been difficult to extend the offer of the means of grace over to the earnest and humble minded without producing a living [?] impression on the minds of others, jealous of their previous distinctions.

36. About 380.

37. I cannot form a very close estimate. About 260. The congregation fell off a short time since for reasons given in answer 52. It has increased again of late.

38. <u>Improvement</u> much needed in the church. A south aisle required and a gallery to be removed. This would give all the additional accommodation required. But little hope of doing it. All in substantial repair - parish averse from such expense and College authorities decline to move.

39. 12 baptisms 5 marriages 13 burials.

40. In 1861 – 11. In 1863, two <u>confirmed at Bishopstone.</u>

41. A statement is laid before the rate payers at the Easter vestry meeting.

42. £9 9s 2d.

43. There is.

44. One. Primitive Methodist. There are 12 <u>families</u> of this denomination. Many members of other families attend occasionally. Many <u>individuals are Independents</u> and there are four <u>Romanists.</u>

45. National daily school, both mixed and infants, average attendance 76. School house of first rate character. Master and mistress both certificated. Two pupil teachers.

46. Aid received from the Government this year £37 17s for 11 months. <u>Lately reduced, by bequest,</u> into income of £31 per annum. Local subscriptions averaging about the same amount.

47. Boys cease to attend generally about 10, girls about 12 or 13. Much taken away from school from local causes, especially for gathering wood in Grovely.

48. Attendance at Sunday schools good, amounting to nearly 100. Both boys and girls attend up to the age of 17 and in some cases beyond it. A <u>bible class</u> for those more advanced, found to answer best, held at the rectory. Catechumens, lately confirmed and ceasing to attend school, come willingly to such classes.

49. Evening school very successful last winter: average attendance 44 and extremely regular, many boys not missing a night for nearly five months and very well conducted. <u>Adult</u> teaching difficult to achieve with all of younger people – great <u>pride</u> among the people of this place. Many anxious to learn but unwilling for their ignorance to be known. Would form a class at the rectory, but I am unable to leave the school. The proposed change of number of days in night school attendance, from 24 to 60, a very hard measure. 40 a much fairer number – 35 the best. It is difficult, generally, to attain a regular attendance throughout the winter. There is a falling off point at Christmas, and this, with so high an attendance as 60, would entirely neutralise the grant, though in general attendance might have been good. I think a representation should be made to Government of the peculiar claims of night schools: the great tax they are on the time and work of the clergy, and their voluntary helpers; the encouragement they deserve; and the great benefit which they confer on the lads themselves. They are the <u>very efficient</u> means of retaining a hold on lads after the age of 16 and of bringing them forward for confirmation. The first year of my residence here my male catechumens numbered 2 -- this year they were <u>22:</u> because this year I <u>know</u> the lads and I could not have known them intimately but for the night school.

50. [Blank]

51. Relief of artisans at Carlisle, collected at desire of Bishop of Carlisle £5 1s. Charmouth Home[2] harvest service £1 14s. Schools £5 16s 7½d. Small benefices fund £5 10s 6d. Not acknowledged in report of the fund. Total £18 2s 1½d.

52. Some local causes have interfered, during the last year, in some measure with the ministry. But they scarcely admit of any remedy save faith and work, with the blessing of the most high. In the place of a very excellent man, the largest farm in the village is now occupied by a dissenter (Congregationalist) and together with his coming, a very powerful preacher of that denomination came to Wilton. This attraction, and the example of the farmer himself, drew away a number of my people to that place. I had succeeded till then in keeping them steadfast, though they plainly told me that my objective was not according to their views. The Congregationalist minister preaches hotter Calvinism, that is, as one of them expressed himself, 'after their palate'. I have a good hope however that a change has taken place in the minds of some of them. They have begun to re-appear in church.

I could venture to ask, whether some organised assistance might not be afforded to the parochial clergy in the matter of preaching. I do not know of any body of worshippers that are as closely restricted to the ministrations of one man as ours are, or any in which so much is required of that one man, as a preacher. I venture to think that especially in a place where sermons are thought of much, the occasional help of other <u>good</u> preachers would be no small advantage. It is not in the power of everyone to preach, always three, four, five or six services every week, fresh, varied and vigorous, calculated to assert and keep the attentions of a truculent, critical and dis-affected congregation, whatever the state of health and occupation and circumstances of the preacher.

Charles Hinxman

[1]The rector had buried his one-day old daughter on March 31st and his wife on April 7th. This may explain the length of this return.

[2]Seaside convalescence was popular in Victorian times. Salisbury General Infirmary, for a time, rented accommodation in the Dorset seaside town of Charmouth for the benefit of patients to take in the sea air. In 1858 the home opened with 47 patients admitted during the first year and 60 in the second.

12. BAVERSTOCK   D. Chalke

1. Baverstock, a rectory.
2. The rector and scholars of Exeter College Oxford.
3. 168.
4. William Edward Hony instituted and inducted in 1827.
5. He has been so resident.
6. In the glebe house.
7. [Blank]
8. He does not.
9. He has not.
10. [Blank]
11. [Blank]
12. [Blank]
13. It does not.
14. [Blank]
15. The church is in perfect repair and provided with all things necessary.
16. It is.
17. Their ordinary duties they perform well but not all the duties comprised in their declaration.
18. No alterations have been made.
19. [Blank]
20. [Blank]
21. Rent charge and glebe about £325 per annum.
22. [Blank]
23. No.
24. The Sunday duty in the church consists of a service at 11.00am and at 3.00 pm. There is a sermon at each of these services.
25. I do.
26. For many years I did so and gave an explanation of a portion in the afternoon

service in Lent but finding that the congregation fell off on those Sundays I have given it up.

27. I do not.

28. There is in general a service on all days for which there is a collect, epistle and gospel appointed. An evening service on one or two days in the week during Lent with a lecture; twice a day in Passion Week with lecture in the evening. No one but my own family can attend a week day service in the morning. When the service is in the evening with a sermon 30 or 40 people attend: ie from ⅕ to ¼ of the population.

29. [a] Yes [b] Yes [c] No [d] Yes [e] No.

30. Other times at intervals of six weeks.

31. I keep such a list.

32. The average number is 34 or one fifth of the population.

33. I have noted the absence of two young men.

34. 40.

35. 31.

36. For 135.

37. About 50 in the morning and 80 in the afternoon exclusive of children.

38. No.

39. 5 baptisms 1 marriage 3 burials.

40. 12.

41. When a collection is made, a receipt from the society is placed on the church door.

42. £11.

43. There is, and it is exhibited at the Easter vestry.

44. There is no dissenting place of worship in the parish, and no professed dissenters, though some go to meeting houses occasionally in other parishes.

45. Yes.

46. I have not.

47. Boys seldom remain after they are 8 years of age. Girls remain until they are 12 or 14.

48. Yes until their confirmation.

49. The boys attend an evening school during the winter months. Not all the success I could wish, but still, I trust with profit to many.

50. I have.

51. Society for promotion gospel £4 7s.   Church Missionary Society £4 6s. Curates aid £2 12s 6d Total £11 5s 6d.

52. I cannot. Though I think the relaxation of parental authority the cause of some of the evils in society in the present day.

William Edward Hony

13. BAYDON   D. Marlborough

1. Baydon, a perpetual curacy.

2. Revd Edwin Meyrick vicar of Chiseldon.

3. 380.
4. William Smith – January 12th 1861.
5. Yes.
6. Yes.
7. [Blank]
8. No.
9. [Blank]
10. [Blank]
11. [Blank]
12. [Blank]
13. No.
14. [Blank]
15. Yes.
16. Yes.
17. Yes.
18. No.
19. [Blank]
20. [Blank]
21. Land at South Marston £100 per annum with £6 tithe from Manor Farm, Baydon – net value £80.
22. [Blank]
23. No.
24. Two full services at 11.00am and 3.00pm with a sermon at each.
25. Yes.
26. No.
27. No: only morning prayers on Wednesday and Friday.
28. On Xmas Day and Good Friday, two services with sermons. On Ascension and all saints' days, morning prayers. Christmas Day and Good Friday a good attendance at other times an average of five persons.
29. [a] Yes [b] Yes [c] No [d] and [e] alternately.
30. On the 1st Sunday of every month.
31. No.
32. From 15 to 20.
33. None.
34. About 15.
35. From 8–10.
36. 164.
37. 50 or 60 as a general congregation independent of about 40 children.
38. No.
39. 15 baptisms 4 marriages 3 burials.
40. 16 in 1861 none since.
41. No.
42. £8 16s 4¾d.
43. No: nothing but my private account of their distribution.
44. One Wesleyan and one Baptist: which comprise about one half the people,

the Wesleyan having the majority.
45. Yes.
46. No.
47. Boys at 9 girls at 11 or 12.
48. Yes.
49. No: I attempted a night school which failed.
50. No.
51. Lancashire operatives £1 2s 9d. Society for prop gospel £1 0s 5d. Small benefice fund £1 8s 4d.
52. [Blank]

William Smith

14. BEECHINGSTOKE.   D. Avebury
1. Beechingstoke a rectory.
2. G H Walker Heneage Esq Compton Bassett Calne.
3. 175 persons.
4. Richard Nicholson July 30th 1858.
5. Yes.
6. In the glebe house.
7. [Blank]
8. No.
9. [Blank]
10. [Blank]
11. [Blank]
12. [Blank]
13. No.
14. [Blank]
15. Yes.
16. Yes.
17. Yes.
18. No.
19. [Blank]
20. [Blank]
21. Tithe rent charge £293. Glebe house and glebe including garden and churchyard 32a 2r 15p.
22. [Blank]
23. Only one.
24. 10.30am and 3.00pm in winter, 10.30am and 6.00pm in summer.
25. Yes.
26. No.
27. No.
28. Xmas Day, Ascension Day, Ash Wednesday, Good Friday twice each day. Friday evenings in Lent. Prayers Wednesday evenings, in Lent prayers and sermon. About 30 attend on Wednesdays in Lent. Good Friday about same as Sunday. The

evening services in the week only the school children and two or three more.

29. [a] Yes [b] Yes [c] Will be (DV) this year [d] Yes [e] No.

30. The 1st Sunday in every month.

31. Yes.

32. 22.

33. 1.

34. About 10.

35. 9.

36. 106 sittings in the nave, eight in the choir.

37. I should think between 60 and 70 but as the greater part of the people live upwards of a mile from the church the attendance of those at a distance is variable and they can only come once in the day. I suppose in numbers it is stationary at present, as removals by death and otherwise have taken away a few of the regular church attendants, but the communicants have considerably increased. (In the village of Beechingstoke the attendance is remarkably more regular and their demeanour in church excellent).

38. Not in regard to church room. I have long contemplated a chapel at Broad Street on account of the distance from the parish church, but am not quite certain as to its expediency.

39. 7 baptisms 3 marriages 5 burials.

40. Ten at the last confirmation.

41. I did so one year and laid it before the vestry but did not repeat it [remaining text is heavily crossed out]

42. £4 2s 3½d to Easter this year. £4 9s. 5d to Easter 1863. £3 19s 4d to Easter 1861.

43. Yes.

44. None. In the village of Beechingstoke there is one dissenter. In Broad Street about 20, Wesleyans and Baptists.

45. Yes.

46. No.

47. Boys about 9 years of age, girls about 12.

48. Yes.

49. I have an influence over some of the choir. I had an evening school, but the boys now go to a master who set up an evening school at Woodborough.

50. I hope to send them in as soon as I can get the parchment.

51. For S.P.G. £1 5s 1d. Sarum Infirmary £1 16s 4d. Augmentation of small benefices 9s.

52. [Blank]

Richard Nicholson

15. BERWICK BASSETT   D. Avebury

1. Berwick Bassett, a perpetual curacy.

2. The Right Reverend the Lord Bishop of Salisbury.

3. 171.

4. Edward John Vicary, May 14th 1861.

5. Yes.

6. In the National School house.

7. [Blank]

8. No.

9. No curate.

10. [Blank]

11. [Blank]

12. [Blank]

13. One church.

14. I do not know when the church was consecrated. The church was dedicated to St Nicholas.

15. The church is in good repair, and provided with all things necessary for the decent performance of divine service.

16. Yes.

17. Yes.

18. No alteration has been made.

19. No chapel of ease.

20. [Blank]

21. The Ecclesiastical Commissioners pay £12 per annum. The Marquis of Lansdown £40 per annum.

22. [Blank]

23. [Blank]

24. There are two full services in the church every Sunday at 11.00am and 3.00pm. There is a sermon after every service; excepting when the Holy Communion is administered.

25. Yes.

26. No.

27. No.

28. Ash Wednesday morning and evening. Every Wednesday and Friday evening during Lent. Good Friday morning and evening, Ascension Day in the evening, Christmas Day morning and afternoon. The attendance is very good.

29. [a] Yes [b] Yes [c] No [d] Yes [e] When it comes on the 1st Sunday in the month.

30. 1st Sunday in the month.

31. No. I always keep the number.

32. No.

33. All have communicated.

34. There were 12 on Easter Sunday. 14 Whit Sunday. 11 Christmas Day.

35. 10/19

36. 120.

37. 172 every Sunday. Increasing.

38. No.

39. 5 baptisms 1 marriage 3 burials.

40. I believe there were 12 confirmed in 1861. None 1862. None 1863.

41. The churchwarden always knows the amount of the collections.

42. £3 19s 0d.

43. Yes.

44. There is no dissenting place of worship. Number of dissenters ten.

45. Yes.

46. No.

47. The oldest boy in my school is 8½ years. The oldest girl is 11¾ years. The boys generally leave about 8 years of age. The girls about 11 or 12.

48. Yes.

49. I have an adult school five evenings every week during the winter. I attend it every night unless prevented. I have found the greatest benefit to attend this school. It is in my opinion the best means of keeping up a good feeling between the clergyman and the young men; and also of keeping them to the church.

50. Yes.

51. A collection was made in my church for the augmentation of the poor livings in this diocese. The sum collected was £1 10s 0d. I do not have many collections in the church as there are only two farmers in this parish and they give liberally to the poor and when called upon for other objects.

52. The dissenters try all they can to get the people away from the church; but this is nothing more than is to be expected. The only thing to be done is to counteract them in every possible manner.

                                                    Edward John Vicary

16. BERWICK ST JAMES   D. Wylye

1. Berwick St James, a vicarage.
2. Lord Ashburton, Bath House, Piccadilly.
3. 290.
4. Charles Lawford, 1847.
5. Resident at Winterbourne Stoke.
6. [Blank]
7. [Blank]
8. Winterbourne Stoke, Sarum.
9. [Blank]
10. [Blank]
11. [Blank]
12. [Blank]
13. No.
14. [Blank]
15. Not in good repair.
16. Yes.
17. Yes.
18. No.
19. [Blank]
20. [Blank]

21. Rent charge commuted at £30. Glebe and other sources £47.
22. [Blank]
23. None.
24. Afternoon at 2.30pm. Sermon always.
25. No.
26. No.
27. No.
28. Friday in Lent. Christmas Day.
29. The Sunday following each of them.
30. 2nd Sunday in October.
31. Yes.
32. 25.
33. None.
34. 20.
35. The same.
36. About 150.
37. I never counted – stationary.
38. No.
39. 9 baptisms 1 marriage 6 burials.
40. 11.
41. No.
42. £1 10s.
43. Yes.
44. No dissenting places of worship. 13 Baptists.
45. Yes.
46. No.
47. Girls about 11, boys at 8.
48. Not long.
49. No.
50. Not yet.
51. No record kept.
52. No.

Charles Lawford

17. BERWICK ST JOHN   D. Chalke

1. Berwick St John, a rectory.
2. The Warden and Fellows of New College Oxford.
3. 499 by the census of 1861.
4. Charles Arthur Griffith. Instituted and inducted May 1855.
5. Yes.
6. In the glebe house.
7. [Blank]
8. No.
9. He is just about commencing such an arrangement.

10. He will shortly be an applicant for licence.

11. George Howard Waterfall, a priest.

12. Nowhere else.

13. Only one church.

14. [Blank]

15. Yes. It was reopened and reconsecrated May 1st 1862.

16. Yes.

17. Yes, but there has been no church rate for five years, owing to the majority of the farms being in dissenting hands and now, an opportunity occurring, by change of two farms in our favour – I desiderate more earnestness in trying to obtain a rate. I still hope we may effect it, but there is an unwillingness to bring it forward perseveringly.

18. No change.

19. [Blank]

20. [Blank]

21. Tithe commuted at £518 and 51 acres of glebe.

22. [Blank]

23. Only one.

24. Full morning service at 11.00am and afternoon at 3.00pm. During summer we have had afternoon prayer at 3.00pm and evening sermon at 6.00pm with bidding prayer, collect and hymns. We propose now a full service with sermon in the evening and prayers in the afternoon.

25. Yes, except the occasional prayers, e.g. that for Parliament is said when the Litany is not used and the Thanksgiving when no church militant.

26. On Fridays in Lent and Advent I have questioned the two first classes of school on the church catechism. I have not catechised on Sundays. It is supposed to keep some persons away.

27. I have not done so.

28. On Wednesdays, Fridays and saints' days there is Morning Prayer at 11.00am. Only five or six on average.

29. Yes on all these and on the Sunday after Easter also.

30. On the 1st Sunday in the month. It is purposed to do so also on the 3rd Sunday.

31. Yes.

32. 56 – viz 20 male and 36 female.

33. Four – three men and one young woman epileptic.

34. 23.

35. 18.

36. 264 – as by measurement allowed at the restoration.

37. No account has been kept. Well filled, all but transepts - the great family living at a distance which thins the afternoon service. The labourers we hope come much more regularly.

38. We have room for all at present who come or are likely to come.

39. 10 baptisms 1 marriage 6 burials.

40. In 1861 – six females and two males at Donhead. In 1862 – one female and

one male at Shaftesbury.

41. On the Sunday following any special collection made in church I notify the amount collected to the congregation. Also I tell the churchwarden the amount of alms collected at each offertory on sacrament Sundays that he may keep his book and compare it with mine. Also about every quarter I report to him the expenditure.

42. The sacramental alms in 1863 amounted to £14 7s 8½d plus a special collection £7 19s 1d. Total £22 6s 9½d.

43. Yes, as shown in question 41.

44. There is an Anabaptist meeting house of long standing in the village and a Primitive Methodist meeting house just across the border but practically in the parish.

45. Yes.

46. I have not put it into connection to Government.

47. At about the age of 11 and 12.

48. In some few cases, but too generally the parents do not interfere and boys become too independent and girls go early to their first place.

49. Alas – I could not, owing to weak health and having no help, but we hope to have an evening school now that we are two of us.

50. Yes.

51. Manchester relief fund three collections – £2 6s 6½d, £1 8s 10½d and £1 9s 9d. Total £5 5s 2d. To the same charity was given also, by consent of the churchwardens, the eucharistic alms for January, February and March, £1 19s 10½d. N.B. These have been reckoned in the report of eucharistic alms. October 11th – Curates Aid Society, preached for and collected by Mr Hammond. The amount accidentally forgotten to be recorded! November 1st – Augmentation of Small Benefices £1 9s 4d.

52. I know no special impediment, except what is from my own weakness, unless it be the influence exerted by dissenting farmers over their workmen. The cases are fewer than they were. An impediment not special but felt everywhere, as far as the experience of some years can speak, is the weak hold of labouring parents over their children after they go to work and leave school. They all seem for a while to be out of reach and control. I have found in former years the evening school to assist in modifying this evil, and I hope much from a restoration of it as remedial. In a parish like mine with long organised dissent there is always a special agitation against confirmation, and (which to dissenters seems analogous) the baptism of adults. I can only meet this by trying to organise and encourage a few earnest church folk to try and influence others for good.

C.A. Griffith

18. BERWICK ST LEONARD   D. Chalke

1. Berwick St Leonard. A rectory.
2. Answered by Mr Grove.
3. Population 45.

4. Answered by Mr Grove.
5. Answered by Mr Grove.
6. Answered by Mr Grove.
7. The curate is J.H. Johnson, residing at East Knoyle.
8. Answered by Mr Grove.
9. [Blank]
10. Curate licensed 24th March 1863.
11. J.H. Johnson, a priest.
12. No.
13. Yes.
14. Berwick St Leonard cum Sedgehill.
15. Yes.
16. Yes.
17. Answered by Mr Grove.
18. No.
19. Answered by Mr Grove.
20. Answered by Mr Grove.
21. Answered by Mr Grove.
22. Answered by Mr Grove.
23. Answered by Mr Grove.
24. One service on a Sunday, morning and afternoon alternately. Morning 10.30am, afternoon 2.30pm. Sermons are preached at these services.
25. Yes.
26. No.
27. No.
28. On Christmas Day, Ash Wednesday and Good Friday. Average attendance 40. This large attendance is owing to the labourers attending, who are not parishioners.
29. [a] Yes [b] Yes [c] No [d] No [e] No.
30. At Midsummer and Michaelmas.
31. No.
32. 8.
33. None.
34. 12.
35. 10. Here I should state that five or six communicants reside in the adjoining parishes.
36. The church will accommodate about 60.
37. The average will be about 22 – continues about the same.
38. No.
39. 1 Baptism 0 Marriages 0 Burials.
40. None.
41. None.
42. Average 7s 9d.
43. Yes.
44. No dissenting place of worship and no dissenters.

45. No.
46. [Blank]
47. [Blank]
48. [Blank]
49. [Blank]
50. Yes.
51. Only one collection made during the past year and that was for the poor benefice augmentation fund when it amounted to 11s.
52. [Blank]

Joseph Holden Johnson

19. BISHOP'S CANNINGS   D. Avebury

1. Bishop's Cannings, a vicarage.
2. The Dean and Chapter of Sarum.
3. 1100 by the census of 1861.
4. William Ewart, 23rd and 24th August 1862.
5. Yes.
6. In a cottage near the church.
7. [Blank]
8. None.
9. None.
10. [Blank]
11. [Blank]
12. [Blank]
13. Only the parish church.
14. [Blank]
15. In fair repair. There is no altar cloth.
16. Yes.
17. According to the prevalent ideas on the subject they do so.
18. None.
19. [Blank]
20. [Blank]
21. Glebe £36. Tithe average £700 per annum. £200 payable to the incumbents of Southbroom and Chittoe and £20 per annum to the school at Bishop's Cannings.
22. [Blank]
23. [Blank]
24. Morning Prayer with sermon at 10.30am. Evening Prayer with sermon at 3.00pm or in summer at 7.00pm.
25. Yes.
26. I have not done so here.
27. No.
28. Morning Prayer and sermon on all festivals at 11.00am. Morning service on Wednesday at 10.00am. Evening service on Friday at 4.00pm.

29. [a] Yes [b] Yes [c] Yes [d] Yes [e] Yes.

30. The 1st Sunday in each month.

31. Yes.

32. 25.

33. None.

34. 20.

35. 14.

36. 300 in the nave of the parish church.

37. I cannot say the average number. It has decidedly increased during the last year.

38. The proposal to seat the transepts giving 120 additional sittings is under consideration.

39. 27 baptisms 5 marriages 23 burials.

40. No record has been kept.

41. I lay it before the Easter vestry.

42. £12 10s.

43. Yes.

44. 1. A meeting of Baptists at Bishop's Cannings. 2. A meeting of Wesleyans at the village of Horton. 3. A meeting of Baptists at Cote. 4. A meeting of Wesleyans at Cote. Probable number 350 to 400.

45. Yes.

46. No.

47. Boys at 8, girls at 11 or 12.

48. Yes, for a time.

49. Evening schools – partially successful.

50. Yes.

51. 18th January 1863 Lancashire distress £6 16s 1½d. 17th May Diocesan Church Building Society £2 7s 9½d. 18th October Pastoral Letter – benefice endowment and parochial association for the Society for the Propagation of the Gospel in Foreign Parts £2 8s 9½d.

52. Bigoted ignorance and prejudice in the minds of the wealthier and better educated laity, rendering them suspicious of the least attempt to impose solemnity to the services of the church or to carry out at all effectively the system of the church. What religious life or activity has existed for many years has been confined to the dissenting sects. The small number of communicants shows how lamentably indifference has prevailed, and I see little hope of improvement until the poor begin to feel more deeply what is offered them in the church.

There being no resident landlord is I consider a serious disadvantage – although Mr Gore is most kind and conscientious – yet the tenants under the Crown having all 21-year leases are perfectly independent. The late revered incumbent (pace tanti viri)[1] gave in to them in everything. My position is one requiring the greatest caution and care.

William Ewart

[1] if so great a man will forgive me

20. BISHOPSTONE D. Chalke

1. Bishopstone St John. A rectory and vicarage annexed.
2. The Earl of Pembroke.
3. 685.
4. Francis Lear M.A. Instituted May 14th and Inducted May 29th 1850.
5. The time prescribed by law, which in his case is 185 days.
6. Yes.
7. [Blank]
8. A canonry of Salisbury.
9. Yes.
10. In 1863.
11. Samuel Richard Dingley, a priest.
12. No.
13. Only one.
14. [Blank]
15. Yes.
16. Yes.
17. Yes.
18. No.
19. [Blank]
20. [Blank]
21. A rent charge commuted at £960 and glebe to the value of £35 per annum.
22. [Blank]
23. No.
24. Morning service at 10.30am and afternoon service at 3.00pm with a sermon at each service. In the summer months the second service is at 6.30pm.
25. Yes.
26. During the Sundays in Lent there has generally been catechising after the 2nd lesson at Evening Prayer, upon some portion of the catechism, with a short sermon in the usual place, upon the same subject. I believe it to be a useful method of instruction.
27. The morning prayers.
28. On all holy days. The attendance is small, besides school children about eight persons.
29. [a] Yes [b] Yes [c] Yes [d] Yes [e] Yes.
30. On the last Sunday in each month.
31. Yes.
32. 120.
33. Only 2 or 3.
34. 60.
35. 45.
36. 310.
37. From 200-300. Rather decreasing.
38. No.
39. 28 baptisms 17 marriages 7 burials.

40. In 1861 – 14 males and 11 females, total 25. In 1862 – 2 females. In 1863 – 18 males and 20 females, total 38.

41. Yes. By affixing the amount to the church door on the Sunday following the collection, and reading out at the Easter vestry the receipts and expenditure of the offertory money.

42. From £12 to £14 per annum.

43. Yes.

44. The Primitive Methodists have a chapel. The number of enrolled dissenters is I should think about 40, but there are many also attend their services.

45. Yes.

46. Yes, by certificated and pupil teachers, by a grant for a teacher's residence, and by grants for books, and now by help under the Revised Code.

47. The boys at 8 or 9 years of age, the girls at 11 or 12.

48. Yes.

49. By an evening school for boys in the winter months, which has been fairly successful.

50. Yes.

51. Lancashire distress, a monthly collection £2 3s 7d. Additional Curates Society £3 3s. Poor benefices fund £2 15s 2d.

52. Besides my own inefficiency, I may mention the early age at which the boys leave school, and the little control that the parents in general exercise over them. Sunday school and night school may help in this matter, but they cannot do much. The popularity of the public house and beer house, especially on Saturday and Sunday evenings, this is most demoralising. Perhaps more frequent, well kept holidays might help to remedy the evil, and especially attention to the comfort of the homes of the poor.

Francis Lear

21. BISHOPSTROW   D. Wylye

1.   Bishopstrow, a rectory.
2.   Sir F.D. Astley. Everleigh House.
3.   268 according to the last census.
4.   John Henry Arnold Walsh, 1859.
5.   Yes.
6.   In the glebe house.
7.   [Blank]
8.   None.
9.   No.
10. [Blank]
11. [Blank]
12. [Blank]
13. No.
14. [Blank]
15. Yes.

16. Yes.

17. Yes.

18. There has been no alteration, unless the substitution of a new for a worn out organ, and a very desirable division of the larger pews, deserve to be named.

19. [Blank]

20. [Blank]

21. The endowments of the benefice arise from rent charge, of which the gross amount in 1863 was £241 6s 7d and from a few acres of glebe which let for £23 10s.

22. [Blank]

23. No.

24. Morning service with sermon at 11.00am. Service with sermon in the afternoon at 3.30pm in winter, in the evening at 6.30pm in summer.

25. Yes – unless indeed the non use of the 'Church Militant Prayer', when there is neither sacrament nor collection, be deemed an omission.

26. No.

27. I have not attempted to have daily service.

28. On Christmas Day and Good Friday, when the congregations are encouraging, and on Ascension Day. On the Wednesday evenings of Advent and Lent, with encouraging numbers. On the Friday mornings in Lent, and the mornings of Holy Week. The attendance has varied from 22 to 4.

29. [a] Yes [b] Yes [c] No [d] and [e] on one of the two.

30. It is administered 12 times in the year, including the above festivals, and on the 1st Sunday in most months.

31. Yes.

32. 84.

33. None, I think.

34. About 47.

35. Nearly 45.

36. About 170 besides the children, and persons in the organ gallery.

37. The Sunday congregations are good, though not generally crowded. Their number I never counted. They do not seem either to decrease or increase.

38. I think not.

39. 9 baptisms 1 marriage 7 burials.

40. 12.

41. Yes.

42. £15 1s 3d.

43. Yes.

44. There is no regular meeting. The village bakehouse is fitted up for worship. I only remember five persons who are avowed dissenters.

45. Yes.

46. No. The schoolroom is private property.

47. About 9 or 10, when the boys go to plow, or Warminster schools, or 12 when the girls become home nurses, or little servants.

48. Yes, especially the males.

49. Our evening school is certainly a success at present: keeping up the acquaintance between the youths and their minister, and at least civilising them.
50. Yes.
51. We have had (as it is my aim to have annually) four collections, viz for distressed manufacturers £5 17s 6d and £4 4s. For the Church Missionary Society £12 12s 8d. For the Irish Church Missions £7 11s 8d. Total £30 5s 10d.
52. I have nothing to add on these points.

H. Walsh

22 BLACKLAND   D. Avebury

1.   Blackland – a rectory.
2.   The Revd J Mayo (I believe).
3.   54 – but some portions of the parish of Calne are also visited and attend the church.
4.   William Maurice Macdonald – 1843.
5.   No – Non-resident by licence.
6.   No.
7.   Fortescue Richard Purvis – resident in the rectory of the adjoining parish – Calstone.
8.   Calstone in this diocese.
9.   Non-resident.
10. [Blank]
11. [Blank]
12. [Blank]
13. No.
14. [Blank]
15. Yes.
16. Yes.
17. As far as my observation goes.
18. None.
19. None.
20. [Blank]
21. Tithe and glebe. Tithe £160.
22. Only one parish in the benefice.
23. No house of residence.
24. Full service with sermon every Sunday morning and evening alternately, and on Christmas Day and Good Friday – 11am and 2.30pm.
25. Most certainly yes.
26. No.
27. No.
28. Christmas Day and Good Friday.
29. Yes – on the following Sunday every alternate year, excepting Ascension Day.
30. It is arranged so as to be administered once in six weeks.
31. Yes – for private use.
32. Attending the church – about 20.

33. I have no information by which to form a judgement on these questions having been but a short time in the parish.

34. [See 33]

35. [See 33]

36. About 120.

37. Between 65 and 70, no certain information. Remains about the same.

38. No further accommodation wanted.

39. 8 baptisms 0 marriages 6 burials.

40. No information.

41. Yes – on the board at the church door.

42. During 1863 - £3 12s 11d.

43. Yes.

44. None in the actual parish – but dissenting worship is performed in a room at a mill in the parish of Calne close at hand.[1]

45. Yes.[2]

46. No.

47. Boys at 9 girls at 11 or 12.[3]

48. Yes – in some instances to above 15 years.

49. Evening school has been tried, but with small success.

50. Not yet – but will before June.

51. Harvest thanksgiving S.P.G. £1 11s. Augmentation of poor benefices £1 0s 7d.

52. Nothing, except the very common impediment of dissent, which tends to produce a feeling that church and chapel are all alike and destroys <u>sound</u> churchmanship.

Fortescue Richard Purvis

[1] Methodists met at Sprays mill in Calstone prior to building a chapel at Theobald's Green in 1866.

[2] There was no school at Blackland. The return refers to the school in neighbouring Calstone.

[3] Purvis also completed the Calstone return; his reply to this question refers to a school there. Warburton says 'There is a school held in a cottage, under a mistress, with 40 scholars, some of whom attend from Blackland (on the confines of which the school is situated) and an outlying district of Calne'.

23. BOSCOMBE   D. Amesbury

1. Boscombe, a rectory.

2. The Lord Bishop of Salisbury.

3. 143.

4. Thomas Taylor, inducted April 27th 1852.

5. Yes.

6. Yes.

7. Resident.

8. No.

9. No.
10. [Blank]
11. [Blank]
12. [Blank]
13. One only.
14. [Blank]
15. Yes.
16. Yes.
17. Yes.
18. No.
19. [Blank]
20. [Blank]
21. Tithes and glebes.
22. [Blank]
23. Only one.
24. Two services. A sermon is preached morning and evening alternately.
25. Yes.
26. No.
27. No.
28. Ash Wednesday, Good Friday and Ascension Day. No exact account kept, the number on Good Friday is generally at the apparent average of Sunday, a satisfactory number attend on the Ascension. The worshippers are fewest on Ash Wednesday.
29. [a] Yes [b] Yes [c] No [d] Yes [e] No.
30. On the 1ˢᵗ Sunday in Advent, the 1ˢᵗ Sunday in Lent, and on the Sunday intermediate between the Feast of Trinity and Advent.
31. No list of communicants is kept, but all are well known.
32. Number of communicants is 33.
33. 5.
34. About 21.
35. About 18.
36. About 65 without crowding inconveniently for worship. (Above 70 were present on the afternoon of Sunday last, April 17ᵗʰ).
37. Between 50 and 60; there is no appearance of decreasing.
38. No.
39. 4 baptisms 1 marriage 2 burials.
40. 3.
41. None of offerings at communion, but collections for extraordinary purposes are generally made known from the pulpit.
42. £2 16s.
43. No.
44. No dissenting place of worship. Three families of dissenters, numbering altogether 17 persons, but the children attend church and school.
45. Yes.
46. No.

47. At about 7.

48. Yes.

49. By an evening school. Five have attended in the winter evenings for the last nine years. There are besides others who are younger.

50. No, but the copies will be sent in a few days.

51. For the distressed manufacturers in the north, £2 13s 5d and £2 6s 4d. For outfit of mechanics etc emigrating to the Canterbury Province of New Zealand 13s 3½d. Also, £2 at Christmas in aid of funds of the Society for the Promotion of the Gospel and £1 12s 6d for the Augmentation of Small Benefices in this Diocese. A sermon also was preached by the Rev T.G. Tower, travelling secretary of the S.P.G., when the sum of £1 6s 8d was collected, which will be forwarded with the subscriptions from the parish at the year's end.

52. No impediment worthy of notice.

T. Taylor

24. BOWER CHALKE or BOWERCHALKE   D. Chalke

Dr Williams could only answer many of these questions by repeating what he has said under 'Broad Chalke'. Therefore, thinking that his Curate may give greater variety, and precision in some details, he ventures to hand on this paper to the Rev John Owen (R.W.)

1. Bower Chalke, a chapelry of Broad Chalke, occupied by Rev John Owen as assistant curate.

2. See Broadchalke for all questions not answered.

3. [Blank]

4. [Blank]

5. [Blank]

6. [Blank]

7. [Blank]

8. See answer no 2.

9. [Blank]

10. Licensed to Bowerchalke in 1861.

11. John Owen, a priest.

12. No other duty.

13. [Blank]

14. Date of consecration unknown. Church of the Holy Trinity, Bowerchalke.

15. In bad repair, ordinary requisites provided.

16. Yes.

17. Yes.

18. No alterations have been made.

19. [Blank]

20. [Blank]

21. [Blank]

22. [Blank]

23. [Blank]

24. Two full services, morning at 10.30am and evening at 3.00pm. Sermons preached.

25. I do.

26. No catechising.

27. No. It has been attempted, but with no success.

28. Christmas Day, Ash Wednesday, Ascension Day and occasional services in Lent. Average attendance about 20.

29. [a] Yes [b] Yes [c] No [d] Yes [e] No.

30. 1st Sunday in every month.

31. I do.

32. 37.

33. About 15.

34. 25.

35. 18.

36. For about 220.

37. 60-70, remains about the same.

38. Great want of further church accommodation might be supplied by enlarging and repewing the church.

39. 17 baptisms 0 marriages 3 burials.

40. 15 in 1861.

41. I do.

42. £2 19s 7d.

43. There is.

44. One meeting house. About 15 regular dissenters, mostly Baptists.

45. There is.

46. I have.

47. Boys between 9 and 10, girls between 13 and 14.

48. For some time, mostly until they are confirmed.

49. I have a boys' night school. Ordinary success.

50. I am about doing so.

51. Collection for the choir. Sum collected was £2 2s 1d.

52. Want of better accommodation; we hope to restore the church shortly. Dissent.

John Owen

25. BOYTON   D. Wylye

1. Boyton, a rectory.

2. Magdalene College Oxford.

3. 393.

4. Richard Zouche Walker. September 26th 1861 and October 19th 1861.

5. Yes.

6. Yes.

7. [Blank]

8. No.

9. No.
10. [Blank]
11. [Blank]
12. [Blank]
13. No.
14. [Blank]
15. Yes.
16. Yes.
17. Yes.
18. None since the restoration in 1860.
19. [Blank]
20. [Blank]
21. Tithe £517, glebe £32, total £549.
22. From Boyton £242 9s 11d, from Corton £306 10s 1d, total £549.
23. No.
24. Full service in the morning at 10.30am. Full service in the evening at 3.00pm in winter, 6.00pm in summer.
25. Yes.
26. No.
27. No. Prayers on Wednesday morning.
28. Christmas Day, Ash Wednesday, Good Friday and Wednesday mornings in Lent. Attendance good on the first three, very bad on the last.
29. [a] Yes [b] Yes [c] No [d] No [e] Yes.
30. On the 1st Sunday in every month.
31. No.
32. About 50.
33. None.
34. 50.
35. 30.
36. Taking in the Lambert chapel, 230.
37. About 150. Lately, attendance has not been so good in the morning.
38. Perhaps a chapel at Corton.
39. 14 baptisms 1 marriage 8 burials.
40. 17.
41. Receipts for collections are put on the church door.
42. No statement is made of the offerings which amount to between £17 and £18.
43. No regular account is kept.
44. Baptist meeting house, about 60.
45. The daily school belongs to Mr Fane, the squire of the parish.
46. [Blank]
47. [Blank]
48. Yes, they are retained.
49. A night school in winter; very fair.
50. Yes.

51. Lancashire distress £5.
52. [Blank]

R. Z. Walker

26. BRADFORD ON AVON CHRIST CHURCH   D. Potterne

1. Christ Church, a perpetual curacy.
2. The vicar of Bradford.
3. [Blank]
4. William Popham, July 1848.
5. Yes.
6. Yes, in the glebe house.
7. [Blank]
8. Chaplain to the workhouse in Bradford.
9. [Blank]
10. [Blank]
11. [Blank]
12. [Blank]
13. No.
14. [Blank]
15. Yes.
16. Yes.
17. Yes.
18. No.
19. Yes, at Christ Church.
20. About 1½ miles.
21. Grant from the Ecclesiastical Commissioners £89. Pew rents about £40.
22. [Blank]
23. Only one.
24. Divine service and sermons every Sunday and Wednesday.
25. Yes, always.
26. Every Friday after prayers children of dissenters thus.
27. Morning prayers at church daily.
28. Every day. From 6 to 12.
29. [a] Yes [b] Yes [c] No [d] Yes [e] Yes.
30. On the 2nd Sunday every month.
31. Yes.
32. 150.
33. All.
34. From 40 to 50.
35. From 30 to 40.
36. 778.
37. From 300 to 400.
38. No.
39. 30 baptisms 12 marriages 32 burials.

40. In 1861 and 1863, 36 viz 24 Christ Church 12 Union [workhouse].

41. Yes.

42. Average 35s each collection.

43. Yes.

44. Four, more than two thirds comprising Baptists, Wesleyans and Independents.

45. Yes.

46. Yes.

47. About 10, a few older.

48. Yes.

49. No.

50. Churchwarden absent – they will be sent up shortly.

51. Organist salary £5 17s 5d. National schools £6 3s 7d. Poor benefice fund £5 6s 4d. For churchwardens' fund for repairs and fuel offertory once a month £1 10s each month.

52. [Blank]

William Popham

27. BRADFORD ON AVON HOLY TRINITY   D. Potterne

1. Bradford on Avon, a vicarage.

2. Dean and Chapter of Bristol.

3. Almost 3200.

4. William Henry Jones, 1851.

5. Yes.

6. Yes.

7. [Blank]

8. [Blank]

9. Yes.

10. In 1863.

11. J.R.C. Miller, a priest.

12. No.

13. Yes. Westwood church is comprised in this benefice. (See separate return).

14. Both are very old churches and the date of consecration is unknown. Bradford, The Holy Trinity, Westwood, St Mary the Virgin?

15. The church is about to be restored immediately.

16. Yes.

17. Yes.

18. No.

19. Yes.

20. 2 miles.

21. Rent charge and glebe rent £601. Fees, Easter offerings etc about £100. Total £701.

22. Bradford £390 Westwood £190 glebe £21, total £601. Subject to rates amounting to about £110 annually and about £52 annually to Queen Anne's

Bounty.

23. [Blank]

24. Full services morning and evening. Sermons at both services.

25. Yes.

26. Not in the church.

27. Daily morning service.

28. Every morning, prayers at 10.30am. About 20 in all. Every Wednesday evening a full service. From 40-80 at various times of the year. All high festivals.

29. [a] Yes [b] Yes [c] Yes [d] Yes [e] Yes.

30. On every Sunday and on the Feast of Circumcision.

31. Yes.

32. About 140.

33. I hardly remember any who have not communicated at all. Several have communicated but seldom. In some few instances they have communicated I am told at Christ Church.

34. The difference is not very perceptible from our having a weekly celebration. The average at [?] day is from 60-74.

35. [See 34]

36. About 800.

37. Morning about 500. Evening about 600-700. I hope it is increasing.

38. Not at present. In the restored church there will be an increase in the available accommodation.

39. No funerals in churchyard – a cemetery for the parish. [The page has been cut off at the bottom and some of the text is lost. No figures have been entered][1]

40. In 1861, 12.

41. An exact account is kept. The expenditure etc for schools is published.

42. £26 3s 5d.

43. Yes.

44. Five in the parish church district. I calculate the dissenters at about half the population at least.

45. Yes.

46. Yes.

47. About 10.

48. Yes to a certain extent, though many go to the dissenting Sunday schools.

49. We have had larger evening schools during the last three winters which have been successful.

50. They will be transmitted before the end of this month.

51. Bath Hospital £10. National schools £13 8s 1d. Society for the Propagation of the Gospel £7 3s 7d. Church expenses £6 14s. Augmenting poor benefices £6 8s 4d.

52. The want of real earnestness among the members of our church has always struck me as the great hindrance to the progress of the church in this place. Dissent is still strong, but we have had many gratifying proofs of their kind feeling towards the church. The great danger of all manufacturing towns is the spirit of free thinking and indifferentism. Our remedy can only be in the prayerful

discharge of our duties in the full belief that we shall ultimately "reap if we faint not".

W H Jones

¹In 1863 there were 46 Baptisms and 10 Marriages.

28. BRAMSHAW   D. Amesbury

1. The perpetual curacy of Bramshaw.
2. The Dean and Chapter of Sarum.
3. Bramshaw, Hants and Wilts, 750. Nomansland, extra parochial, 148.
4. Alan Brodrick. Licensed August 1860.
5. Yes.
6. Yes.
7. [Blank]
8. No.
9. No.
10. [Blank]
11. [Blank]
12. [Blank]
13. The school chapel at Fritham; not consecrated.
14. [Blank]
15. It may be termed in repair, but is in a poor and miserable state for this wealthy parish.
16. Yes.
17. Yes.
18. No.
19. No.
20. Fritham is distant 3½ miles.
21. Net income £150 from tithes, land and house, Queen Anne's Bounty, Easter offerings etc.
22. [Blank]
23. [Blank]
24. Sunday duty – two full services in the parish church. One at Fritham every Sunday evening necessitating a walk of 5 miles or more thither and back. Sermon at all these. Morning Prayer every Wednesday. Evening service with sermon every Friday. Service on all the festivals and during Holy Week.
25. The whole service.
26. No catechising.
27. No daily morning and evening prayers in the church.
28. On Wednesdays, Fridays, saints' days and the great festivals and on fast days. Attendance very good on Good Friday and Christmas Day, not on Ash Wednesday and other days.
29. [a] Yes [b] Yes [c] No [d] Yes [e] Yes.
30. The 1st Sunday in each month.
31. I am making a fresh one.

32. Speaking roughly, 80 or 90.

33. Very few, if any.

34. 60 or 70.

35. 50.

36. About 300 at Bramshaw and 100 at Fritham.

37. Increasing I think, but I have no method of counting them.

38. Many complaints are made of the inefficient accommodation and a new church is most desirable.

39. 26 Baptisms 6 Marriages 17 Burials.

40. In 1861 − 47. In 1864 − 31.

41. Every Christmas a list is placed on the church door.

42. £16 16s.

43. Yes.

44. A Wesleyan, a Baptist and a Primitive Methodist meeting house, besides several praying houses where meetings are held.

45. There is a daily school supported and managed solely by one of the resident gentry − G Eyre Esq.

46. The whole system of schools at Bramshaw as at present administered does not adequately provide for the daily and Sunday and evening schools and as the clergyman is not asked or permitted to have the least voice in the management and regulation of the school, he is utterly unable to superintend the education of the parish as he would wish. In the school he is powerless.

47. [See 46]

48. [See 46]

49. [See 46]

50. [Blank]

51. A collection was made for the establishment of a parochial coal club after a harvest thanksgiving, collection £6 odd, and on behalf of foreign missions, £5 odd.

52. Drunkenness, dress and dissent. Want of a new church. A school chapel at Nomansland. Funds for a curate and the present silly way of managing the school are great difficulties. Also, an increase of the Episcopate which might enable our Father in God to pay an annual visit to each parish in his diocese which is of course at present an utter impossibility.

Alan Brodrick

29. BRATTON   D. Wylye

1. Bratton.

2. Vicar of Westbury, Westbury, Wilts.

3. 741.

4. Richard Pyper, January 29th 1859.

5. He has.

6. Yes since last August.

7. [Blank]

8. No.
9. No.
10. [Blank]
11. [Blank]
12. [Blank]
13. Only one church.
14. [Blank]
15. In good repair.
16. It is.
17. They do.
18. No alterations.
19. [Blank]
20. [Blank]
21. House, about three acres of land and an endowment of £300 from the Ecclesiastical Commissioners.
22. [Blank]
23. No.
24. Two full services at 10.30am and 3.00pm each Sunday. Sermons preached at each except when Holy Communion is administered.
25. Yes.
26. I do not.
27. Only during the seasons of Advent and Lent when there is a service at 9.00am every day and at 10.00am on saints' days and holidays.
28. Daily during Advent and Lent and on saints' days and holidays – about 12 persons attend.
29. [a] Yes [b] Yes [c] Yes [d] Yes [e] Yes.
30. The 1st Sunday in every month.
31. I keep a private memorandum.
32. About 50.
33. Ten of the above have not attended.
34. 36.
35. 30.
36. 212.
37. 150 in the afternoons and 70 in the morning.
38. Not at present.
39. 15 baptisms 1 marriage 9 burials.
40. 26 in 1861.
41. Yes.
42. £20 18s 2d.
43. Yes.
44. A large Baptist chapel – there are at least 400 dissenters in the parish.
45. There is a National mixed school, a large British school and a dissenting infant school.
46. I have.
47. About 10 years.

48. Not always.

49. Night school and singing classes with good success.

50. Not yet.

51. Sick £6 18s. Lancashire relief £8 3s. National Society £2. Small benefices £2 10s. S.P.G. £1 6s 6d. Total £20 17s 6d.

52. Dissent. With God's help to quietly persevere.

Richard Pyper

30. BREMHILL & FOXHAM   D. Avebury

1. Bremhill alias Bremble. A vicarage endowed with the rectorial tithes.

2. The Right Revd the Lord Bishop of Salisbury.

3. 1172.

4. Charles Amyand Harris MA. Collated Feb 24th and inducted Mar 20th 1863.

5. Residence did not commence until May 23rd 1863.

6. In the glebe house.

7. Resident.

8. The rectory of Highway annexed to Bremhill (see return) and the archdeaconry of Wilts, in this diocese.

9. Revd William Feltham. Priest. Licensed Nov 22nd 1861. Revd Cecil Edward Fisher. Priest. Licensed Feb 18th 1864.

10. [See 9.]

11. [See 9.]

12. Mr Feltham is curate of Highway.

13. The chapelry of Foxham. Date of consecration and dedication unknown. The church of Highway (see return).

14. [See 13.]

15. Bremhill church in good repair and duly provided. Foxham chapel in repair and provided but should be rebuilt.

16. Yes. Bremhill and Foxham.

17. Yes.

18. No alteration.

19. Baptisms and burials, but not marriages at Foxham.

20. Foxham 3½ miles. Highway 6 miles.

21. Bremhill – glebe (gross rental) £398. Cottage (Gross rental) £5. Rent charge (commuted value) £90. Money payments in lieu of tithe £145 15s. [Total] £638 15s. Foxham glebe £1. Highway see return.

22. [See 21.]

23. One at Bremhill. (See Highway return).

24. Bremhill. Summer 11.00am 6.00pm. Winter 10.30am 3.30 or 3.00pm. [Both] with sermon. Foxham 11.00am or 3.00pm alternate Sundays with sermon. Highway. (See return).

25. Yes.

26. No.

27. At Bremhill 10.00am daily.

28. Foxham 11.00am on Holy Days: with sermon Christmas Day, Good Friday, Ascension. Evening service with sermon Fridays in Advent; Wednesdays in Lent. Bremhill Christmas Day and Good Friday as on Sunday. Ascension Day morning service. Friday evening in Lent and every evening in Passion Week with sermon. Attendance (of adults) when no sermon. Foxham – Bremhill 5. With sermon Foxham 30 Bremhill 45.

29. [a] Yes [b] Yes [c] Not hitherto [d] Yes [e] No. At Bremhill and Foxham.

30. At Bremhill 1st and 3rd Sunday of the month. At Foxham eight times a year.

31. Yes.

32. 120 at Bremhill and Foxham.

33. About 10.

34. Bremhill 40. Foxham 16.

35. Bremhill 24. Foxham 16.

36. Bremhill 330. Foxham 150 but not available on account of pews.

37. Bremhill about 240 including children. Foxham about 90 including children.

38. At Foxham the pew accommodation is wretched. Much benefit would arise if by a territorial rearrangement the churches of Foxham, West Tytherton and Kellaways could be made available for the population between the Wilts & Berks Canal and the river Avon.

39. Bremhill 27 baptisms 4 marriages 17 burials. Foxham 14 baptisms 6 burials.

40. 54 at Bremhill and Foxham in 1863. No record of 1861 and 1862.

41. Yes.

42. Bremhill £11 10s 4d. Foxham £6 4s 3d.

43. Yes.

44. Moravian chapel with middle and poor school Tytherton. Wesleyan chapel at Spirt Hill. Cottage meetings of Baptists and Mormonites at Charlcott. The inhabitants of Tytherton chiefly Moravians, of Spirt Hill chiefly Wesleyan or Baptist.

45. At Bremhill and Foxham and a good dame school at Charlcott.

46. At Bremhill.

47. Boys about 9. Girls about 11.

48. Partially.

49. There are evening schools at Bremhill and Charlcott November to February but not largely attended and chiefly by boys under 19.

50. They are in preparation.

51. A sermon was preached at Bremhill and Foxham for the poor benefices' augmentation fund. Collection at Bremhill £2 19s.

52. The chief impediment consists in the population being distributed in hamlets distant from one another and from the parish church; while the Moravian chapel at Tytherton and the Wesleyans at Spirt Hill are of ready access to those hamlets. Charlcott, Tytherton and Foxham would benefit by being rearranged as ecclesiastical districts.

C.A. Harris

31. BRITFORD   D. Chalke

1. Britford, a vicarage.
2. Dean and Chapter of Salisbury.
3. 410.
4. Richard Humphrey Hill, January 1850.
5. Yes.
6. Yes.
7. [Blank]
8. No.
9. [Blank]
10. [Blank]
11. [Blank]
12. [Blank]
13. [Blank]
14. [Blank]
15. Yes.
16. Tolerably.
17. Yes.
18. No.
19. [Blank]
20. [Blank]
21. Tithe rent charge, gross amount £312.
22. [Blank]
23. [Blank]
24. Two, morning and afternoon, 10.30am and 3.00pm. The sermon preached alternately.
25. Yes.
26. No. The arrangements in the church not calculated for the venture.
27. No.
28. On the festivals and fasts when the vicar's health permits it.
29. [a] Yes [b] Yes [c] No [d] No [e] Yes.
30. Every seven weeks.
31. Of the number – not of names.
32. About 80 – most of whom attend the neighbouring churches of Alderbury, Nunton, Homington, Coombe and East Harnham.
33. [A figure has been entered and crossed out]
34. 21.
35. 21.
36. 300.
37. 80 to 100. Very stationary for some years past.
38. No.
39. 10 baptisms 5 marriages 10 burials.
40. In 1861 I believe the number was 20 besides eight from the workhouse.
41. Yes, by affixing the list to the church door and by means of the churchwardens.
42. £6 18s.

43. A regular account is kept.

44. None – a very few Wesleyans.

45. Yes.

46. No.

47. At about 10.

48. Some of them.

49. [Blank]

50. They await the signatures of the churchwardens.

51. For poor benefices in the diocese £1 17s. For the distress in Lancashire £14 2s.

52. I must remark that the custom of pulling down houses (10 having been pulled down within a few years) is beginning to tell upon our population. There must prove a great decrease in all the items I have answered, as well as in our school. It is a great mistake.

R.H. Hill

32. BRIXTON DEVERILL   D. Wylye

1. Brixton Deverill, a rectory.

2. The Lord Bishop of Salisbury, The Palace, Salisbury.

3. 230.

4. Emmanuel Strickland, 1858.

5. Yes.

6. Yes.

7. [Blank]

8. No.

9. No.

10. [Blank]

11. [Blank]

12. [Blank]

13. No.

14. [Blank]

15. Yes.

16. Yes.

17. Yes.

18. The chancel has been lengthened 14 feet, a new vestry has been built, and the nave re-seated by a faculty.

19. [Blank]

20. [Blank]

21. Tithe rent charge and glebe. The apportionment of rent charge is £385 and the rent of the glebe £60 per annum.

22. [Blank]

23. [Blank]

24. Morning and evening service at 10.30am and 6.00pm. Sermons are given at these services.

25. Yes.
26. No.
27. No.
28. On Holy-days. Ten adults besides 30 schoolchildren.
29. [a] Yes [b] Yes [c] Yes [d] Yes [e] Yes.
30. On the 1st Sunday of the month.
31. Yes.
32. 31.
33. None.
34. 22.
35. 18.
36. 130.
37. 80 – neither.
38. No.
39. 7 baptisms 1 marriage 7 burials.
40. In 1861, seven.
41. Yes.
42. In 1863 £3 18s.
43. Yes.
44. None. About a dozen who belong to the Primitive Methodists.
45. Yes.
46. No.
47. 10.
48. Yes.
49. Evening schools. Respect for the clergyman and his office.
50. Yes.
51. Church Missionary Society £2 4s. Distress in Lancashire £6 18s 5½d. Irish Church Missions £2 7s ½d. Benefice augmentation fund £2 10s 2d. S.P.G. £2 4s 1d. Total £16 3s 9d.
52. The indifference of the labourers to their religious duties.

Emmanuel Strickland

33. BROAD CHALKE   or BROADCHALKE   D. Chalke

1. Broadchalke, a vicarage.
2. Provost and Fellows, King's College Cambridge.
3. 800 in Broadchalke and 500 in Bowerchalke.
4. Rowland Williams. January 1859, I believe.
5. Yes.
6. Yes.
7. [Blank]
8. No.
9. Has recently had occasional assistance from Revd Mr Wilson at Fisherton, Revd Mr Darland at Sarum and Revd Mr Williams at Endless St. The last named, Revd Mr Williams, is likely to do the Sunday duty for three months.

10. [Blank]

11. [Blank]

12. [Blank]

13. Yes.

14. Broadchalke church and Bowerchalke chapel. The rest of the question relates to a time prior to my incumbency.

15. Church, yes, chapel but middling.

16. Now being done.

17. Yes, so far as appears necessary.

18. Stoves have been employed. Chandeliers are employed to give light.

19. Yes.

20. Two miles.

21. Vicarial tithes £147, glebe land £60, total £207 exclusive of the chapel.

22. Bowerchalke £100, absorbed by curate and other charges.

23. One at each place.

24. 10.30am and 3.00pm, full services in both. In summer, in the mother church, at 6.00pm instead of 3.00pm.

25. Never any part of it, but read it. [The word 'say' in the question has been underlined and quotation marks added].

26. Sometimes in Lent I hear the catechism and ask a few of the plainest possible questions. Probably, it does more good than harm.

27. Reasonable hindrances, and especially the want of a congregation, occur habitually.

28. Every Friday evening with sermon. Attendance 25 in winter, barely 10 in summer.

29. [a] Yes [b] Yes [c] No [d] Yes [e] Yes.

30. 1st Sunday in each month, unless very near a high festival.

31. In the tablets of my mind.

32. About 30 in Broadchalke.

33. Not many.

34. 25.

35. 21.

36. I can only guess; perhaps 400 or 500 in the church, 200 or 250 in the chapel.

37. I will guess it at 150, or, 200 with children. If any sensible change, it is increase, not diminution.

38. At Bowerchalke there is very great need of enlarging and improving the chapel.

39. 25 baptisms 6 marriages 25 burials.

40. Was there a confirmation? My means of knowing are not equal to those of the Right Revd Bishop, who doubtless received lists.

41. Yes, usually from the pulpit or otherwise.

42. An average of 9s each sacrament.

43. Yes, of the amount and of the distribution.

44. One 'Independent' chapel, rebuilt as bicentenary. One 'Primitive's' chapel. The majority of the population attend church and meeting at their fancy.

45. Yes.

46. <u>Yes, and found it work eminently for the advantage of the school. The Revised Code gave our school new life.</u>

47. About 10.

48. In some cases, yes.

49. I have found night classes for boys, or young men, very useful; almost the only practical instrument of good here, as regards the diffusion of information.

50. I hope to do so.

51. The only object for which I felt inclined to collect, was the Infirmary at Salisbury, to which useful charity my parishioners resort largely.

52. Besides the general tendency of English rustics to consider extempore prayer and emotional preaching as more properly 'religious' than any liturgical or organised system, the more 'special impediments' to my own ministry, and to the welfare of the church, have arisen from episcopal litigation. If it would be too strong, or hardly gracious, to describe the whole process as an enforcement of the theology of Laud in the spirit of Titus Oates, it must at least be considered as an introduction of the most inappropriate test possible for either literary fact or opinion. It has exhibited a bishop professing to honour the Bible, yet labouring to close it against the people; pleading 'loyalty' to a Protestant church as an excuse for urging an almost idolatrous materialism as regards the sacraments: and more than one eminent person, whose position was judicial, assuming the character of a partisan. I say nothing of the coarser weapons employed by episcopal allies in the press: but must confess, that a growing mistrust of episcopal justice and consistency has lessened in me that spirit of confiding obedience which is so charming an ingredient in the ministerial character.

Rowland Williams

34 BROAD HINTON   D. Avebury

1. Broad Hinton. A vicarage.

2. The Revd G.E. Howman, Barnesley, Cirencester.

3. 430 or rather below.

4. The Revd William Corkson, I believe in 1835.

5. No.

6. No, but in the Island of Jersey.

7. The Revd John Thomson, yes.

8. Yes, Hungerford, diocese of Oxford.

9. [Blank]

10. [Blank]

11. [Blank]

12. [Blank]

13. No.

14. [Blank]

15. Yes.

16. Yes.

17. Yes.

18. No.

19. [Blank]

20. [Blank]

21. [Blank]

22. [Blank]

23. No.

24. Two services at 11.00am and at 3.00pm with sermons.

25. Yes.

26. Not since last visitation. I catechised in church publicly for many years, but the practice was never popular here. The children of the parish are so well trained in the catechism and liturgy at day school and Sunday school that so far as they are concerned this practice would not benefit them, although it would the adults.

27. No, as in a rural parish like this the labourers would not attend.

28. On Christmas Day, Circumcision, Epiphany, Ash Wednesday, all the Wednesdays and Fridays during Lent, Good Friday and Ascension Day. On the Nativity and Death of our Lord the attendance is the same as on a Sunday, but on other occasions not above three or four grown up persons besides the school children.

29. [a] Yes [b] Yes [c] No [d] Yes [e] No.

30. On 1st Sunday in Lent, 4th Sunday after Trinity, 9th ditto, 16th ditto. On the 1st Sunday in Advent, in all eight times a year.

31. Yes.

32. About 40.

33. About 10.

34. About 25.

35. About 18.

36. For 319 although the population is under 430.

37. About 150 am and about the same pm. Stationary, but <u>more decided in their principles and more religious.</u>

38. No. There is <u>too much</u> since Broad Town church was built and the parish divided into two sections.

39. 11 baptisms 4 marriages 8 burials.

40. In 1861 there were 19 confirmed. None in 1862 or in 1863.

41. Only of the collections when receipts are put on a board in the church porch.

42. £2 8s 9d.

43. A regular account is kept for my own use.

44. A private house is used as a meeting house by a tailor who calls himself a Bible Christian, or Baptist. There may be about 50 persons who dissent from the church, and some call themselves Primitive Methodists, some Wesleyans, some Baptists or Brethren, and some Mormonites. The Baptists are the greatest enemies to my ministry and oppose me greatly in preparing candidates for confirmation. The preacher whose cousin is going to be confirmed tore the catechism on confirmation he was learning and threw it into the fire in presence of the uncle and aunt.

45. Yes.

46. No.

47. Nearly all the boys of labourers go to work about 7, and some go to bird scaring at 6. The low wages of labourers oblige their children to work at a very early age for 1/6 a week.

48. Yes, up to about 13 or 14 when the boys especially fancy themselves too big to attend school.

49. Yes, by an evening school, but they come only for secular instruction, and not for religious, still such schools are good.

50. Yes.

51. For the S.P.G. collection £1 18s 5½d. For Augmentation of Small Benefices £1 2s 3d.

52. The numerous sects about, and their different opinions cause numbers of the parishioners to believe there is no good in religion at all, and therefore they absent themselves from church all together. – None, excepting a faithful discharge of clerical duties and a holy life, with daily prayer for God's Blessing.

John Thomson

35. BROAD TOWN D. Avebury

1. Christ Church, Broad Town a perpetual curacy.

2. Vicar of Broad Hinton and vicar of Clyffe.

3. 473.

4. A[lexander] J W Morrison.

5. Yes.

6. Yes.

7. [Blank]

8. No.

9. No.

10. [Blank]

11. [Blank]

12. [Blank]

13. No.

14. [Blank]

15. Yes.

16. Yes.

17. Yes.

18. No.

19. [Blank]

20. [Blank]

21. £30 from Clyffe £10 from Broad Hinton £60 from Ecclesiastical Commissioners £24 from Bounty Board.

22. [Blank]

23. No.

24. Morning commencing at 10.30am, afternoon from Michaelmas to Easter commencing at 3.00pm. Evening from Easter to Michaelmas commencing at

5.30pm.

25. The whole.

26. No. Having practiced catechising in former parishes I consider its advantages to be very great but the prejudice against it in Broad Town has rather so deterred me from attempting it.

27. Yes, until prevented lately by illness from attending church.

28. On Ash Wednesday, Good Friday and Ascension Day. The attendance on Ash W and Ascension Day and G Friday is about 50. On Good Friday morning the farmers who attend church require their labourers to attend and it is then about 150.

29. [a] Yes [b] Yes [c] Yes [d] Yes [e] Yes.

30. On the 1st Sunday of the month.

31. Yes.

32. 22.

33. Two – one from illness.

34. 18.

35. 15.

36. 240.

37. 60. Stationary.

38. No.

39. 0 baptisms 2 marriages 4 burials.

40. In 1861- 15. In 1863- one.

41. Yes.

42. On an average 5s 6d a Sunday.

43. Yes.

44. One meeting house of Primitive Methodists. Several cottage meetings of Wesleyans and Primitives. There are a few Baptists. 400 dissenters at least and of the remainder I do not think there are 30 who do not go to meetings as well as to church.

45. Yes.

46. [Blank]

47. Boys at about 7 or 8. Girls stay till 12 generally.

48. Yes, but the church Sunday school is limited to 27.

49. No. And from the results favourable to the church of adult and evening schools in the neighbouring parishes I am not encouraged to do so.

50. Yes.

51. For the Society of the Propagation of the Gospel £0 19s 3d. For the Augmentation of Poor Benefices £2.

52. The systematic combination of the dissenters – their long possession of this district and the dreadful laxity of the prevailing opinion and habits as to the relations of the sexes. Any attempt to improve and correct these opinions and habits drives the people seemingly to a firmer association with dissent. In this parish there is scarcely any form or mode of sin between the sexes which has not its living representative. I believe that a revival of discipline and the exclusion from Christian burial of such offenders would greatly tend to winning back many

to the church by impressing the people with a sense of reality of the church's system.

A J W Morrison

36. BROMHAM   D. Avebury
1. Bromham, a rectory.
2. The present rector.
3. 1174.
4. Edward Betenson Edgell. Instituted and inducted in June 1857 having been previously curate; priested in 1843.
5. Yes.
6. In the rectory.
7. [Blank]
8. No.
9. No.
10. [Blank]
11. [Blank]
12. [Blank]
13. No.
14. [Blank]
15. It is in good repair having been restored in 1842.
16. The old churchyard has been closed excepting vaults by Order in Council and a cemetery – an acre in extent has been provided and consecrated. It is walled all round and in good order.
17. Yes.
18. No alteration has been made either in church or chancel since the last visitation, except that the organ has been removed into the chancel.
19. The cemetery is so near the church that no chapel was required.
20. [Blank]
21. From commuted tithe and glebe. The gross amount derived from both sources being about £920.
22. [Blank]
23. No.
24. Two full services at 11.00am and 3.30pm. During the <u>summer</u> months the second service is in the evening at 6.00pm.
25. Yes.
26. No.
27. No.
28. On Christmas Day and Good Friday there is full morning service in the church and an evening in the schoolroom the church not being lighted at night – where there is a full attendance. There are prayers in the church during Lent on the Conversion of St Paul, Holy Thursday, the Epiphany.
29. [a] Yes [b] Yes [c] Yes [d] Yes [e] Yes.
30. The Holy Communion is administered eight times in the year – Christmas

Day, Easter Day, Trinity Sunday, 7th after Trinity, 14th after Trinity, Advent Sunday and one other Sunday, so as to make it about every six weeks.

31. No.

32. About 65.

33. All have I believe during the year.

34. 45.

35. 40.

36. [Blank]

37. The church is well attended and the attendance has certainly increased.

38. No.

39. 36 baptisms 8 marriages 22 burials under the average.

40. None since the last confirmation.

41. No.

42. The alms for 1863 amounted to £7 10s.

43. No regular book is kept.

44. There are three dissenting chapels, Baptist, Wesleyan and Primitive Methodist. The dissenters form about a third I should think of the population.

45. There is a daily boys' and girls' school.

46. No.

47. The boys, as soon as they are able to earn anything, are removed – about 9 or 10 years of age. The girls remain longer.

48. Some attend Sunday school after leaving the day school.

49. I have had a night school for young men during the winter months November to March. The attendance at which amounted to above 50.

50. The copies are made and will be sent immediately.

51. For the Lancashire operatives and the propagation of the gospel society. For the former the collection was £10, for the latter £6.

52. What in country parishes one sees most is the lack of co-operation on the part of the laity – gentry and farmers. No interest is shewn either in parish matters, or the schools, or the spiritual welfare of the poor. More in every way might be done if this co-operation could be secured.

Edward B. Edgell

37. BROUGHTON GIFFORD   D. Potterne

1. Broughton Gifford, a rectory.

2. The Lord Chancellor.

3. Under 600 – perhaps 10 or 12 under.

4. John Wilkinson, 1848.

5. Yes.

6. Yes.

7. [Blank]

8. No.

9. No.

10. [Blank]
11. [Blank]
12. [Blank]
13. One church.
14. [Blank]
15. Yes.
16. Yes.
17. Yes.
18. No.
19. [Blank]
20. [Blank]
21. Tithe rent charge and glebe lands.
22. [Blank]
23. One only.
24. Two services. One at 10.30am another at 3.00pm. A sermon at each.
25. Yes.
26. No.
27. No.
28. On the chief Holy Days.
29. [a] Yes [b] Yes [c] Yes [d] Yes [e] Yes.
30. On the 1st Sunday in each month.
31. No.
32. 18.
33. All have communicated.
34. 18.
35. 15.
36. 420.
37. 200. Stationary. The population is decreasing.
38. No.
39. 16 baptisms (5 of these are not infants – they are the children of the chief farmer in the parish) 2 marriages 11 burials.
40. In 1861, 21.
41. Yes, at the church door.
42. During the year 1863 £10 5s.
43. Yes.
44. Two. Baptist (endowed) chapel, and Wesleyan chapel. Two thirds are dissenters.
45. Yes.
46. Yes for building, not for annual support.
47. 10 for boys, 12 for girls.
48. Not generally. The Baptists have a good Sunday school. Their day school has been closed by the improved church day school.
49. Yes – much success.
50. Yes.
51. Lancashire distress £6 14s. Collection for small benefices augmentation 18s 6d.

52 [Blank]

John Wilkinson

38. BULFORD   D. Amesbury
1. Bulford, a perpetual curacy.
2. Anthony Southby M.D.
3. Males 179, females 191. Total 370, dwellings 80.
4. Thomas Darnton Milner[1] L.L.B., after Michaelmas 1852.
5. No!
6. No glebe house. Non resident.
7. John James Scott, Exeter College Oxford M.A.
8. No!
9. [Blank]
10. [Blank]
11. [Blank]
12. [Blank]
13. One church only.
14. [Blank]
15. In tolerable repair and all things necessary are provided.
16. Yes!
17. Yes!
18. None as far as I can ascertain!
19. [Blank]
20. [Blank]
21. £75.
22. [Blank]
23. No glebe house.
24. Divine service, morning at 11.00am and afternoon at 3.00pm, sermons delivered at both services. When the Lord's Supper is celebrated the sermon is omitted.
25. Certainly!
26. Yes! After the 2nd Lesson in the afternoon, during Lent. Some part of the church catechism, repeated by Sunday scholars, accompanied by scripture proofs. It has been productive of good results.
27. No! To obtain even two or three for daily prayer would be impossible; men, women and children being all employed in farm labour from sunrise to sunset.
28. On all the minor festivals, and on Wednesdays in Lent. The churchwarden's and clergyman's families, the day school and a few communicants.
29. [a] Yes [b] Yes [c] Yes [d] Yes [e] Yes.
30. On the 1st Sunday of every month.
31. Yes.
32. 37 in 1863 – 29 additional up to Easter 1864, total 66.
33. Not any to my knowledge have omitted.
34. All the above mentioned are regular attendants. Out of 28 confirmed in

March, all but 5 presented themselves at Easter – 14 of whom came for the second time.

35. About 25 monthly.

36. 260. Seats in pews 166, free seats 36, total 202. School seats 45, gallery 12, total 57. Total 259.

37. Nearly 100 in the morning and 50 more in the afternoon. Certainly increasing, especially in the afternoon.

38. None whatever.

39. 16 baptisms since August 1st and one previous to that date in 1863. 2 marriages. 9 burials in 1863.

40. 1861 – none, 1862 - none, 1863 – 15 females and 13 males in March.

41. Yes!

42. From August 1st to April 3rd inclusive £4 12s 3d.

43. Yes!

44. One meeting house of the sect of Independents. About 112.

45. Yes!

46. The school being supported by Dr Southby, he declines all interference.

47. At the age of 10 years at the latest. They enter at 3 years. Some leave at 7 or 8 for farm labour.

48. Yes. By the aid of prize tickets and rewards as encouragement for lessons and regular attendance.

49. An adult evening school for farm lads and plough boys, between 13 and 21 years, has been held at my private residence from October to January twice a week.

50. Yes.

51. For S.P.G. £3 in October and for the Augmentation of Small Benefices in the Diocese £3 in December.

52. The Independent meeting house, endowed, and its resident minister, who professedly administers baptism and the Lord's Supper to the detriment of the church. He has been living in a house specially built for the dissenting minister, for the last 20 years in Bulford, and from this one circumstance alone possesses considerable influence in the village, while there is no parsonage, or any house fit for a clergyman to reside in. Remedy – a parsonage, in order to secure a resident clergyman and one likely to be permanent. Until this can be effected, I would recommend that the clergyman, incumbent of Milston, be invited to accept the curacy, being resident within a mile of Bulford church.

John James Scott M.A.

¹ The correct spelling is Millner (see Crockford's and Cambridge Alumni)

Mem: The Sunday School Scholars have increased from 34 in August last to 53 on the books, April 17th 1864. Sunday April 17th attendance at school and church 45. At church this afternoon (including the school) 112 persons. The absence of many are accounted for, during the lambing season, which extends from January to May.

	Bibles	Test	Prayer B
Mrs Southby's gift to School	13	13 large 12 small	13 large 12 small
Presented to new communicants after confirmation	25		
Purchased by parishioners	9	6	31
Total	47	31	56

Grant from Parent Society (S.P.C.K.) £3 <u>tracts in circulation.</u>
Mrs Southby's gift to the school £1 13s.
To April 17th – total purchased from Salisbury (Depot) and paid for £6 10s.
Total £8 3s.

39. BULKINGTON   D. Potterne
1. Bulkington, a chapel of ease to Keevil.
2. [Blank]
3. 260.
4. [Blank]
5. [Blank]
6. [Blank]
7. J.M. Tandy, not resident.
8. [Blank]
9. [Blank]
10. The assistant curate is not licensed.
11. [Blank]
12. [Blank]
13. [Blank]
14. [Blank]
15. Yes.
16. Yes.
17. Yes.
18. No.
19. Baptisms and burials.
20. 2 miles.
21. Rent charge.
22. Tithes commuted at £101.
23. No.
24. Morning service with sermon at 10.30am, afternoon service with sermon at 3.00pm.
25. I have reason to believe the curate does.
26. No.
27. [Blank]
28. Good Friday and Christmas Day.
29. At the great festivals.

30. [Blank]
31. I have no information on these questions.
32. Ditto.
33. Ditto.
34. Ditto.
35. Ditto.
36. About 120 or 130.
37. [Blank]
38. No.
39. 7 baptisms 4 burials.
40. I am not able to say from Bulkington.
41. The former curate did so.
42. I am unable to say.
43. I do not know.
44. A Wesleyan meeting house.
45. Yes.
46. No.
47. As early as 8 years old.
48. Very few.
49. An evening school has recently been opened.
50. [Blank]
51. I received no information of the collections in Bulkington.
52. [Blank]

William Henry Pooke

40. BURBAGE   D. Marlborough

1. All Saints Burbage, a vicarage.
2. The Bishop of Salisbury.
3. 1603.
4. Thomas Stanton M.A. 1852.
5. Yes.
6. Yes.
7. Resident.
8. No.
9. Yes.
10. 1863.
11. Hugh Stowell, priest.
12. No.
13. No.
14. [Blank]
15. Yes.
16. Yes.
17. Yes, as they are usually understood.
18. No.

19. No chapels.

20. [Blank]

21. Rent charge commuted at £363 and about 7 acres of glebe.

22. All one.

23. No.

24. Two full services with sermons every Sunday at 10.30am and 3.00pm.

25. Yes.

26. Yes, in Lent. Standing on the chancel step I take small portions of the catechism for scriptural proof and explanation. Very useful for adults when they come and most useful to the children.

27. I have tried it at different times, but the congregations are most unsatisfactory in number.

28. Christmas Day, Lent, Good Friday, Ascension Day, etc.

29. Christmas Day, Easter Day, Whit Sunday or the Feast of Trinity.

30. 1st Sunday in the month.

31. Yes.

32. About 100.

33. Most have done so.

34. About 40.

35. About 30.

36. About 560.

37. Nearly full and increasing.

38. A district church or chapel is wanted between Steep and Ram Alley, i.e. at the north end of the parish.

39. 64 baptisms 11 marriages 25 burials.

40. In 1861 31 males and 35 females.

41. Yes.

42. £12 5s 10d in 1863.

43. Yes.

44. There is a small Wesleyan meeting built about 40 years. There are few dissenters and these diminish both in number and importance.

45. Yes. National and infants both very well attended. There is also a large Sunday school. In all about 300 scholars.

46. Yes.

47. About 10 or 11.

48. Yes, many of them.

49. There are three or four evening schools in the parish kept privately by churchmen.

50. Mine is regularly sent, but this year has not yet been dispatched.

51. Society for Propagation of the Gospel £4 3s 1d. Ruri-Decanal offertory for Augmentation of Poor Benefices £1 4s 3d. Augmentation of Poor Benefices £3 15s 3d.

52. The navvies have been our torment for the last two years. The beer shops are a perpetual impediment to the growth of morality and religion. A Freehold Land Society is erecting cottages and injuring the parish, by introducing many

worthless characters who would not otherwise be admitted. We thus have two new beer shops.

Thomas Stanton MA

41. BURCOMBE   D. Wilton
1. Burcombe, a perpetual curacy.
2. The Revd C.B. Pearson, Knebworth, Herts.
3. 400.
4. Revd Edward Fiennes Trotman. March 1858.
5. Yes.
6. In the glebe house.
7. [Blank]
8. None.
9. No.
10. [Blank]
11. [Blank]
12. [Blank]
13. There is attached (though not necessarily) the chaplaincy of the Hospital of St John.
14. [Blank]
15. Yes.
16. Yes.
17. There is only <u>one</u> churchwarden at Burcombe. He does his duty well.
18. None.
19. No.
20. The chapel of the alms house is one mile distant.
21. From Queen Anne's Bounty £40. Prescriptive payment at Burcombe £11. Tithe rent charge on Ugford £30. Total £81 per annum. The emoluments of the chaplaincy are not endowments, but at the will of the priory.
22. [Blank]
23. Only one, at Burcombe.
24. In Burcombe parish church, morning prayer at 10.30am and evening prayer at 3.00pm. Sermons are given at both services.
25. Yes.
26. I do not.
27. I do not.
28. On Christmas Day, Ash Wednesday, Good Friday and Ascension Day. Christmas Day and Good Friday are observed as Sunday. Ash Wednesday and Ascension Day are <u>ill-observed.</u> Through Lent and Advent I have morning prayer on Wednesdays and Fridays, evening prayer with a course of sermons on Thursdays. The evening services are well attended – not so the morning services.
29. [a] Yes [b] Yes [c] No [d] Yes [e] Yes.
30. On the 1st Sunday in every month.
31. I do.

32. 55.

33. Two. My experience is that among the agricultural poor, when once they are prevailed on to become communicants, they are most regular in attendance on the holy communion.

34. 35.

35. 25.

36. The parish church will seat 192.

37. About 160. The congregation is regular and stationary.

38. Not at present.

39. 9 baptisms 2 marriages 4 burials.

40. 18 young people.

41. I circulate a printed statement of all offerings, collections and charities, at the end of each year, which I have reason to believe meets with approbation.

42. In 1861, before monthly communion was established, the alms amounted to £8 17s 6d. In 1862, £17 18s 1d. In 1863, £13 1s 2d.

43. Yes.

44. There are no dissenting places of worship. In a hamlet called Ugford, lately severed from South Newton and added to Burcombe, nearly all the people, to the number of 30, are Primitive Methodists or Independents. This I ascribe to their former isolation from their parish church.

45. There is a daily school.

46. I have not yet placed the school under Government inspection, owing to the insufficiency of the buildings. I hope ere long to be able to build schools and school house, and with it to introduce a new system.

47. Girls at the age of 12 years. Boys at the age of 8 and sometimes younger.

48. Yes – girls will stay in the Sunday School under a good teacher to the age of 17 – and boys over 16 years.

49. I have been successful in night schools, having had during 1860, 1861 and 1862 young men ranging from 12 years to 28. I find now that they consider they have learnt enough and require other inducements to keep them in the night school. Music is one of the greatest inducements. The night school proper is now attended by boys to the age of 16.

50. I have.

51. Diocesan Church Building Society £2 8s 7d in 1862 and £1 in 1863. Church Missionary Society £3 1s in 1862 and £2 8s 6d in 1863. S.P.G. £8 0s 6d in 1862 and £5 1s 5d in 1863. National Society for Education £1 5s 9d in 1862. Lancashire Relief Fund £4 18s 1½d in 1862. Home Missions £2 2s 1½d in 1863. Small Benefices £1 1s 6d in 1863. Infirmary £1 2s in 1863. The difference in the collections of 1862 and 1863 is to be accounted for mainly by the departure from the parish of a most liberal family, who lived at Burcombe House.

52. [Blank]

Edward Fiennes Trotman

42. BUTTERMERE   D. Marlborough

1. Buttermere, a rectory.
2. The Bishop of Winchester.
3. 120-130.
4. Rev N Dodson. Admitted 1818.
5. He is non resident.
6. [Blank]
7. Rev J H Dixon is curate and does not reside in the parish.
8. The incumbent is also rector of Abingdon in the diocese of Oxford.
9. [Blank]
10. [Blank]
11. [Blank]
12. [Blank]
13. No.
14. [Blank]
15. Yes.
16. Yes.
17. Yes.
18. No.
19. [Blank]
20. [Blank]
21. Tithes and about two acres of glebe. Gross about £300 per annum, if not exactly so.
22. [Blank]
23. [Blank]
24. On alternate Sundays, morning service at 10.30 am and evening service at 5.30pm. Every other Sunday evening service at 5.30pm. Sermons at each service.
25. Yes.
26. No.
27. No.
28. On Good Friday congregation generally 50 or 60. Sometimes more.
29. Holy Communion is administered at Christmas, Easter, Whitsuntide, the Feast of Trinity and Michaelmas.
30. [Blank]
31. No, the number being so small.
32. 11.
33. None.
34. 9 or 10.
35. [Blank]
36. About 80.
37. About 38, perhaps 40. I am unable to say that it is either increasing or decreasing. The position of the church renders any increase extremely unlikely.
38. No.
39. 3 baptisms 0 marriages 2 burials.
40. Four in 1861.
41. Yes.

42. Usually from 5/- to 6/-.

43. A regular account is kept but not in a special book.

44. Meetings of Primitive Methodists are held in a private house. There are probably not more than two persons who would not come to church, but there are very many more who would go to meetings.

45. No daily school. An attempt to establish one having failed in consequence of the general preference for Fosbury school when the children are received.

46. [Blank]

47. [Blank]

48. Partially.

49. No adult or evening schools.

50. Yes.

51. Society for the Propagation of the Gospel 13s 6d. Fund for Augmentation of Small Benefices in the diocese of Salisbury – collection not in church – amount £5 15s.

52. It is not easy to answer this question, as different obstacles appear to predominate at different times. But at present there appears to be no special hindrance.

J H Dixon

43 CALNE cum HOLY TRINITY   D.Avebury

1. Calne a vicarage.

2. The Bishop of Salisbury.

3. 5106.

4. John Guthrie Feb 1835.

5. He has.

6. He has.

7. [Blank].

8. He does not.

9. He has three – all licensed.

10. [See 11].

11. Rev George Davenport priest licensed Jan 1863. Rev S Cavan priest Sep 1864. Rev G Collis deacon.

12. Rev S Cavan is chaplain to the Union [workhouse]

13. It does comprise one other church – Holy Trinity.

14. The church was consecrated on March 17th 1852 by the name of Holy Trinity.

15. The church (parish) is now under a complete restoration.

16. [Blank].

17. They do.

18. The church is now in the act of restoration under a faculty per the Bishop.

19. They are.

20. About half a mile or not so much.

21. Rent charge with glebe.

22. [Blank].

23. No.

24. In parish church morning service at 10.45am, evening service 6.30pm. In Trinity church morning service at 10.45am, evening at 3.00pm. Sermon preached in all.

25. Always.

26. Not lately.

27. Only on Wednesdays, Thursdays, Fridays and saints' days.

28. Service Wednesday, Thursday, Friday weekly. Saints' days and all festivals of the church.

29. [a] Yes [b] Yes [c] Not yet [d] Yes [e] Yes.

30. On the 1st, 2nd and 3rd Sunday of each month.

31. I do.

32. [Blank].

33. [Blank].

34. [Blank].

35. 90 or 100.

36. [Blank].

37. The church is now under going such an alteration that I am unable to answer these questions.

38. [Blank].

39. 83 baptisms 26 marriages 68 burials.

40. 70 in 1862. Church being under alteration no confirmation in 1863.

41. Always.

42. [Blank].

43. There is.

44. There are four dissenting chapels.

45. There are five.

46. We have.

47. Between 12 and 13.

48. A certain.

49. We have evening schools and adult.

50. Yes.

51. The various schools of the parish – church missionary school (Sunday) PC aid society.

52. [Blank].

John Guthrie

44 CALSTONE WELLINGTON D. Avebury

1. Calstone Wellington a rectory.

2. The Marquis of Lansdown.

3. 36. Besides which about 300 of the neighbouring population of Calne are visited and attend this church and that of Blackland.

4. William Maurice Macdonald, 1841.

5. Non-resident by licence.

6. No.

7. Fortescue Richard Purvis residing in the rectory house.
8. Blackland in this diocese.
9. Non- resident.
10. [Blank]
11. [Blank]
12. [Blank]
13. Only one church.
14. [Blank]
15. Yes.
16. Yes.
17. Yes.
18. No.
19. No chapel.
20. [Blank]
21. Tithe £192 with a few acres of glebe.
22. Only one parish.
23. Only one residence.
24. Morning or evening alternately with Blackland at 11am and 3pm. Full service with sermon.
25. Yes, always.
26. No.
27. No – except during Lent on Wednesday evening and during Passion week every evening.
28. Christmas Day, Ash Wednesday, Good Friday, Ascension Day. Every Wednesday during Lent. Every day during Passion week except Saturday. There is a fair attendance for the populace.
29. Yes, or on the next Sunday every alternate year with Blackland except Ascension Day.
30. It is arranged so as to be administered once in six weeks.
31. Yes, for private use.
32. About 23 attending the Calstone church.
33. To the best of my knowledge all have attended during the year.
34. 17 average.
35. 17 average.
36. 175.
37. About 80.
38. No – ample room.
39. _ baptisms 0 marriages _burials.[1]
40. No information.
41. Yes, a statement is always placed at the church door.
42. £3 12s 5½d.
43. Yes.
44. None actually in the parish. But the dissenters meet in a room at a mill in the parish of Calne, close adjoining Calstone.
45. Yes.

46. No.
47. Boys at 9, girls at 11 or 12.
48. Yes, and some boys to 15 years.
49. An evening school was tried, but I understand the success was not great.
50. Will do so within the time appointed by law.
51. Harvest thanksgiving £3 15s 3d. Augmentation of poor benefices £1 2s 1d.
52. The existence of dissent is found to produce a feeling destructive of <u>sound</u> churchmanship among the poor and tends to make the poor and untaught discontented and neglectful.

Fortescue Richard Purvis

[1] The curate wrote the words 'baptisms' and 'burials' without adding any numbers, suggesting he intended to look at the registers, but forgot. The figures are 5 baptisms, 0 marriages, 1 burial.

45. CHARLTON ALL SAINTS   D. Wilton

1. All Saints Charlton, a perpetual curacy.
2. Revd Prebendary [Richard] Payne.
3. 304.
4. William Esdaile Burkitt BA Oxon Aug 25th 1860.
5. Yes.
6. Yes.
7. [Blank]
8. No.
9. No.
10. [Blank]
11. [Blank]
12. [Blank]
13. No.
14. [Blank]
15. Yes.
16. Yes.
17. Yes.
18. No.
19. Yes [crossed out]
20. [Blank]
21. Queen Anne's Bounty £33. Winchester College £25. Rev Prebendary Payne £25. Total £83.
22. [Blank]
23. No.
24. Morning at 11.00am and evening at 6.00pm with a sermon at each.
25. Yes, invariably – including prayer for the church militant.
26. No.
27. No, for lack of a congregation.

28. Wednesdays, Fridays and all Holy Days at 10.00am, average attendance besides children six. Evening service on Thursdays during Lent and Advent with sermon, average attendance 25.

29. [a] Yes [b] Yes [c] Yes [d] Yes [e] Yes.

30. On the 2nd Sunday in each month and on the feast of the dedication of the church.

31. Yes.

32. 55 in all.

33. Six of the above did not communicate during 1863.

34. 25.

35. 18.

36. About 200, besides school children.

37. About 100 adults and 50 children. It has not decreased in spite of the exertions of the dissenters – though two large families and some other regular attendants have left and been succeeded by dissenters.

38. No.

39. 11 baptisms 4 marriages 6 burials.

40. 1861 -5. 1862 -10. 1863 – 5.

41. Yes, full particulars are given in the Charlton Almanack – a copy of which is given gratuitously to every family in Charlton – and the amounts are also laid before the vestry at Easter.

42. 1861 - £ 18 6s 3½d. 1862 - £22 7s 3½d. 1863 – £20 3s 3d.

43. Yes.

44. A Wesleyan meeting house – provided by Lord Folkestone. There are about 30 regular dissenters, but many more frequently go to meetings as well as to church.

45. Yes.

46. Yes.

47. 13 or 14.

48. A few – both of boys and girls.

49. Yes, a night school is kept by the parson for the four winter months and is very well attended and also pays its own expenses, leaving a small surplus for prizes.

50. Yes.

51. During last year a collection was made for the 'Sarum Church Union Society' amounting to £3 14s 4½d. In consequence of the Bishop's Pastoral being received just at this time no collection could be made last year for the 'Small Benefice Fund' but will be shortly. The amount collected between Nov 1862 and Easter 1863 for the Lancashire relief fund was £27 6s 3¾d and during 1863 for SPG £11 17s 9d. Church expenses 12s 6d.

52. The exertions of the Wesleyans who are now much encouraged by Lord Folkestone having given them a site for a meeting house immediately opposite the church.

William Esdaile Burkitt

46. CHARLTON ST. PETER   D. Potterne

1. Charlton, a vicarage.
2. The Dean and Chapter of Christ Church, Oxford.
3. 220.
4. Arthur Baynham. November 1852.
5. Yes.
6. Yes.
7. Resident and no curate.
8. No.
9. No curate.
10. [Blank]
11. [Blank]
12. [Blank]
13. One church.
14. [Blank]
15. Yes.
16. Yes.
17. Yes.
18. No.
19. No chapel.
20. [Blank]
21. Tithe commuted at £132; and £30 a year money payments.
22. Only one parish.
23. Only one glebe house.
24. Two full duties every Sunday. One at 11.00am, the other at 3.00pm in winter and 6.00pm in summer. Sermons delivered at each service.
25. Yes.
26. No.
27. No, because I consider that there are reasonable hindrances.
28. On Christmas Day, Good Friday and Ascension Day. On the former festivals the attendance as on Sunday, but on Ascension Day small.
29. [a] Yes [b] Yes [c] No [d] No [e] Yes.
30. Inclusive of the above, the Holy Communion is administered 12 times a year.
31. Yes.
32. 14.
33. All have.
34. In this parish there is no variation between the attendance at the great festivals and on other occasions. The average may be set at 11.
35. [See 34]
36. About 145.
37. About 80 or 90 attend on the Sunday in the course of the two services. The congregation remains much the same as it has always been.
38. No.
39. 4 baptisms 1 marriage 5 burials.
40. In 1861, six persons were confirmed.

41. No, but it can be seen at any time on application, which however is never made.

42. Between £3 and £4.

43. Yes.

44. No dissenting place of worship in the parish. About ten per cent of the population are dissenters (Anabaptists). I mean the adult population.

45. Yes.

46. No.

47. Between 9 and 10.

48. Not regularly – their attendance after the age specified depends upon their getting work.

49. I tried an evening school for three years but the result did not answer my expectations and a variety of circumstances led to its discontinuance for the present.

50. Yes.

51. The Society for the Propagation of the Gospel 16s. The Salisbury Infirmary £2 4s 2d.

52. The prevalence of dissent, especially that most malignant form of it – the Anabaptist, which prevails in this neighbourhood in its general and particular form.

A. Baynham

47. CHERHILL   D. Avebury

1. Cherhill, a perpetual curacy.
2. Bishop of Salisbury.
3. 364.
4. W. C. Plenderleath, 1860.
5. Yes.
6. Yes.
7. [Blank]
8. No.
9. No.
10. [Blank]
11. [Blank]
12. [Blank]
13. No.
14. [Blank]
15. Yes.
16. Yes.
17. Yes.
18. Restoration according to specifications sent to the Bishop by authority of a faculty.
19. [Blank]
20. [Blank]

21. £200 charge on rectorial tithes.

22. [Blank]

23. No.

24. Mattins, Litany, altar service and sermon in morning at 10.30am. Evensong and sermon at 2.30pm.

25. Yes.

26. No.

27. I do not say them daily, being reasonably hindered.

28. On all the greater festivals and fasts. Also on every Friday evening (with lecture) during Advent and Lent. At latter services average attendance from 50 to 75 per cent of Sunday congregations.

29. [a] Yes [b] Yes [c] No [d] Yes [e] No.

30. Once in every month.

31. Yes.

32. 38.

33. Former communicants two. Become communicants this year, and included in above number three.

34. 20.6

35. 19.

36. [Blank]

37. The position of pulpit being changed, I am no longer able to count the congregation.

38. No.

39. 11 baptisms 6 marriages 6 burials.

40. I had not come into residence in 1861. None have been confirmed in 1862 or 1863.

41. No.

42. In 1863 £3 1s 10½d.

43. Yes.

44. Two small Primitive Methodist meeting rooms but attendants at which consider themselves church people and some of them are communicants. Also some 10 or 12 Baptists.

45. Yes.

46. No.

47. Girls about 13. Boys about 9, to go to parish school of next parish, which possesses a master, there being at present only a mistress at Cherhill. This however incumbent is trying to alter.

48. Yes.

49. Adult and evening school has been tried unsuccessfully by incumbent, assisted by young tradesman.

50. Yes.

51. For improvement of church plate £6.

52. [Blank]

W Charles Plenderleith

48. CHICKLADE   D. Chalke

1. Chicklade, a Rectory.
2. The Marquis of Bath, Longleat.
3. 120.
4. John Cooke Faber, 1839.
5. Yes.
6. Yes.
7. [Blank]
8. No.
9. No.
10. [Blank]
11. [Blank]
12. [Blank]
13. No.
14. [Blank]
15. Yes.
16. Yes.
17. Yes.
18. No.
19. [Blank]
20. [Blank]
21. Tithe rent charge and glebe land.
22. [Blank]
23. There is a small farmhouse on the glebe besides the rectory house.
24. Morning and evening services at 11.00am and 3.00pm in the winter, 11.00am and 6.00pm in the summer with a sermon at each service.
25. Yes.
26. No.
27. There are no morning or evening prayers said daily.
28. Ash Wednesday, Good Friday, Ascension Day and Christmas Day. About 60 attend on Good Friday and Christmas Day. About 10 on the other days.
29. [a] No [b] Yes [c] No [d] Yes [e] No.
30. Sunday after Christmas Day and on three other Sundays, so that it shall be administered once in two months nearly.
31. No.
32. 28.
33. 2.
34. 23.
35. 16.
36. 174.
37. 60 – steady.
38. No.
39. 6 baptisms 2 marriages 3 burials.
40. None.
41. I place the receipts on the church door.

42. £3 11s 2d.
43. Yes.
44. None.
45. Yes.
46. No.
47. Boys about 13, girls 17 or 18.
48. Generally for some time.
49. No.
50. Yes.
51. Lancashire relief fund, Church Missionary Society and Pastoral Aid Society.
52. [Blank]

John Faber

49. CHILMARK   D. Chalke

1. Chilmark, a rectory.
2. The Earl of Pembroke, Wilton House.
3. 642.
4. Charles Tower, February 8th 1843.
5. Yes.
6. Yes.
7. [Blank]
8. No.
9. No.
10. [Blank]
11. [Blank]
12. [Blank]
13. No.
14. [Blank]
15. Yes.
16. Yes.
17. Yes.
18. No.
19. [Blank]
20. [Blank]
21. From rent charge and 24 acres of land, £426.
22. [Blank]
23. No.
24. Morning Prayer at 10.30am, afternoon at 3.00pm, on Sundays when Holy Communion is administered or when a Holy Day falls on a Monday, Evensong on the Sunday at 6.30pm. No sermon on the mornings when Holy Communion is administered, but a sermon in the afternoon and evening.
25. Yes.
26. Yes, every Sunday afternoon during Lent, I catechise without notes on some portion of the catechism, having during the week prepared the children, and applying where suitable the Sunday services, I think it must do good, though it is

not popular as it makes the service longer, for I have a sermon besides.

27. Morning Prayer but not evening except on Wednesdays and Fridays in Lent, on all Fridays and on Holy Days.

28. Every day, when at home, and not hindered by illness or otherwise, I have Morning Prayer, but not more than three or four persons attend except my own family and six schoolchildren who come in turn. More persons come on Wednesdays and Fridays.

29. [a] Yes [b] Yes [c] Yes [d] Yes [e] Yes.

30. On the Sunday after Christmas Day, and on Low Sunday, and on the 1st Sunday in every month.

31. Yes.

32. About 119.

33. 29.

34. At Christmas about 34, at Easter 49, on Ascension Day 12, on Whit Sunday 15, Trinity Sunday 20.

35. About 27.

36. 320.

37. About 85 besides as many schoolchildren in the morning, the church is generally nearly full in the afternoon, and a great many come when there is evening service. The additional evening service has brought several to church who were very irregular before, otherwise the attendance is much the same as it has been for the last few years.

38. There is no further accommodation needed.

39. 22 baptisms, viz 11 males and 11 females, 3 marriages, 10 burials, viz 4 males and 6 females.

40. In 1861 there were 27 from this parish, 14 males and 13 females confirmed at Dinton; in 1862, two females at Salisbury Cathedral; in 1863, two females at the Cathedral – note- also three females from the parish confirmed in London.

41. Yes, I always bring the account of offertory collections to the vestry meeting on Easter Monday.

42. In 1861, £7 7s 10d. In 1862, £8 9s 10½d. In 1863, £8 11s 5d besides special collections, those for 1863 noticed under question 51.

43. Yes.

44. One at Ridge for Calvanistic Baptists. About 25 persons have been immersed according to their forms, but several others who come to church occasionally, also go to the meeting house. There is one Roman Catholic family in the parish.

45. Yes.

46. Yes and received £46 9s lately for the day and night school.

47. The boys at 9 or 10 cease to attend the day school regularly, the girls at 11.

48. Several of the girls and a few of the boys.

49. Yes, I have had evening schools for many years. This last year, I had a girls school of about 18 and a boys school of upwards of 20, attended regularly by Mrs Tower or one of my daughters and myself when well, as also being under the charge of a certificated master and a mistress (uncertificated).

50. They are made out, and will be sent by the next post if the churchwarden is

at home to witness my signature tomorrow.

51. For the Curates' Aid Society on Whit Sunday collected £1 9s. In aid of the augmentation of poor benefices on November 15th collected £2 1s.

52. [Blank]

Charles Tower

50. CHILTON FOLIAT　D. Marlborough

1. Chilton Foliat, a rectory.
2. E W L Popham Esq, Littlecote, Hungerford
3. 720.
4. John Leyborne Popham. 1835.
5. Yes.
6. Yes.
7. [Blank]
8. No.
9. Yes.
10. Trinity ordination in 1863.
11. C[alcraft] N[eeld] Wyld, a deacon.
12. No.
13. No.
14. [Blank]
15. Yes.
16. Yes.
17. Yes.
18. No.
19. [Blank]
20. [Blank]
21. Tithes, rent charge and glebe.
22. [Blank]
23. No.
24. Two full services with sermon. Morning service at 11.00am and evening service at 3.00pm.
25. Yes.
26. Yes during Lent. The first class in the Sunday school are examined in the catechism and the result of their answers is given by the examiner to the congregation. It is in my judgement a very important and effective method of instruction.
27. I say the Morning Prayer in the parish church.
28. Every day in the parish church.
29. [a] Yes [b] Yes [c] Yes [d] Yes [e] Yes.
30. On the second and last Sunday in the month.
31. Yes.
32. 150.
33. About 24.

34. 90.

35. At the 11.00am service 40. At the 8.30am service 20.

36. 300.

37. From 200 to 250. It does not increase nor decrease much.

38. No.

39. 19 baptisms 6 marriages 11 burials.

40. In 1861 41 persons confirmed. In 1863 six persons by the Bishop of Oxford.

41. The amount of collection made at any time is always posted on the church door the next Sunday following.

42. Amount of sacramental alms £36 17s 6d.

43. An account is kept.

44. One Wesleyan chapel. About 24 persons Wesleyans or Independents.

45. Yes.

46. Yes.

47. Boys 8-10, girls 12.

48. Yes.

49. A night school. The success very encouraging.

50. No, but it shall be done.

51. January 18th third collection for distress in Lancashire £11 12s 1d. February 8th fourth collection for distress in Lancashire £7 16s 1d. July 19th collection for S.P.G. £8 8s. September 20th collection for Reading hospitals £12 13s 2d. November 1st collection for the augmentation of small livings £6 6s 2½d.

52. [Blank]

J. L. Popham

51. CHIRTON   D. Potterne

1. Chirton, a vicarage.

2. The Lord Chancellor.

3. [Blank]

4. George Ellis Cleather. Instituted, August 12th 1862. Inducted, August 14th 1862.

5. Yes.

6. Yes.

7. [Blank]

8. No.

9. No.

10. [Blank]

11. [Blank]

12. [Blank]

13. No.

14. [Blank]

15. There is some repair necessary in the roof of the south side of the nave, which is to be executed during the ensuing summer. There is a due provision of all things necessary for the decent performance of divine service.

16. Yes.

17. Yes.

18. No.

19. [Blank]

20. [Blank]

21. The gross amount of the income for 1863 was £232 11s 1d derived from rent charge, rental of glebe, and allotment land.

22. Chirton – tithe rent charge £135 2s 6d. Rent of glebe £8 15s. Rent of allotments £17 19s.
Conock – tithe rent charge £70 14s 7d. Total £232 11s 1d.

23. No.

24. Morning service at 10.30am and afternoon service at 3.00pm. During the summer months, there is a service in the evening at 6.00pm instead of the afternoon service. At each of these services a sermon is preached.

25. Yes.

26. No.

27. No.

28. On Christmas Day, Feast of Epiphany, every Wednesday and Friday in Lent. Every day in Holy Week, Easter Monday and Easter Tuesday, Holy Thursday, Whitsun Monday and Whitsun Tuesday, and on all saints' days. On Christmas Day and Good Friday the average Sunday congregation, on other days an average of 14 or 16 persons.

29. [a] Yes [b] Yes [c] No [d] No [d] No.

30. On four other Sundays in the year at equal intervals.

31. Yes.

32. 62.

33. To the best of my knowledge and belief all have communicated at least once, and the greater number at least four times during the year 1863.

34. At Christmas 30, at Easter 40.

35. About 30.

36. The church contains 208 sittings.

37. In the morning 60 or 70, afternoon 150. During the summer months the congregation is generally very large averaging nearly 200. The congregation during the whole year keeps up steadily, neither increasing visibly nor diminishing.

38. No.

39. 11 baptisms 3 marriages 12 burials.

40. There were no candidates in 1862 and 1863. For 1861 I have unfortunately lost my list, but, if my memory serves me truly, there were over 20 candidates.

41. No printed account is published, but the amounts of offerings and collections are always made known to the churchwardens.

42. The amount for 1863 was £7 16s 4d. For 1862, £7 5s 10d. For 1861, £8 12s 4d.

43. Yes.

44. There are no dissenting places of worship in this parish, nor at present are there any dissenters resident here.

45. Yes.

46. No.

47. The boys usually leave for the fields at 10 years of age. The girls remain until 13 or 14.

48. Many of both sexes are retained till nearly the period of confirmation.

49. Yes, by a night school for boys only. Having the sole superintendence of the night school, and not having been in good health, I have been obliged for the two winters past to close it, but I hope next winter to be able to re-open it. It was very fairly attended and was on the whole successful.

50. Copies of the registers will be sent to the diocesan registry forthwith.

51. A collection on behalf of the fund for the augmentation of poor benefices amounting to £2 1s.

52. There is no opposition to church principles in this parish, there being no dissenters in it, and the feeling of churchmen being decidedly high. But there is one sad impediment to my ministry, viz the existence of three beer-houses. Drunkenness prevails to a lamentable extent, and is, in fact, the crying sin of the parish. For this I see no remedy except an alteration of the Beer Law. None of the respectable inhabitants will sign for the annual beer licence, but as long as small rate-payers are empowered to do so, they will use that power, and there can be no hope of a diminution of the mischief consequent thereupon.

G. Ellis Cleather M.A.

52. CHISLEDON   D. Marlborough

1. Chisledon, a vicarage.

2. Henry Calley Esq. Burderop Park, Swindon.

3. 1206.

4. Edwin Meyrick. February 1847.

5. He has been resident.

6. He has resided in the glebe house.

7. Resident.

8. He does not possess any other benefice.

9. He has an assistant curate.

10. Licensed March 1864.

11. C. T. Salusbury. He is a deacon.

12. He performs no other duty, except a little assistance to the incumbent in tuition.

13. Only one church.

14. Dedicated to the Holy Cross.

15. The church is in good repair, though the walls are much out of the perpendicular. It is duly provided.

16. The churchyard is well fenced and kept.

17. They do.

18. Several pews have been replaced by open seats. My only authority for doing this was a general permission from the late Rural Dean.

19. No chapel of ease.

20. [Blank]

21. Glebe land £110. Rent charge £106. Subject to rates, taxes, Queen Anne's Bounty debt and curate's salary.

22. Only one parish.

23. Only one glebe house.

24. Two services in the church at 11.00am and 3.00pm in winter, 6.00pm in summer. A sermon at each.

25. I do.

26. I do not catechise publicly in church.

27. I do not.

28. On Wednesdays and Fridays in Lent and on the chief festivals.

29. [a] Yes [b] Yes [c] No [d] No [e] Yes.

30. On nine other Sundays, which are printed each year in the Chisledon Almanack.

31. I do not keep a written list.

32. Rather more than 50.

33. I think all have communicated either at the church or in their houses.

34. About 45.

35. About 30 or 35.

36. The children being seated down the centre of the nave and benches in the chancel filled, there is accommodation for nearly 400.

37. About 250 or 300 including children. About stationary, but much affected by the weather, as the hamlets are distant.

38. The parish is scattered in hamlets. I think there is no need of enlarging the parish church. I have a congregation averaging 80 in a room at Coate, nearly 3 miles from the church.

39. 32 baptisms 6 marriages 29 burials.

40. I cannot find my list of those confirmed in Chisledon church in 1861. None have been confirmed since.

41. I affix the receipts to the church door.

42. For 1863 £16 1s 4d.

43. A regular account is kept.

44. Primitive Methodist and Wesleyan. I cannot estimate their number. Very many of them come to church.

45. There is a daily school.

46. We cannot take advantage of the aid offered.

47. Boys leave at 8, 9 or 10. Girls at 11 or 12.

48. We retain some in the Sunday school.

49. We have several night schools. I think they do good.

50. I have sent the copies.

51. S.P.G. Total from sermon, meeting and collection £18 11s 6d. Poor benefices fund. Total including 10s sent afterwards, £5.

52. I should mention that our National School is kept entirely by contributions.

Edwin Meyrick.

53. CHITTERNE ALL SAINTS WITH ST MARY D. Wylye

1. Chitterne All Saints with St Mary.
2. Bishop and Dean and Chapter alternately.
3. 710.
4. George Richards. October 1862.
5. Yes.
6. Yes.
7. [Blank]
8. No.
9. [Blank]
10. [Blank]
11. [Blank]
12. [Blank]
13. No.
14. [Blank]
15. Yes.
16. Yes.
17. Yes, with one exception.
18. Church newly built by faculty.
19. [Blank]
20. [Blank]
21. Glebe and corn rents £340.
22. Chitterne All Saints £160, St Mary £180, total £340.
23. No.
24. Full services on Sundays at 10.30am and 3.00pm.
25. Yes.
26. No.
27. No.
28. Ash Wednesday and Thursday evenings during Lent. Good Friday. Ascension Day. Average attendance 150.
29. [a] Yes [b] Yes [c] No [d] Yes [e] Yes.
30. Quinquagesima Sunday, 5th Sunday after Trinity, 12th after Trinity, 19th after Trinity and 25th after Trinity.
31. Yes.
32. About 80.
33. Cannot say.
34. 50.
35. 50.
36. 530.
37. 300 adults and nearly 200 schoolchildren. Much increased since the new church was opened.
38. No.
39. 36 baptisms 3 marriages 13 burials.
40. 46.
41. Yes.

42. £6 2s 8d.
43. Yes.
44. One, number very small; no particular denomination, if any, probably Baptists.
45. Yes.
46. No.
47. Boys at 8 years, girls 10 to 11.
48. Generally.
49. Evening school; attendance pretty good.
50. Not yet.
51. For Salisbury Infirmary £6 8s 6d.
52. No.

George Richards

54. CHITTOE D. Avebury
1.   Chittoe, a perpetual curacy.
2.   The Lord Bishop of Salisbury.
3.   600.
4.   Meredith Brown, October 16th, 1845.
5.   No.
6.   Partly at Nonsuch in the parish of Chittoe, and partly at Bath by licence from the bishop.
7.   Rev W A Richmond. Yes.
8.   No.
9.   [Blank]
10. April 1863.
11. William Alexander Richmond. He is a priest.
12. No.
13. No.
14. [Blank]
15. Yes.
16. Yes.
17. Yes.
18. No.
19. Yes.
20. [Blank]
21. The Ecclesiastical Commission and rent charges on Spy Park and an estate at Bishops Cannings, amounting together to £120.
22. [Blank]
23. [Blank]
24. Two full services with sermons at 11.00am and 3.30pm in winter and at 6.00pm in summer.
25. Yes.
26. No.
27. No.
28. On Christmas Day, Good Friday, Ascension Day, Wednesdays and Fridays in Lent and every day in Holy Week. 40.

29. [a] Yes [b] Yes [c] No [d] Yes [e] Yes.

30. On the 1st Sunday in every month.

31. Yes.

32. 55.

33. None.

34. 35.

35. 30.

36. 200.

37. 180; it increases.

38. Not at present, but I expect there to be.

39. 17 baptisms 2 marriages 9 burials.

40. In 1861 about 20 but I regret that I have mislaid the record. In 1862 none, in 1863 two.

41. Yes, all collections except the offertory at Holy Communion.

42. £20.

43. Not of late, but it shall be done in future.

44. One Baptist and one Primitive Methodist. Probably 150 including the late addition of Sandy Lane.

45. Yes.

46. Yes.

47. 10.

48. Yes, generally.

49. Yes, at an evening school in the winter, but not with much success.

50. Yes.

51. For Bath Hospital £4 17s 6d. For the Society for the Propagation of the Gospel £12 12s 6d.

52. No.

Meredith Brown

55. CHOLDERTON   D. Amesbury

1.   Cholderton, a rectory.

2.   Oriel College Oxford.

3.   191.

4.   Charles Peter Chretien. Instituted 9th and inducted 12th January 1861.

5.   Yes.

6.   In the glebe house.

7.   [Blank]

8.   No.

9.   No.

10. [Blank]

11. [Blank]

12. [Blank]

13. No.

14. [Blank]

15. Yes.
16. Yes.
17. Yes.
18. No.
19. [Blank]
20. [Blank]
21. Tithes of Cholderton £265, of Eltham (in part) £245 14s 6d. Land about £5. These amounts are gross. The <u>net</u> value is about £430.
22. [Blank]
23. No.
24. Mornings at 10.40am, afternoons at 2.40pm. There are sermons on all afternoons and alternate mornings.
25. As a rule, I read the whole service. I make at times some small omissions which have received the sanction of custom.
26. I rarely catechise and can say nothing definite of my method or its result.
27. It is not my practice to say daily prayer in church.
28. On Ash Wednesday, Good Friday, during Holy Week daily, Ascension Day, Wednesday evenings in Lent and generally on saints' days. The average attendance may be 20 including children.
29. It is administered <u>either</u> on Whit Sunday or Trinity Sunday, not on both. It is not administered on Ascension Day. It is administered on the other days mentioned.
30. It is administered, in all, eight times in the year; the first Sunday in Advent and Quinquagesima being two of the days of administration.
31. Yes.
32. 36 (approximately).
33. 7 (approximately).
34. 20 (approximately).
35. 18 (approximately).
36. 126.
37. About 80, stationary.
38. No.
39. 11 baptisms 2 marriages 3 burials.
40. 14.
41. It is my custom to announce the amount at the beginning of the sermon following the collection.
42. In 1863 it was £15 6s 11½d.
43. Yes.
44. There is no dissenting place of worship in the parish. There is one professed dissenter of no ordinary denomination.
45. Yes.
46. Yes.
47. Boys about 9, girls about 13.
48. Yes.
49. I have had a night school for boys and young men, on a small scale. It has

worked, I think, satisfactorily.
50. Yes.
51. Fund for augmenting small livings £2 19s 7d.
52. I have no extraordinary impediment to mention.

Charles P. Chretien

56. CHUTE   D. Marlborough
1. Chute, a vicarage.
2. The Lord Bishop of Salisbury, Palace, Salisbury.
3. 238.
4. S[amuel] Cosway, 1838.
5. Yes.
6. In the vicarage house.
7. [Blank]
8. No.
9. No.
10. [Blank]
11. [Blank]
12. [Blank]
13. No.
14. [Blank]
15. Yes.
16. Not very well fenced.
17. In many respects.
18. No.
19. [Blank]
20. [Blank]
21. Rent charge, after deducting the rates, under £250 per annum.
22. [Blank]
23. No.
24. Morning and evening service, morning at 11.00am and evening at 3.30pm during nine months, and at 3.00pm during three months. There is a sermon given at each service during nine months, and one sermon during three.
25. Yes.
26. Yes. Simply hearing the catechism in the church and asking some questions. The parents are satisfied, and instructed.
27. No.
28. On every Wednesday during Lent, and on Good Friday, Ascension Day and Christmas Day. The average attendance during Lent besides the school children, is very small indeed.
29. [a] Yes [b] Yes [c] No [d] Yes [e] Yes.
30. On the 1st Sunday of every month.
31. Yes.
32. 60.

33. None.
34. 18 (on Trinity Sunday 27 communicated).
35. 15.
36. 200.
37. 150. About the same.
38. No.
39. 14 baptisms 8 marriages 12 burials.
40. In 1861, 27. In 1862 and 1863, none.
41. No.
42. In 1863 £20 4s 8½d. In 1862 £17 11s 7d. In 1861 £26 14s 4d.
43. Yes.
44. There is a small dissenting place of worship on the borders of the parish. Of no fixed denomination. About 30 Baptists, Wesleyans etc. etc. etc. The greater number are Baptists.
45. Yes.
46. Yes.
47. 8 years old. The girls rather older.
48. Some, with much difficulty.
49. Yes. Tolerably good.
50. Yes.
51. In the last year, all has been expended on the poor of the parish, for which object the collections were made.
52. No.

S. Cosway

57. CLYFFE PYPARD D. Avebury

1. Clyffe Pypard, a vicarage.
2. H.N. Goddard Esq, Clyffe Pypard Manor House, Wootton Bassett.
3. 540.
4. Charles William Bradford. Instituted Sept 22nd and Inducted Sept 26th 1863.
5. No, being instituted here in Sept 1863.
6. [Blank]
7. [Blank]
8. No.
9. No.
10. [Blank]
11. [Blank]
12. [Blank]
13. Does not comprise more than one church.
14. [Blank]
15. Fairly good and is duly provided here.
16. Yes.
17. Yes.
18. No.

19. [Blank]
20. [Blank]
21. Tithe £560 per annum.
22. [Blank]
23. [Blank]
24. Morning Prayer with Litany and communion service with sermon at 11.00am. Evening Prayer and sermon at 3.00pm in winter and at 5.30pm in summer.
25. Yes.
26. I have not catechised publicly as yet.
27. No.
28. Hitherto on Tuesdays and Fridays Morning Prayer. Average number from 10 to 15.
29. [a] Yes [b] Yes [c] No [d] Yes [e] No.
30. Hitherto about one Sunday in six or eight.
31. Yes.
32. I have not, as yet, accurately ascertained.
33. [Blank]
34. From 40 to 45.
35. About 30.
36. [Blank]
37. [Blank]
38. [Blank]
39. 19 baptisms 7 marriages 8 burials.
40. [Blank]
41. [Blank]
42. £8 18s.
43. Yes.
44. One meeting house of Primitive Methodists. A few Baptists also in the parish.
45. Yes – two. One free and endowed the other supported by children's pence and voluntary contributions.
46. Not as yet.
47. Boys about 9. Girls about 14.
48. Yes, a fair number.
49. [Blank]
50. Yes.
51. For the augmentation of poor benefices £2 6s 6d.
52. Many of the questions I am unable to answer owing to the short time of my residence here.

C.W. Bradford

58. CODFORD ST MARY D. Wylye

1. Codford St Mary, a rectory.
2. President and scholars of St John the Baptist College Oxford.
3. 400.

4. John William Hammond, 5th July and 11th July 1861.
5. Yes.
6. Yes.
7. [Blank]
8. [Blank]
9. [Blank]
10. [Blank]
11. [Blank]
12. [Blank]
13. Only one church.
14. [Blank]
15. Yes.
16. Yes.
17. [Blank]
18. [Blank]
19. [Blank]
20. [Blank]
21. Tithes £355 18s. Glebe 44 acres.
22. [Blank]
23. [Blank]
24. Morning at 11.00am, afternoon with a sermon at 3.00pm.
25. [Blank]
26. [Blank]
27. [Blank]
28. [Blank]
29. [a] Yes [b] Yes [c] No [d] Yes [e] No.
30. [Blank]
31. No.
32. [Blank]
33. [Blank]
34. [Blank]
35. [Blank]
36. [Blank]
37. [Blank]
38. [Blank]
39. 10 baptisms 1 marriage 7 burials.
40. [Blank]
41. [Blank]
42. [Blank]
43. [Blank]
44. [Blank]
45. [Blank]
46. [Blank]
47. [Blank]
48. [Blank]

49. [Blank]
50. Yes.
51. [Blank]
52. After very serious reflection and a careful perusal of pages 10, 11 and 12 of your Lordship's Charge of 1861, I have endeavoured to answer these questions to the best of my ability. If these answers are not as full or as satisfactory as your Lordship would expect, I respectfully request your Lordship not to come to the conclusion that this is owing either to want of courtesy to yourself personally or to want of respect for the office which you hold.

John William Hammond

59. CODFORD ST PETER   D. Wylye

1. Codford St Peter, a rectory.
2. Pembroke College Oxford.
3. 350.
4. H[enry] Wightwick, 1841.
5. Yes.
6. Yes.
7. [Blank]
8. No.
9. No.
10. [Blank]
11. [Blank]
12. [Blank]
13. No.
14. [Blank]
15. Under repair.
16. Under repair.
17. Yes.
18. Under repair.
19. [Blank]
20. [Blank]
21. £460 tithes. £10 glebe.
22. [Blank]
23. No.
24. Prayers at 11.00am. Prayers and a sermon at 3.00pm
25. Yes.
26. No.
27. No.
28. Christmas Day, Ash Wednesday, Passion Week, Good Friday and Ascension Day.
29. [The answer is yes on three occasions, but it is difficult to determine which three].
30. Michaelmas.

31. Yes.
32. 40.
33. Nearly all.
34. 40.
35. [Blank]
36. Under repair.
37. 230.
38. Under repair.
39. 7 baptisms 5 marriages 7 burials.
40. 2.
41. Generally fix amount to the church door.
42. Average 35s each administration.
43. No.
44. No.
45. Yes.
46. Yes.
47. About 12.
48. Yes.
49. We sit 100 hours night school each year. Average attendance 50.
50. No.
51. We collect from house to house for local charities also for the S.P.G. Society with an annual meeting. Collection about £20 for local charities and about £8 for the Society.
52. No.

                                                            H. Wightwick

60. COLLINGBOURNE DUCIS   D. Marlborough

1. Collingbourne Ducis, the benefice is a rectory.
2. The Marquis of Ailesbury, Savernake Park, Marlborough.
3. By the census of 1861 the population amounted to 553 persons.
4. Francis Henchman Buckerfield. Instituted February 21st 1862, inducted March 4th 1862.
5. He was resident from the 1st May 1863.
6. He resided in a hired house in the parish from the 1st May 1863 and entered in the occupation of the glebe house on the 10th October 1863.
7. During the incumbent's non-residence his curate was the Rev T A Penruddocke who was resident.
8. He does not.
9. He has no assistant curate.
10. [Blank]
11. [Blank]
12. [Blank]
13. The benefice comprises but one church.
14. [Blank]

15. The church is in tolerable repair. The pulpit was removed and destroyed under the incumbency of my predecessor and has not been replaced. In other aspects provision is made for the decent performance of divine service.

16. Yes.

17. They do.

18. The chancel was rebuilt by the late rector and I believe, completed previously to your Lordship's last visitation. There has been no alteration either as to the fabric or in the manner of fitting up during my incumbency.

19. [Blank]

20. [Blank]

21. Tithe rent and glebe: the gross amount of the former in 1863 was £671 16s. The gross amount of the latter was £110.

22. [Blank]

23. There is but one glebe house.

24. There are two full services in the church at the hours (respectively) of 11.00am and 3.00pm. A sermon is preached at each service.

25. Yes.

26. I do not catechise publicly.

27. No.

28. On the greater festivals of Christmas Day and Ascension Day I have morning and evening services with sermon, and also on Good Friday. With the exception of Holy Thursday, the attendance on these days is much the same as on Sundays. I have Morning Prayer in the church at 10.00am on all Fridays in the year and on saints' day. In Lent I say in addition Morning Prayer at 10.00am on Wednesdays and have Evening Prayer with a sermon in the evening. In Holy Week I have Morning Prayer daily and Evening Prayer and a sermon on Wednesday and Thursday. The morning congregation on week days consists of a few aged poor, occasionally of one or two members of the more respectable families and of part of my own household. The evening services in Lent were more fully attended.

29. The Holy Communion is administered on Christmas Day and the Sunday following, on Easter Day and its octave, on Whit Sunday and the Feast of Trinity.

30. On the 1st Sunday in the month.

31. I do.

32. I have no means of judging accurately, no list of communicants having been left by my predecessor, but I should estimate them as exceeding 80 in number.

33. Probably about 20. 66 persons resident in the parish have communicated in 1863.

34. The average of 1863 has been 29 at the great festivals.

35. At other seasons 17 8/9.

36. The church would in its present state probably accommodate 250 persons. But it is badly arranged and so many would scarcely find accommodation unless admitted to the pews of the wealthier parishioners.

37. The average number of attendants at church would not probably much exceed 150, but the congregations are more numerous in the afternoon than at the morning service. I do not think the congregation is decreasing.

38. There is great want of a better arrangement and re-distribution of the sittings in the church. The church should be partially rebuilt and wholly re-seated.

39. 18 baptisms 4 marriages 18 burials.

40. In 1861 – 35, in 1862 – 9, total 44.

41. I do.

42. £10 3s 7½.

43. Yes.

44. There is a small chapel belonging to the Primitive Methodists. There are also dissenters of the Baptist and Wesleyan Methodist denominations who attend chapels in neighbouring parishes. The whole number of dissenters may probably be nearly 200.

45. There is a daily school.

46. I have.

47. Few remain beyond the age of 12 and the larger number, especially of the boys, leave between 10 and 11.

48. A few, chiefly girls, continue to attend the Sunday school.

49. I have had an evening school for boys and young men during each of the two winters of my incumbency which have been attended on an average by about 20.

50. I have.

51. A collection was made on Sunday 28th September in aid of the Society for the Propagation of the Gospel amounting to £2 8s. And again on the 3rd Sunday in Advent in aid of the diocesan fund for augmenting benefices amounting to £1 12s 5d. The former was made on the occasion of a public thanksgiving for the abundant harvest.

52. [Blank]

F H Buckerfield

61. COLLINGBOURNE KINGSTON   D. Marlborough

1. Collingbourne Kingston, a vicarage.

2. Dean and Chapter of Winchester.

3. 904.

4. Charles Harwood Poore, July 1839.

5. Yes.

6. In the vicarage house.

7. [Blank]

8. No.

9. No.

10. [Blank]

11. [Blank]

12. [Blank]

13. No.

14 [Blank]

15. Yes.

16. Yes.

17. Yes.

18. The chancel has had a new roof and been re-seated, by arrangement of the Ecclesiastical Commissioners and the lessee of the rectorial tithes.

19. [Blank]

20. [Blank]

21. Tithe rent charge of vicarage average net income £270.

22. [Blank]

23. The rectorial glebe house, distinct from the vicarage, situated close to the church and occupied by the tenant of the glebe – 105 acres. The vicar has no land apportioned to him.

24. Morning 11.00am afternoon 3.00pm, at each of which services a sermon or lecture is given.

25. Always.

26. No.

27. No.

28. Christmas Day, Good Friday, Ash Wednesday, Wednesdays and Fridays during Lent, every day during Passion Week. Very few persons attend the Lenten services. They may average from 18 to 24.

29. [a] Yes [b] Yes [c] No [d] No [e] Yes, on Trinity Sunday.

30. At intervals of about seven weeks in addition to the above.

31. Not of the names, but of the numbers.

32. About 70.

33. From 55 to 60.

34. 40 to 45.

35. 30.

36. 400 (children included). If required the accommodation might be increased.

37. Including children, 300. Decidedly increasing since the restoration of the church.

38. No.

39. 26 baptisms 6 marriages 39 burials. [The burials] being nearly treble the yearly average. The cause, fever, especially scarlet fever among the little children.

40. In 1862 about 37.

41. Yes, the receipt of the money transmitted is affixed to the principal church door.

42. £3 15s 1d.

43. Yes, with number of communicants.

44. Wesleyan meeting house, Primitive meeting house. I should say more than one third of the population are dissenters.

45. Yes.

46. Yes.

47. Boys at 8, girls at 12 or 13. Some very few continue in school up to 14 years of age.

48. Not very many of late years. They are under less parental control than they used to be.

49. For three or four years I had an evening school but could not continue it for

want of funds.

50. No, but will transmit them before the end of the present month.

51. Distressed manufacturers collected £7 19s 4d. Society for the Propagation of the Gospel – after two sermons – collected £3 0s 4¾d.

52. Dissent accompanied by a very hostile spirit towards the church, and earnest efforts to prejudice the minds of the children in their Sunday schools, against her ordinances, especially that of confirmation. I can suggest no remedy. School work has for some time taken the place of the morning service at the Wesleyan meeting house, in which views, as I have reason to believe, <u>opposed to the church</u> are carefully inculcated.

Charles Harwood Poore

62. COOMBE BISSETT   D. Chalke

1. Coombe Bissett, a vicarage.

2. The Honble and Revd Lord Charles Paulett, prebendary of Salisbury.

3. 339.

4. Henry Smith Pollard, July 28th 1857.

5. Yes.

6. In the glebe house.

7. [Blank]

8. Yes – the perpetual curacy of Homington in the diocese of Salisbury.

9. There is no glebe house and is distant less than a mile from Coombe Bissett.

10. 18 months ago.

11. The Revd D.H. Sawyer, a priest.

12. The curate is licensed to Coombe Bissett cum Harnham and also to Homington.

13. The chapelry of West Harnham.

14. [Blank]

15. Yes.

16. Yes.

17. Yes.

18. No.

19. There are no chapels in the parish.

20. [Blank]

21. Rent charge £160, money payment £50.

22. Coombe Bissett rent charge £160. Money payment from prebendal estate at West Harnham £50 per annum.

23. No.

24. Morning and evening service every Sunday with a sermon only in the evening.

25. Yes.

26. No.

27. No.

28. Wednesday and Friday morning during Lent and every Thursday evening

during that season. Between 40 and 40[1] persons Christmas Day and Good Friday.

29. [a] Yes [b] Yes [c] No [d] Yes [e] Yes.

30. The 1st Sunday in every month.

31. Yes.

32. 48.

33. All.

34. 25.

35. 16.

36. 250.

37. About 200. It is increasing.

38. No.

39. 8 baptisms 4 marriages 8 burials.

40. 22.

41. No.

42. £6.

43. Yes.

44. There are no dissenting places of worship in the parish but many of the parishioners go to a Primitive Methodist chapel situated in the adjoining parish who nevertheless attend the parish church once on the Sunday.

45. Yes.

46. Yes.

47. About 10.

48. In some measure.

49. An evening school during the winter which was well attended.

50. I am about to do so.

51. S.P.G. £1 12s. Harvest sermon £4. Poor benefices fund 9s 6d.

52. [Blank]

Henry Smith Pollard

[1] The two figures are correct.

63. COMPTON BASSETT   D. Avebury

1. Compton Bassett, a rectory.

2. The Lord Bishop – Salisbury.

3. 370.

4. John William Clarke – 17th Sept 1862. 15th Nov 1862.

5. Yes.

6. Yes.

7. [Blank]

8. No.

9. No.

10. [Blank]

11. [Blank]

12. [Blank]

13. No.

14. [Blank]

15. No. The report of the Rural Dean will, I believe, specify what is needed in the way of repairs; but the main fabric is, as regards the nave, in an unsound state.

16. Yes.

17. Yes, in the usual way.

18. None of any importance.

19. [Blank]

20. [Blank]

21. Commuted rent charge £558 13s 4d.

22. [Blank]

23. [Blank]

24. Two full services, with sermon at each, morning at 11.00am, afternoon at 3.00pm.

25. Yes.

26. No – I have not yet introduced the custom, but hope to do so when the chancel is adapted for it.

27. No.

28. Christmas Day, Ascension Day, Circumcision, Good Friday, Ash Wednesday, all the saints' days in the year, and Wednesdays and Fridays in Lent. On the great days the services are attended as on the Sunday. On other days by about 14 persons.

29. [a] Yes [b] Yes [c] No [d and e] alternately.

30. On the 1st Sunday in each month.

31. Yes.

32. 66.

33. Very few, if any. I think there are none.

34. 40.

35. 30.

36. 210, and children.

37. 170 – increasing.

38. Yes, especially for the children, another aisle.

39. 10 baptisms 3 marriages 11 burials.

40. None in 1862-3; in 1861 I am unable to say.

41. No.

42. [Blank]

43. Yes.

44. None. I think about 5 Independents.

45. Yes.

46. Yes.

47. Boys about 10, girls at 13 or 14.

48. Yes, some of them.

49. By evening schools. Moderate success.

50. No; the last return made at Midsummer.

51. S.P.G. £6 15s (besides annual subscriptions making a total of £14 7s 5d). Augmentation of small benefices £3 7s 8d. Offertory alms £20 12s.

52. Nothing, but my own want of diligence and faithfulness; but which I trust to remedy, as time goes on, by increased efforts to promote the success of the ministry which I have received. In this particular parish there is much rather to help, than to impede, the work of the ministry. The church feeling around us is also decidedly good.

J W Clarke

64. COMPTON CHAMBERLAYNE   D. Chalke

1. Compton Chamberlayne, a vicarage.
2. Charles Penruddocke Esq, Compton Park.
3. 348.
4. Arthur Whitmarsh Phelps. Instituted March 24th 1863, inducted May 9th 1863.
5. Yes.
6. In the glebe house.
7. [Blank]
8. No.
9. No.
10. [Blank]
11. [Blank]
12. [Blank]
13. No.
14. St Michael.
15. Yes.
16. Yes, so far that nothing can get into the churchyard.
17. Yes.
18. No.
19. [Blank]
20. [Blank]
21. £20 yearly from the rector, 2 two acres of land. £67 10s chantry tithe at Tisbury. There is also a lectureship of £30 a year founded by Alexander Thistlewaite Esq A.D. 1621, on account of certain sermons to be preached in the parish church of Compton as long as the place remains in the hands of the Penruddockes.
22. [Blank]
23. No.
24. Morning prayers at 11.00am and afternoon prayers and sermon at 3.00pm.
25. Yes, except that the Litany alone is said on the week day evening service.
26. No.
27. [Blank]
28. Christmas Day, Ascension Day, Good Friday, Ash Wednesday, first Monday in May, some Sundays, Thursday evenings in winter. About 45.
29. [a] Yes [b] Yes [c] Yes [d] Yes [e] Yes.
30. Last Sunday in the month.
31. Yes.
32. 42.

33. 2.
34. 31.
35. 18.
36. 180.
37. 100, about stationary.
38. No.
39. 10 baptisms 2 marriages 4 burials.
40. 21 prepared by myself and two prepared by others.
41. No.
42. £10 9s.
43. Yes.
44. None.
45. Yes.
46. No, because it is entirely supported by the squire of the parish as his own park school.
47. Girls about 14, boys about 9.
48. Yes.
49. Evening schools, not any great success.
50. Yes.
51. Lancashire fund £4 4s. Church Pastoral Aid £3 6s. Infirmary £3 16s 1d. Small benefices £2 16s 9d. Total £14 2s 10d. Meetings – Church Missionary £1 5s 6d. Jews' Society £3. Irish Church Missions £8 10s.
52. [Blank]

Arthur W Phelps

65. CORSLEY D. Wylye

1. Corsley, a rectory.
2. The Marquess of Bath, Longleat, Wilts.
3. About 1200.
4. James Hay Waugh, November 1844 and April 1845.
5. Yes.
6. In the glebe house.
7. [Blank]
8. No.
9. None.
10. [Blank]
11. [Blank]
12. [Blank]
13. No.
14. [Blank]
15. Yes.
16. Yes.
17. Yes.
18. None.

19. Answered in no 13.

20. [Blank]

21. Glebe land and money payment in lieu of tithes, and a payment on St Thomas Day by the patron.

22. [Blank]

23. Only one.

24. Sunday duty 10.30am and 3.00pm, sermons at each.

25. Yes. Save by the omission of the prayer for the church militant.

26. I do not. The experiment did not answer the congregation being averse to the practice.

27. I do not.

28. Friday morning prayers no attendance besides school children ten. All Wednesdays during Lent, Easter sermon – two services with homilies during holy week, save Saturday. Holy Thursday H[oly] C^m [Communion] full service with sermon in the evening. Average attendance during Lent 25.

29. [a] Yes [b] Yes [c] Yes [d] Yes [e] Yes. Average attendance 50.

30. The 1st Sunday in the month.

31. Yes, and of their attendance.

32. 157, being an eighth of the whole population.

33. On looking through the roll I find seven only who have not communicated and of these, four are sick and have communicated since.

34. 70.

35. 65.

36. 800.

37. 250-350. Decreasing manifestly owing to the decrease in the population during my incumbency of 19 years. The population has fallen 25 per cent.

38. Far from any want.

39. 42 baptisms 12 marriages 11 burials.

40. In 1861, 26 females and 23 males.

41. Yes, a notice is posted at each entrance.

42. £15 9s.

43. Yes, with the names of the recipients and the amount given.

44. Two actually in the parish, Wesleyan and Baptist. Two virtually in the parish being separated by the street only in Chapmanslade. These are Baptists and Independents. Perhaps in Corsley there may be 300 dissenters. The Wesleyans are falling in to the church in measure [?].

45. Yes.

46. I have no aid whatever annually from the government. The master is uncertificated.

47. 10 to 11.

48. Yes, increasingly so.

49. We have for five months October – March a capital night school – average attendance 40 – 50, at which Mrs Waugh, my niece and myself regularly attend.

50. I have.

51. Wylie Missionary Association £2. S.P.G. for Bishop of Cape Town £9 14s 1d.

Augmentation of Small Benefices £2 4s 11d. Total £13 19s.
52. [Blank]

J. H. Waugh, March 29th 1864

66. CROCKERTON   D. Wylye
1. Longbridge Deverill vicarage, with Crockerton and Monkton Deverill chapels.
2. Marquis of Bath.
3. Included in Longbridge Deverill. Total 1178.
4. William David Morrice, 1852.
5. Yes.
6. Yes.
7. [Blank]
8. No.
9. Yes, two.
10. 1859 and 1860.
11. H.C. de St Croix, Priest, 1859. William Slatter, Priest, 1860.
12. No.
13. Yes, three.
14. Longbridge Deverill S.S. Peter and Paul, date of consecration unknown. Crockerton Holy Trinity, 1845. Monkton Deverill, dedication and date unknown.
15. Crockerton, yes.
16. Yes.
17. Yes.
18. No.
19. Baptisms and burials.
20. Monkton 3 miles, Crockerton 1½ miles.
21. Vicarial tithe, modus and land in Somerset.
22. Monkton Deverill tithe £6, Glebe 0. Longbridge Deverill tithe £158, glebe 9 acres, say £18. Crockerton 0.
23. No.
24. Longbridge Deverill 10.30am and 3.00pm. Crockerton 10.30am and 6.30pm. Sermons at all services. Monkton Deverill 11.00am and 2.30pm.
25. Yes.
26. Yes. Good effect. Course of seasons.
27. Yes at Longbridge and Crockerton, not at Monkton.
28. Daily, three besides children.
29. [a] Yes [b] Yes [c] Yes [d] Yes [e] Yes.
30. Monthly.
31. Yes.
32. 38.
33. 7.
34. 18.
35. 17.

36. Longbridge Deverill say 350, Crockerton say 450 (including gallery, disused), Monkton Deverill say 120.

37. Crockerton, say 230 in the evening; increasing.

38. No.

39. Crockerton 23 baptisms 0 marriages 6 burials.

40. Crockerton 9 in 1861, none in 1862 or 1863.

41. Yes, occasionally.

42. £10 0s 1d.

43. Yes.

44. Independents, and just outside the parish, Baptists. More than ¾ go occasionally, but there are not many members.

45. [Blank]

46. Yes.

47. 10 boys and 11 girls.

48. Girls, yes, boys, occasionally.

49. At Longbridge Deverill.

50. In preparation.

51. Parochial schools 17s 5d. Augmentation of poor benefices £1 4s 9d.

52. Dissent. I may also mention the necessity of having three sponsors (none of them parents) as creating a great difficulty.

W.D. Morrice

67. DAMERHAM   D. Chalke

1. Damerham, a vicarage.

2. The Right Honble The Earl of Chichester, Stanmore Park, Sussex.

3. 698 in 1861.

4. William Owen M.A. Instituted Sept 17th 1862, inducted Sept 19th 1862.

5. Yes.

6. Yes.

7. [Blank]

8. No.

9. No curate.

10. [Blank]

11. [Blank]

12. [Blank]

13. No.

14. [Blank]

15. Yes.

16. Yes.

17. Yes.

18. No.

19. [Blank]

20. [Blank]

21. Gross for 1863, tithe rent charge in Damerham £228, share of ditto of Martin

£69, Damerham glebe say £120, Martin ditto £29, Fees £3, Total £449. Nett for 1863 about £330.

22. [Blank]

23. No.

24. Two full services every Sunday 10.30am and 3.00pm, 6.00pm or 6.30pm according to the season of the year. Sermon or lecture at all the services.

25. Yes.

26. Yes, once a month, after the ordinary prayers for the 2nd service. I deliver a short address either upon some doctrine, or grace, or virtue or sin and then ask questions upon the subject of last month's lecture. I have reason to believe it to be very useful to the old as well as to the young.

27. No.

28. On Christmas Day, the 1st of January, Good Friday and Ascension Day – 150 to 180. (The week day evening service with lecture I hold in the school room on Thursdays).

29. On Easter Sunday only.

30. On the 1st Sunday in every month.

31. Yes.

32. 61 in 1863.

33. Four.

34. About 40 on Easter Sunday.

35. 7/12 in 1863.

36. 340 including seats for children.

37. About 260; increasing.

38. No.

39. 16 baptisms 3 marriages 12 burials.

40. None since September 1862 when I was instituted to the living. No confirmation held since then.

41. Yes.

42. In 1863 £5 1s.

43. Yes.

44. A Congregationalist chapel, a Baptist chapel and a Primitive Methodist chapel all in the village of Damerham. A Wesleyan chapel in a hamlet about 2 miles from the church. (About 130 dissenters in all including children. Many of these occasionally attend the church services).

45. Yes.

46. Yes.

47. Between 10 and 11.

48. The girls generally go to service when they leave the day school. The lads after a while, as a rule, cease to attend the Sunday school when they have left the day school.

49. Yes, by an evening school each winter since I have been here. On the whole encouraging. 33 attended one winter, 17 the other. Eight presented themselves for examination by H M Inspector and all passed in each subject.

50. Yes.

51. For the Lancashire operatives £6 1s 6¼. For the Church Missionary Society £3 12s 9¾d. At the thanksgiving sermons for day and Sunday schools £5. Total £14 14s 4d.

52. The influence of dissent is obviously the serious impediment to the work of the Church of England pastor. In years gone by, dissent struck its roots deeply in this parish, and although I have good reason to believe that the people are gradually returning to the Church of England, still the process is a slow one. The dissenting day school is all but closed, but certain wealthy dissenters residing in other parts of the country contribute largely towards the support both of the chapels and schools and so contrive to keep the spirit of dissent alive in a few. The injury to the young of both sexes is evident, for in the first place, I have reason to know that a license of behaviour is allowed at some of the chapels which would not be borne at the church, and conduct which is known to the clergyman, and which would be commented upon by him affectionately but plainly were he their teacher, is not known or noticed by the dissenting teachers who do not reside in the parish. I trust that the rule I at present act upon, to regard all as my flock, and in sin, sickness and sorrow not to inquire what people are, may be by the grace of God followed by happy results. There is little or no bitterness towards the C of E. A church rate is easily levied and the two occasional preachers who reside in Damerham accept very cordially my pastoral visits. 'Be not overcome of evil, but overcome evil with good' seems to be the precept to pray for grace to carry out. It is right that I should add that there are certain things to encourage me in my grave responsibilities as the pastor of the souls of this parish.

1.   The day schools number 132. 72 were presented for examination by H. M. Inspectors, all but five passed in all subjects, the remaining five in two or one subject.

2.   93 children of the Sunday school received prizes in the presence of many parents and friends, and since then some have joined the church Sunday school.

3.   The young men who attended the evening classes have made great progress, and behave generally reasonably well in the parish.

4.   The appeal to the farmers to allow their labourers to attend church on Good Friday has been cordially responded to – the church was nearly full this Good Friday and the greater part were men.

5.   Notwithstanding the awful calamity of the fire which deprived 150 people of their homes in a few hours no one was driven to the Union, and our Societies have not suffered. The amount raised for the Church Missionary Society was about £4 more than on the previous year. The poor are particularly ready to give – 115 pieces of copper were given on the Thanksgiving Sunday.

6.   The people take collecting boxes for Missions and other objects pretty freely – 28 boxes are now out.

7.   The people show an increasingly intelligent interest in the services of the church, specially in that of Holy Baptism.

8.   The manners and morality of the people are decidedly improving.

9.   The number of active workers assisting the minister is increasing.

10. The farmers' families attend a week day service more generally.

These are among the encouraging signs I have to mention for which I desire humbly yet heartily to thank God. For if aught is ever done to benefit a single soul it must be from first to last the work of this Holy Spirit, condescending it may be, to use man as agent.

William Owen

68. DERRY HILL　D. Avebury

1. The new parish of Christ Church, Derry Hill, a perpetual curacy.
2. The vicar of Calne. Vicarage, Calne.
3. 1388 census 1862, but soon, by a rearrangement of boundaries, to be reduced to 1230.
4. Henry Mordaunt Fletcher, November 1856.
5. Yes.
6. Yes.
7. [Blank]
8. No.
9. No.
10. [Blank]
11. [Blank]
12. [Blank]
13. Within its boundaries are, besides the parish church, two consecrated chapels; one within Bowood House, the other, the mausoleum of the Lansdowne family, but they are neither of them served by the incumbent.
14. [See 13]
15. Yes.
16. Yes.
17. Very well – according to the conventional standards.
18. The organ has been, under the authority of a faculty, removed to the west gallery from the north east corner of the nave.
19. Neither baptisms nor marriages are performed in either of the consecrated chapels above mentioned. The burial service of the church is performed at the mausoleum when required.
20. [Blank]
21. The Benefice is endowed with £100 per annum by the Ecclesiastical Commissioners under an Order of Council; and with £10 per annum from the same body under an arrangement made with the Dean and Chapter of Salisbury on the transfer by the Chapter to the Commissioners of certain estates. And the fees for marriages, burials and churchings. Easter offerings have been collected since the formation of the new parish.
22. [Blank]
23. No.
24. Two services – morning at 10.30am. Evening at 3.30pm in winter, at 6.30pm in summer. Sermons are preached at both services, except when there is catechising

when the catechising takes the place of the sermon.

25. Yes.

26. During Lent 1864. Following the church catechism my own opinion is that it is much more useful than a sermon, but it is not popular.

27. Yes.

28. [Blank]

29. [a] Yes [b] Yes [c] Yes [d] Yes [e] Yes.

30. Generally on the 1st Sunday in each month and on the 3rd Sunday in each month.

31. No, but I purpose to do so.

32. I cannot say with exactness enough to justify an entry.

33. [Blank]

34. In 1863 the following numbers communicated: Easter 28, Ascension 18, Whit Sunday 24, Trinity 13, Christmas 32. Easter 1864 – 39 communicants.

35. The average number of communicants during 1863 has been exclusive of the great feasts 20. The celebration on the 3rd Sunday of the month is at 8.00am. There were in 1863 17 celebrations.

36. For 540 worshippers.

37. 200. I fear rather decreasing, but it is difficult to say.

38. No.

39. 27 baptisms 5 marriages 27 burials.

40. In 1863 two persons at Bremhill church.

41. Yes. By posting the receipts on the church doors.

42. £21 6s 7½d in 1863. The whole amount collected at the offertory made every Sunday in 1863 was £51 5s 1¾d.

43. Yes.

44. Five places. Two Baptist, two Primitive Methodist, one Wesleyan Methodist. Each has a large number of frequenters.

45. Yes.

46. Yes.

47. At 11.

48. For a short time.

49. Evening school with considerable success.

50. Yes.

51. Bath Hospital £4 4s 8½d. Society for the Propagation of the Gospel in Foreign Parts £8 6s 2¾d. Salisbury poor benefice aid fund £2 3s 3¼d.

52. [Blank]

Henry M. Fletcher

69. DEVIZES ST JOHN   D. Potterne

1. St John Devizes, a rectory.

2. Lord Chancellor.

3. 1906.

4. William Henry Teale. November 1861.

5. Yes.
6. Yes.
7. [Blank]
8. No.
9. Yes.
10. September 1863.
11. Walter Hook. Deacon.
12. No.
13. Two parishes under one incumbent.
14. St John and St Mary.
15. Yes.
16. Yes.
17. Yes.
18. Nave partly rebuilt and entirely re-seated by faculty.
19. [Blank]
20. [Blank]
21. Tithe, glebe and poor rates. Net income under £300.
22. [Blank]
23. [Blank]
24. 11.00am and 7.00pm.
25. Yes.
26. No.
27. Morning Prayer daily, Evening Prayer Friday with sermons.
28. About 30 daily, more on Friday evenings.
29. [a] Yes [b] Yes [c] Yes [d] Yes [e] Yes.
30. Monthly. Every Sunday during Advent and Lent (8.00am).
31. No.
32. 120.
33. 100.
34. 80.
35. 70.
36. 714.
37. Usually full and frequently crowded. Increasing.
38. Not at present. 154 free sittings have been obtained by the late enlargement of the church.
39. 47 baptisms 11 marriages 25 burials.
40. 27, 35, 30. [Numbers crossed out] confirmed in St Mary's church.
41. [Blank]
42. £38 2s. £36 15s. £36 18s 4d.
43. Yes.
44. One Independent meeting house.
45. Three – boys, girls and infants.
46. Yes.
47. 11.
48. In some instances.

49. Night school for men and boys; successful.

50. Not yet. Always sent in June.

51. May 5th re-opening of church £63 8s 11d. June offertory at visitation £7 5s 7d. Aug 16th Additional Curates Society £8 13s 11d. Sept 20th town schools £6 16s 5d. Nov 8th S.P.G. £13 17s 6½d. Dec 17th Small benefice fund £6 17s 5½d. Total £106 19s 10d.

52. [Blank]

W.H. Teale

70. DEVIZES ST MARY   D. Potterne

1. St Mary, Devizes.
2. The Lord Chancellor.
3. 2685.
4. William Henry Teale, November 1861.
5. Yes.
6. Yes.
7. [Blank]
8. [Blank]
9. Yes.
10. September 1863.
11. Walter Hook. Deacon.
12. No.
13. [Blank]
14. [Blank]
15. Yes.
16. Yes.
17. Yes.
18. No.
19. [Blank]
20. [Blank]
21. [Blank]
22. [Blank]
23. No.
24. Morning service at 11.00am, evening at 3.00pm.
25. Yes.
26. No.
27. [Blank]
28. Wednesday evening prayers at 4.00pm. 20.
29. [a]Yes [b] Yes [c] No [d] Yes [e] Yes.
30. Third Sunday in the month.
31. No.
32. 80.
33. 60.
34. 50.

35. 40.
36. 650.
37. Church generally fairly full.
38. No.
39. 72 baptisms 19 marriages 26 burials.
40. Confirmations for both parishes have been held in St Mary's church for these years. 27, 35, 30.
41. [Blank]
42. 1861 £18 10s 7d. 1862 £21 17s 5½d. 1863 £16 16s 9d.
43. Yes.
44. Two. Baptist and Wesleyan.
45. Three, open to St John's and St Mary's.
46. Yes.
47. 11.
48. In some cases.
49. Evening school; successful.
50. Always sent in June.
51. Jan 18th Lancashire distress £10 11s 10½d. Aug 16th Additional Curates Society £4 2s 1½d. Sept town schools £3 10s 7d. Nov S.P.G. £1 19s 1d. Dec poor benefices fund £2 6s 7½d. Total £22 10s 3½d.
52. [Blank]

W.H. Teale

71. DILTON D. Wylye
1. As Dilton is in no respect a <u>separate</u> incumbency or cure of souls, and, (with slight exception) the answers are involved in those which it was necessary to give in the paper referring to the parish of Westbury, I have made no separate return on this paper.

Henry H Duke, Vicar of Westbury with Dilton

72. DILTON MARSH D. Wylye
1. Dilton Marsh, a perpetual curacy.
2. The Lord Bishop.
3. 1561.
4. Charles Frederick Hyde, 12th May 1862.
5. Yes.
6. In the glebe house.
7. [Blank]
8. No.
9. No.
10. [Blank]
11. [Blank]
12. [Blank]

13. No.
14. [Blank]
15. Yes.
16. Yes.
17. Yes.
18. No.
19. [Blank]
20. [Blank]
21. Six acres of glebe and £286 from the Ecclesiastical Commissioners. Gross value £300.
22. [Blank]
23. [Blank]
24. Morning Prayer at 10.45am and Evening Prayer at 6.00pm with a sermon at each service.
25. Yes, except in Advent and Lent when the Litany and Catechism form a third service on Sunday afternoon at 3.00pm. (Subjects up to the present time the Catechism in the Morning and Evening Prayer).
26. With G[eorge] Herbert I value 'catechising' highly as calculated to infuse a competent knowledge of salvation in every one of my parishioners.
27. [Blank]
28. In Advent and Lent, daily Evening Prayer and twice a day on Wednesdays and Fridays at 10.45am and 7.00pm and on all the festivals and fasting days of the year.
29. [a] Yes [b] Yes [c] Yes [d] Yes [e] Yes.
30. On the 1st Sunday in the month.
31. Yes.
32. 81.
33. 3.
34. 48.
35. 34.
36. 600.
37. The church is two thirds full. I believe the congregation is on the increase.
38. Yes, at Chapmanslade by erection of a school chapel.
39. 34 baptisms 11 marriages 10 burials.
40. In March 1864 there were 24.
41. Yes.
42. In 1863 £16 14s 8¼d.
43. Yes and also of the mode of expenditure.
44. Two Baptist meeting houses and two Independent meeting houses. Two thirds.
45. Yes.
46. Yes, last report 24th March 1864 'The discipline of the school is very good and the work, as far as it goes, is carefully done'. Grant £47 14s 4d.
47. 10 years.
48. In many cases.
49. Yes. Most satisfactory results have flowed from them. Many have been drawn

to Sunday school and church.

50. Yes.

51. Church expenses £23 9s 11¼d. S.P.G. £19 5s 10¼d. Augmentation of poor benefices society £2 2s.

52. As I have so lately communicated with your Lordship on this subject, I will not trouble you with any further remarks.

Charles F. Hyde

73. DINTON cum TEFFONT MAGNA   D. Chalke

1. Dinton cum Teffont Magna, a vicarage.
2. President and Fellows of Magdalene College Oxford.
3. Dinton 509. Teffont 292.
4. James Charles Stafford, June 1841.
5. Yes.
6. In the glebe house.
7. [Blank]
8. No.
9. Yes.
10. In October 1863.
11. Rev E.H. Lloyd, a priest.
12. No.
13. A church and a chapel.
14. Dinton St Mary. Date of consecration not known – to whom the chapel was dedicated not known.
15. Yes.
16. Yes.
17. Yes.
18. No.
19. Baptisms and marriages.
20. Under a mile and a half.
21. Rent charge and glebe.
22. The whole arises from Dinton.
23. No.
24. Morning and afternoon at both. Sermon, or lecture, or catechising at Dinton. Ditto at Teffont except at Morning Prayer the first Sunday in the month. Other times when the curate comes to Dinton to assist in the Holy Communion.
25. Yes.
26. Yes, twice a month. I endeavour to illustrate some portion of the church catechism from the collect, epistle, gospel and lessons.
27. I have discontinued for three years from failing health.
28. Wednesdays, Fridays, saints' days, Ember and Rogation Days.
29. [a] Yes [b] Yes [c] Yes [d] Yes at Teffont [e] Yes.
30. The 1st Sunday in the month generally.
31. Yes.

32. 120. More in the parish have communicated but not very lately.

33. 12 in Dinton.

34. Easter 60. Ascension 32. Trinity absent. Christmas 34.

35. Barely 40.

36. Dinton 344 or thereabouts, including children in the chancel under the tower. Teffont 182 including seats in the chancel.

37. From 150 to 200, steady. Much depends upon the weather, as the population is scattered and lies wide.

38. As the Teffont people no longer occupy the Teffont transept, there is room for the poor; otherwise there would not be, there not being a proportional number of open sittings.

39. 16 baptisms not including Teffont. 2 marriages not including Teffont. 14 burials including Teffont.

40. 23 in Dinton, 10 in Teffont.

41. Yes.

42. £11 2s 2½d.

43. Yes.

44. None in Dinton. In Teffont a Primitive Methodist chapel.

45. Yes.

46. No.

47. Boys at 11, girls at 12.

48. Yes.

49. A night school; fairly attended.

50. Yes.

51. Lancashire fund £5, Teffont 14s. Parish Church Building Society £2 2s 11½d, Teffont 14s 10d. Small benefices £7 0s 4d, Teffont £1 15s 2d. S.P.G. parochial £10 7s, Teffont £1 4s.

52. The Ranters during the summer hold meetings on the village green but they have no meeting house yet. See Teffont Magna.

J. C. Stafford

74. DONHEAD ST ANDREW   D. Chalke

1. Donhead St Andrew, a rectory.

2. Rev. R.B. Bourne, as above.

3. 830.

4. R[obert] B[urr] Bourne, July 1856.

5. He has.

6. He has.

7. [Blank]

8. He does not.

9. He has.

10. November 1858.

11. George Henry Preston, a priest.

12. He does not.

13. It does not.

14. [Blank]

15. It is.

16. It is.

17. They do.

18. None.

19. [Blank]

20. [Blank]

21. [Blank]

22. [Blank]

23. There is not.

24. Morning service at 11.00am and sermon. Afternoon service at 3.00pm and sermon.

25. Yes.

26. On Wednesday and Friday after prayers if the school children are examined in the lessons, sometimes psalms. The parts of the catechism with which the psalms and lessons have connection are introduced. I think this better, among our people, than catechising on Sunday. All the people stay. On Sunday it appears wearisome to some. It makes out the hour satisfactorily, likewise the [?].

27. Not except on Wednesday and Friday, when there is a service, and on saints' days. Children of the upper classes of the school attend (say) 36; other persons (say) five or six, more or less, but the above may be called an average. On Christmas Day, Epiphany and Ascension Day considerably more, and in the evenings of the week before Easter Day. I don't include among these my family.

28. [Blank]

29. [a] Yes [b] Yes [c] No [d] Yes [e] Yes.

30. At intervals of never less than six weeks. Sometimes less, for instance, Advent Sunday and Christmas Day.

31. A list of communicants or supposed communicants (at any time) is kept.

32. 110.

33. 13: of these full five have communicated at their houses.

34. Between 62 and 63. They are not used to come both on Trinity Sunday and Whit Sunday.

35. 49.

36. Nearly 400, if they sat very close.

37. Sunday April 10th there were at morning service 132 and afternoon 154. Sunday 17th April, morning 131 afternoon 158. This may be called about an average, except on a wet Sunday. As Roman Catholics regularly become tenants of houses when vacant, we should be rather decreasing, but we keep up fairly. Most of the houses are Lord Arundell's.

38. There is not.

39. 19 baptisms 4 marriages 9 burials.

40. In 1861 there were 31.

41. Yes. I suppose by this question 'sacramental alms' is not meant.

42. Last year, £13 11s.

43. There is.

44. None in the parish. There are Independents who go to 'Birdbush' which has existed since the Civil War – 93. Roman Catholics who go to Wardour (see answer to no 38) – 123. This enumeration includes their children.

45. There is.

46. No – we have a very good master, but he is not certificated.

47. In the daily school are two above 14, two over 13 and six over 12. But of these some are [?] farmers' sons: very few or no poor people's children stay after 10½.

48. Not generally after 12½; they do come to this age. I get some to my house on a Sunday, but they do not like sitting with the school children. It is 'ut quimus, quando ut volumus not licet'.[1]

49. For three years we have had evening schools, chiefly of adults. As a worthy neighbouring clergy prognosticated they did not do well after three years. Last year we had none.

50. They will be duly transmitted by the churchwarden in May.

51. [Blank]

52. All the holders of lands, with very few exceptions, (three only of any account, and these small farmers) are Roman Catholics. The consequence is we get no church rate and no subscriptions to the school. Patience seems the only practicable remedy for what is thus cast upon me in the way of extra exertion.

R.B. Bourne

[1] 'When we cannot act as we wish, we must act as we can' (Terence)

75. DONHEAD ST MARY   D. Chalke

1. Donhead St Mary, a rectory.

2. New College Oxford.

3. According to the last census 1482.

4. R[ichard] W[hite] Blackmore, July 1847.

5. Resided the whole of the last year.

6. Yes, in the glebe house.

7. [Blank]

8. No.

9. He has.

10. 15th July 1863.

11. M[atthew] M[ortimer] Ffinch, a priest.

12. No.

13. There are two – one the mother church of St Mary and a chapel of ease, St John the Evangelist, for the hamlets of Charlton, Ludwell and the three Coombs. The consecration of the first about the same time as the Cathedral, the second in 1839.

14. [See 13]

15. Yes.

16. Yes.

17. Yes.

18. No.

19. Baptisms and burials but not marriages.

20. 1½ miles.

21. Rent charge and glebe, net amount £850.

22. There is only one parish.

23. Only one glebe house.

24. Two full services every Sunday at the mother church and the same at the chapel of ease. At the mother church 11.00am and 3.00pm, at the chapel of ease the same in winter and in the summer at 11.00am and 6.00pm.

25. Yes.

26. No – the catechism is taught in the schools.

27. No.

28. Saints' days and holidays. 35 average at the mother church, 65 at the chapel of ease.

29. [a] Yes [b] Yes [c] Yes [d] Yes [e] Yes.

30. Every month.

31. Yes.

32. 140.

33. Perhaps about 20.

34. About 100.

35. No perceptible difference.

36. In the church of St Mary 314 exclusive of the vestry occupied by the school children. In the chapel of ease of St John the Evangelist 603.

37. The numbers in a scattered village like this vary so much in different seasons of the year and are so much influenced by the state of the weather that it is impossible to give an average – rather increasing.

38. [Blank]

39. 35 baptisms 12 marriages 23 burials.

40. 22 persons confirmed in 1861. None in 1862 or 1863.

41. Yes.

42. At the church of Donhead St Mary £9 13s 8d. At the chapel of ease £19 10s 9½d.

43. Yes.

44. An Independent meeting house, a Wesleyan and a Primitive – about 20. Roman Catholics about 150. Independents and others who entirely absent themselves from the church. The remainder are baptised, married and buried by the church and about 2/3 of the whole number attend her services.

45. There are two daily schools, one near the church at Donhead, the other near the chapel.

46. Yes, for that of Charlton and Ludwell.

47. From 8 to 14.

48. Yes.

49. There is an evening school which has been well attended.

50. Yes.

51. For the clergy fund £4 10s 2d.

52. Allow me to remark that the three meeting houses mentioned in answer to no 44 are supported by the neighbouring parishes of Donhead St Andrew and Semley and as well as by Donhead St Mary and that the reason of them having been all built here is that free land for their erection is not to be procured in the other neighbouring parishes.

R.W. Blackmore

76. DOWNTON   D. Wilton

1. Downton, a vicarage.
2. Warden and Fellows of Winchester College.
3. 2400.
4. Richard Payne, November 1841.
5. Yes.
6. Yes.
7. [Blank]
8. No.
9. Yes.
10. February 9th 1864.
11. William Carmichael Porter, a priest.
12. No.
13. A church at Nunton.
14. Downton St Lawrence.
15. Yes.
16. Yes, fairly.
17. Yes.
18. Chancel re-roofed and re-seated by faculty.
19. [Blank]
20. [Blank]
21. The vicarial tithe at Downton commuted at £700 gross. Nunton £80. And a beneficial holding of the great tithes of Nunton worth £130 gross. Payments from the College £7.
22. [See 21]
23. The vicarage at Downton and a cottage fit for a labourer at Nunton.
24. At Downton 10.30am and 3.00pm with sermons at each service. In the summer, prayers at 3.00pm and a full service at 6.00pm. At Nunton 11.00am and 3.30pm with sermon.
25. Yes.
26. No.
27. I consider a large, scattered parish at all times a reasonable hindrance when there would be no congregation.
28. At Downton, prayers on Wednesdays, Fridays and Holy Days. Daily in Lent and twice a day in Passion Week.
29. [a] Yes [b] Yes [c] Yes [d] Yes [e] Not necessarily.
30. 1st Sunday in the month.

31. Yes.
32. About 150.
33. 120 persons communicated at Downton besides strangers in 1863 and about 20 received the communion at Lent.
34. Christmas Day and Whit Sunday 24. Ascension Day 8. Easter Day 57.
35. 38.
36. 750 at Downton.
37. 400 including children. Not much variation the last year.
38. No.
39. 45 baptisms 12 marriages 31 burials.
40. 76.
41. Yes.
42. £18 5s 10d in 1864.
43. Yes.
44. 3 Baptist Chapels, 1 Wesleyan Methodist, 1 Wesleyan Reformed, 1 Primitive Methodist. Also Dr Welch's own house. Perhaps 500 members including children, where parents are members, and as many more occasional hearers. Two thirds are Baptist.
45. Yes.
46. For the girls' school, not the boys.
47. About 10.
48. Less so, I think, than a few years ago, but still to a certain extent, in the case of boys an attendance once a day.
49. A night school has been opened but with no great success. During the last winter it was confined to those who attended the Sunday school.
50. Yes.
51. Parent and Diocesan Church Building Society £5 2s 10d. Collection for warming the church £6 1s 9d. Collection for schools £13 2s 4d. Poor benefice augmentation fund £6.
52. Nothing new. The abnegation of all parental authority and the want of a better arrangement for the attendance upon cattle including sheep on the Sunday.

Richard Payne

77. DRAYCOT FOLIAT   D. Marlborough
1. Draycot Foliat, a rectory.
2. M.A. Thorowgood, West Brixton, Surrey.
3. 21 or 22.
4. George Eastman. Instituted December 14th 1858, inducted January 8th 1859.
5. No. Non-resident by licence of the bishop.
6. No glebe house.
7. Edwin Meyrick, curate, resident at Chiseldon.
8. No.
9. Not resident.
10. [Blank]

11. [Blank]
12. [Blank]
13. No.
14. [Blank]
15. [Blank]
16. [Blank]
17. No churchwardens.
18. No church.
19. No church or chapels.
20. [Blank]
21. Tithe commuted at £180 per annum. Deductions – rates, taxes and curate's stipend.
22. But one parish.
23. No glebe house.
24. No church.
25. [Blank]
26. [Blank]
27. [Blank]
28. [Blank]
29. [Blank]
30. [Blank]
31. No.
32. 1 or 2.
33. The communicants are regular.
34. [Blank]
35. [Blank]
36. No church.
37. [Blank]
38. No.
39. None.
40. 1.
41. No church.
42. [Blank]
43. [Blank]
44. No dissenting place of worship. One family consisting of eight or nine persons are Baptists.
45. No.
46. [Blank]
47. [Blank]
48. [Blank]
49. [Blank]
50. No parish registers except at Chiseldon.
51. No church.
52. No.

George Eastman B.D.

78. DURNFORD   D. Amesbury
1.   Durnford, a vicarage.
2.   The Lord Bishop of the diocese.
3.   553.
4.   John Newton Hinxman. 1849.
5.   Yes.
6.   In the glebe house.
7.   [Blank]
8.   No.
9.   No.
10. [Blank]
11. [Blank]
12. [Blank]
13. No.
14. [Blank]
15. The church is not in good repair.
16. A new iron fence is being erected.
17. Moderately so.
18. Not any.
19. There are no chapels.
20. [Blank]
21. The sources are rent charge £105, one grant from the Ecclesiastical Commissioners £30 per annum, ditto £22 per annum and 32 acres of glebe.
22. [Blank]
23. No.
24. There are two full services in the church on the Lord's Day at 10.30am and 3.00pm with sermons.
25. The prayer for the church militant and the offertory sentences are omitted usually.
26. No.
27. Not daily.
28. On the principal fasts and festivals. The number varies from 30 to 100.
29. [a] Yes [b] Yes [c] No [d] Yes [e] No.
30. On five other Sundays in the year.
31. Not of all the communicants, as, in consequence of the wide extent and straggling nature of the parish, and the church being at one end, the parishioners are obliged to attend divine service at three other churches, where many of them also receive the Holy Communion.
32. The probable number is about 80.
33. [Blank]
34. Between 30 and 40 at the parish church.
35. About 26.
36. About 250.
37. About 120.
38. A chapel at the south end of the parish is wanted.

39. 20 baptisms 1 marriage 5 burials.
40. 19.
41. There is no public statement issued.
42. £13 7s 2d.
43. Yes.
44. There is a small Wesleyan meeting house. The number is uncertain.
45. Yes.
46. No.
47. The boys at 7 and 8, the girls at 12 and 13.
48. Yes, some of them.
49. By an evening school with tolerable success.
50. Yes.
51. Collections have been made for the Society for the Propagation of the Gospel, for the Jews' Society and harvest thanksgiving to the Infirmary Fund.
52. The remoteness of the parish church from the bulk of the population and the straggling nature of the parish generally.

J.N. Hinxman

79. DURRINGTON   D. Amesbury

1. Durrington.
2. The Dean and Chapter of Winchester.
3. By last census 436.
4. Charles Snelling Ruddle. February 22nd 1863.
5. Yes.
6. Resident in the parish. No glebe house exists.
7. [Blank]
8. No.
9. No.
10. [Blank]
11. [Blank]
12. [Blank]
13. No.
14. [Blank]
15. Yes.
16. Yes.
17. Yes.
18. No.
19. [Blank]
20. [Blank]
21. Charge of £70. One sack of wheat and one sack of malt payable by the lessee of the tithe. £42 from the Ecclesiastical Commissioners. £13 from Queen Anne's Bounty. Total £125.
22. [Blank]
23. There is none.

24. Morning at 11.00am and afternoon at 3.00pm or 6.30pm in summer. A sermon at each.

25. Yes.

26. No.

27. [Blank]

28. On Holy Days; and a weekly service including a lecture from October to Easter. At morning service about 12; at evening service about 100.

29. [a] Yes [b] Yes [c] No [d] No [e] No.

30. On the 1st Sunday of each month.

31. Yes.

32. 135.

33. I am not able to say – not having entered upon my incumbency till after the celebrations of January and February.

34. 40.

35. 40.

36. 340.

37. Morning 150, evening 270. Stationary.

38. No.

39. 6 baptisms 1 marriage 8 burials.

40. In 1861 approximately 35.

41. No.

42. £10 15s 6½d.

43. Yes.

44. One chapel – Congregationalist. Four families of Congregationalists and one of Wesleyans.

45. Yes.

46. Yes.

47. About 11.

48. Several lads attend who are employed as plough boys.

49. The evening school in the past winter had an average attendance of about 20. I have lately established a Sunday evening class for young men and lads, and a fortnightly bible class for young women and girls. Both are fairly attended.

50. Yes.

51. Salisbury Diocesan Church Building Association £2 3s 3d. For the building fund of a church in a poor district in Deptford £1 17s 2d. Augmentation of small benefices in this diocese £3. Foreign Missions, S.P.G. and Church Missionary Society £3 16s 9d. Total £10 17s 2d.

52. [Blank]

Charles S Ruddle

80. EAST COULSTON D. Potterne

1. East Coulston, a rectory.

2. The Lord Chancellor.

3. 120 or thereabouts.

4. Henry C. Dishon, June 1858.
5. Yes.
6. In the glebe house.
7. [Blank]
8. No.
9. No.
10. [Blank]
11. [Blank]
12. [Blank]
13. No.
14. [Blank]
15. Yes.
16. Yes.
17. Yes.
18. No.
19. [Blank]
20. [Blank]
21. About £270. £170 from rent charge the remainder from glebe.
22. [Blank]
23. No.
24. Two full services in the church on Sunday. Mornings at 11.00am, afternoons at 3.00pm, always sermons.
25. Yes.
26. No.
27. No.
28. Occasional services in winter always good attendances.
29. [a] Yes [b] Yes [c] No [d] Yes [e] No.
30. On the 2nd Sunday in the month.
31. No.
32. About 20.
33. Can't say.
34. The same as on Sundays.
35. [Blank]
36. About 80.
37. About 60 – stationary.
38. No.
39. 8 baptisms 2 marriages 3 burials.
40. 1861 four persons.
41. No.
42. About £3.
43. Yes.
44. A small meeting house for Baptists.
45. Yes.
46. No. It is chiefly supported by myself.
47. About 12.

48. To some extent.

49. No.

50. Yes.

51. Church Missionary Society, Jews Society, Irish Church Missions, average collection about £1.

52. The supineness and worldliness of the laity. I can suggest no remedy and can only hope to see a more practical religion springing up among us.

Henry C. Dishon

81. EAST GRAFTON   D. Marlborough

1. Perpetual curacy of S. Nicholas East Grafton, in the parish of Great Bedwyn.

2. The vicar of Great Bedwyn (legally).

3. 1046.

4. George Stallard M.A. 9th August 1855.

5. Yes.

6. Yes.

7. Resident.

8. No.

9. No.

10. [Blank]

11. [Blank]

12. [Blank]

13. No.

14. [Blank]

15. Yes.

16. Yes.

17. Yes.

18. No.

19. [Blank]

20. [Blank]

21. From the Ecclesiastical Commissioners £95. Dividends on £501 5s 1d from Queen Anne's Bounty £15 0s 8d. And a voluntary payment by the Marquis of Ailesbury to the present incumbent.

22. [Blank]

23. [Blank]

24. Morning 10.30am with sermon. Afternoon 3.00pm with sermon. During Advent, Lent and all the high festivals at 6.30pm with sermon. Wednesday and Friday evenings at 7.00pm with sermons.

25. Yes.

26. At festivals and before confirmation. After catechising a lecture or address is delivered to the congregation on the subject for the day with evident benefit to the hearers.

27. During Lent at 9.00am. During the year on Wednesday and Friday evenings at 7.00pm.

28. Christmas Day★, two full services. Ash Wednesday**, two full services. Maundy Tuesday, Wednesday and Thursday, two services with sermons every evening. Good Friday★, two full services with sermons. Holy Thursday★★, two full services with sermons. Wednesday morning★ in Whitsun week with sermon. Monday★ after Trinity Sunday, with sermon. ★ - very large congregation ★★ - good congregation.

29. [a] Yes [b] Yes [c] Yes [d] Yes [e] Yes.

30. Advent Sunday, Holy Thursday, Festival of Circumcision and every 1st Sunday in the month.

31. Yes.

32. 110.

33. [Blank]

34. 44.

35. 34.

36. 500.

37. [Blank]

38. The very scattered state of the population, in five hamlets each two miles from the other and from the church, might benefit from lectures in a school room (licensed).

39. 27 baptisms 8 marriages 12 burials.

40. [Blank]

41. Yes. Receipts with statements of all collections are placed on the church doors and accounts exhibited at the Easter vestry.

42. For 1863, £16 3s 8d.

43. Yes.

44. A Wesleyan Methodist meeting house at Wilton. Primitive Methodist meeting house at West Grafton.

45. Yes, a National School.

46. A certificated master, mistress and pupil teacher. We have received a capitation grant.

47. About 12.

48. But few.

49. Night school. Above 30 have attended.

50. [Blank]

51. Society for the Propagation of the Gospel £4 6s 9d. Harvest thanksgiving for the aged poor £4 10s.

52. [Blank]

George Stallard

82. EAST GRIMSTEAD D. Amesbury

1. West Dean with East Grimstead annexed; a rectory.

2. Rev. Henry Glossop, Silver Hall, Isleworth, Middlesex.

3. Total 450.

4. G[eorge[G[oodwin] P[ownall] Glossop[1], 1861. Inducted 10th June.

5. Yes.

6. In the rectory.

7. [Blank]

8. No, the two parishes are one benefice.

9. No licensed curate, but the rector of West Grimstead helps.

10. [Blank]

11. Rev. T. Morse, a priest.

12. Yes, rector of West Grimstead.

13. A church at West Dean and a chapel of ease at East Grimstead.

14. East Grimstead – Holy Trinity; about 1856, West Dean – St Mary's; part of it 1250.

15. At East Grimstead, yes.

16. Yes.

17. Yes.

18. A lectern is used and kneeling benches have been placed in the chancel by me, G.G.P.G., rector.

19. At E. Grimstead there are baptisms but no burials.

20. E. Grimstead is about 2½ miles from Dean.

21. [Blank]

22. West Dean rent charge £410 plus glebe £100 plus a house. East Grimstead rent charge £215 plus glebe £37. Total value £762 plus the rectory.

23. No.

24. At E. Grimstead there is only one service with sermon on Sundays and that is always in the afternoon. There is an occasional administration of the Holy Communion there at 9.00am and in Lent there is an evening service with sermon on Fridays at 7.00pm.

25. Yes in the evening, but in the morning I do not say the prayer for the church militant.

26. No, except before confirmation when I found the church the best place for a confirmation class.

27. No.

28. East Grimstead chapel on Fridays in Lent, Good Friday and Ascension Day. In West Dean on Wednesdays in Lent, Good Friday and Ascension Day.

29. At West Dean [a] Yes [b] Yes [c] No [d] Yes [e] Yes. At East Grimstead [a] Yes [b] Yes [c] Yes [d] No [e] No.

30. At Dean on the 1st Sunday in each month.

31. No.

32. At East Grimstead about 12, at Dean about 30.

33. None that I know of.

34. 10 and 25.

35. 9 and 20.

36. Grimstead holds 75 to 80 well. Dean holds 160 with much discomfort.

37. Grimstead 60, Dean 100-120.

38. Yes, Dean church must be rebuilt.

39. 8 baptisms 2 marriages 3 burials.

40. None.

41. No.

42. In 1862 £1 7s 4d and in 1863 £2 13s 11d, which is nearly double the year before.

43. No.

44. At East Grimstead there is a chapel for the reformed Wesleyans. There are very few who do not <u>sometimes</u> attend this chapel.

45. Yes.

46. They offer me nothing <u>at East Grimstead</u> because my mistress is not certificated by them.

47. Girls go at 13, boys at 9.

48. Not very long, for I have not a sufficient staff of teachers.

49. At East Grimstead there is a small evening school and at Dean a better one.

50. Yes.

51. East Grimstead church collections for poor benefices 7s 8½d. For the S.P.G. 11s 11d.

52. Dissent deprives me of the sympathy and of the <u>personal assistance</u> of the best people in my parish, so that those who are the most able to help me as 'teachers' regard me rather as an opponent than as their true and only pastor. I propose as a remedy to have a resident curate and more frequent services in East Grimstead. I have great difficulty about getting a curate to live at East Grimstead. Unmarried men do not like to 'keep house' and married men want a regular parsonage which I have not got here.

G.G.P. Glossop

¹ Third son of Henry Glossop.

83. EAST HARNHAM   D. Chalke

1. East Harnham, a perpetual curacy.

2. The vicar of Britford.

3. About 350.

4. Arthur Philip Morres, July 1861.

5. Yes.

6. In a rented house in The Close.

7. [Blank]

8. He is chaplain to the Alderbury Union [workhouse]

9. No.

10. [Blank]

11. [Blank]

12. [Blank]

13. No.

14. The church was dedicated to All Saints in the year 1854.

15. Yes.

16. Yes.

17. Yes.

18. No alterations. A stand for the choir in the chancel and two stained windows in the nave have been added.

19. In East Harnham church (but not in the Alderbury Union chapel, the building being unconsecrated).

20. [Blank]

21. In all £110 with fees additional. From vicarial tithes at Har[nham] £46. From rent charge on rectorial charge £30. From the Ecclesiastical Commissioners £30. Fees varying £4. Total £110.

22. [Blank]

23. There is no glebe house.

24. Full services with sermons, at 10.30am and 6.30pm. Full service with sermon (morning and evening alternate) at the Alderbury Union chapel.

25. Yes.

26. No.

27. There is daily morning service, without intermission, at 8.30am in the church.

28. Besides the daily services at 8.30am, during Advent and Lent there are evening services at 7.00pm with sermon on Thursdays. On saints' days, the morning service is at 10.30am. Attendance at daily morning service from 6 to 12. At evening lectures from 15 to 40. The morning prayers are read at the Alderbury Union at 10.30am on Thursdays.

29. [a] Yes [b] Yes [c] No [d] Yes [e] Yes.

30. The 1st Sunday in every month.

31. Yes.

32. 49.

33. All have.

34. On Christmas Day 17. On Easter Day 44. On Whit Sunday 17. On Trinity Sunday 10.

35. Average number throughout the year 24.

36. By the plan of the church 220.

37. Fair average attendance. Morning attendance the thinnest, but rather on the increase, evening attendance good.

38. [Blank]

39. 9 baptisms 2 marriages 14 burials.

40. 10 in 1861 by the Rev Tupper Carey. None in 1862 or 1863.

41. The sum collected is placed on the church door.

42. £14 6s 2d during the year 1863.

43. Yes.

44. From 25 to 40, chiefly Primitive Methodist.

45. Yes.

46. Yes, a grant for 1863 being £30 8s 6d.

47. Girls 13 or 14, boys 10 or 11.

48. Partially.

49. There is a night school during the winter months for boys, average attendance from 10 to 14.

50. Yes.

51. February 22nd Church Quarterly £7 13s 10½d. May 17th Church Quarterly £6 4s. August 2nd Church Quarterly £8. October 25th harvest thanksgiving £3. November 15th Church Quarterly £5 6s 6d. Gold £11, silver £17 12s 8d, copper £1 11s 8½d. Total £30 4s 4½d.

52. Nothing except the usual impediments, which must necessarily arise from the vicinity of a large town and two large public houses in so small a place.

Arthur P Morres

84. EAST KENNETT   D. Avebury

1. East Kennett, a perpetual curacy.
2. John Mathews Esq, Chieveley.
3. About 70.
4. William Collins Badger, Sept 23rd 1863.
5. Yes, the right time since being licensed.
6. In the parsonage.
7. Resident.
8. Only the chaplaincy to the Marlborough Union [workhouse]
9. [Blank]
10. [Blank]
11. [Blank]
12. [Blank]
13. No.
14. [Blank]
15. Yes.
16. Yes.
17. Yes, I believe so.
18. Church rebuilt.[1]
19. [Blank]
20. [Blank]
21. £58 a year rent charge with the hope of £50 a year more.
22. [Blank]
23. No.
24. Two services, one at 10.30am the other at 6.00pm every Sunday and sermons at both.
25. Yes.
26. No.
27. No.
28. Christmas Day and Good Friday.
29. I propose its administration on those days.
30. Generally through the year all together I propose once a month.
31. [Blank]
32. Only nine at present.
33. [Blank]
34. [Blank]

35. [Blank]
36. About 103.
37. About 35 in the barn.[2]
38. No.
39. 4 baptisms 0 marriages 7 burials.
40. [Blank]
41. I have been in the habit of doing so.
42. I should think about £2 a year from what I have heard.
43. Yes, now.
44. Two Baptists.
45. Yes.
46. No.
47. From 11 to 14 years of age.
48. [Blank]
49. Yes. I hold an evening class of 12 men and boys and find them very attentive.
50. They are sent.
51. None made.
52. [Blank]

W.C. Badger[3]

[1] The church was rebuilt in 1863.

[2] During the rebuild services were held in a barn.

[3] While at East Kennett, Badger entered into controversy with Bishop Hamilton whose tractarian views he found unacceptable. *See* Wilts. Tracts, xcii, no. 6.

85. EAST KNOYLE D. Chalke

1. East Knoyle, a rectory.
2. The Rt Rev the Lord Bishop of Winchester, Farnham Castle, Surrey.
3. 1034.
4. Crosbie Morgell, April 1848.
5. Always resident through the year 1863.
6. Always.
7. [Blank]
8. None.
9. An assistant curate.
10. No licence granted to the last curate, because of particular circumstances. The present curate will shortly be licensed.
11. The Rev Thomas Hills, priest.
12. His services are confined to East Knoyle.
13. It does not.
14. [Blank]
15. Quite so.
16. Perfectly well.
17. They do efficiently.
18. No alteration since the last visitation.

19. [Blank]

20. [Blank]

21. Rectorial rent charge, glebe land, a summer lease, a rectorial manor: estimated net value of the whole £850.

22. [Blank]

23. [Blank]

24. During the winter months three Sunday services at 11.00am, 3.00pm and 6.30pm. During the summer months two Sunday services at 11.00am and 6.00pm. Always with a sermon or lecture.

25. When there are three services the 6.00pm is Litany only: otherwise the whole service is said without omission.

26. In the church there is no catechising. If it were attempted the answers of the children would not be heard by the congregation and it is believed the practice would in this parish be no exception to the result elsewhere – a very thin attendance at church.

27. I have never made this my practice.

28. Until the last winter there has always been an evening service on the Wednesday – discontinued owing to the smallness of the attendance. There are services on Christmas Day and an attendance of 250: on Ash Wednesday 200: on Good Friday 250: on Holy Thursday under 100.

29. [a] Yes [b] Yes [c] No [d] Yes [e] No.

30. So that there is an administration once a month.

31. Not a nominal list.

32. Probably 100 persons have communicated some time or other: but I do not account the number over 80, who may be considered communicants.

33. Perhaps some 10.

34. Perhaps 56 to 60.

35. From 45 to 50.

36. 400.

37. 220. Stationary.

38. No want.

39. 17 baptisms which is far below the average. 11 marriages which is above average. 21 burials which is about average.

40. In 1861, 30 adults.

41. It has been generally done every year in a printed statement circulated through the parish.

42. About £20.

43. Yes of receipts and disbursements.

44. There [is] a place for those of the Independent persuasion and another for those calling themselves Primitives: there are about 70 persons, adults, professing themselves dissenters, some having families: the chapels have congregations no doubt exceeding this number, especially as they draw persons from other parishes.

45. We have a daily National School.

46. We have under the new code lately obtained a grant which will probably reach over £40.

47. The mechanic class and farmers' children remain with us up to 14 and 15: labourers' boys leave between 8 and 10, girls remain to 12 or 13.

48. In some cases: but farm duties on Sundays commonly interfere.

49. We have a successful evening school: attended by all who would if they could come Sundays and by several adults (males) besides.

50. It is now just the time when the returns are made.

51. Society for the Propagation of the Gospel. Church Missionary Society. Pastoral Aid Society. Jews Society. Bishop's Pastoral Letters. County Infirmary.

52. Religious apathy as regards religion generally. The enormous sum expended in support of the Independent establishment in the village by a rich manufacturer in a neighbouring town[1], impedes the welfare of the church. The lax discipline of the Independent school renders our strictness distasteful to many. The profanation of Good Friday and other holy-days by large bodies of persons from other parishes making it a feasting day at the chapel of the Primitives. Occasional camp meetings during the summer of dissenters. The only remedies I can suggest are those founded upon Acts 20: 20, 21[2] and the maintenance of discipline and giving the best education we can in the school.

[No signature]

[1] Charles Jupe of Mere.

[2] 'And how I kept back nothing that was profitable unto you, but have shewed you, and have taught you publickly, and from house to house. Testifying both to the Jews, and also to the Greeks, repentance toward God, and faith toward our Lord Jesus Christ'.

86. EASTON, or EASTON ROYAL   D. Marlborough

1. Easton Royal, a donative.
2. The Marquess of Ailesbury, Savernake Forest.
3. Between 4 and 5 hundred.
4. David Llewellyn, March 1839.
5. He has been always resident since 1839.
6. In a house belonging to Lord Ailesbury.
7. [Blank]
8. No, but he is licensed chaplain to the Union workhouse at Pewsey.
9. Yes.
10. In 1858.
11. Arthur J. C. Llewellyn[1], a priest.
12. He performs one at Oare and lives there at present by permission of the bishop.
13. No.
14. [Blank]
15. Yes.
16. Yes.
17. Yes.
18. No.

19. Yes.

20. [Blank]

21. No legal endowment of any kind, but I have no reason to complain of the annual salary paid me[2] by the patron the Marquess of Ailesbury.

22. [Blank]

23. There is no glebe house.

24. Two, 10.30am and 6.00pm, a sermon at each service.

25. Yes.

26. In the school room.

27. No.

28. Christmas Day, Ash Wednesday, Wednesdays in Passion Week and Good Friday. Church well attended on Christmas Day and Good Friday.

29. Christmas Day, Easter Day, Whit Sunday and Michaelmas.

30. [Blank]

31. Yes.

32. Between 20 and 30.

33. [Blank]

34. 20.

35. [Blank]

36. 190.

37. From 80 to 100.

38. [Blank]

39. 15 baptisms 3 marriages 9 burials

40. 25 in 1861.

41. No.

42. £1 14s.

43. Yes.

44. A Wesleyan meeting house.

45. Yes.

46. No.

47. 8.

48. Partially.

49. A night school.

50. Yes.

51. For the augmentation of poor livings 17s and for the Society for the Propagation of the Gospel in Foreign Parts £1 5s 3d.

52. I am not able to mention anything which specially impedes my own ministry or the welfare of the church around me, nor to suggest a remedy, except it be earnest prayer to God for an outpouring of the Holy Spirit, to enable us with one mind and one mouth to glorify God, even the Father of our Lord Jesus Christ.

David Llewellyn

[1] First son of David Llewellyn

[2] £120 according to Crockford's

87. EBBESBOURNE WAKE   D. Chalke

1. Ebbesbourne Wake, a perpetual curacy.
2. The Bishop of the Diocese.
3. 326.
4. Tupper Carey, June 24th 1861.
5. Resident at Fifield Bavant.
6. No.
7. None.
8. Yes, Fifield Bavant (q.v.)
9. No.
10. [Blank]
11. [Blank]
12. [Blank]
13. Only one church.
14. St John the Baptist.
15. In fair repair.
16. Yes.
17. Fairly.
18. No, not to my knowledge.
19. [Blank]
20. [Blank]
21. £61 from the Ecclesiastical Commissioners and £19 last year from the Subchanter.
22. [Blank]
23. No.
24. Morning at 10.30am, evening at 6.00pm. 1st Sunday in the month afternoon at 3.00pm. Sermons at each service.
25. The Litany on the 1st Sunday in the afternoon, full service at other times.
26. The offices of baptism and catechism during the last year. Disliked by the congregation.
27. No.
28. In Advent and Lent there is an evening service. Morning Prayer Friday morning in Lent. 30 persons in the evening, 4 in the morning.
29. [a] Yes [b] Yes [c] No [d] No [e] No.
30. Last Sunday in the month.
31. Yes.
32. 34.
33. 2.
34. 20.
35. 16.
36. 278.
37. 40. Keeps the same.
38. No.
39. 5 baptisms 3 marriages 5 burials.
40. Six girls, boys one in 1861.

41. No.
42. £7 13s 5½d.
43. Yes.
44. An Independent Chapel. 230 dissenters.
45. Yes.
46. Not required.
47. At 9.
48. Very few.
49. Yes – the evening school has nearly failed.
50. Not yet, they are sent in before the visitation.
51. Home Missions £1 14s 2d. Poor benefice fund £3 13s. Society for the Propagation of the Gospel £1 8s. Total £5 15s 2d.
52. Nothing can be done till there is a resident clergyman in the village, the neglect of the church having confirmed the people in dissent.

Tupper Carey

88. EDINGTON   D. Potterne

1. Edington, a perpetual curacy.
2. Simon Watson Taylor Esq, Erlestoke Park, nr Devizes.
3. 994.
4. Samuel Littlewood, 4th Sept 1826.
5. Yes.
6. He has resided in a house rented at a small rent of the patron situated in the parish of Edington.
7. [Blank]
8. No.
9. He has no assistant curate.
10. [Blank]
11. [Blank]
12. [Blank]
13. No.
14. [Blank]
15. Yes.
16. Yes.
17. Yes.
18. No.
19. [Blank]
20. [Blank]
21. Queen Anne's Bounty, fees, and stipendiary payment by lay impropriator amounting all together to £160 a year.
22. [Blank]
23. [Blank]
24. Two full services at the church, morning service beginning at 10.30am, afternoon beginning at 2.30pm. A sermon preached at each.

25. Yes.
26. No.
27. No.
28. Every Wednesday, morning prayers, except during the winter months. Only two or three attend besides the school children and our own family. Prayers on Ascension Day. Two full services on Good Friday and Christmas Day.
29. The Holy Communion is administered on Christmas Day, Easter Day, Whit Sunday and the Sunday after Michaelmas Day.
30. No other.
31. No, but I know them all.
32. About 50.
33. Four or five on account of illness.
34. About 40.
35. [Blank]
36. 600 or more.
37. Between 300 and 400 in the afternoon; not so many in the morning – increasing.
38. No.
39. 15 baptisms 11 marriages 18 burials.
40. 17 in 1861.
41. The churchwardens make the collection and can certify to the amount of the same.
42. Last year £6 17s 8d.
43. Yes.
44. There is a Wesleyan chapel at Tinhead in my parish. I cannot say the probable number, for many of them attend church and chapel. The denominations are Wesleyan and Baptist.
45. Yes, two daily schools, one for girls and an infant school for little boys and girls.
46. No.
47. 12 years of age or 13.
48. But very few of them.
49. No, except that my daughter has a scripture class, only few attend.
50. Yes.
51. One collection for the Bath Mineral Water Hospital, which amounted to £3 18s 1d.
52. Yes. There are no school rooms, and we are obliged to rent two cottages, consequently there is no place where the children or any of the parishioners can be assembled together.

Samuel Littlewood B.D.

89. ENFORD   D. Potterne
1.   All Saints, Enford, a vicarage.
2.   The Governors of Christ's Hospital.

3. 950.
4. Just Henry Alt M.A. instituted Nov 1833. Inducted Jany 1834.
5. Yes.
6. Yes.
7. [Blank]
8. No.
9. Yes.
10. May 1860.
11. Rev George Keith Fennell. A priest.
12. No.
13. No.
14. [Blank]
15. Yes.
16. Yes.
17. Yes.
18. Yes. New books. New hangings to the pulpit and reading desk, carpets and mats. Chairs for the communion table, an alms box presented by the ladies of the parish and the vicar.
19. [Blank]
20. [Blank]
21. Farm land. £450.
22. [Blank]
23. No.
24. Full service morning and afternoon. In the morning at 10.30am and in the afternoon at 3.00pm.
25. Yes.
26. No.
27. No. The parish is too scattered.
28. On Wednesdays and Fridays in Lent. Two services on Good Friday, and in the morning on Holy Thursday. 6 or 8.
29. [a] Yes [b] Yes [c] No [d] Yes [e] No.
30. The 1st Sunday in the month.
31. No.
32. 30.
33. All.
34. 20 to 24.
35. 12 to 18.
36. 650.
37. 160. Stationary.
38. No.
39. 32 baptisms 8 marriages 24 burials.
40. 42.
41. The curate does not.
42. About £6.
43. No.

44. A chapel on Sir Edmund Antrobus's property. Baptists.
45. Yes.
46. No. The school belongs to Lady Antrobus.
47. 10 or 11.
48. Very seldom.
49. No.
50. Yes.
51. Bath Hospital £6 16s 7d. S.P.G £4 18s 1d.
52. [Blank]

Just Henry Alt M.A.

90. ETCHILHAMPTON   D. Avebury

1. All Cannings rectory.
2. The Lord Ashburton. The Grange, Alresford, Hants.
3. 250.
4. Thomas Anthony Methuen. Instituted in 1809.
5. Yes.
6. Yes.
7. [Blank]
8. Yes, Garsdon Rectory near Malmesbury in the diocese of Gloucester.
9. Yes.
10. 1856.
11. Henry Hoare Methuen[1], in priest's orders.
12. No.
13. Yes, Etchilhampton.
14. Date so remote that it can scarcely be ascertained.
15. Yes.
16. Yes.
17. Taking the word 'duties' in its most extended sense, I can make but a qualified reply.
18. No.
19. Yes.
20. The chapel is about 2 miles from it.
21. Tithes – the amount varies according to the average price of wheat, that I cannot make an exact reply, but the income arising to the rector for Etchilhampton is from £250 to £260.
22. [Blank]
23. [Blank]
24. Two services, with sermons, on every Sunday at 10.30am and 2.30pm.
25. Yes.
26. No.
27. No.
28. On the day appointed in the Prayer Book ie the festivals and on Good Friday.
29. [a] Yes. [b] Yes. [c] No. [d] No. [e] Yes.

30. On the 1st Sunday of every month.
31. Yes! I do.
32. <u>About</u> 15-20.
33. <u>Few</u> – I am compelled thus <u>generally</u> to reply.
34. 15-20.
35. Much the same.
36. For 150 at least.
37. About 130; it is not diminishing.
38. No.
39. Some 8 baptisms. One couple married. 3 or 4 burials.
40. In 1861 there were six persons.
41. No.
42. In 1863 £6 14s.
43. Yes!
44. None.
45. Yes.
46. No.
47. About 10 to 12 years of age.
48. Some few are thus retained.
49. A night school, which has done some good.
50. Yes.
51. For the Pastoral Aid Society £1 6s 10d.
52. The existence of a considerable and highly prejudiced body – the Particular Baptists.

I am, my Dear Lord, your Lordship's faithful & obedient Thomas Anthony Methuen, Rector
March 29th 1864

¹ Second son of Thomas Methuen

91. EVERLEIGH   D. Marlborough

1. Everleigh, a rectory.
2. Sir F.D. Astley, Bart., Folkestone, Kent.
3. 276.
4. Symeon Taylor Bartlett, 1857.
5. Yes.
6. Yes.
7. [Blank]
8. No.
9. No.
10. [Blank]
11. [Blank]
12. [Blank]
13. No.
14. [Blank]

15. Yes.
16. Yes.
17. Yes.
18. No.
19. [Blank]
20. [Blank]
21. Tithe rent charge and glebe commuted to £700 per annum.
22. No.
23. [Blank]
24. 10.45am and 3.00pm, sermons at both services.
25. Yes.
26. No.
27. No.
28. Good Friday, Christmas Day, Ash Wednesday. 50 to 80.
29. [a] Yes [b] Yes [c] No [d] Yes [e] Yes.
30. None.
31. No.
32. 30 to 45.
33. None.
34. 34.
35. [Blank]
36. 150 to 200.
37. 130, stationary.
38. No.
39. 14 baptisms 3 marriages 8 burials.
40. In 1861. May 16th males 12 females 18.
41. No.
42. About £1 10s.
43. No.
44. None.
45. Yes.
46. No, not required.
47. 10 or 12.
48. Yes, partially.
49. Not for two years past. Very little [success].
50. Yes.
51. None.
52. Nothing.

Symeon T Bartlett LLD

92. FARLEY   D. Amesbury

1. Farley: a chapelry of the parish of Alderbury forming with Pitton a separate parish for civil purposes.
2. The Lord Bishop of Salisbury.

3. 241.
4. The Revd Newton Smart. Prebendary and Rural Dean. 1843.
5. [Blank]
6. In the glebe house at Alderbury.
7. [Blank]
8. No.
9. Yes.
10. March 28th 1863.
11. John Farnham Messenger. A priest. (Revd Henry Barton the resident curate of Pitton is also junior curate of Farley).
12. He is Sub-Warden of Farley Hospital.
13. Yes.
14. Alderbury church. Consecrated 1858. Dedicated by the name of St Mary. Pitton chapel. [Blank]. St Peter. Farley chapel. [Blank]. [Blank].
15. Yes. There is need of a larger altar table.
16. Yes.
17. Yes.
18. No.
19. Yes.
20. Farley chapel distant about 3½ miles from the mother church.
21. Tithe rent charge, reserved rents, glebe, Queen Anne's Bounty, Ecclesiastical Commissioners. £367 4s.
22. From Alderbury £216 10s. From Pitton and Farley £122 18s. Conjointly £27 16s 8d.
23. No.
24. Full morning and evening service. Morning service at 10.30am. Afternoon service at 2.30pm. Sermons at both services.
25. Yes.
26. No. I distrust my own skill and fear therefore that the practice might not be to the edification of the general congregation.
27. I have daily Morning Prayer in the chapel attached to Farley Hospital which is open to the inhabitants of Farley and which they are invited to attend.
28. Morning Prayer and Evening Prayer with sermon, on all festivals, also on Ash Wednesday and Good Friday. Morning Prayer with Litany on Wednesday and Friday during Lent and Advent and Evening Prayer with sermon by various preachers on Wednesday evenings in Lent and Advent. Daily Morning Prayer during Holy Week. About 20 persons (exclusive of the school children) attend the morning services and 55 there in the evening.
29. [a] Yes. [b] Yes. [c] No. [d] Yes. [e] Yes.
30. On the 1st Sunday in every month.
31. Yes.
32. 75.
33. 4.
34. 45.
35. 30–35.

36. Ample accommodation for the whole parish.

37. In morning 100; in aft 120. No marked change.

38. No.

39. 10 baptisms. 4 marriages. 3 burials.

40. In 1861 – 8. None in the two following years.

41. Yes.

42. From March 1863 to March 1864 £6 6s 4½d.

43. Yes.

44. A small Wesleyan chapel, a wooden temporary building. From 20 to 30 decided dissenters, though a good many more attend chapel as well as the church. All Wesleyans except one Baptist and one Presbyterian.

45. Yes.

46. No.

47. About 12 years of age.

48. Yes; the boys in a 1st class held at the school. The girls in a class taught by my wife and held in my house.

49. I have had a night school which met with fair success. It was open 4 months, (3 nights a week) and I had 11 scholars. More would have attended but owing to special circumstances this last year a good many lads were working at long distances from home.

50. Yes.

51. For the S.P.G. £1 2s 6d. For the small benefices aug[mentation] fund 10s.

52. The frequent change in the resident clergyman since the Revd the vicar ceased to reside in Farley, and the absence of resident gentry have no doubt to some considerable extent impeded the church's work in this parish; still on the whole things go on well. Having, by the kind permission of the vicar on taking charge of the parish introduced the practice of a monthly celebration of the Holy Communion I have to record as a subject for deep thankfulness, that the number of communicants has steadily and largely increased, so much so that 59 different persons communicated this year within the octave of Easter. I am no less pleased to add that out of the 21 persons who were confirmed in Feby 1864, 17 have already become communicants (all but two having received more than once) and nearly all promise to come regularly to the Holy Table. Of the remaining four, two have hitherto been prevented communicating but intend to do so ere long.

J. Farnham Messenger M.A.

In countersigning the returns made by Mr Messenger for Farley I gladly bear my testimony to the value of his services as senior curate of Pitton and Farley.

Newton Smart

93. FIFIELD BAVANT   D. Chalke

1. Fifield Bavant, a rectory.

2. Marquis of Bath.

3. 33.

4. Tupper Carey. June 21st 1861.
5. Yes, absent two months from illness, known to the Bishop.
6. Yes, in the glebe house.
7. [Blank]
8. Yes, the adjoining one of Ebbesbourne Wake.
9. No.
10. [Blank]
11. [Blank]
12. [Blank]
13. One church.
14. St Martin – date unknown of consecration.
15. Yes, in fair repair.
16. Yes.
17. Yes.
18. None.
19. [Blank]
20. [Blank]
21. Tithes commuted at £146. 20 acres of glebe, £20 from Lord Bath.
22. [Blank]
23. No.
24. Afternoon service at 2.30pm except the first Sunday in the month, when morning service and Holy Communion are performed. Sermon always preached.
25. Yes.
26. No.
27. Yes, but not Evening Prayer.
28. Besides the above, the services in Lent and Advent are at 10.00am when about three persons attend. Wednesday evenings when 18 people attend.
29. [a] Yes [b] Yes [c] No [d] Yes [e] No.
30. 1st Sunday in the month.
31. Yes.
32. 16.
33. All have once or more.
34. 12. No difference from that below.
35. 12.3.
36. 33.
37. 24. Keeps much the same.
38. No.
39. 1 baptism 0 marriages 2 burials.
40. One girl only in 1861.
41. No.
42. £8 11s 6d.
43. Yes.
44. None. One family are dissenters, Independents.
45. No. The only children, three, are dissenters.
46. [Blank]

47. [Blank]

48. [Blank]

49. [Blank]

50. Not yet.

51. Poor benefice fund £1 0s 6d. Society for Propagation of the Gospel 12s 8d. Total £1 13s 2d.

52. The non-observance of the Sunday and the stables being attended at the same time as the service. A general movement for closing the stables etc during the time of divine service.

Tupper Carey

94. FIGHELDEAN   D. Amesbury

1. Figheldean, a vicarage.

2. The Lord Bishop of Salisbury.

3. 472.

4. Henry Caswall, 1848.

5. Yes.

6. Yes.

7. [Blank]

8. No.

9. No.

10. [Blank]

11. [Blank]

12. [Blank]

13. No.

14. [Blank]

15. Yes.

16. Yes.

17. Yes.

18. The church was re-opened after a complete restoration on May 9th 1860.

19. [Blank]

20. [Blank]

21. £350 tithes, £7 10s rent. Vicarage house is worth £20 per annum.

22. [Blank]

23. There is a good cottage fit for the residence of a curate, in the vicarage garden.

24. Morning service at 11.00am. Afternoon in winter at 3.00pm, evening in summer at 6.00pm. Sermons are given at these services.

25. Yes.

26. No, by reason of deafness.

27. There is no daily service in the church.

28. On all the principal festivals and fasts. The congregation is much the same as on Sundays.

29. [a] Yes [b] Yes [c] Yes [d] Yes [e] No.

30. Four Sundays besides.

31. Yes.

32. 60.

33. The above have all communicated during the year 1863 – no others are counted.

34. 46 at Easter, 35 at Christmas, 39 at Whitsuntide.

35. 36.

36. About 280.

37. The church is pretty well filled. The congregation fluctuates very little; indeed, the attendance is generally encouraging as to number.

38. No.

39. 16 baptisms 1 marriage 11 burials.

40. 21.

41. Yes.

42. The average is 13 guineas a year.

43. Yes.

44. One ranting meeting, seating 50 persons.

45. Yes.

46. Yes.

47. Girls about 11 or 12, boys about 7.

48. Some of them.

49. Yes, in evening schools.

50. Not yet.

51. May 13th, Church Building Society £1 15s 8½d. July 5th S.P.G. £1 4s 4d. October 21st S.P.G. and Pongas Mission £6 17s. Total £9 17s 0½d.

52. In this neighbourhood there is much proclivity towards low forms of dissent among the poor people. This may be counteracted by rendering the church and its services more attractive as for instance by introducing a better style of music and interesting the parishioners generally in the singing and practicing. I have found the parish library very useful also. Here the people pay a penny a month each towards the purchase of the books and when we remit £5 to S.P.C.K. that society doubles it and gives us £10 worth of books. We have done this three times and now have a large number of volumes which are fully appreciated and carefully read. We have 70 or 80 subscribers, all poor people.

Henry Caswall

95. FISHERTON ANGER D. Wilton

1. The rectory of Fisherton Anger.

2. Bishop of Carlisle, the Dean of Gloucester, Rector of Bath, Revd C. Bridges and John Deacon Esq.

3. [Blank]

4. [Blank; Augustus Bernard Handley arrived Sept 1864]

5. [Blank]

6. [Blank]

7. [Blank]

8. [Blank]
9. [Blank]
10. [Blank] John Ramsay M'Dowell
11. [Blank]
12. [Blank]
13. No.
14. [Blank]
15. Yes.
16. Fairly kept, but not well fenced.
17. Yes.
18. A seat added in the chancel for the choir.
19. [Blank]
20. [Blank]
21. [Blank]
22. [Blank]
23. [Blank]
24. 10.30am full service with sermon. 3.00pm till lately with sermon. 6.30pm full service with sermon.
25. Always.
26. No.
27. No.
28. Epiphany. Wednesdays and Fridays during Lent, Good Friday and Ascension Day. Wednesdays and Fridays in Lent about 25, exclusive of school children. Other days about 200.
29. [a] Yes [b] Yes [c] No [d] Yes [e] Yes.
30. 1st Sunday in each month.
31. [Blank]
32. About 112.
33. I believe all have.
34. About 64.
35. 50.
36. 660.
37. Increasing.
38. Yes. We had hoped to increase by adding a double aisle.
39. 60 baptisms 10 marriages 46 burials.
40. [Blank]
41. No.
42. About £12 per year.
43. The curate kept an account of his share; he does not know if the rector did.
44. One Wesleyan Methodist and one Primitive Methodist.
45. Yes.
46. Yes.
47. About 13.
48. In some instances.
49. [Blank]

50. [Blank]

51. Society for the Promotion of the Gospel about £6; Church Missionary Society about £4; National School £10; infant school £5; cotton famine [no amount entered].

52. [Blank]

J. Ramsay M'Dowell

96. FISHERTON DE LA MERE   D. Wylye

1. Fisherton de la Mere, a vicarage.
2. John Davis, Fisherton de la Mere.
3. 390.
4. Thomas John Davis. November 1854.
5. Yes.
6. Glebe house.
7. [Blank]
8. No.
9. Resident. No curate.
10. [Blank]
11. [Blank]
12. [Blank]
13. One church.
14. [Blank]
15. Yes.
16. Yes.
17. Yes.
18. In the year 1861. The chancel was rebuilt but by the power of a faculty.
19. Baptisms, marriages and burials are performed in the church.
20. [Blank]
21. £150.
22. [Blank]
23. No.
24. Sunday duty 11.00am and 3.00pm. One sermon after the afternoon service.
25. Yes.
26. No.
27. No.
28. Wednesday and Friday during Lent. Christmas Day, Ash Wednesday and Good Friday.
29. [a] Yes [b] Yes [c] No [d] Yes [e] No.
30. 1st Sunday in every month.
31. Only as to numbers.
32. [Blank]
33. [Blank]
34. From 24 to 30.
35. From 17 upwards.

36. In the body of the church about 170 filled. The chancel being filled with school and choir.
37. [Blank]
38. [Blank]
39. 10 baptisms 2 marriages 9 burials.
40. In 1861 – 8 boys and 9 girls. None in 1862 or 1863.
41. When called upon at the annual vestry.
42. The average sum is from £8 to £10 per annum.
43. Yes.
44. None.
45. Yes.
46. No.
47. About the age of 11 years.
48. Yes.
49. Not yet.
50. Yes.
51. Infirmary and propagation of the gospel.
52. [Blank]

Thomas John Davis

97. FITTLETON with HACKLESTON or HAXTON   D. Potterne

1. Fittleton with Hackleston, Wiltshire. A rectory.
2. The President and Fellows of St M. Magdalene College, Oxford.
3. The population is 392, according to the census of 1861.
4. Thomas Pearse. Instituted 10th April 1855. Inducted 24th April 1855.
5. He has been resident during the last year the time prescribed by law.
6. In the glebe house.
7. [Blank]
8. No.
9. No.
10. [Blank]
11. [Blank]
12. [Blank]
13. One church.
14. [Blank]
15. The church is in good repair and duly provided with all things necessary for the decent performance of divine service.
16. Yes.
17. Yes.
18. No alterations.
19. There is no chapel.
20. [Blank]
21. Tithe rent charge commuted at £461 7s 8d and glebe land 30 acres.
22. One parish.

23. One glebe house.

24. Morning service at 11.00am; afternoon service at 3.00pm in the summer and at 2.30pm in the winter, with sermon at each.

25. The whole service without omissions.

26. Yes – publicly after the second lesson at the afternoon service, out of church catechism, which I consider instructive for the adults as well as the school children.

27. No.

28. On Christmas Day, Ash Wednesday, Fridays during Lent, Ascension Day. Large congregation on Good Friday. Average Sunday congregation on Christmas Day. Very few (except the schoolchildren) on the other days.

29. [a] Yes [b] Yes [c] No [d] and [e] alternately.

30. On three other Sundays in the year.

31. No.

32. Communicants 33.

33. About 3.

34. 20.

35. 18.

36. For 150 besides 60 Sunday school children.

37. The average number at the morning service is 50. At the afternoon service, 70 besides the Sunday school children. The congregation continues about the same.

38. No.

39. 13 baptisms 0 marriages 6 burials.

40. Persons confirmed in 1861, 19, and in 1864, 19.

41. Yes. A statement of the collections for special purposes is placed at the church door; but not of the sacramental alms.

42. The amount of sacramental alms for the year 1863 was £3 0s 3d.

43. Yes. I keep a regular account of them in a book for that purpose.

44. None, but there are about 30 dissenters in this parish, chiefly Baptists.

45. Yes, there is a daily school.

46. No.

47. The boys at about the age of 8, the girls at about the age of 12.

48. Yes, most of them.

49. Yes. There is an evening school for boys during the winter months, which has been pretty well attended and been found useful.

50. Yes.

51. For S.P. Gospel in F. Parts[1] collection £1 10s. For the Salisbury Infirmary collection £3.

52. [Blank]

Thomas Pearse

[1]Society for the Propagation of the Gospel in Foreign Parts

98. FONTHILL BISHOP   D. Chalke

1. Fonthill Bishop, a rectory.

2. Bishop of Winchester.

3.   183.
4.   Barton Bouchier, 1858.
5.   Yes.
6.   In the glebe house.
7.   [Blank]
8.   Not any.
9.   No curate.
10. [Blank]
11. [Blank]
12. [Blank]
13. Only the parish church.
14. [Blank]
15. Yes, though I trust to have it restored to its original condition.
16. Yes.
17. Yes.
18. None.
19. [Blank]
20. [Blank]
21. Tithes about £240 in the gross and seven acres of glebe.
22. [Blank]
23. [Blank]
24. Twice every Sunday at 10.30am and 3.30pm. Full service with sermon.
25. Always.
26. No, we have a small number of children and as I attend three times every week to instruct the children and have a night school twice every week, I do not see the need.
27. I do not.
28. Good Friday and Christmas Day, about the same numbers as on the Sunday.
29. [a] Yes [b] Yes [c] No [d] Yes [e] No.
30. Bimonthly.
31. No.
32. About 33. The highest number is 42, the lowest 27. I am alluding to the average attendance.
33. I do not believe any.
34. About the same number at festivals and other seasons.
35. [Blank]
36. About 100 or 120.
37. About 70. I think it is rather <u>decreasing</u> than <u>increasing,</u> but it is nearly the same.
38. At present no enlarged accommodation is needed.
39. 3 baptisms 2 marriages 4 burials.
40. 9.
41. No.
42. Between £5 and £6 per annum.
43. There is a regular account of receipts and expenditure kept by myself.

44. There are no dissenting places of worship.
45. Yes.
46. We have no aid from the Committee of Council. Our school is entirely supported by voluntary subscription.
47. As soon as they can earn a penny in the fields.
48. Only two or three.
49. We have a night school twice a week during the winter months. About 12 young men and boys.
50. Yes.
51. Church Missionary, Lancashire distress. Church Pastoral Aid and Irish Missions. I do not recollect the amount collected.
52. [Blank]

Barton Bouchier

99. FONTHILL GIFFORD   D. Chalke

1.   Fonthill Gifford, it is a rectory.
2.   The Marquess of Westminster, Motcombe House, Dorset.
3.   430.
4.   William Coxe Radcliffe, April 1839.
5.   Yes.
6.   In the glebe house.
7.   [Blank]
8.   No.
9.   No.
10. [Blank]
11. [Blank]
12. [Blank]
13. Only one church.
14. [Blank]
15. The present church is about to be replaced by a new one, for which a faculty has been granted.
16. The wall-fence of the churchyard will be repaired or rebuilt.
17. [Blank]
18. [Blank]
19. [Blank]
20. [Blank]
21. Tithes commuted at £320 per annum and glebe lands worth about £50.
22. It consists of only one parish.
23. No.
24. Two full services at 10.30 am with a sermon, 2.30pm with a sermon.
25. Yes.
26. No.
27. No.
28. On Christmas Day, Ash Wednesday, Good Friday and Ascension Day. About

the same number as on a Sunday.

29. [a] Yes [b] Yes [c] No [d] Yes [e] Yes.

30. Generally on three other Sundays, but on no especial days.

31. No.

32. About 50.

33. All have communicated either privately or in church.

34. There is no perceptible difference in the numbers of those who attend on these occasions.

35. [See 34]

36. In the present church there is accommodation for 168. The new one will accommodate 232.

37. About 80 in the morning and 140 in the afternoon, not including school children.

38. The new church – see answers to questions from 15-18 – will afford sufficient accommodation.

39. 7 baptisms 2 marriages 9 burials.

40. 23.

41. No.

42. £3 14s 11d.

43. Yes.

44. One, belonging to the Independents. There are very few professed dissenters, but many, who regularly attend the church, would also go at other times to any dissenting meeting house.

45. Yes.

46. No.

47. The boys at about 10 and the girls at 12 years of age.

48. Yes, until they are confirmed, with a few exceptions, as long as they reside in the parish.

49. Not lately.

50. No, but they will be shortly forwarded to the registrar.

51. For the Salisbury Infirmary £4 0s 1d.

52. Nothing of an especial character.

W. Coxe Radcliffe

100. FOSBURY   D. Marlborough

1. Christ Church, Fosbury, (ecclesiastical district formed of portions of the parishes of Shalbourne and Tidcombe) a perpetual curacy.

2. There are four trustees, patrons, viz R.C.L. Bevan Esq, Fosbury House near Hungerford; S. Bevan Esq ditto; Hon. A. Kinnaird M.P.; Rev R.G. Bryan, Fosbury, Hungerford.

3. About 350.

4. Reginald Guy Bryan, Christmas 1856.

5. Yes.

6. Yes, in the glebe house.

7. [Blank]
8. No.
9. No.
10. [Blank]
11. [Blank]
12. [Blank]
13. No.
14. [Blank]
15. Yes.
16. Yes.
17. Yes.
18. No.
19. [Blank]
20. [Blank]
21. The interest of £1062 8s 4d consol 3% and of 40 shares of the Birmingham Canal Company producing £160 per annum at 4%.
22. [Blank]
23. No.
24. Morning service with sermon at 10.30am, evening service with sermon at 2.45pm or 6.00pm.
25. Yes, excepting omissions by accident or through infirmity.
26. No.
27. I do not say the morning and evening prayers daily in the church.
28. On Good Friday and Christmas Day, attendance not quite 100.
29. [a] Yes [b] Yes [c] No [d] and [e] not always.
30. On the 1st Sunday in every month.
31. Yes.
32. 46 (increased since 1861).
33. All communicate, I believe, more than once in each year.
34. About 25, more or less according to the weather. Some have a long way to come.
35. About 25.
36. About 200.
37. Rather less than 100. Perhaps rather decreasing.
38. No.
39. 5 baptisms 4 marriages 5 burials.
40. Four in 1861.
41. Yes.
42. £7 7s 9½d.
43. Yes.
44. None. There are two Baptists, one Congregationalist and two families of Primitive Methodists.
45. Yes.
46. Yes.
47. Boys at 8 or 9, girls at about 12.

48. Not for long.
49. Yes with varying success.
50. Yes.
51. Church Missionary Society £4 11s 4d. London Jews Society £1 19s. Other collections have been made at schoolroom meetings.
52. Besides my own failings and those common to us all, the people suffer from some of the special disadvantages of poverty, viz ignorance and consequent want of interest in the study or exposition of Holy Scripture. Also, they are the more tempted to acts of dishonesty, such as poaching, or taking sticks from their employer's hedge. A good scriptural education will, I trust, be one great means, with the Divine blessing, of effecting an improvement in the rising generation. I am confirmed in my determination to admit only communicants as sponsors: this rule of our church cannot easily be carried out, it is true; yet, in respect of it, we may deal 'suaviter in modo, fortiter in re'[1], and thus endeavour to be free from the charge of encouraging an utterly inconsistent profession.

Reginald G. Bryan

[1] 'gently in manner, firmly in action'

101. FOVANT   D. Chalke

1. Fovant, a rectory.
2. The Earl of Pembroke, Wilton House.
3. 600.
4. Wellesley Pole Pigott, September 28th 1836.
5. No.
6, At Bemerton.
7. The Revd Edward Henry Elers. He is resident.
8. Yes, in the diocese of Salisbury.
9. He is non-resident.
10. [Blank]
11. [Blank]
12. [Blank]
13. No, only one church.
14. [Blank]
15. The church is in good repair, and provided with all things necessary for the decent observance of divine service according to law.
16. Yes.
17. Yes.
18. The church and chancel have been restored under the authority and faculty of the Bishop.
19. There are no chapels in the parish.
20. [Blank]
21. Rent charge and glebe. Rent charge £460, glebe £60.
22. [Blank]

23. There is only one glebe house.

24. Matins at 11.00am, Evensong at 3.00pm in the winter and 6.00pm in the summer. Sermons at each service.

25. The whole service is said with the exception of the church militant prayer after the morning sermon.

26. No.

27. No.

28. On all saints' days, festivals, Holy Week, Ash Wednesday and certain days in Lent at which services the congregation varies from 10 to 100 besides children.

29. Not on Ascension Day, and only on one of the two feasts of Trinity and Whitsuntide.

30. On the 1st Sunday in each month.

31. Yes.

32. It varies from 30 to 42.

33. None.

34. 40.

35. 30.

36. 240 besides the sittings for the children.

37. Matins 160, Evensong 290, and keeps about the same.

38. No.

39. 24 baptisms 2 marriages 5 burials.

40. 22.

41. The amount of alms offered is posted after Holy Communion on the church door.

42. £5 12s.

43. An account is kept of them in a book together with the other parish charities.

44. One. 35. Ranters.

45. Yes.

46. Not at present, but we hope to be so shortly.

47. Boys leave at 9, girls at 12 years old.

48. Yes.

49. An evening school is held for three months in winter, three nights a week, for 1½ hours each night. It is fairly attended and moderate progress made. The 1½ hours are spent ½ hour reading, ½ hour writing and ½ hour summary.

50. Yes.

51. For an organ £40. For poor benefice fund 10s.

52. The welfare of many of the poorer people would be improved bodily, and I believe spiritually too, were their cottages more adapted to their decent comfort.

Wellesley Pole Pigott

102. FROXFIELD   D. Marlborough

1. Froxfield, a vicarage.

2. The Chapter of Windsor.

3. About 600.

4. T.G.P. Atwood, inducted 1828.
5. He has.
6. In the rectory.
7. [Blank]
8. No.
9. [Blank]
10. [Blank]
11. [Blank]
12. As curate of the Widows' Chapel.[1]
13. No.
14. [Blank]
15. Yes.
16. Yes.
17. Yes.
18. No.
19. No.
20. [Blank]
21. £127. Stipend paid by the rector £28, the rest from Queen Anne's Bounty and Parliamentary Grant Fund account.
22. [Blank]
23. A rectory and vicarage, adjoining.
24. Two duties on Sunday at the parish church, one sermon, and one full service at the Widows' Chapel.
25. Yes.
26. Yes, in the church catechism.
27. No.
28. On Christmas Day and Good Friday. Average attendance about 250.
29. [a] Yes [b] Yes [c] No [d] Yes [e] Yes.
30. On the Sunday before and after Michaelmas, and the Sunday after Christmas.
31. Generally of the poor.
32. In the church, from 30 to 45. In the Widows' Chapel about 40.
33. I do not know any.
34. The number stated above.
35. [Blank]
36. 200 at the church and about 80 at the Widows' Chapel.
37. In attendance on the morning service about 100, at the evening about 170.
38. Occasionally, but I do not see how the church could be enlarged.
39. 10 baptisms 3 marriages 15 burials.
40. None in 1862 or 1863. The number in 1861 I do not remember.
41. Only to the churchwardens.
42. £5 15s.
43. I keep a regular account of the receipt and expenditure.
44. One small cottage, Wesleyans, very few in number.
45. No, our children go to Bedwyn Parva.
46. [Blank]

47. About 12.

48. Some of them, but they are generally employed in the farmers' service.

49. [Blank]

50. Not yet.

51. We made collections for the Lancashire fund and the augmentation of small livings, but I do not recollect the sums realised.

52. No, except the smallness of my means.

Thomas G Atwood

¹ Duchess of Somerset's Hospital, founded in 1694, originally for 15 clergy and 15 lay widows.

103. FUGGLESTONE ST PETER   D. Wilton

1. Fugglestone St Peter with Bemerton St John, a rectory.

2. The Earl of Pembroke, Wilton House.

3. About 650.

4. Wellesley Pole Pigott, August 6th, 1836.

5. Yes.

6. In the glebe house.

7. [Blank]

8. Yes, Fovant St George, diocese of Salisbury.

9. Yes.

10. Sept 20th 1863.

11. The Hon and Revd Henry Bligh, a deacon.

12. No.

13. Yes.

14. Bemerton – Dec 13th 1860, dedicated to St John the Evangelist. Fugglestone St Peter – date of consecration unknown.

15. Yes.

16. Yes.

17. Yes.

18. No.

19. Yes.

20. The chapel of St John the Evangelist is about 1¼ miles from the church of Fugglestone St Peter.

21. Tithes £450.

22. The tithes are included in the parish of Fugglestone St Peter.

23. Only one, situated at Bemerton.

24. Matins 10.30am and evensong 2.30pm on alternate Sundays at Fugglestone and Bemerton, and evensong at 6.30pm every Sunday at Bemerton, with sermons at each service.

25. The whole service is said with the exception of the church militant prayer after morning sermon.

26. No.

27. No.

28. On all saints' days, festivals, Holy Week, every Wednesday and Friday in Lent, and every Friday during the year. From 20 to 200.

29. On all these days except Ascension Day, which we propose to begin this year.

30. On the 1st Sunday in each month.

31. Yes.

32. 120.

33. None.

34. About 80.

35. About 65.

36. Fugglestone 200. Bemerton 325.

37. At Fugglestone about 160. At Bemerton about 280. Decidedly increasing since Bemerton church has been built.

38. No.

39. 21 baptisms 6 marriages 11 burials.

40. In 1861 there were 26 − 15 females. In 1862, one female. In 1863, two, one female and one male.

41. The amount of collections are posted on the church door on the Sunday after they are made.

42. In 1861, £13 1s 10d. In 1862 £13 6s 8d. In 1863 £14 5s.

43. An account of them is kept in a book, as well as other parish charities.

44. There is no dissenting place of worship in the parish.

45. Yes.

46. Yes.

47. Boys about 10, girls about the same age; perhaps earlier as many are employed in the Wilton carpet manufacturing.

48. Yes. The girls usually to the age of 17 and the boys to 16.

49. An evening school is held during four winter months, two nights in the week for 1½ hours each night. It is well attended and good progress made. The time is spent in reading, writing and summing.

50. Yes.

51. For lighting the church £5 1s; for the increase of small benefices £3 10s 4d; for the Society for the Promotion of the Gospel £2 5s 6d.

52. By the great increase of buildings at Bemerton much dissent has been imported from other parishes. A new public house also has had a bad influence. The only remedy to these evils must be increased efforts on our parts to counteract these baneful tendencies.

Wellesley Pole Pigott

104. GREAT BEDWYN cum ST. KATHARINE'S   D. Marlborough

1. Great Bedwyn, a vicarage.

2. The Marquess of Ailesbury, Savernake Forest, Marlborough.

3. 1252 by the census of 1861 (independently of East Grafton district). Of these about 170 belong to the district of St Katharine's.

4. John Dryden Hodgson. Instituted 4th May 1855. Inducted 5th May 1855.

5. Yes.

6. In the house appointed by the Bishop.

7. [Blank]

8. No.

9. Yes.

10. Licensed 11th June 1862.

11. Robert Clarke Caswall. A priest.

12. He has officiated also in the churches of St Katharine and Christ Church Savernake Forest.

13. Yes, for the present.

14. Great Bedwyn, St Mary the Virgin, date of consecration unknown. Savernake Forest, St Katharine Virgin and Martyr, consecrated 24th September 1861.

15. Yes.

16. Yes.

17. Yes.

18. None.

19. Baptisms and burials at St Katharine's Church. And one marriage was performed there by special licence on 15th October 1863.

20. About 1¾ miles.

21. Tithe rent charge commuted at £212. Parliamentary Grant £34 5s 8d. Queen Anne's Bounty £26.

22. [Blank]

23. No.

24. At St Mary, Gt Bedwyn: 8.30am communion service once a month. 10.30am morning service with sermon. 3.00pm evening service with sermon and baptisms. 6.30 or 7.00pm evening service with sermon during part of the year. At St Katharine's, Savernake: 11.00am morning service with sermon. 3.30pm evening service with sermon and baptisms.

25. Yes.

26. Yes. On the Sunday afternoons in Advent, before a confirmation and after the second lesson, with a lecture on the same subject after the prayers. I think catechising in church is desirable at special seasons as in Lent and Advent, on the approach of a confirmation, but not throughout the year.

27. Not daily throughout the year.

28. Every Wednesday and Friday throughout the year. Every holy day. A daily morning service through Lent. Daily morning and evening services with sermons in Holy Week. Average attendance about 30. (More in Lent). At St Katharine's church: two services and a sermon on the Circumcision, Epiphany, Ash Wednesday, Ascension Day and each day in Holy Week. Three services with sermons on Good Friday. One service on every saints' day. Extra morning and evening services and sermons in Lent and Advent. Attendance varying in morning from 12–20, in the evenings from 40 to 70 or 80.

29. At St Mary's: [a] Yes [b] Yes, twice [c] Yes [d] Yes [e] Yes. At St Katharine's [a] Yes, twice [b] Yes, twice [c] Yes [d] Yes [e] Yes.

30. At St Mary's on the first and third Sunday in the month. At St Katharine's

on the first Sunday in each month. Advent Sunday, Sunday after Christmas, Low Sunday, Anniversary of Consecration.

31. Yes.

32. 115, and 90 in the district of St Katharine's.

33. Nine sick persons at home only. Two in St Katharine's district.

34.

St Mary's	1861	1862	1863	1864
Christmas	30	38	32	
Easter	108	81	67	74
Ascension	13	25	11	
Whitsuntide	23	23	28	
Trinity	18	23	18	

At St Katharine's, in 1863, 62 at Christmas and 90 at Easter. In 1864, 60 at Easter.

35. St Mary's 24. St Katharine's 20.

36. At St Mary's, seated for 450 (would hold 1000). At St Katharine's, seated for 300 (would hold 350).

37. At St Mary's, 250, stationary. At St Katharine's, 160, stationary.

38. No.

39. 45 baptisms 7 marriages 24 burials at the two churches.

40. In 1861, 27 males, 22 females = 49 at Great Bedwyn church. In 1862 none. In 1863, 21 males, 29 females = 50 at St Katharine's church.

41. Generally.

42. In 1863, at Great Bedwyn church, £12 15s 11¼d. At St Katharine's church from 14th May 1863 to Low Sunday 1864, £19 12s 6½d.

43. Yes.

44. One small meeting house. Perhaps twelve families, chiefly Wesleyans.

45. Yes, three, at Great Bedwyn, St Katharine's and Crofton.

46. Yes.

47. Boys about 10 or 11. Girls about 12 or 13.

48. A certain number till confirmation, and a few after it for a time.

49. Yes. The night school for men and boys during the winter months continues to succeed well. From 50 to 60 attend. There is also a night school at St Katharine's, well attended.

50. Yes.

51. At Great Bedwyn church. Fund for augmentation of small benefices £3 12s. Society for Propagation of the Gospel £2. The church institute £1 1s 6d. At St Katharine's Church. Fund for augmentation of small benefices £6. Society for Propagation of the Gospel £8. Pongas Mission £3 3s. Diocesan choral association £10 12s 7½d.

52. [Blank]

John D Hodgson

105. CHALFIELD MAGNA or GREAT CHALFIELD   D. Potterne

1. Chalfield Magna, a rectory.
2. Lady Burrard, Yarmouth, Isle of Wight.
3. About 17.
4. Rev George Mullins. Inducted Jan 18th, 1858.
5. No.
6. Resides at Oxford.
7. G.L. Farthing. No.
8. Possesses no other benefice.
9. [Blank]
10. June 26th, 1863.
11. G.L. Farthing, a deacon.
12. As assistant curate at Atworth, and mathematical master at Shaw House school.
13. No.
14. [Blank]
15. Tolerable repair, but there is room for some improvement in the furniture of the church.
16. Yes.
17. Yes.
18. No alterations have been made.
19. [Blank]
20. [Blank]
21. Tithe rent charge commuted at £164 and glebe land, rental £15.
22. [Blank]
23. No glebe house.
24. One service on Sundays: winter at 11.00am, summer alternately at 11.00am and 6.00pm. Sermons are preached.
25. Yes.
26. I do not catechise.
27. No.
28. Christmas Day and Good Friday.
29. The Holy Communion is administered 6 times in the year, not always on the feasts mentioned in Q.29.
30. [Blank]
31. No.
32. About 9.
33. I am not aware that any of them have omitted communicating.
34. About 6.
35. Ditto.
36. About 125.
37. About 25. It may be increasing.
38. No.
39. 3 baptisms 0 marriages 0 burials.
40. I am informed there were none.

41. No.
42. I believe they would amount to about one guinea.
43. No.
44. No dissenting place of worship, there are no dissenters.
45. No.
46. [Blank]
47. [Blank]
48. There is no Sunday school.
49. [Blank]
50. Yes.
51. For a harmonium to be used in church. Collection in church about 12s. For expenses connected with playing the instrument, collection 14s ½d.
52. [Blank]

George Lax Farthing

106. GREAT CHEVERELL   D. Potterne

1. Great Cheverell, a rectory.
2. The Rev. R.M. Atkinson, Bath.
3. About 590.
4. Robert Moulton Atkinson. Inducted Nov 27th 1841.
5. I believe so.
6. In the glebe house.
7. The curate W.H. Schwabe is now resident during the absence of the incumbent.
8. Not that I am aware of.
9. [Blank]
10. [Blank]
11. [Blank]
12. [Blank]
13. Only one church.
14. [Blank]
15. Pretty fair.
16. I should say so.
17. I should say that they do.
18. I am not aware of any.
19. [Blank]
20. [Blank]
21. I do not know.
22. [Blank]
23. Only one glebe house.
24. Morning service at 10.30am, evening service at 3.00pm, sermon on both occasions.
25. Yes.
26. No.

27. No.

28. Christmas Day and Good Friday; I believe on no other days.

29. Only at Easter, Midsummer, Michaelmas, Christmas Day; <u>four</u> times in the year.

30. [Blank]

31. No.

32. On the last two occasions about 20 have attended.

33. I cannot say.

34. [Blank]

35. [Blank]

36. About 150 I think independent of the school children.

37. I cannot say.

38. Yes, by enlarging the church.

39. 14 baptisms 2 marriages 12 burials.

40. In 1861 it appears 11 persons were confirmed.

41. No.

42. I do not know.

43. I think not.

44. There is one dissenting meeting house. I cannot form an opinion as to the number of dissenters most seem to be Baptists or Mormons.

45. Yes.

46. No.

47. The boys leave at about 9 or 10 years of age some sooner the girls a little later.

48. A good many of them.

49. We have had an evening school for boys and young men during the winter months with <u>moderate</u> success.

50. Yes.

51. [Blank]

52. Having been resident only during the last two months of the year 1863 I am not able to give full or explicit answers to many of the above questions.

W.H. Schwabe

107. GREAT WISHFORD or WISHFORD MAGNA   D. Wylye

1. Wishford Magna, a rectory.

2. The Earl of Pembroke, Wilton House.

3. About 400; 372 at the last census.

4. Thomas Boughton Buchanan. Instituted June 4th 1863 and inducted June 15th 1863.

5. Resident since institution.

6. In the glebe house.

7. [Blank]

8. No.

9. No.

10. [Blank]

11. [Blank]
12. [Blank]
13. One church only.
14. The church is named after St Giles.
15. It is at present undergoing restoration.
16. Yes.
17. Yes.
18. No.
19. [Blank]
20. [Blank]
21. The sources of endowment are tithe and glebe; about £480 gross in amount.
22. [Blank]
23. No.
24. At present there are three full services in the licensed school room, and Holy Communion at 8.00am except on the first Sunday in the month when it is after morning service. Holy Communion is celebrated in the chancel, a part of which is bound off for that purpose. Morning Prayer at 11.00am, afternoon at 3.00pm, evening at 6.30pm.
25. Yes.
26. No.
27. No. The parish church is undergoing restoration.
28. Ash Wednesday, and the greater festivals morning and evening. Fridays in Advent and Lent, Evening Prayer with lecture also throughout Holy Week. Ash Wednesday about 30. Good Friday (as Sunday). Weekly evening service about 120 on an average.
29. [a] Yes [b] Yes [c] No [d] Yes [e] Yes.
30. At present every Sunday at 8.00am. On the 1st Sunday in the month after Morning Prayer.
31. One is in the course of formation.
32. Between 40 and 50.
33. I cannot answer this question.
34. Between 30 and 40.
35. Between 20 and 30. At present there is only room for 16 in the chancel. But the weekly celebration gives ample opportunity for all. The attendance thereat averages about eight.
36. The licensed room will hold (with children) 150.
37. It is generally full at present.
38. Yes, but the want will be fully met by the restoration now in progress.
39. 20 baptisms 4 marriages 13 burials.
40. I cannot answer this question.
41. The account of the church offerings and charities is shown once a year to the churchwardens.
42. For the half year from June to December £4 13s 9d.
43. Yes.
44. There is one small room. There are perhaps 12 dissenters, Wesleyans and

Independents.

45. Yes.

46. No; the school is endowed.

47. Boys at 8 years, girls at 10.

49. Yes, evening schools during the winter and weekly bible classes. Both have been hitherto successful.

50. Yes.

51. During the half year ending December 31ˢᵗ, collections were made for the Society for the Propagation of the Gospel and for the diocesan society for the increase of small benefices. The sums collected were £3 13s 2½d and £1 5s respectively.

52. The greatest hindrance to the efficient carrying out of the church system in such a parish as mine seems undoubtedly to be the want of power to divide the existing services. Agricultural labourers cannot find a spare half hour, though they might find a spare two minutes, out of their breakfast hour. Indeed daily service in such a parish as this is simply an impossibility (at any rate in the mornings) unless the clergyman is content with such a congregation as his own household may supply. Since the pulling down of my church I have had a service for the workmen employed on it, in a corner of the churchyard which has been excellently attended, but then that service has not lasted more than 10 minutes. If there was any authorised way of dividing or shortening the daily service, I am sure it would be of the greatest use in agricultural parishes.

T.B. Buchanan

108. HAM   D. Marlborough

1. Ham, a rectory.

2. The Bishop of Winchester.

3. [Blank]

4. Charles Sumner Burder. Instituted February 27th 1864 and inducted March 19ᵗʰ 1864.

5. [Blank]

6. [Blank]

7. [Blank]

8. No.

9. [Blank]

10. [Blank]

11. [Blank]

12. [Blank]

13. No.

14. [Blank]

15. Yes.

16. Yes.

17. Yes.

18. [Blank]

19. [Blank]
20. [Blank]
21. Rent charge.
22. [Blank]
23. No.
24. Two full services and sermons at 11.00am and 3.00pm.
25. Yes.
26. [Blank]
27. [Blank]
28. [Blank]
29. [Blank]
30. [Blank]
31. [Blank]
32. [Blank]
33. [Blank]
34. [Blank]
35. [Blank]
36. [Blank]
37. [Blank]
38. [Blank]
39. [Blank]
40. [Blank]
41. [Blank]
42. [Blank]
43. [Blank]
44. Not any.
45. Yes.
46. [Blank]
47. [Blank]
48. [Blank]
49. [Blank]
50. [Blank]
51. [Blank]
52. [Blank]

Charles S. Burder

109. HEDDINGTON   D. Avebury
1. Heddington [a Rectory].
2. Revd Francis H Du Boulay, Heddington, Calne.
3. 358.
4. Francis H Du Boulay, instituted June 1853, inducted July 1853.
5. No.
6. No.
7. Rev W H Schwabe.

8. No.
9. [Blank]
10. [Blank]
11. [Blank]
12. [Blank]
13. No.
14. [Blank]
15. Yes.
16. Yes.
17. Yes.
18. No.
19. [Blank]
20. [Blank]
21. The tithes are commuted at £268. There are 15 acres of glebe.
22. [Blank]
23. No.
24. Morning service at 10.30am and afternoon at 3.00pm, with sermons.
25. At the prayers on Wednesdays and Fridays I frequently omit the exhortation.
26. Occasionally.
27. No.
28. On Wednesdays and Fridays throughout the year. And on all saints' days and holy days. In addition, on Tuesday evenings during Lent and Advent and daily during Holy Week. On week day mornings seven or eight besides children. In the evening between 30 and 40.
29. Yes with the exception of Ascension Day when it is administered on the Sunday next after.
30. On the 1st Sunday in each month.
31. Yes.
32. 67
33. 9.
34. 31.
35. 21.
36. 190.
37. The number seems to me about stationary – average rather over 100.
38. I think not.
39. 11 baptisms 1 marriage 3 burials.
40. 14.
41. Yes.
42. £6 8s 4½d.
43. Yes.
44. There is one chapel in the parish. About 50 or 60 Wesleyan Methodists.
45. Yes.
46. Yes.
47. Boys about 10, girls about 12.
48. Yes.

49. Yes, a night school has been held here for many years. Last year the attendance was about 20.

50. Not yet.

51. Foreign missions £2 10s. Bath Hospital £2 2s. Education (Salisbury Board) £1. Education (National Society) £1. Parish school improvement £12 0s 6d. Church expenses £3 6s 5d. Augmentation of (small) benefices 18s 6d.

52. This parish being a long one and the Wesleyans having for some time past opened a Sunday school at their chapel which is about half way down the parish, I have found some difficulty in keeping the day school children to the church Sunday school. The objection of the parents being in no case on account of doctrinal teaching, but on the score of convenience and from the fact that more reading is taught at the Wesleyan school. For some time I winked at the non-appearance of some of the day scholars on Sunday but finding that the habit was increasing, I have lately been obliged to take a more decided line, requiring all who come to the day school, if old enough, to come also on Sundays. This rule, though it has caused the removal of three or four children, will I hope in the end work well.

Francis H Du Boulay

110. HEYTESBURY D. Wylye

1. Heytesbury with Knook and the prebend of Tytherington; a vicarage and perpetual curacy.

2. Formerly the Dean, but now the Lord Bishop of Salisbury.

3. Heytesbury with Tytherington about 1200, Knook 220.

4. John Knight, 1836.

5. Yes.

6. In the Heytesbury Hospital as Custos thereof.

7. [Blank]

8. No.

9. Yes.

10. 1863.

11. Richard Gawler Mead, a priest.

12. Only for the above named places.

13. One church at Heytesbury, one prebendary chapel at Tytherington, one church or chapel at Knook.

14. Consecration unknown. Heytesbury St Peter and St Paul, Knook St Margaret, Tytherington St James.

15. Provided with all things necessary but not in good repair.

16. Yes.

17. Yes as they are usually discharged.

18. Only necessary repair to tower and outer walls by order of vestry.

19. No marriages or burials at the prebendary chapel at Tytherington, only baptisms.

20. Knook one mile, Tytherington 1¼ miles.

21. Heytesbury land £75, Queen Anne's Bounty £18, Ecclesiastical Commissioners £160, rental payment by Lord Heytesbury, total £268; Knook land £60, Ecclesiastical Commissioners £40, total £100, gross £368; Prebend of Tytherington Ecclesiastical Commissioners £80, gross £448.

22. [See 21]

23. No glebe houses.

24. Two full services with sermon at Heytesbury; one at Knook and Tytherington.

25. Yes.

26. No – this is done in the schools.

27. On Holy Days, Wednesdays and Fridays in Advent and Lent with an evening lecture on Fridays in Lent.

28. School children 160, adults at prayer about 30. On Christmas Day and Good Friday, congregations as on Sunday and at evening lectures in Lent about 130.

29. [a] Yes [b] Yes [c] No [d] Yes [e] No at Heytesbury.

30. On the 1st Sunday in each month at Heytesbury, quarterly at Knook and Tytherington.

31. Yes.

32. About 110 at Heytesbury, 20 at Knook, 10 at Tytherington.

33. About one half communicate monthly; very few have omitted communion during the whole year.

34. Heytesbury 70, Knook 16, Tytherington 8.

35. Heytesbury 60, Knook 15, Tytherington 7.

36. Heytesbury 500, Knook 150, Tytherington 60.

37. Heytesbury 400, Knook 100, Tytherington 40.

38. Heytesbury church wants opening out to the chancel which is shut off by Lord Heytesbury's pew.

39. Heytesbury baptisms with Tytherington 31, Knook baptisms 2. Heytesbury marriages 2, Knook marriages 2. Heytesbury burials 29, Knook burials 3.

40. In 1861 there were 37.

41. Not generally.

42. About £16 at Heytesbury, £1 10s at Knook, £1 at Tytherington.

43. A private account is kept.

44. One dissenting chapel for Independents, occasional rooms occupied by Plymouth Brethren, Baptists and Ranters. Numbers unknown.

45. Yes.

46. Yes.

47. Boys seldom remain regular until more than 9 years. Girls seldom remain regular until more than 10 or 11 years.

48. Many do continue for some years.

49. Adult and evening schools at Heytesbury during the winter are very well attended and are doing much good. Number in attendance from 50 to 60.

50. Not yet.

51. Church Missionary Society sermon and meeting £5 12s 2d. Organ expenses £8 6s. Society for the Propagation of the Gospel £6 2s 8d. Small benefice increase £5 1s 6d. Clothing Club £6 18s 10d. Total £32 1s 2d.

52. The state of Heytesbury church is greatly in the way of ministerial usefulness but will I trust soon be improved.

John Knight

111. HEYWOOD   D. Wylye

1. Heywood, a perpetual curacy.
2. H.G.G Ludlow Esq, Heywood House.
3. 540.
4. Robert L Armstrong, licensed October 1862.
5. Yes.
6. He has resided in a house assigned to the minister but not a glebe house.
7. [Blank]
8. No other benefice.
9. No.
10. [Blank]
11. [Blank]
12. [Blank]
13. [Blank]
14. [Blank]
15. It is in good repair.
16. Yes.
17. Yes.
18. No alterations, except that we use oil lamps in the time of evening service in place of candles as before.
19. Yes.
20. [Blank]
21. £32 per annum from a sum invested in Queen Anne's Bounty. £70 per annum from Mr Ludlow and about £15 per annum from pew rents.
22. [Blank]
23. [Blank]
24. Two services each Sunday, commencing at 10.30am and 6.00pm with a sermon at each.
25. Yes.
26. Not in the church, but in the school every Sunday afternoon. I catechise on the gospel for the day and think it tends to instruct the young.
27. No. There would be no possibility of getting an attendance here.
28. Ascension Day, Ash Wednesday, the last day of the year besides Good Friday and Christmas Day. The average attendance about 30 or 40 on the former occasions and 60 or 70 on Good Friday and Christmas Day.
29. [a] Yes [b] Yes [c] No [d] Yes [e] No.
30. None.
31. I do not keep a regular list as I know them all.
32. 39 or 40.
33. I should say four or five of that number have not communicated during the

past year.

34. About 30.

35. From 20 to 27 – sometimes less.

36. 400 or thereabouts can be accommodated in the church.

37. In the evening the church is full; in the morning the congregation averages from 100 to 120 or 150. The congregation is increasing.

38. I do not consider that we need any further church accommodation at present, though if we had more seats to let, we could I think let them.

39. 12 baptisms 4 marriages 6 burials.

40. None have been confirmed since I was appointed in October 1862. I have not a list of those who were confirmed <u>before</u> I came.

41. I made a statement at the close of last year of the sums which had been contributed by the congregation in the year.

42. Last year they amounted to £8 0s 5d.

43. Yes.

44. There is one dissenting chapel belonging to the Independents. The number of dissenters is considerable, about 150 or 200.

45. Yes.

46. Yes, we derive aid from the Committee of Council.

47. About 12 or 13 years, though some remain longer.

48. Some stay in the Sunday school after they have ceased attending every day.

49. Yes. I have an evening school from October till March for young men. About 30 attended last year.

50. Yes.

51. There have been collections for the Pastoral Aid Society coll: £4; for the Jews £5; for the Church Missionary Society £3 17s 5d. As a thanksgiving for the bountiful harvest £5.

52. Nothing occurs to me of a special character under this head beyond that coldness and deadness in the people which all have to contend against. Perhaps this is not so fitting a place to mention it, but I cannot forebear saying to your Lordship, with reference to one of the above subjects – the endowment of the benefice – that it would have been most acceptable if the Ecclesiastical Commissioners could have increased it consistently with their rules, as the incumbent's usefulness and comfort would be much promoted thereby.

Robert L Armstrong

112. HIGHWAY D. Avebury

1. Highway, a rectory.

2. The Right Revd the Lord Bishop of Salisbury.

3. By census 121. Now 130.

4. Charles Amyand Harris M.A. Collated February 24th and inducted March 21st 1863 by virtue of induction to Bremhill.

5. Residence at Bremhill commenced May 23rd 1864.

6. No. At Bremhill vicarage.

7. Revd William Feltham resident at Charlcutt in Bremhill parish.
8. The rectory of Highway is annexed to Bremhill.
9. See Bremhill return.
10. See Bremhill return.
11. See Bremhill return.
12. Mr Feltham officiates at Foxham chapel. See Bremhill return.
13. No.
14. [Blank]
15. In repair and provided, but the church requires restoration or rebuilding.
16. Yes.
17. There is only one churchwarden. Yes.
18. No.
19. [Blank]
20. Highway is 6 miles by carriage road from Bremhill.
21. Rent charge (commuted value) £170. Glebe £38. Cottage £3.
22. See 21. See Bremhill return for Bremhill and Foxham.
23. There is a dilapidated labourer's cottage once (it is said) the glebe house.
24. At 11.00am and 3.00pm alternately with sermon.
25. Yes.
26. No.
27. No.
28. Christmas Day, Ash Wednesday, Good Friday and Ascension Day. On the first and third 60, on the second and fourth about five.
29. It is administered eight times a year and on the festivals if possible.
30. See 29.
31. No.
32. 8.
33. None.
34. 5.
35. 5.
36. About 80.
37. 50. Number stationary.
38. The church requires rearrangement and enlargement as there is an unsightly gallery and the schoolchildren occupy the chancel.
39. 7 baptisms 0 marriages 3 burials.
40. In 1863 − 3. No record of 1862.
41. [Blank]
42. £1 16s 9d.
43. Yes.
44. There is no dissenting chapel but many attend those at Goatacre in the neighbourhood.
45. A small dame school of about 18. Kept by Caroline Clifford a cripple girl of 20.
46. No.
47. 9.

48. Yes.

49. The parish clerk has kept a night school in winter on his own account to which several resort.

50. They are in preparation.

51. For the 'small benefices augmentation fund' collection 5s 2d.

52. A resident minister is much required, as the people are chiefly engaged in field work far from home and are therefore comparatively difficult of access by occasional visits from a distance.

C.A. Harris

113. HILL DEVERILL   D. Wylye

1. Hill Deverill, a perpetual curacy.
2. The prebendary of Hill Deverill, the Rev E.B. Elliott, Brighton.
3. 149.
4. John Powell, May 17th 1858.
5. Yes.
6. No glebe house. At Boreham, Warminster.
7. [Blank]
8. No.
9. No.
10. [Blank]
11. [Blank]
12. [Blank]
13. No.
14. [Blank]
15. Yes.
16. Yes.
17. Yes.
18. No.
19. [Blank]
20. [Blank]
21. £76. Consisting of a reserved rent from the Duke of Somerset of £20 and a gift from the Duke of £10, and £46 from land in Somersetshire purchased with money from Queen Anne's Bounty.
22. [Blank]
23. [Blank]
24. Twice on Sunday at 10.30am and 3.00pm. Sermons are preached at these services.
25. Yes.
26. No. The children attend Longbridge church and school.
27. I would do so if I could live in the parish.
28. Christmas Day, Ash Wednesday, Good Friday and Ascension Day. About 40.
29. [a] Yes [b] Yes [c] Yes [d] Yes [e] Yes.
30. The last Sunday in the month.

31. Yes.

32. 17.

33. One through being bedridden and one through old age. Two in all.

34. 11.

35. 10.

36. 150.

37. 50. It remains about the same.

38. No.

39. 3 baptisms 0 marriages 3 burials.

40. 6.

41. The sum is fixed on the church door.

42. £3 3s 4d.

43. Yes.

44. There is no meeting house in the parish. About 14. Ranters.

45. No; the children attend Longbridge Deverill school, as I have no school house or place to hold a school.

46. [Blank]

47. About 12.

48. Yes; they remain at the Sunday school at Longbridge Deverill.

49. Yes; I joined the night school at Longbridge Deverill for five years, but I find there is a strong feeling against attending a place out of their own parish existing.

50. Yes.

51. Missions £2 10s. Poor benefices £2 10s.

52. Nothing but dissent, and that does not exhibit a very hostile spirit. Of the 149 population about 80 live near the church, and about 20 two miles off. The remainder live at a much greater distance and attend either Horningsham church and school, or Maiden Bradley church and school. The average attendance at church of course does not include the children at Longbridge school or the persons and children at the churches and schools I have just mentioned.

John Powell

114. HILMARTON   D. Avebury

1. Hilmarton, a vicarage.

2. The Crown.

3. 780.

4. Francis Goddard 1858.

5. Yes.

6. Yes.

7. No curate.

8. No.

9. No.

10. [Blank]

11. [Blank]

12. [Blank]

13. No.

14. [Blank]

15. Yes, in everything.

16. Yes, with especial care.

17. Yes.

18. I do not think any material alterations have been made except that the floors have throughout the church been matted.

19. They are performed in the church alone.

20. [Blank]

21. Except the vicarage house and the grounds, which are 4 acres, the whole endowment consists of tithes.

22. [Blank]

23. No

24. Service in church on Sunday at 11.00am and 3.00pm and a sermon is preached in both services. In the summer the afternoon service is moved to 6.00 pm.

25. Yes.

26. No.

27. No.

28. On saints' days, Christmas Day, Good Friday, Ascension Day and every Friday evening in Advent and Lent there is a service with sermon. The Sunday congregation in morning and evening service throughout the summer numbers about 600 persons united. In winter not so many. Week day evening services are attended by about 60 persons each service.

29. [a] Yes [b] Yes [c] No [d] Yes [No].

30. Every 1st Sunday of the month.

31. Yes, after every communion.

32. 48 including invalids.

33. I think nearly all have communicated last year.

34. About 20.

35. No difference.

36. About 350 including children.

37. Our church is always full and has always been so since I have been here.

38. No.

39. 27 baptisms 9 marriages 16 burials.

40. In 1861 – 23, in 1862 – none, in 1863 – 1.

41. At the conclusion of every year a full statement is made and affixed to the church door of every parish or charitable fund and its expenditure. All the receipts for all collections are in like manner so affixed at the time the collection is counted.

42. The sacramental alms amounted to £8 18s.

43. A regular account of them is kept and account[ed] for to the parish as above stated.

44. The regular dissenting places of worship are two, one at Goatacre and one at Hilmarton. The former Independents, the latter Baptists.

45. We have an excellent day school with good master and mistress.

46. We have never required Government aid in my time.

47. The age varies according to the requirements of the agriculturists, boys generally leave at about 10 years of age, girls from 12 to 15.

48. We retain a great many in the Sunday schools to a later age of 16-18 years.

49. We have large evening schools, which during the last winter have been attended by about 53 scholars chiefly above 16 and under 25 years of age. The most encouraging results have followed the night school system in this parish.

50. [Blank]

51. [Blank]

52. Better attendance of late in men of that age at church, more regularity of conduct generally, and better preparation especially for confirmation.

Francis Goddard

115. HILPERTON cum WHADDON D. Potterne

1. Hilperton cum Whaddon, a rectory.

2. Walter Long Esq M.P. Rood Ashton, Trowbridge, Wilts.

3. 103.

4. Thomas Henry Tait 7th Dec 1861 instituted. 19th Dec 1861 inducted.

5. Yes.

6. In the glebe house.

7. [Blank]

8. No.

9. No.

10. [Blank]

11. [Blank]

12. No.

13. Yes.

14. Hilperton and Whaddon.

15. Yes.

16. Yes.

17. One churchwarden only is a communicant.

18. The church and chancel have been heated underground, the stoves and piping removed. The organ gallery also was lowered. Gas fittings have also been put into the church and chancel and the interior of the chancel cleaned. The space within the altar rails was covered with encaustic tiles and otherwise beautified. The Rural Dean inspected and approved of what was done. The fabric has not been interfered with.

19. Yes.

20. [Blank]

21. Tithe and glebe £418.

22. Hilperton £259 Whaddon £159.

23. No.

24. At Hilperton. Morning Prayer, Litany, communion service at 10.30am, Evensong at 6.30pm on three Sundays in the month. On the other Sunday, there

is in addition to the above, a choral afternoon service at 3.45pm. At Whaddon. Service every Sunday at 2.30pm. There are always sermons except at the choral service.

25. Except in evenings in Lent and Advent where sometimes I have Litany and sermon.

26. No.

27. I began daily service and kept it in for some time but could get no attendance. I shall commence it again and keep it in during the summer.

28. All festivals and other holy days and twice a day on Wednesdays and Fridays in Advent.

29. At Hilperton on all these days and at Whaddon with the exception of Ascension Day.

30. On the last Sunday in each month and on every Sunday which is a festival or saints' day and on Sundays within octaves.

31. No, but I remember who are.

32. [Blank]

33. One only. Four regular communicants have left the parish since June.

34. Not more than at other times, say 14.

35. About 14.

36. [Blank]

37. Rather increasing.

38. No.

39. 11 baptisms 3 marriages 18 burials.

40. None since my induction.

41. No.

42. Under £5 per annum.

43. No but they are kept separate from all other money.

44. One Baptist meeting house and one Wesleyan meeting house. When I first came to the parish I consider that at least two thirds of the population if not more were dissenters.

45. Yes.

46. Yes.

47. 11 years.

48. Yes.

49. An evening school commencing in September and ending in May. It is pretty well attended.

50. Yes.

51. The Society for the Propagation of the Gospel, Additional Curates' Aid Society and for the endowment of churches in Connaught.

52. The chief people in the place who should have set a good example have led most immoral lives and there has been no church layman who has taken any interest whatever in the spiritual well being of the place or its inhabitants. The bulk of those who went to church I found to be dissenters in heart and doctrine disbelieving Baptismal Regeneration and the real presence in the Holy Eucharist (by the latter expression I mean) not believing that the faithful communicant

is a partaker of Christ in partaking of that sacrament but looking at attendance at Holy Communion merely in the light of professing oneself a member of the establishment as of any other sect. I have I hope been careful not to startle people but to put forward truths to them gradually as they have been able to bear them.

Thomas Henry Tait

116. HINDON   D. Chalke

1. Hindon. A rectory and perpetual curacy.
2. The Lord Chancellor.
3. 604.
4. Robert Graves Walker, Spring 1855.
5. Yes.
6. Elsewhere a house given to the incumbent.
7. [Blank]
8. No.
9. No.
10. [Blank]
11. [Blank]
12. [Blank]
13. No.
14. [Blank]
15. Yes.
16. Yes.
17. Yes.
18. No.
19. Yes.
20. [Blank]
21. Sources three, tithe rent charge, trust property and Queen Anne's Bounty. Amount already returned.
22. [Blank]
23. Not any.
24. Two full services at 10.30am and 6.00pm, sermons after each service.
25. Always according to Rubric.
26. No.
27. [Blank]
28. Christmas Day and Good Friday.
29. [a] Sometimes [b] Yes [c] No [d] and [e] on one or the other.
30. On the 1st Sunday of every second month.
31. Yes.
32. 39.
33. Perhaps four.
34. About 20.
35. About the same.
36. I think 350.

37. I have not counted the congregation lately; it is as formerly.
38. No.
39. 15 baptisms 2 marriages 15 burials.
40. Not any.
41. [Blank]
42. £4 19s 6d.
43. Yes.
44. Independent and Methodist (Primitive).
45. Yes.
46. Yes.
47. About 12 years to 13 years.
48. For a time.
49. No.
50. No.
51. [Blank]
52. [Blank]

Robert Graves Walker

117. HOLT   D. Potterne
1.   Holt. A perpetual curacy.
2.   Dean and Chapter of Bristol.
3.   809.
4.   Charles Turner. August 1st 1850.
5.   Yes.
6.   In his own hired house.
7.   [Blank]
8.   No.
9.   Yes.
10. 25th November 1863.
11. Richard Umfraville Lambert. In priest's orders.
12. No.
13. No.
14. [Blank]
15. With the exception of the tower which is considerably out of repair, the fabric is in a sound state, yes.
16. Yes.
17. Yes.
18. No.
19. [Blank]
20. [Blank]
21. Tithe £160 gross £110 net income.
22. [Blank]
23. No glebe house at all.
24. Two full services every Sunday. Morning and afternoon 10.30am and 3.00pm.

Sermons are preached at every service.

25. Yes.

26. No.

27. No. Except on saints' days and during Lent.

28. [Blank]

29. [a] Yes [b] Yes [c] No [d] Yes [e] Yes.

30. On the 1st Sunday in every month.

31. Yes.

32. 70 attend during the year. The average attendance is about 40.

33. [Blank]

34. 40.

35. 40.

36. 500.

37. 200 – increasing.

38. No.

39. 11 baptisms 3 marriages 16 burials.

40. 14 in 1863.

41. No.

42. £10.

43. Yes.

44. A large Independent chapel. About two thirds of the population have dissented.

45. Yes.

46. No.

47. About 12 years.

48. Some.

49. No.

50. Yes.

51. National school £3 16s. Propagation of the gospel £2.

52. The chief drawback is the prevalence of dissent.

Richard U. Lambert

118. HOMINGTON   D. Chalke

1. Homington, a perpetual curacy.

2. The Dean and Chapter of Salisbury Cathedral.

3. 155.

4. Henry Smith Pollard, October 12th 1857.

5. There is no glebe house, but the incumbent resided at Coombe Bissett – distant from Homington less than a mile.

6. At Coombe Bissett.

7. [Blank]

8. Yes – the vicarage of Coombe Bissett cum West Harnham in the diocese of Salisbury.

9. Yes.

10. 18 months ago.

11. Duncombe Herbert Sawyer, a priest.

12. Yes, curate to the parish of West Harnham.

13. One church.

14. [Blank]

15. Yes.

16. Yes.

17. Yes.

18. No.

19. [Blank]

20. [Blank]

21. The parsonage farm of 150 acres and a rent charge of £17 per annum.

22. [Blank]

23. [Blank]

24. One full service every Sunday afternoon with a sermon and two full services with a sermon every alternate Sunday morning at 10.30am and 3.00pm.

25. Yes.

26. No.

27. I have not done so for want of a congregation to attend the church.

28. Christmas Day and Good Friday.

29. The Holy Communion is administered every six weeks and care is taken to have it administered on the days mentioned in no 29.

30. Every six weeks.

31. Yes.

32. [Blank]

33. [Blank]

34. [Blank]

35. [Blank]

36. 150.

37. The congregation is a most fluctuating one – it is really impossible to say whether it is increasing or decreasing. Some Sundays the church is full, the next nearly empty. The truth is dissent is deeply rooted and nearly all who come to the church in the morning go to the chapel in the evening.

38. [Blank]

39. 4 baptisms 3 marriages 4 burials.

40. 8 in 1864.

41. No.

42. £1 10s.

43. I keep a regular private account myself.

44. Primitive Methodists dissenting chapel. I am really unable to say what may be the number of dissenters in the parish.

45. No. The children of this parish attend the Coombe National School.

46. [Blank]

47. About 10 years of age.

48. There is a very excellent Sunday school.

49. [Blank]
50. I am about to do so.
51. Thanksgiving sermon £1 18s.
52. The prevalence of deep rooted dissent of many years standing.

Henry Smith Pollard

119. HORNINGSHAM   D. Wylye
1.   Horningsham, a perpetual curacy.
2.   The Bishop of the diocese.
3.   1067.
4.   James John Jacob, 1858.
5.   Yes.
6.   Yes.
7.   [Blank]
8.   No.
9.   No.
10. [Blank]
11. [Blank]
12. [Blank]
13. No.
14. [Blank]
15. Yes.
16. Yes.
17. Yes.
18. The church has been fitted with standards and coronae for lighting.
19. [Blank]
20. [Blank]
21. A farm at Brewham[1] £80; Ecclesiastical Commissioners £20; Lord Bath from agreement with Ecclesiastical Commissioners £50; Lord Weymouth benefaction £30; William Archer's benefaction £30. Gross income £210.
22. [Blank]
23. [Blank]
24. Morning service with sermon at 10.30am, afternoon service with sermon at 3.00pm, a Litany service with sermon at 6.30pm.
25. Yes.
26. No.
27. No.
28. We have Morning Prayer every Wednesday and Friday and on saints' days. Daily Morning Prayer during Lent. Evening service on Wednesday in Lent and Advent. Average attendance in the morning six besides schoolchildren, evening 60.
29. [a] Yes [b] Yes [c] No [d] Yes [e] No.
30. The 1st Sunday in each month.
31. Yes.

32. 83.

33. None.

34. 40.

35. 35.

36. 600.

37. I should think in the morning 120 besides 100 schoolchildren. In the afternoon 350 besides 100 schoolchildren. In the evening 180.

38. No.

39. 27 baptisms 5 marriages 17 burials.

40. 33.

41. I affix to the church doors the receipts after collections have been made.

42. £8 8s 6d in 1863.

43. Yes.

44. One – Independent. There are not very many avowed dissenters but many more who attend the meeting house occasionally.

45. Yes.

46. Yes.

47. About 10 years old.

48. Not very much.

49. We have an evening school from Michaelmas to the 1st day of Lent. There are classes at the parsonage which have been successful.

50. No – but I shall in a day or two.

51. Society for the Propagation of the Gospel. The poor benefices.

52. I find that my parishioners at that part of the parish which is near the meeting house are for the most part dissenters. I should be glad if I could make arrangements for a Sunday service amongst them.

James J Jacob

[1] A parish on the Wiltshire, Somerset border, next to Stourton.

120. HUISH or HEWISH   D. Marlborough

1. Huish, a rectory.

2. The Marquis of Ailesbury and other noblemen and gentlemen, trustees of Froxfield College, Wilts.

3. The village population is 66, the scattered parish population 133.

4. William Bleeck, February 1830.

5. He has so been, every year since 1830.

6. Yes in the glebe house.

7. He has no curate.

8. Not at all.

9. Has no assistant curate.

10. Has none.

11. Has none.

12. Has none.

13. No, only one church.

14. One church.

15. Very good in every respect.

16. Yes.

17. Only <u>one</u> churchwarden who does all the duties of his office well.

18. None at all.

19. No chapels.

20. No chapel.

21. Rent charge variable: see 'Sarum Almanack' for amount.

22. One parish only.

23. Only one.

24. Two Sunday services take place in the parish church every Sabbath Day at 10.30am and 3.00pm and always with sermons.

25. Yes.

26. No.

27. No.

28. On Christmas Day and Good Friday. Attendance depends on <u>weather;</u> some days a dozen, some days 40.

29. On Christmas Day, Easter Day, St John Baptist's Day and on Michaelmas Day, or <u>near</u> the latter two.

30. None.

31. No.

32. Six, more or less.

33. All of them, most probably.

34. Same as at other times.

35. No variation.

36. 100, more or less.

37. At a rough guess 40: there it stands. The rest go to the Methodist chapel or Oare new church for convenience.

38. No: <u>plenty of room.</u>

39. 4 baptisms 2 marriages 5 burials.

40. Not one.

41. None.

42. About <u>one pound</u> all together.

43. No.

44. One Methodist chapel, comprising Wesleyans and Ranters; well attended for convenience sake, all the <u>outlying</u> population attending it.

45. No.

46. No.

47. As soon as they can earn <u>a shilling a week.</u>

48. They will come a <u>little</u> longer.

49. None.

50. Not yet; but will do so <u>in due time.</u>

51. None at all; none but the <u>poor and penniless.</u>

52. <u>Want of Spirituality.</u> None but the remedy <u>from 'above'</u>, which is lightly regarded in these days of <u>externals</u> and <u>trumperies.</u> 'Every good gift and every

perfect gift 'is from above'.

William Bleeck

121. IDMISTON   D. Amesbury

1. Idmiston cum Porton, a vicarage.
2. The Lord Bishop of the diocese.
3. It is given as amounting to 542.
4. William Dowding, July 1862.
5. Yes.
6. In a house called the rectory.
7. [Blank]
8. No.
9. No.
10. [Blank]
11. [Blank]
12. [Blank]
13. A church and a chapel.
14. Idmiston church is dedicated to All Saints, Porton to St Nicholas.
15. The church is in bad repair at Idmiston, at Porton it is in fair condition. Both church and chapel have all things necessary for divine service.
16. Fairly fenced and I strive to keep it in order.
17. Yes.
18. Merely the benches furnished with a back, railing for the choir and matting and hassocks for kneeling.
19. There are no burials at Porton, but burials as well as baptisms and marriages are solemnised at Idmiston.
20. About one mile.
21. Vicarial tithe apportionment.
22. It is all collected together twice a year.
23. No.
24. There are three full services every Sunday at 10.30am, 2.30pm and 6.00pm. On the Sunday there are two services at Idmiston and one at Porton and the next Sunday it is vice versa.
25. When a baptism occurs, having repeated the Creed at the ministration of baptism, I do not repeat it again.
26. At Porton, when I have since my coming begun a Sunday school in the chancel, I endeavour so to instruct the children and to make it instructive to all present.
27. Litany on Friday mornings.
28. Christmas Day, Good Friday and Ascension Day. Prayers on saints' days, and in the Ember week, and in Lent and on Friday evenings in Lent. Full service with a sermon.
29. The Holy Communion is always ministered on Christmas Day, Easter Day, Whit Sunday and Trinity Sunday, either at Idmiston or Porton, according to a

regular course, and on the Sunday following in which ever church it was not in the festival.

30. The Holy Communion is administered 14 times in the year. Last year it was eight times at Idmiston and six at Porton including the festivals, reckoning the year from <u>Advent.</u>

31. Yes.

32. It has, I am thankful to say, much increased. Eight were added this Easter, four at each place. 26 at Idmiston.

33. All who I have enumerated.

34. I do not find that there has been an increase generally at the great festivals, but there certainly was last Easter Day for the 22 communicants.

35. [Blank]

36. 120 in the body of the church, 16 in the gallery, 10 in a part called the vestry, 4 in the chancel, 42 children; total 192.

37. I never recollect a larger number, but I wish it was larger.

38. When the church is restored the seats will be better arranged to accommodate.

39. 9 baptisms 2 marriages 13 burials. Thus in the whole parish there were 15 baptisms, 3 marriages and 13 burials.

40. In 1861 there were 24 confirmed and in 1863 there were 31.

41. Yes, at the Easter vestry.

42. £1 15s 3d.

43. Yes.

44. A meeting house called a Wesleyan. There are few who never go to church but only to meeting. Several go to church and meeting and a few go nowhere.

45. Yes.

46. Not yet.

47. Boys as soon as they can get work. Girls are frequently called away by their mothers to give assistance.

48. Yes.

49. I had evening schools last winter both at Idmiston and Porton, offering at least six evenings, three at each place.

50. Yes.

51. For the poor benefices, there were also collections for missions after a meeting held in Oct in the school room.

52. There are 11 houses at Shripple, appertaining to Idmiston, the children from which go to school at Winterslow, either at Middle Winterslow or to the infant school at Shripple (in Winterslow). There are two communicants from Shripple at Winterslow church and there were two candidates for confirmation from Shripple who also were prepared for confirmation by the clergyman at Winterslow. I go over and visit my flock there but as they go to new Winterslow church then also every Sunday evening, and every Wednesday except in the harvest service in the school church at Shripple and they are 4½ miles from me I do not see them here on Sundays.

William Dowding

122. IMBER   D. Potterne
1. Imber, a perpetual curacy.
2. Marquis of Bath, Longleat, Warminster.
3. 382.
4. William Dyer M.A. August 1841.
5. Yes.
6. He has so resided.
7. [Blank]
8. No other.
9. No such assistance.
10. [Blank]
11. [Blank]
12. [Blank]
13. One church only.
14. [Blank]
15. Yes.
16. Fairly.
17. Yes.
18. Very trifling, only in furtherance of former Rural Dean's suggestions for uniformity of pewing.
19. [Blank]
20. [Blank]
21. Q.A. Bounty £47 18s 4d. Marquis of Bath £60. Rent of 7 acres of land £10. Total £117 18s 4d subject to income tax.
22. [Blank]
23. [Blank]
24. Morning service at 10.30am, evening service at 3.00pm and in the summer at 6.00pm. Sermons at both services.
25. Entirely so.
26. Did so for many years, but obliged to yield to clamour, by discontinuing the practice.
27. Utterly impracticable.
28. Christmas Day, Good Friday and Ascension Day in the evening. From 20 to 60.
29. The Sunday after Christmas Day, Easter Day, Whit Sunday and after Harvest.
30. None.
31. Yes.
32. 19. I have lost 11 during the last 7 years from death and removal.
33. Only one.
34. About 15.
35. [Blank]
36. About 250.
37. Varies very much, from 50 to 130.
38. No such want.
39. 7 baptisms 0 marriages 5 burials.

40. 4.
41. Yes, always, subsequently on the church doors.
42. £2 0s 1d.
43. Yes.
44. Yes, one, of the Anabaptist persuasion. A great proportion of the humbler class frequent it, none of the upper class.
45. Yes.
46. No.
47. About 10 years of age.
48. Yes, generally.
49. For want of proper assistance, the evening school is suspended.
50. This will be done within a few days. Omitted for want of parchment forms.
51. Oct 4th 1863 for Salisbury Infirmary £2 11s 1d. Dec 13th 1863 for augmentation of small livings £1 4s 9½d. Collection and subscriptions to S.P.G. £4 2s 2½d.
52. The prevalence of a low species of dissent, under the Anabaptist form. The attendance at church when I came here, in 1841 was very small, and although it has much increased, much time and patience, as well as prudence are needful to a more hopeful state of things. A better example, and greater personal interest, in the employers of labourers is desirable.

William Dyer

123. KEEVIL   D. Potterne

1. Keevil cum Bulkington, a vicarage.
2. The Dean and Chapter of Winchester.
3. 730.
4. William Henry Pooke, 1839.
5. Yes.
6. Yes.
7. [Blank]
8. No.
9. Yes.
10. Not licensed.
11. John Mortimer Tandy, a deacon.
12. Master of [Grammar] School in Devizes.
13. One church and chapel of ease.
14. Christ Church, Bulkington, consecrated 1860.
15. Yes.
16. No.
17. They do.
18. No.
19. Baptisms and burials only.
20. 2 miles.
21. Rent charge and an endowment of £50 per annum for the curate of Bulkington.

22. Rent charge £162 13s, £25 paid by the Ecclesiastical Commissioners annually.
23. One only.
24. Morning service with sermon at 10.30am, afternoon service with sermon at 3.00pm.
25. Yes.
26. No.
27. No.
28. On Ash Wednesday, Good Friday, Ascension Day and Christmas Day.
29. [a] Yes [b] Yes [c] No [d] Yes [e] Yes.
30. On the 1st Sunday in Lent, the 1st Sunday in Advent, Michaelmas and the 1st Sunday in August.
31. No.
32. [Blank]
33. [Blank]
34. About 20.
35. There is little or no difference.
36. More than 300.
37. In a scattered village it is hardly possible to say. I should say increasing.
38. None.
39. 9 baptisms 4 marriages 10 burials.
40. For Keevil 16.
41. Yes.
42. £3 2s 11d.
43. Yes.
44. One. Impossible to say.[1]
45. Yes.
46. No.
47. 8 years.
48. Very few.
49. Evening school for youths above 15 has been opened with success.
50. They are nearly ready.
51. For the Lancashire distress fund and Bath Hospital.
52. [Blank]

William Henry Pooke

[1] A Wesleyan Methodist chapel was built and licensed in 1833. The average congregation in 1851 was 75.

124. KINGSTON DEVERILL   D. Wylye
1. Kingston Deverill, a rectory.
2. Marquess of Bath, Longleat.
3. 376 by the last census – 414 when I came 18 years ago.
4. David Malcolm Clerk, February 17th 1846.
5. Yes.
6. In the glebe house.

7. [Blank]
8. No – he is Honorary prebend of Wells Cathedral.
9. [Blank]
10. [Blank]
11. [Blank]
12. [Blank]
13. No.
14. [Blank]
15. Yes.
16. Yes.
17. Yes.
18. No.
19. [Blank]
20. [Blank]
21. Land in extent about 347 acres at present let on lease to the Marquess of Bath for the sum of £324 a year.
22. [Blank]
23. No more than one.
24. Two full services, at 10.30am and 3.00pm, sermons preached at both.
25. Yes.
26. During Lent on the Wednesdays and Fridays in the morning service after Litany is ended. I question the school children on the catechism and lecture them on it on the saints' days and other fasts and festivals when there is no regular sermon. I also catechise the children on the same subject. I cannot say any very marked good has been the result.
27. I do not.
28. Christmas Day, Ash Wednesday, Good Friday, Ascension Day two full services at the normal times – fairly attended. On Wednesday and Friday mornings in Lent at 9.30am and at 7.00pm on both these days in the evenings in Lent – not well attended this year. In the evening perhaps 30 persons are present on Friday evening for about eight months in the year. Latterly not well attended or the mornings of every festival when but few persons attended, seldom eight besides children(?).
29. [a] Yes [b] Yes [c] No [d] Yes [e] No.
30. The last Sunday in every month.
31. No – only of their numbers on each occasion.
32. It has varied considerably from 16 or 18 to 36 at each communion. There are probably 40-46 who sometimes attend.
33. All these have attended during the year 1863 (save two – there was reason why they did not).
34. I don't think there is any great difference in the attendance at the great festivals; probably there are one or two more at Christmas.
35. [Blank]
36. About 230 including children, might find room.
37. Mornings adults 50-60, children 50, total 100-110. Afternoons adults 100,

children 50, total 150. It varies with the seasons and has altered but little from year to year i.e. <u>on the Sundays</u>; the <u>weekday</u> congregations have lessened very visibly.
38. No.
39. 17 baptisms 2 marriages 3 burials.
40. In 1861 – I believe 12, but my list is incomplete for that year.
41. No.
42. £9 19s 2½d.
43. I keep an exact account of the portion which I take. I know nothing of the portion (½) I give to the churchwardens attending at the sacrament of the Lord's Supper.
44. There is a Wesleyan chapel and Ranters meet in some house or other every Sunday. The chapel is small but in the evenings there are nearly enough I believe to fill it.
45. Yes.
46. I never have as yet, hope to do so next year.
47. About 11.
48. In <u>some few</u> instances the boys till 12, the girls until they are about 14 years old.
49. I always have an evening school during the winter months.
50. Not as yet.
51. One for the Salisbury Infirmary. There is generally one collection made during the year for some charitable object or other, seldom more than one.
52. General indifference to religion and carelessness. I know not save increased earnestness, informing (?) and toil (ministerial) – alas too slackly (?) bestowed – earthly troubles and cares deadening one's efforts (?).

D.M. Clerk

125. KNOOK   D. Wylye

1. Knook is I believe only a chapelry to Heytesbury a vicarage, or perpetual curacy if separate.
2. See answers in Heytesbury paper.
3.
4. John Knight 1836.

The rest of the return is blank.

John Knight

126. LANDFORD   D. Amesbury

1. Landford, a rectory.
2. The Dowager Countess Nelson, Landford, Wiltshire.
3. 260 when the last census was taken.
4. Henry Girdlestone, April 1833.
5. Yes.

6. In the glebe house.

7. Resident.

8. Yes. The rectory of Colton St Andrew, Norwich.

9. Yes.

10. 3rd December 1858.

11. Francis Gurney Girdlestone[1]. Priest's orders.

12. No.

13. No.

14. [Blank]

15. Yes.

16. Yes.

17. Yes.

18. No alterations.

19. No chapels.

20. [Blank]

21. Tithes about £220. Rent from glebe farm £66. Amount £286.

22. The benefice is composed of but one parish.

23. No.

24. Morning and Evening Prayers at 11.00am and 3.00pm respectively, and a sermon is preached at each of these services.

25. Yes.

26. No catechising.

27. No.

28. Every saints' day and Holy Day in the year there is morning service at 11.00am, at which service there is an average attendance of 18. During the seasons of Advent and Lent, there are special evening services on Fridays, average attendance 100.

29. [a] Yes [b] Yes [c] No [d] Yes [e] No.

30. The 1st Sunday of every month.

31. Yes.

32. 80.

33. None.

34. 50.

35. Average monthly attendance of the last year was 41.

36. Including children, there is accommodation for 200.

37. Average morning attendance, including children, about 110. Afternoon about 160. This is a fair average of the 5 years past and the numbers continue the same.

38. No further accommodation needed at present.

39. 11 baptisms 2 marriages 4 burials.

40. 13.

41. The amount of collections is always declared by a notice attached to the church screen, used for all public notices, and also printed on the notice page of the 'Landford Parish Magazine'.

42. £19 0s 10d for the year ending 1863.

43. Yes.

44. We have no chapel of any dissenting sect in the parish, but there is a cottage

in the place, the owner of which holds a licence to hold meetings at his dwelling house for public worship: and such meetings are held every Thursday evening and twice on Sunday. They term themselves Wesleyan Methodists. We have not more than a dozen bona fide dissenters.

45. Yes.

46. Yes. We received a grant of £22 during the past year.

47. Average age 12.

48. Yes.

49. A night school is held during four months in the year. The same is well attended, and the scholars appear willing and anxious to keep up the instruction received at the day school.

50. Yes.

51. During the earlier months of 1863 the sum of £20 15s was collected at the church, in aid of the Manchester relief fund. For the Society for the Propagation of the Gospel £8 7s 4½d was collected at the church. Total £29 2s 4½d.

52. [Blank]

[No signature]

¹ Son of Henry Girdlestone

127. LAVERSTOCK   D. Amesbury

1. Laverstock.

2. The vicars of Salisbury Cathedral.

3. 470 including the asylum.

4. [Blank]

5. [Blank]

6. No glebe house.

7. [Blank]

8. [Blank]

9. [Blank]

10. [Blank]

11. [Blank]

12. [Blank]

13. No.

14. [Blank]

15. Yes.

16. Yes.

17. [Blank]

18. No.

19. [Blank]

20. [Blank]

21. [Blank]

22. [Blank]

23. [Blank]

24. Morning at 10.30am, afternoon at 3.00pm, sermons at both.

25. Yes.

26. No.

27. No. In Advent and Lent, only Morning Prayer.

28. Wednesday and Friday mornings, Friday evening; four or five. All fasts and festivals of the church.

29. [a] Yes [b] Yes [c] Yes [d] Yes [e] No.

30. 1st Sunday in every month.

31. Yes.

32. 42.

33. 4.

34. No increase. Easter 1864 – 32.

35. 24.

36. 240 including seats for school children.

37. 100. Decreasing in the afternoon service.

38. No.

39. 15 baptisms 1 marriage 8 burials.

40. In 1863 – one.

41. Yes.

42. [Blank]

43. No.

44. One at Ford. Dissenting meetings are held in a cottage at Laverstock. Between 80 and 90 Independents, reformed Wesleyans and Ranters.

45. Yes.

46. Yes.

47. 13.

48. Not many.

49. An evening school with a little success.

50. Yes.

51. Society for the Propagation of the Gospel £6 12s, for the parochial school £6 19s, for the choir £2. Total £15 11s.

52. A spirit of indifference and opposition to church ordinances fostered by dissent and encouraged by one or two nominal churchmen.

J.P. Greenly[1]

[1] John Prosser Greenly, curate of Laverstock. In 1861 he was living in The Close with his parents.

128. LIMPLEY STOKE. Potterne

1. Limpley Stoke, a perpetual curacy.

2. The Dean and Chapter of Bristol.

3. 330 in 1861 – probably a few more now.

4. Francis Stephen Forss. Instituted October 11th 1862, inducted October 18th 1862.

5. Yes.

6. No glebe house – resided in the united parish of Winsley.

7. [Blank]
8. He has the united parishes of Winsley cum Limpley Stoke.
9. He has an assistant curate.
10. April 8th 1863.
11. Charles L Hardman a priest.
12. No.
13. Two churches.
14. Not known.
15. Yes.
16. Yes.
17. Yes.
18. No.
19. [Blank]
20. [Blank]
21. Tithe rent charge and surplice fees, net £147 per annum.
22. £117 Winsley and £30 Limpley Stoke.
23. No glebe house.
24. Two full services at each church on a Sunday. Time 11.00am and 6.15pm at Winsley and 11.00am and 3.00pm at Limpley Stoke. Sermons after each service at both churches.
25. Yes.
26. No.
27. No.
28. Christmas Day, Ash Wednesday, Good Friday and Ascension Day. 20 persons.
29. [a] Yes [b] Yes [c] Yes [d] Yes [e] Yes.
30. Every sixth Sunday.
31. Yes.
32. 20.
33. They have all.
34. 16½.
35. 14.
36. 90.
37. 70 to 80. About the same now – there has been a large increase.
38. Yes, by enlarging the church.
39. 10 baptisms 2 marriages 4 burials.
40. [Blank]
41. Yes.
42. £4 14s 11d.
43. Yes.
44. A Baptist Chapel and a Chapel in connection with the hydropathic establishments.
45. Yes.
46. Not for three or four years.
47. Boys about 8 or 10, girls about 12.
48. Yes.

49. An evening school during the winter months – moderate.
50. Yes.
51. Church Missionary Society £1 15s 3d. For the school £3 12s 10d.
52. The want of church accommodation by enlarging the church.

F.S. Forss

129. LITTLE BEDWYN   D. Marlborough

1. Bedwyn Parva, a vicarage.
2. The Marquess of Ailesbury, Savernake House, Marlborough.
3. 400.
4. John Worthington. Instituted 23rd April 1862. Inducted 20th June 1862.
5. Yes, except for the time he received licence for non-residence.
6. Yes.
7. [Blank]
8. No.
9. No.
10. [Blank]
11. [Blank]
12. [Blank]
13. No.
14. [Blank]
15. Yes.
16. Yes.
17. Yes.
18. No.
19. [Blank]
20. [Blank]
21. Tithe rent charge and a small portion of glebe. Gross income £290.
22. [Blank]
23. No.
24. Service with sermon morning and evening. 11.00am and 3.00pm in winter, 11.00am and 6.00pm in summer.
25. No.
26. No.
27. No.
28. On the great festivals and special services, during Lent, Advent and on New Year's Day.
29. Yes.
30. The 1st Sunday of every month.
31. Have not made one at present.
32. About 40.
33. Three.
34. About 20.
35. 13.

36. About 150.

37. 70 exclusive of children.

38. No.

39. 11 baptisms 3 marriages 12 burials.

40. Do find in the parish book any list of persons confirmed since 1859.

41. Yes.

42. From July 30th (when I resided) to December 31st £7 4s 9d.

43. Yes.

44. An Independent chapel and a meeting in a cottage of Wesleyans. About 30 souls.

45. Yes.

46. Yes.

47. From 7 to 11.

48. Some of them.

49. Yes, with fair success.

50. No, was not aware it was required.

51. Since I came into residence there have been collections for the S.P.G and for augmentation of poor benefices.

52. [Blank]

John Worthington

130. LITTLE CHEVERELL   D. Potterne

1. The rectory of Cheverel Parva.

2. The Earl of Radnor or his son The Hon E.P. Bouverie.

3. About 200.

4. J[ohn] R[oles] Fishlake, 1823.

5. Resident.

6. In the glebe house.

7. [Blank]

8. No.

9. Yes.

10. Licensed in 1863.

11. H[enry] M[owld] Robinson, a priest.

12. None whatever.

13. One church only.

14. [Blank]

15. Yes.

16. Yes.

17. Yes.

18. None.

19. [Blank]

20. [Blank]

21. About 190 acres of land in lieu of tithe.

22. [Blank]

23. [Blank]

24. Two services at 11.00am and 3.00pm. A sermon at the latter.

25. Of course.

26. No public catechism in the church. The children attend a Sunday school an hour before each service.

27. No daily morning or evening prayers in the parish, the population being engaged in agricultural labour.

28. There is a service on Christmas Day and Ash Wednesday, and evening service at 7.00pm on saints' days and the Wednesdays in Lent.

29. On the Sunday after Christmas Day, on Easter Day, on Trinity Sunday and on three other Sundays as most convenient.

30. [See 29]

31. I keep no list as I know every communicant.

32. About 20.

33. None.

34. Above 20.

35. Below 20.

36. There is accommodation for all the inhabitants.

37. About 80 on Sunday mornings and about 130 on Sunday evening. If there is any difference it increases.

38. No want of further accommodation.

39. 12 baptisms 2 marriages 2 burials.

40. In 1861 15. In 1862 and 1863 none.

41. Yes – when it concerns them.

42. In 1863 £3 4s 2d.

43. A regular account is kept.

44. No dissenting place of worship. Three dissenters in the parish.

45. Yes.

46. Yes. The day school and evening classes are both under Government inspection.

47. About 11.

48. Yes, always.

49. We have been particularly successful in having an evening school from Oct 1863 to Mar 1864.

50. Copies of the parish registers are invariably given in at the Bishop's and Archdeacon's visitation.

51. Besides the sacramental alms, 10s 6d was collected for lighting and warming the church during the evening services.

52. [Blank]

J.R. Fishlake

131. LITTLE LANGFORD   D. Wylye

1. Langford Parva, a rectory.

2. Earl of Pembroke, Wilton House.

3. 56 (in 1861, 39).
4. Edward Hill M.A. Instituted 6th May 1863 and inducted 15th May 1863.
5. Resident from the end of June.
6. In the glebe house.
7. [Blank]
8. None.
9. None.
10. [Blank]
11. [Blank]
12. [Blank]
13. No.
14. [Blank]
15. In the course of rebuilding.
16. Not at present.
17. No, because being himself never present at Holy Communion, he cannot present non-communicants at Easter. Canon CXII.
18. The church and chancel rebuilt under the authority of a faculty.
19. No chapels.
20. [Blank]
21. Tithe rent charge £145 and a few acres of glebe.
22. [Blank]
23. Only one.
24. Morning service with sermon at 11.00am. Evening service with sermon at 6.00pm.
25. Yes.
26. Yearly at certain seasons (Lent and saints' days) but catechising is suspended for the present on account of the inconvenience of the temporary room.
27. Yes, the morning prayers.
28. Daily; average attendance <u>five.</u>
29. [a] Yes [b] Yes [c] Yes [d] Yes [e] Yes.
30. Monthly (when there are sufficient communicants).
31. Yes.
32. Six (Easter 1864).
33. Two, but there was not one communicant in the parish last summer.
34. Six at Easter.
35. The same.
36. For 80 in the new church.
37. Morning 20. Evening 35. More would attend if there were accommodation for them in the licensed room. N.B.
38. No.
39. 3 baptisms 0 marriages 3 burials.
40. One only I believe.
41. Yes.
42. £1 2s (in the half year).
43. Yes.

44. None.
45. No.
46. No.
47. [Blank]
48. [Blank]
49. An evening school of a very small number, but so far successful.
50. Yes.
51. None.
52. The smallness of the population is an impediment, especially the heathen state of the people, not one of whom ever bowed the knee in worship, or witnessed a public baptism in the parish church, or knew what was meant by Holy Communion.
N.B. Some of the answers are necessarily vague on account of the peculiar transitional state of the parish both as regards its inhabitants and its church arrangements.

Edward Hill

132. LONGBRIDGE DEVERILL   D. Wylye

1. Longbridge Deverill vicarage, with Monkton Deverill and Crockerton chapels.
2. Marquis of Bath.
3. 1178.
4. William David Morrice, 1852.
5. Yes.
6. Yes.
7. [Blank]
8. No.
9. Yes, two.
10. 1859 and 1860.
11. Revd Henry de St Croix, priest, 1859. Revd William Slatter, priest, 1860.
12. No.
13. Yes, three.
14. Longbridge Deverill S.S. Peter and Paul, date of consecration unknown. Monkton Deverill, dedication and date unknown. Crockerton Holy Trinity, 1845.
15. Yes.
16. Yes.
17. Yes.
18. No.
19. Yes, except that there are no marriages at Crockerton.
20. Monkton 3 miles, Crockerton 1½ miles.
21. Vicarial tithe. Land in Somerset. A modus.
22. Monkton Deverill tithe £68, Glebe 0. Longbridge Deverill tithe £158, glebe 9 acres, say £18. The land in Somerset belongs to the benefice as a whole.

23. No.

24. Longbridge Deverill 10.30am and 3.00pm. Monkton Deverill 11.00am and 2.30pm. Crockerton 10.30am and 6.30pm. Sermons at all services.

25. Yes.

26. Yes. The course of the seasons. With tolerable effect.

27. Yes.

28. Daily. About eight besides children.

29. [a] Yes [b] Yes [c] Yes [d] Yes [e] Yes.

30. Monthly. Early communion weekly.

31. Yes.

32. At Longbridge church, 88.

33. 3.

34. 35.

35. 37.

36. Longbridge Deverill 350 (?) Crockerton 450 (?) Monkton Deverill 120 (?)[1]

37. Say, Longbridge Deverill 300 in the afternoon, Crockerton 200 in the evening, Monkton 70 in the afternoon. It may be more; it is certainly not decreasing.

38. No.

39. 15 baptisms 3 marriages 9 burials.

40. In 1861 − 16, in 1862 − 2, in 1863 − 0.

41. Occasionally.

42. Exclusive of collections (Art:51) £22 1s 1¼d.

43. Yes.

44. In the village of Longbridge, Primitive Methodists. Very few 'joined members', but many frequent it.

45. Yes.

46. Yes.

47. Boys 10, girls 11.

48. Yes, generally.

49. Yes. Great success.

50. In preparation.

51. Home Missions £3 4s 10d. Parochial schools £1 13s 0½d. Augmentation of poor benefices £2 4s 2d.

52. Dissent and indifference seem our principal difficulties. More earnestness in our work, and closer dealing with individuals seem under God's blessing, to be our remedies. I may mention also the necessity of having three sponsors (none of them parents) as creating a great difficulty.

W.D. Morrice

[1] The question marks are the incumbent's, to indicate his estimation of the accommodation.

133. LUDGERSHALL   D. Amesbury

1. Ludgershall, a rectory.

2. W. Maund Esq, Guernsey.
3. 580.
4. Revd J[ohn] Pannel, 1825.
5. He has leave of non-residence.
6. There is no glebe house.
7. Revd W[illiam] H[enry] Awdry. Resident.
8. No.
9. [Blank]
10. [Blank]
11. [Blank]
12. [Blank]
13. No.
14. [Blank]
15. Yes.
16. Yes.
17. Yes.
18. No.
19. [Blank]
20. [Blank]
21. The tithe rent charge in 1863 was £457 19s 10d.
22. [Blank]
23. There is none.
24. Morning service at 11.00am and evening service at 3.00pm with sermons.
25. Yes.
26. No.
27. No.
28. On the 20th June, saints' days, Ash Wednesday, Good Friday and on Friday evenings.
29. [a] Yes [b] Yes [c] Yes [d] and [e] alternately.
30. Once a month.
31. Yes.
32. About 120, including those who were confirmed this year, some 20.
33. About 10 have not.
34. 31.
35. 24.
36. About 240.
37. 150. It is not decreasing.
38. No.
39. 18 baptisms 1 marriage 10 burials.
40. In 1861 – 22 males and 20 females.
41. Yes.
42. In 1861 - £45 15s 1d. 1862 - £34 0s 5¼d. 1863 - £21 17s 6¼. In 1863, money which used to be distributed as alms has been applied to the soup kitchen fund. This will account for the apparent decrease.
43. Yes.

44. Two, one Baptist and one Independent. There are about nine of the former and twelve of the latter denomination.
45. Yes.
46. Yes.
47. Boys at 10, girls at 13.
48. Generally.
49. By evening schools which have been fairly attended. Some of the older lads are making good progress.
50. Yes.
51. S.P.G. £1 9s 2½d. Sarum Infirmary £1 18s 9d. Diocesan Society for the Augmentation of Small Benefices £2. Total £5 7s 11½d.
52. [Blank]

W.H. Awdry

134. LYNEHAM   D Avebury

1. Lyneham. A perpetual curacy.
2. G. H. W. Heneage Esq Compton Bassett Calne.
3. 1034.
4. John Duncan. 11th May 1859.
5. Yes.
6. Yes.
7. [Blank]
8. No.
9. [Blank]
10. [Blank]
11. [Blank]
12. [Blank]
13. No.
14. [Blank]
15. Yes.
16. Yes.
17. Yes.
18. Yes, under the authority of a faculty. Complete restoration of the church, including rebuilding the chancel. Improvement of the churchyard.
19. [Blank]
20. [Blank]
21. Moduses. Queen Anne's Bounty. Ecclesiastical Commission. Rent charge. Easter Dues. Small glebe. Surplice ones. Under £150 gross.
22. [Blank]
23. No.
24. Morning and Evening Prayer in the parish church. Evening Prayer in a licensed school room at Clack. Hours: 11.00am, 3.00pm, 6.30pm. A sermon is preached at each service.
25. Yes. At Clack the Litany is used.

26. Yes. After the second lesson in the afternoon, the children stand up before the minister, who questions them, generally on some event connected with the day. If conducted so as to keep up attention, and not continued too long; it is very instructive to the adult congregation.

27. No.

28. On all the important festivals. On Wednesdays and Fridays in Advent and Lent. Morning congregations in the week are small. Evening congregations average from 60 to 80.

29. [a] Yes [b] Yes [c] No [d] Yes [e] Yes.

30. On the 1st Sunday in every month.

31. Yes.

32. 37.

33. None.

34. 26.

35. 18.

36. 250 in the parish church. 120 in the licensed room at Clack.

37. I cannot say precisely. I hope it is increasing at Clack.

38. Yes. By building a church at Clack and providing a suitable endowment.

39. 23 baptisms (41 in the year 1862) 6 marriages 22 burials.

40. 25.

41. Yes: in part and to a certain extent.

42. In 1863 £11 0s 4½.

43. Yes.

44. Three. A Baptist chapel at Clack. A Primitive Methodist chapel at Clack. A Primitive Methodist chapel at Tockenham.

45. Yes. There are two; one at Lyneham and one at Clack.

46. Yes: for both.

47. Girls at 13 – boys from 8 to 10.

48. Yes.

49. Yes. An evening school is most profitable; especially if religious instruction is systematically given by the clergyman.

50. Yes.

51. For the Lancashire operatives £6 15s 3d. For the Society for the Propagation of the Gospel £4 19s 1d. For the augmentation of small benefices £4 6s 6d. For the alms for the poor £11 0s 4½d. Total £27 1s 2½d.

52. 1. My own infirmity. 2. Dissent. 3. Want of a church and resident minister at Clack.

John Duncan

135. MADDINGTON   D. Wylye

1. Maddington, a perpetual curacy.

2. L.P. Maton Esq, Maddington.

3. 396.

4. Frederick Bennett. 1851.

5. Yes.

6. Yes.

7. [Blank]

8. Yes, Shrewton, diocese of Sarum.

9. Yes.

10. 1860.

11. Samuel Chamberlain, a priest.

12. By your Lordship's permission he assists in the services of Shrewton. He performs no other duty.

13. No.

14. [Blank]

15. Yes.

16. Yes.

17. Yes.

18. No.

19. [Blank]

20. [Blank]

21. Stipend paid by lay impropriator £60. Interest of £200 money Royal Bounty Fund £6 10s. Surplice fees about 15s.

22. One benefice.

23. No.

24. Two full services with sermon at 11.00am and 6.00pm.

25. Yes.

26. No.

27. No.

28. On all Holy Days full service with sermon at 7.00pm. The same on Thursdays in Advent and Fridays in Lent. During Holy Week, morning prayer at 11.00am.

29. [a] Yes [b] Yes [c] No [d] Yes [e] No.

30. The 1st Sunday in each month.

31. Yes.

32. 61.

33. One.

34. At Christmas 23, Easter 30 and Whit Sunday 31.

35. 19.

36. About 260.

37. 130 to 150 in the morning, 180 and sometimes 200 in the evening. The evening congregation is not so large as it was in consequence of there being an evening service in Shrewton church.

38. No.

39. 7 baptisms 2 marriages 4 burials.

40. In 1861 – 18, in 1862 – 2, none in 1863.

41. Yes, by a notice in the church porch. At the Easter vestry I produce the accounts of all parochial charities.

42. In 1861 - £4 16s 6d. In 1862 - £5 18s. In 1863 - £5 18s.

43. Yes.

44. None. There are about 70, principally Baptists, the remainder Wesleyans who have seceded from the Baptists.
45. Yes – united with Shrewton.
46. Yes.
47. Boys at 11 or 12, girls at 12 or 13.
48. Yes.
49. Yes – by an evening school for boys. This has now been in operation for 16 years, and my experience is that it succeeds in exactly inverse ratio to the excellence of the education which is given to the boys at the day school.
50. Yes.
51. Expenses of the evening service £2 1s 1d. Salisbury Infirmary £2 12s 7d. Society for the Propagation of the Gospel £1 12s 10d.
52. [Blank]

Frederick Bennett

136. MAIDEN BRADLEY   D. Wylye

1. Maiden Bradley.
2. Dean and Chapter of Christ Church, Oxford.
3. 653.
4. Richard Rowley, 1862.
5. Resident.
6. In the glebe house.
7. [Blank]
8. [Blank]
9. No assistant curate.
10. [Blank]
11. [Blank]
12. [Blank]
13. One church.
14. [Blank]
15. In good repair.
16. Yes.
17. Yes.
18. [Blank]
19. [Blank]
20. [Blank]
21. From the Duke of Somerset, lessee of tithes £80. Bounty office £51 2s. Rent of glebe land at Somerton £13. Total £144 2s.
22. [Blank]
23. One glebe house.
24. Morning Prayer with sermon at 11.00am. Evening Prayer with sermon at 3.00pm.
25. Whole service.
26. [Blank]

27. [Blank]

28. Morning Prayer at 11.00am on Holy Days. Schoolchildren attend and an average of four adults.

29. [a] Yes [b] Yes [c] No [d] Yes [e] No.

30. On the 1st Sunday in the month.

31. Yes.

32. About 60.

33. [Blank]

34. 36.

35. 26.

36. [Blank]

37. [Blank]

38. [Blank]

39. 23 baptisms 9 marriages 5 burials.

40. In 1861, 31 confirmed.

41. The receipt for moneys collected is affixed to the church door.

42. £15 4s 3d.

43. Yes.

44. One chapel. A few regular dissenters. Many who attend both church and chapel.

45. Yes.

46. [Blank]

47. Boys at 10. Girls at 12.

48. To a certain extent.

49. Evening school at present seems not to have been successful.

50. Yes.

51. For the United Hospital Bath £3. For S.P.G. £3.

52. [Blank]

Richard Rowley

137. MANNINGFORD ABBOTS   D. Marlborough

1. Manningford Abbots, a rectory.

2. Sir F.D. Astley, Bart. Folkestone, Kent.

3. About 139.

4. Edward Everett, instituted March 14th inducted 16th 1857.

5. Yes.

6. Yes.

7. [Blank]

8. No.

9. No.

10. [Blank]

11. [Blank]

12. [Blank]

13. One church.

14. [Blank]

15. Yes.
16. Badly fenced at present, but we hope soon to repair it.
17. Yes.
18. The chancel was rebuilt in 1861. The greater part of the church was rebuilt in 1863 and 64. A faculty was obtained for the same in 1861. Want of funds prevented the completion of the church at an earlier period.
19. [Blank]
20. [Blank]
21. Tithe commuted at £315. Glebe between 14 and 15 acres value £28 per annum.
22. [Blank]
23. [Blank]
24. Two full services at 11.00am and 3.00pm with sermon at each service.
25. Yes.
26. No.
27. No.
28. On Christmas Day, Ash Wednesday, Good Friday and Ascension Day. On Christmas Day and Good Friday from 50 to 60 persons attend on other days very few.
29. On Christmas Day or the Sunday after. On Easter Day. More usually Trinity Sunday [rather than Whit Sunday].
30. On three other Sundays in the course of the year it is also administered.
31. Yes.
32. 17.
33. All have communicated.
34. 13.
35. The same.
36. 85, including the chancel.
37. About 60, rather on the increase.
38. No.
39. 4 baptisms 2 marriages 2 burials.
40. I regret that I have mislaid my list.
41. The receipt for the amount collected is always affixed to the church door.
42. £1 4s 1d.
43. Yes.
44. No dissenting place of worship.
45. Yes.
46. No.
47. Boys between 8 and 9 years old. Girls between 11 and 12.
48. Yes.
49. No.
50. Yes.
51. Not any.
52. [Blank]

Edward Everett

138. MANNINGFORD BRUCE   D. Marlborough

1. Manningford Bruce, a rectory.
2. Alexander Grant, Manningford.
3. 260 about.
4. Alexander Grant, 1845.
5. Yes.
6. Yes.
7. None.
8. No.
9. None.
10. [Blank]
11. [Blank]
12. [Blank]
13. No.
14. [Blank]
15. I cannot say that the church is in 'good' repair.
16. Not 'well' fenced on one side.
17. I should say that the churchwarden does not discharge his duties in that he does not attend his parish church for divine worship.
18. None.
19. No chapels.
20. [Blank]
21. Tithe rent charge commuted annual value £296 19s 7d. Land estimated annual value £10 7s.
22. [Blank]
23. One house only.
24. Ordinarily Matins at 10.30am with sermon every alternate Sunday. Evensong at 2.30pm with sermon always. Communion on the first Sunday in each month at 9.00am followed by Matins and Litany and sermon at 11.00am and Evensong at 3.00pm. One Sunday in each quarter and on all great festivals – High Celebration of Blessed Sacrament at 11.00am with sermon. This service having been preceded by Matins at 9.00am.
25. [Blank]
26. No. I believe that no method of instruction equals catechising.
27. I do not say daily the Morning and Evening Prayers in the parish church; I feel I am reasonably hindered in the use of Common Prayer for want of a congregation; but I look for the removal of the Protestant Rubric prohibiting the celebration of the communion without the presence of a congregation.
28. Wednesdays and Fridays. Average attendance about two. Vigils and saints' days average attendance about five.
29. [a] Yes [b] Yes [c] Yes [d] Yes [e] Yes.
30. On the 1st Sunday in each month. Also on the octave of Christmas and Low Sunday.
31. Yes.
32. 14 communicate at the parish church; the number drawn away to other

churches is, I hear, considerable.

33. 14 have communicated in my church during the year 1863.

34. About 8.

35. About 5.

36. About 110.

37. About 70 – congregation stationary.

38. If the present large square boxes were replaced by proper open pews the church would be far better attended.

39. 4 baptisms 2 marriages 4 burials.

40. 13.

41. Yes.

42. From Easter 1863 to Easter 1864 £3 4s 3½d.

43. Yes.

44. A Methodist conventicle; perhaps two-thirds (4/6) of the people are dissenters. Baptists or Fatalists, and Methodists with Upavon Crook-ites.[1]

45. None belonging to the church.

46. [Blank]

47. [Blank]

48. [Blank]

49. [Blank]

50. I think not.

51. Manchester cotton distress – 17s 3d. Church missions abroad (Hawaii) - £1 1s 10¾. Warming and lighting own church - £2 14s 4d. Augmentation of small benefices in the diocese of Salisbury – 9s 10d.

52. One great hindrance to my ministry, and a standing scandal to the church in these parts is the habitual reception of my parishioners to communion at Upavon – and especially as the continuance of the evil is assumed by the public to have the sanction of the bishop. I would suggest that question no 32 be made more explicit by adding 'resident' after the word 'communicants'; and that it be extended to the enquiry whether, if any, how many persons not resident in the parish have been commonly admitted to communion during the last year.

Alexander Grant

[1]This is probably an irreverent reference to Henry Crook, the vicar at Upavon.

139. MARDEN   D. Potterne

1. Marden, a vicarage.

2. The Dean and Canons of Bristol.

3. [Blank]

4. John Benson Skipper, A.D. 1845.

5. Yes.

6. In the glebe house.

7. No curate.

8. No.

9. No curate.
10. [Blank]
11. [Blank]
12. [Blank]
13. But one church.
14. [Blank]
15. Yes.
16. Yes.
17. Yes.
18. None.
19. No chapel.
20. [Blank]
21. Tithe rent charge commuted at £175. Bounty money paid out in ground rents £14.
22. One parish.
23. [Blank]
24. Morning service at 11.00am with sermon. Evening service at 3.00pm with sermon.
25. Yes.
26. No.
27. No.
28. Ash Wednesday, Good Friday, Ascension Day, Christmas Day.
29. [a] Yes [b] Yes [c] No [d] and [e] either.
30. About twice in the year.
31. Not their names but their number.
32. 16.
33. None.
34. 14.
35. Much the same.
36. 200.
37. 50 or 60.
38. No.
39. 4 baptisms 1 marriage 6 burials.
40. 11.
41. Yes.
42. [Blank]
43. Yes.
44. None.
45. Yes.
46. No.
47. Boys at 9, girls at 11.
48. Girls generally until they enter service. Few boys, as they have to attend horses.
49. No.
50. Yes.

51. Collection for S.P.G. Sept 27th 1863, £2 6s 9d.

52. No, except the difficulty of steering clear of quarrels with certain parishioners while defending the cause of the widow and fatherless and refusing to grovel before a purse-proud man.

J.B. Skipper

140. MARKET LAVINGTON   D. Potterne

1. Market or East Lavington, a vicarage.
2. The Dean and Chapter of Christ Church, Oxford.
3. 1583 by the last census.
4. Thomas Pearson, instituted Aug 1st 1860.
5. Yes.
6. In the glebe house.
7. [Blank]
8. No.
9. No.
10. [Blank]
11. [Blank]
12. [Blank]
13. No.
14. [Blank]
15. Yes.
16. Yes.
17. Yes.
18. The nave of the church has been restored; that is, the roof which had been closed, has been opened, and thoroughly repaired, the walls etc repaired and the whole church re-pewed. A faculty was obtained for this purpose.
19. [Blank]
20. [Blank]
21. Vicarial tithes £310 per annum, glebe £72 per annum.
22. [Blank]
23. [Blank]
24. Morning prayers and sermon at 10.30am. Evening prayers and baptisms if any at 3.00pm. Evening prayers and sermon at 6.00pm.
25. Yes.
26. During Lent I examine the children in the church catechism, every Sunday after the second lesson in the afternoon service, requiring explanation, texts from scriptures etc.
27. I say the morning service in the church daily during nine months in the year, and on Wednesdays and Fridays during the winter months. And there is morning service on all holy days.
28. On Christmas Day and on Good Friday there are nearly as many as on Sundays. On Ash Wednesday say 40 in the morning, and a 100 in the evening when there is a lecture. On Ascension Day about 30. On other Holy Days eight

or ten.

29. [a] Yes [b] Yes [c] Yes [d] Yes [e] Yes.

30. On the 1st Sunday in every month.

31. No.

32. About 80.

33. Very few of these have not communicated. Probably not more than three or four, as I have administered the Holy Communion privately to invalids who were unable to come to church.

34. 55.

35. 37.

36. The estimate of the architect was for 410 when the church was re-pewed. That is, in the pews, but with benches and chairs in aisles, the church will hold 520.

37. The average number on a Sunday morning is about 400, including the school children, in the evening 500. I do not think it is increasing or diminishing.

38. I think a church in the hamlet of Easterton would be desirable, if the necessary funds could be raised.

39. 63 baptisms 9 marriages 39 burials.

40. In 1861, 59 were confirmed, and in 1863, 48. There was no confirmation for this parish in 1862.

41. I inform the churchwardens and any of the parishioners who feel an interest in the subject, of the amount of each collection.

42. £14 19s 7d without reckoning collections for particular objects.

43. Yes.

44. Two. There are probably about 400 dissenters, chiefly Baptists and Independents.

45. Yes.

46. Yes.

47. About 10 years of age or under, on an average.

48. Yes, some attend the Sunday school till they are 14 or 15 years of age.

49. Yes, we have an evening school during the winter months, which has succeeded fairly.

50. Yes.

51. For National Schools of the parish collected £13 3s 3d. For Society for the Propagation of the Gospel in Foreign Parts £4 18s 4d. For augmentation of small benefices in the diocese of Sarum £1 17s 6d. For coal for the poor of the parish £4 12s 5½d. N.B. The above were the only collections in the year 1863, as in the previous year our people were somewhat drained by collections in church and from house to house, for the restoration of the church. Since the present year (1864) commenced, we have had a collection for the Diocesan Church Building Society, which amounted to £4 10s, and one for the Incorporated Society which amounted to £3 6s 6d.

52. [Blank]

Thomas Pearson

141. MARLBOROUGH ST MARY   D. Marlborough

1. St Mary's Marlborough, a vicarage.
2. The Bishop of the diocese.
3. By the census of 1851 - 2149, of 1861 – 1903. There is good reason for thinking one of these is a mistake.[1]
4. Edward B Warren, December 1851.
5. Yes.
6. Yes.
7. [Blank]
8. No.
9. Yes.
10. Trinity Sunday 1863.
11. O[ctavius] G[eorge] D[alhousie] Perrott. Deacon.
12. Assistant master in the R F[2] Grammar School in this parish.
13. One church, and a moiety of the mortuary chapel.
14. The parish church was dedicated to St Mary the Virgin probably in the 12th century. The mortuary chapel in 1861 to [blank].
15. Yes.
16. Yes.
17. Yes.
18. No.
19. No chapels, except one for burials.
20. Less than half a mile.
21. Tithes £25. Estate £24. Fees £7. Ground rent £40. Small endowments £8. Total £104.
22. [Blank]
23. No.
24. Two full services every Sunday and on the chief festivals at 11.00am and 6.30pm. Extra services in Lent and Advent. Prayers every Friday morning at 9.15am. And on the 3rd Sunday in every month a service at 3.00pm at which baptisms are celebrated.
25. Yes.
26. No.
27. No.
28. Morning Prayer on Fridays at 9.15am average attendance 10. On saints' days, service at the same hour, average attendance 50.
29. [a] Yes [b] Yes [c] No [d] Yes [e] Yes.
30. On the 1st Sunday in every month.
31. No.
32. Probably 250.
33. Say 50.
34. 60.
35. 40.
36. 800 including schools.
37. 500. Decreased for the last two years, from various local causes.

38. No.

39. 47 baptisms 11 marriages 25 burials in 1863.

40. 1861 – 13. 1862 – 7. 1863 – none.

41. No.

42. £26 in 1863.

43. Yes.

44. One Independent, one Wesleyan, one Primitive Methodist. One room licensed for Particular Baptists and one for Plymouth Brethren. As to numbers, there are 83 dissenting families, and allowing an average of five to a family it gives 415 dissenters. All together there are in the parish 370 families.

45. Yes.

46. Yes.

47. Both boys and girls at about 10.

48. Yes to some extent.

49. Evening schools have been tried, but without success.

50. It has been done.

51. Lighting the church - £2 10s. For the repairs of St Peter's - £5 4s 2d. National schools - £9 0s 6d. Augmentation of small benefices - £5 6s 1d. National Society - £5 5s 11d. Total £27 6s 8d.

52. [Blank]

Edward Warren

¹ The figures given in VCH III are 1851 – 2129; 1861 – 1903.
² Royal Free.

142. MARLBOROUGH ST PETER   D. Marlborough

1. St Peter Marlborough, a rectory.

2. The Lord Bishop of the diocese.

3. 1552 the last census.

4. Townley Wm Dowding, Nov 25ᵗʰ 1859.

5. Yes.

6. Yes.

7. [Blank]

8. No.

9. No.

10. [Blank]

11. [Blank]

12. [Blank]

13. No.

14. [Blank]

15. Yes.

16. Yes.

17. Yes as far as is customary.

18. Yes. A portion of the fabric has been rebuilt and the whole of the interior

re-pewed under the authority of faculty granted of the bishop of the diocese.

19. [Blank]

20. [Blank]

21. Pew rents £90, Ecclesiastical Commissioners £76, rent of land £20, Tithe £20. The amount of pew rents will be less for the future on account of an increased number of free sittings.

22. [Blank]

23. No.

24. Two full services morning at 11.00am and evening at 6.30pm.

25. Yes.

26. No.

27. No.

28. Morning Prayer on Wednesdays, Fridays and holy days 12-20 present besides school children. Special services in Lent and Advent 100 to 200 persons. Full services twice on Good Friday and Christmas Day, also on the evenings of H Epiphany, Ascension Day, last day of the year.

29. [a] Yes [b] Yes [c] No [d] Yes [e] Yes.

30. Last Sunday of the month.

31. Yes.

32. 160/180.

33. Perhaps 25.

34. 80 to 109.

35. 55.

36. 600, though practically not more than 500 are accommodated owing to the system of pew letting.

37. 450 to 500. As far as regards free sittings the number is increasing.

38. No. Not if all the seats were practically available.

39. 40 baptisms 6 marriages (this small number may have been partly owing to the church having been closed during half the year, during which time marriages were solemnised in the town hall). 20 burials.

40. In 1861- 16, in 1862- 34, in 1863 - 1, - no confirmation at St Peter's.

41. Only with reference to the schools. The particulars of other collections are kept in a book which is subject to the inspection of the churchwardens. This year probably a statement of all collections will be made public, though it has never hitherto been customary to do so.

42. £48 including two special offerings.

43. A regular account kept in a book set apart for that purpose.

44. No dissenting place of worship in the parish except a room used by Plymouth Brethren. Many of the shopkeepers are Independents or Wesleyans.

45. Yes.

46. Yes.

47. From 12 to 14.

48. Yes, in a measure.

49. A flourishing night school conducted chiefly by a layman of the parish.

50. They are copied out and will be sent next week.

51. Lancashire three collections £15 9s 6d. Good Friday for the poor £1 1s 10d. A missionary sermon June 14ᵗʰ £4 10s. Church opening June 25ᵗʰ £105. Thanksgiving sermon Oct 11ᵗʰ £21 8s 4d. Pongas Mission Oct 25ᵗʰ £10. S.P.G. sermon Nov 15ᵗʰ £12 13s 6d. Schools of parish Dec 20ᵗʰ £15. Total £185 3s 2d.

52. The number of public houses as mentioned before and the custom of keeping them open of a Sunday evening. A working man's hall it is hoped may lead to an improvement of the moral and religious habits of the people and counteract in a measure the mischief caused by the public houses.

Townley W Dowding

143. MARTIN   D. Chalke

1. Martin, a perpetual curacy.
2. The Rev William Owen.
3. Population 574.
4. G[eorge] W[arwick] B[ampfylde] Daniell, 1854.
5. Yes.
6. Yes.
7. [Blank]
8. None.
9. No.
10. [Blank]
11. [Blank]
12. [Blank]
13. [Blank]
14. [Blank]
15. Tolerable, yes.
16. No.
17. Negatively so.
18. No.
19. [Blank]
20. [Blank]
21. Tithe £64.
22. [Blank]
23. One.
24. Two full duties, 10.30am and 3.00pm, two sermons preached.
25. [Blank]
26. Not publicly, but I purpose doing so.
27. No.
28. On all the feast days and every day thro' Lent.
29. [a] Yes [b] Yes [c] Yes [d] Yes [e] Yes.
30. On the 1st Sunday of every month.
31. No.
32. 18.
33. All have attended.

34. 18.

35. In winter 10 to 12 in summer about 15.

36. 380.

37. 120 – decreases considerably in winter.

38. No.

39. 3 baptisms 6 marriages 24 burials.

40. 3.

41. The receipts are in my possession.

42. About 36s.

43. No.

44. Two – 200 – Ranters and Independents.

45. There is.

46. No.

47. Between 8 and 10.

48. The girls but not the boys.

49. I had an adult evening school four evenings in the week. Well attended and a good success.

50. Yes.

51. Salisbury Infirmary, the Society for the Propagation of the Gospel in Foreign Parts and the British and Foreign Bible Society.

52. The church being very exposed in winter, there is a great falling off of the congregation to the chapels. Stoves are needed in the church.

G.W.B. Daniell

144. MELKSHAM   D. Potterne

1. Melksham, a vicarage.

2. The Dean and Chapter of Salisbury.

3. 4251.

4. George Hume, instituted and inducted July 1825.

5. Yes.

6. In the glebe house.

7. [Blank]

8. Not any other benefice.

9. He has an assistant curate.

10. In 1857.

11. E[dward] T[homas] W[atson] Thomas, in priest's orders.

12. He has no other duty whatever.

13. It does.

14. The chapelry of Seend – date of consecration uncertain, dedicated to Holy Cross. The chapelry of Erlestoke – the church dedicated to St Mary, date not known.

15. The parish church is in good repair and provided with everything necessary.

16. It is well fenced, and as far as possible, being a thoroughfare, it is well kept.

17. They do.

18. No alteration has taken place.

19. These services are performed in both of the chapels.

20. The distance of Seend is 3½ miles, of Erlestoke, 10 miles.

21. The tithes were commuted at £900 Melksham and £315 Seend.

22. Melksham £900 Seend £315 Erlestoke glebe £50.

23. There is one glebe house only.

24. Services in the mother church are held on Sundays at 10.30am and 6.00pm. At Seend – at the same hours during the summer, during the winter the second service is at 3.00pm. At Erlestoke the times of divine service are 10.30am and 3.00pm. Full service each time throughout the year.

25. Yes.

26. Public catechising is not adopted.

27. There is not daily morning service.

28. On every Wednesday and on the great festivals and fasts of the church. The number attending averages 35 or 40.

29. [a] Yes [b] Yes [c] No [d] Yes [e] Generally.

30. On Good Friday and on the 1st Sunday in every month.

31. I have not done so.

32. Speaking from memory and without having recourse accurate statement of numbers – I should say 100.

33. I am not aware that there has been entire neglect of the Lord's supper on the part of any members.

34. One average may be taken, about 50 or 60.

35. [See Q34]

36. In the parish church about 900 or 950. In Seend Chapel 550. In Erlestoke 300.

37. It is stationary. Including children, about 700 or 750.

38. There is, owing however to the scattered nature of the population, increased church accommodation could only be supplied by means of a schoolhouse, a church or chapel in one of the outlying hamlets.

39. 66 baptisms 9 marriages 59 burials.

40. To the best of my recollection, 33 persons were confirmed in this parish in 1861 – nothing since.

41. The sums collected on behalf of different societies are made public at the annual meetings held in favour of such societies. The sacramental alms are distributed by the clergy and are not made known to the members of the congregation.

42. £28 8s 5d.

43. Yes.

44. There are Baptist, Wesleyan, Independent and Friends places of worship and several offshoots from these. The dissenters probably are a moiety of the population. The hamlets are large and distant and are supplied with dissenting places of worship and they become thus cut off from the church.

45. Yes.

46. I have to some extent.

47. The girls are removed as early as 11, the boys remain to 13.

48. To some extent, not however after 18.

49. Evening schools have been in use in the parish for the last three years during the winter months. There is no lack of attendance on the part of the scholars, the difficulty lies in providing teachers.

50. Yes.

51. Jan 7th Patagonian Mission £2 0s 3d. March 22nd Society for the Promotion of Christianity Amongst the Jews £6 19s 6d. June 21st Church Missionary Society £8 9s 11½d. Aug 23rd Bath United Hospital £9 14s 7½d. Oct 18th for the augmentation of small livings £9 10s. Dec 13th Teach(ing?) Church Mission £9 10s 3½d.

52. [Blank]

I am, my Lord, your Lordship's Obedient Servant, George Hume

145. MERE   D. Wylye

1. Mere, a vicarage.
2. The Bishop of the diocese.
3. 2476.
4. Charles Henry Townsend September 1861.
5. Yes.
6. In a rented house.
7. [Blank]
8. No.
9. Yes.
10. February 21st 1864.
11. Charles Edward Hornby, a deacon.
12. No.
13. No.
14. [Blank]
15. Yes.
16. Yes.
17. Yes.
18. No alteration in the church. In the chancel, six seats which were inconveniently placed, facing the east with their backs to the congregation, have been removed to the south side of the chancel. As far as I remember, the Rural Dean was certified of the fact.
19. [Blank]
20. [Blank]
21. From tithes. The gross amount is £400, the net value (as at present without a house) under £300.
22. [Blank]
23. There is no glebe house. The old vicarage having been sold and the Ecclesiastical Commissioners not having as yet commenced a new one.
24. Sunday duty is Morning Prayer with sermon at 10.30am and Evening Prayer with sermon at 6.00pm.
25. Yes.

26. I have not done so as yet.

27. No, I have not done so as yet, (except during Lent), as I have been single handed.

28. Every Wednesday Morning Prayer at 11.00am. Friday evening there is Evening Prayer with a short sermon at 7.00pm. Morning Prayer on saints' days and holy days; about 50 persons may attend such services.

29. [a] Yes [b] Yes [c] Yes [d] Yes [e] No.

30. On the 1ˢᵗ Sunday in every month.

31. Yes.

32. 82.

33. All of these have communicated during the past year.

34. About 50.

35. About 35.

36. 580.

37. Average number as far as I can learn is between 400 and 500. Sometimes in the evening the church is quite full.

38. I could wish that the church accommodated more; since the church, as restored, in consequence of the removal of several galleries, affords fewer sittings than it did before. This want may be in some measure supplied by increased services. There is only a small chapel of ease in one of the outskirts of the parish, but the living, unless endowed more fully from the rectorial tithes, which I believe will shortly fall into the Commissioners hands, cannot bear any additional expense. Indeed, it is inadequate now to the population; to take one item, the vicar's poor rate is £52 a year.

39. 34 baptisms 11 marriages 25 burials.

40. There has been no confirmation in my time except that which has just taken place, April 4ᵗʰ 1864.

41. I place the amount of each collection on the church door, at the end of the year.

42. Amount of sacramental alms during the year 1863, £15 3s 7¾d.

43. Yes.

44. There is an Independent chapel, a Wesleyan chapel, and a room used by the sect of Plymouth Brethren and a room used by some Quakers. The amount of dissenters of all denominations would be I should suppose 1400 – chiefly Independents.

45. Yes.

46. The schools are under Government but we must simply be losers under the revised code, as we have so few children to present for capitation.

47. They leave mostly between 8 and 10.

48. Yes, we get very fair Sunday schools.

49. We have adult evening schools from November to the end of March – not very successful.

50. No – I will do so.

51. Collections have been made in the church during the past year for the Sunday schools, the day schools, for the Church Missionary Society, for Society for

Promoting Christianity amongst the Jews, for the Society for the Propagation of the Gospel.

52. The overbearing influence of dissent, which has been allowed for many years past to flourish and abound. Most of the people follow the leading Independent dissenter[1], a silk manufacturer, who employs some 500 or 600 hands, and utterly despise the church and her ministrations thus any way to replace the church in her proper position must necessarily be a work of time, and of patient persevering labour.

Charles H Townsend

[1] Charles Jupe

146. MILDENHALL   D. Marlborough

1. Mildenhall, a rectory.
2. Charles Soames Esq, Coles Park, Buntingford.
3. 460.
4. Charles Soames[1], May 1861.
5. Yes.
6. In the glebe house.
7. [Blank]
8. No.
9. No.
10. [Blank]
11. [Blank]
12. [Blank]
13. No.
14. [Blank]
15. Yes.
16. A new fence is in course of erection.
17. Yes.
18. No.
19. [Blank]
20. [Blank]
21. Tithe rent charge £740 and glebe land 150 acres.
22. [Blank]
23. No.
24. Morning and afternoon, 11.00am and 3.00pm, sermon at each.
25. Yes.
26. Yes.
27. No.
28. Good Friday, Ascension Day, Christmas Day, Whit Tuesday and every Wednesday in Lent.
29. [a] Yes [b] Yes [c] No [d] Yes [e] No.
30. Four Sundays in the course of the year.
31. Yes.

32. 65.
33. I cannot say.
34. About 30.
35. About 26.
36. 218.
37. 125.
38. No.
39. 13 baptisms 1 marriage 6 burials.
40. 12.
41. Generally on the Sunday following.
42. £5 10s 9d.
43. Yes.
44. None.
45. Yes.
46. No.
47. Boys 8, girls 12.
48. Yes.
49. Night school for boys with fair success.
50. Yes.
51. Collection for fund for augmenting small livings in the diocese £2 3s 7½d.
52. [Blank]

Charles Soames

¹ Son of the patron

147. MILSTON   D. Amesbury

1. Milston, a rectory.
2. C.E. Rendall Esq, Brigmerston House.
3. About 130.
4. Frederick Adolphus Radcliffe, instituted and inducted January 1863.
5. Yes.
6. Yes.
7. [Blank]
8. No.
9. No.
10. [Blank]
11. [Blank]
12. [Blank]
13. No.
14. [Blank]
15. Yes.
16. Yes.
17. Yes.
18. None during my incumbency.
19. [Blank]

20. [Blank]

21. Land and rent charge £315.

22. [Blank]

23. No.

24. A morning service with sermon at 10.30am. An afternoon service with sermon at 2.30pm.

25. Yes.

26. No.

27. No.

28. Wednesdays and Friday mornings in Lent and Ascension Day. The attendance in Lent generally very small indeed.

29. The Holy Communion is administered at Christmas, Easter and Whitsuntide, once between Christmas and Easter and twice between Whitsuntide and Christmas.

30. [See 29]

31. No. I object to the practice.

32. Between 30 and 40.

33. [Blank]

34. About 25 (exclusive of the eight who have been recently confirmed).

35. [See 34]

36. About 100.

37. In the afternoon the church is often nearly full but the morning attendance is variable.

38. [Blank]

39. 3 baptisms 0 marriages 0 burials.

40. 8.

41. No.

42. The alms at Holy Communion from Easter 1863 to Easter 1864 amount to £4 11s 3½d.

43. Yes.

44. None.

45. Yes.

46. We have not wished for government aid.

47. 9.

48. Yes.

49. Yes.

50. Not yet.

51. For the augmentation of the income of poor benefices.

52. [Blank]

Frederick A Radcliffe

148. MILTON LILBOURNE D. Marlborough

1. Milton Lilbourne, a vicarage.

2. Rev J Henry Gale, Milton nr Pewsey, Wilts.

3. Between 600 and 700.
4. John Henry Gale, June 1846.
5. Yes.
6. At glebe house.
7. Incumbent resident, no curate.
8. None anywhere.
9. Resident and no curate of any kind.
10. [Blank]
11. [Blank]
12. [Blank]
13. One church.
14. Nos. sub (see questions below?)
15. The church is not in good repair by any means, but is duly provided with the things in question.
16. Yes.
17. I hope so.
18. No.
19. No chapel.
20. No chapel.
21. Rent charge, glebe land and augmentation from Queen Anne's Bounty.
22. One parish.
23. One glebe house.
24. Full service at 11.00am. Full service at 3.00pm or else during the summer months at 6.00pm.
25. I have never made any alterations in the service and am not aware that I cut any short.
26. Never.
27. No.
28. Ash Wednesday may be half a dozen or perhaps less, according to circumstances. Good Friday – good attendance. Christmas Day – good attendance.
29. Sacrament of the Lord's Supper administered six times a year. At Christmas, Easter and Whitsuntide and at intervals between each.
30. See 29.
31. No.
32. Various according to circumstances.
33. Cannot say.
34. From 20 to 40.
35. See 34.
36. About 400.
37. Congregations vary according to weather etc. Sometimes the church is pretty full, at others nearly empty.
38. No.
39. 20 baptisms 2 marriages 22 burials.
40. I gave up a list at the last confirmation in '61; I did not keep a copy.
41. All public money accounts under my charge are open for inspection by

anyone interested in them, and regularly kept, I trust.

42. About £5.

43. See Q41.

44. I believe there is one small dissenting chapel in this parish: and <u>as in all country villages,</u> people come to church and go to the chapel and are not very particular respecting the chapel doctrines.

45. Yes.

46. I have not asked for any aid.

47. As soon as they are able to go out to work.

48. Sometimes.

49. There are several private evening schools in the parish during the winter months.

50. Yes.

51. Thank offering for harvest collection £2 2s in aid of the Bath Water Hospital.

52. [Blank]

J Henry Gale

149. MONKTON DEVERILL   D. Wylye

1. Longbridge Deverill vicarage, with Monkton Deverill and Crockerton chapels.

2. Marquis of Bath.

3. Monkton Deverill is 205.

4. William David Morrice, 1852.

5. Yes.

6. No glebe house at Monkton Deverill.

7. [Blank]

8. No.

9. Yes, two.

10. 1859 and 1860.

11. Henry C de St Croix, priest. William Slatter, priest.

12. No.

13. Three.

14. Longbridge Deverill S.S. Peter and Paul, date not known. Crockerton Holy Trinity, 1845. Monkton Deverill, dedication and date not known.

15. Monkton Deverill yes.

16. Yes.

17. Yes.

18. No.

19. At Crockerton, baptisms and burials. At Monkton Deverill, baptisms, marriages and burials.

20. Monkton 3 miles, Crockerton 1½ miles.

21. Vicarial tithe, modus and land in Somerset.

22. Monkton Deverill tithe £60, glebe 0. Longbridge Deverill tithe £158, glebe 9 acres, say £18. The land in Somerset belongs to the benefice as a whole.

23. No.
24. Longbridge Deverill 10.30am and 3.00pm. Monkton Deverill 11.00am and 2.30pm. Crockerton 10.30am and 6.30pm. Sermons at all services.
25. Yes.
26. Yes. Good effect. Christian seasons.
27. Yes.
28. Daily. About eight, besides children, at Longbridge Deverill and Crockerton. Not at Monkton.
29. [a] Yes [b] Yes [c] Yes [d] Yes [e] Yes.
30. Monthly.
31. Yes.
32. Monkton Deverill 16.
33. One.
34. 8 2/3rds.
35. 7 1/9th.
36. Longbridge Deverill 350 (?) Crockerton 450 (?) Monkton Deverill 120 (?).[1]
37. Monkton Deverill say 70.
38. No.
39. 1 baptism 1 marriage 3 burials.
40. 1861 – 6, none in 1862 or 1863.
41. Occasionally.
42. £4 7s 7½d.
43. Yes.
44. Primitive Methodists meet in a room. Most of the lower orders go occasionally, because the preacher is the grocer, and they are all in his debt.
45. Yes.
46. No.
47. Boys 9, girls 12.
48. Girls, yes. Boys, hardly ever.
49. Yes. Considerable.
50. In preparation.
51. Society for Propagation of the Gospel £1 5s 8½d. Poor benefice augmentation fund £1 6s 5d.
52. Dissent.

W.D. Morrice

[1] The question marks are the incumbent's, to indicate his estimation of numbers.

150. MONKTON FARLEIGH   D. Potterne

1. Monkton Farleigh, a rectory.
2. The Lord Bishop of Salisbury.
3. 382.
4. Alfred Earle. Collated March 26th 1863, inducted April 2nd.
5. Yes.
6. The glebe house.

7. [Blank]
8. No.
9. No.
10. [Blank]
11. [Blank]
12. [Blank]
13. No.
14. [Blank]
15. Yes.
16. Yes.
17. Yes.
18. No.
19. [Blank]
20. [Blank]
21. Rent charge £192 and 26 acres of glebe and a payment of £10 from estate.
22. [Blank]
23. No.
24. In the morning at 11.00am and in the afternoon at 3.00pm. Sermons at both services.
25. Yes.
26. I hope to commence next Sunday. My plan will be to prepare my first class in day school and first class in Sunday school during the week and to catechise for 20 minutes before afternoon service as many people are in the habit of coming to service some time before 3. I hope in this way to be able to instruct many.
27. No.
28. Wednesdays and Fridays in Lent and Advent. Every Friday. And all the saints' days and holy days. In Lent the evening service fairly attended by more than a third of the Sunday congregation, a gradual increase in these services during Lent.
29. [a] Yes [b] Yes [c] Yes [d] Yes [e] Yes.
30. Every 1st Sunday in the month.
31. Yes.
32. 71.
33. All have. I have only returned three who to my own knowledge have communicated since my incumbency.
34. 55.
35. 30.
36. 220, including children.
37. In the afternoon the church is full, in the morning ⅔ full. It is not decreasing; I hope the reverse.
38. No.
39. 0 baptisms 1 marriage 6 burials.
40. I have no lists for these years. In 1864 there were 33.
41. Yes.
42. Since my residence, £10 2s 2½d.

43. Yes.
44. None.
45. Yes.
46. No.
47. The boys about 9. As soon as the boys can intimidate a rook they leave. The girls remain till 14 or 15. In a few cases the late lady of the manor Mrs Abbott gave great encouragement to the elder girls.
48. 16 has hitherto been the outside age of Sunday scholars. I hope to amend this.
49. Yes, but not successful. The lads work late and at a distance.
50. Yes.
51. Augmentation of poor benefices £3 17s 8d. S.P.G. Society £6 14s.
52. [Blank]

Alfred Earle

151. NETHERAVON   D. Potterne

1. Netheravon, a vicarage.
2. The Lord Bishop of Salisbury.
3. 547.
4. Francis Jackson Blandy. 1838.
5. Yes.
6. In the glebe house.
7. [Blank]
8. No.
9. Yes.
10. 1856.
11. William Henry Heaven. Priest.
12. No.
13. No.
14. [Blank]
15. Yes, with the exception of the tower, which is about to be repaired.
16. No.
17. Yes.
18. The chancel has been restored by the Ecclesiastical Commissioners.
19. No chapels.
20. [Blank]
21. £131.
22. [Blank]
23. No.
24. Morning Prayer, the litany, ante communion and sermon at 11.00am. Evening Prayer and sermon at 3.00pm.
25. On the days when the Holy Communion is administered, there is no sermon in the morning.
26. No.
27. No.

28. On Wednesdays, Fridays and Holy days there is morning service. On each day in Holy Week, morning and afternoon service. Average attendance of adults about 20.

29. [a] Yes [b] Yes [c] Yes [d] No [e] Yes.

30. On the 1st Sunday in the month except when it immediately precedes or follows one of the great festivals.

31. Yes.

32. 80.

33. None, but about 10 have become communicants since the commencement of this year.

34. 37, but the average is low taking into consideration the small attendance on Ascension Day.

35. About 32.

36. About 200.

37. About 150.

38. No.

39. 19 baptisms 2 marriages 17 burials.

40. 26 males, 14 females, in 1861.

41. Yes.

42. £18 9s 4½d.

43. Yes.

44. Two chapels, Baptists and Primitive Methodists.

45. Yes.

46. No.

47. Boys about 8 to 10, girls 10 to 12.

48. Some of them.

49. Yes. The usual number of night school boys and men is about 30.

50. Yes.

51. For the distress in the north £10 2s 3d. For Salisbury Infirmary £7 1s 3d. For small benefice fund £5 5s 7½d. For S.P.G. £2 19s 8d.

52. [Blank]

F.J. Blandy

152. NEWTON TONY D. Amesbury

1. Newton Tony, a rectory.
2. The President and Fellows of Queens' College Cambridge.
3. 351.
4. John Newton Peill. Instituted June 23rd 1853, inducted July 16th 1853.
5. Yes.
6. Yes.
7. [Blank]
8. Not any.
9. [Blank]
10. [Blank]

11. [Blank]

12. [Blank]

13. Only one church.

14. [Blank]

15. Yes – in good repair and duly provided with all things necessary.

16. Yes.

17. Yes.

18. Not any.

19. [Blank]

20. [Blank]

21. Tithe commutation £441 with about 41 acres of glebe.

22. [Blank]

23. No.

24. Sunday duty – morning at 10.45am and afternoon at 2.45pm except in summer months when it is evening at 6.00pm. Always a sermon or lecture after each.

25. Yes.

26. I do not.

27. I do not.

28. Two services with sermons as on Sundays on Christmas Day and Good Friday. Evening service and a sermon on every Wednesday during Lent. Morning prayers on Ash Wednesday. Morning Prayer and a sermon in the evening on Ascension Day. In the morning services the attendance is very small indeed – perhaps three beyond our own household and the children of the parish school. In the evening the attendance is very good – upwards of 100.

29. [a] Yes [b] Yes [c] No [d] Yes [e] No.

30. About five or six times on the 1st Sunday of the month, so that it be at least once in two months.

31. No I do not – they are all known by me.

32. 37 up to the end of 1863 exclusive of those who have during the present year been confirmed.

33. Not any of them.

34. 31.

35. 26.

36. 234.

37. I do not exactly know, but I think about 150 in the forenoon and 200 in the afternoon or evening. There is no perceptible variation.

38. Not any.

39. 12 baptisms 1 marriage 13 burials.

40. 19.

41. The receipts sent by the respective treasurers are fixed on the notice board in the church porch.

42. £11 9s 8d.

43. There is a regular account kept until the whole has been expended, the balance at the end of each year being spent in coals for the poor.

44. There are no dissenting places of worship and I am not aware of any family

absenting themselves from church through religious scruples.

45. Yes, a parochial school, mixed.

46. No, I have not. There was a building grant.

47. The boys leave or become half-time scholars soon after 7 years of age. The girls leave as soon as they are strong enough to nurse a baby.

48. Yes, if they remain in the parish. The morning Sunday school is well attended by plough boys.

49. The evening school from the middle of October to the commencement of barley sowing is well and regularly attended.

50. The lists were made out on 5th January and I expect the parish churchwarden transmitted them.

51. Church Missionary Society £3 5s 6d. Augmentation of small benefices 19s 3d. The parish schools £3 19s 8d. Total £8 4s 5d.

52. The want of education – very few of the adult population can read the Book of Common Prayer. When a man is married he does not like to attend a night school and one of the best remedies would be an Act of Parliament not allowing children under 12 or 14 years of age to be employed in farm labour.

John Newton Peill

153. NORTH BRADLEY   D. Potterne

1. North Bradley, a vicarage.

2. Winchester College.

3. About 1700.

4. Harry Lee, 1828.

5. [Blank]

6. In the vicarage house.

7. The curate's name is Geoffrey Samuels and he is resident.

8. None other.

9. Mr Samuels is assistant curate.

10. 30th January 1862.

11. Geoffrey Samuels.

12. None other and nowhere.

13. There is a chapel which takes about 4 or 500 population.

14. It is a district chapel by name Christ Church Road.

15. Perfectly – in every respect.

16. It is not well fenced.

17. They do not.

18. The church and chancel have been rebuilt.

19. They are.

20. About 3 miles.

21. Tithe rent charge about £640 per annum.

22. It is one parish, but three districts.

23. Only one at N Bradley near the church.

24. Two full services on Sunday at each church and chapel.

25. Certainly.
26. We do not.
27. We do not.
28. At all the chief festivals. Very few attend except on Good Friday.
29. [a] Yes [b] Yes [c] Yes [d] Yes [e] No.
30. Every 1st Sunday in the month.
31. Not regularly.
32. About 30 to 40.
33. I cannot say exactly.
34. About 25 to 30.
35. About 20.
36. 300.
37. 150.
38. Increasing.
39. 20 baptisms 10 marriages 9 burials.
40. [Blank]
41. I do not, as it chiefly comes from myself.
42. [Blank]
43. My curate kept an account and delivered it to me. I leave the whole of it to his disposal.
44. [Blank]
45. There is.
46. I have not.
47. About 10.
48. Yes – to a great degree.
49. I have not, having tried it in vain.
50. [Blank]
51. My curate having just left without giving me any information on this and some of the above points, while I was absent for a month or two, I cannot give the information required accurately.
52. Want of co-operation by one of the churchwardens and the fear of offending dissenters by both of them. Since writing some of these answers which I deferred till I could go back to my living, having been absent through illness this year. My curate has left very unceremoniously.

Harry Lee

154. NORTH NEWNTON   D. Avebury

1. North Newnton, a vicarage.
2. Rev S Stockwell, Wylye rectory, Heytesbury.
3. About 360.
4. A W Radcliffe, April 18th 1843. Inducted May 6th 1843.
5. Yes.
6. Within the limits of his benefice in a rented cottage.
7. [Blank]

8. No.
9. No.
10. [Blank]
11. [Blank]
12. [Blank]
13. One church and one licensed school house.
14. St James.
15. Yes.
16. Yes.
17. Yes.
18. Yes, the church has been restored and chancel also – and a faculty granted for the same.
19. All performed at the parish church.
20. [Blank]
21. Tithe rent charge £76 per annum.
22. [Blank]
23. [Blank]
24. One full service at the parish church at 11.00am and one at the licensed school house at 3.00pm, according to the time of year.
25. Yes.
26. No.
27. No.
28. Ash Wednesday, Good Friday, Ascension Day, Christmas Day. About 50 persons attend.
29. [a] Yes [b] Yes [c] No [d] Yes [e] No.
30. Four other times besides as the church was under repair.
31. [Blank]
32. About 19 or 20.
33. None.
34. The usual average.
35. 10 or 12.
36. About 150.
37. About 100 – much as before.
38. No.
39. 15 baptisms 3 marriages 3 burials.
40. In the year 1861 five persons.
41. The receipt of the amounts received are placed on the church door.
42. The whole year £2 17s 6½d.
43. Yes for our private use.
44. One, Primitive Methodist. About 40.
45. Yes.
46. No.
47. From 10 to 12.
48. Sometimes.
49. Yes, by a night school for boys which only lasted a few weeks.

50. Yes.
51. £2 (?) collected for the S P G Society.
52. The over indulgence of parents in allowing the young people to do as they like after the age of 12.

Alston William Radcliffe

155. NORTH TIDWORTH   D. Amesbury
1. Holy Trinity, North Tidworth. A rectory.
2. The Crown.
3. 350 souls.
4. James Francis Turner. February 1859.
5. He has.
6. He has resided in the glebe house.
7. [Blank]
8. [Blank]
9. [Blank]
10. [Blank]
11. [Blank]
12. [Blank]
13. [Blank]
14. [Blank]
15. It is in average condition.
16. It is fenced and steps are being taken to improve its condition.
17. They do.
18. None.
19. [Blank]
20. [Blank]
21. Tithe rent charge £320 and glebe lands 15 acres £15.
22. [Blank]
23. There is but one house on the glebe.
24. From Advent to Holy Trinity Sunday, morning with sermon. Afternoon without. Evensong with lecture. From Holy Trinity Sunday to Advent, M S [morning service] and afternoon with sermons.
25. I do.
26. I have done so, but the very early age at which most children are removed from the teaching I found to be a most powerful hindrance to the reality of the thing.
27. Daily Morning Prayer.
28. All Holy Days. Scarcely more than two or three attend beyond my own household and the choir.
29. [a] Yes [b] Yes [c] Yes [d] Yes [e] Yes.
30. At intervals averaging six weeks.
31. I know them all.
32. 36.

33. 24 on an average.
34. About 30.
35. [Blank]
36. 100, not including children.
37. It scarcely fluctuates perceptibly.
38. [Blank]
39. 10 baptisms 0 marriages 6 burials.
40. In 1863 − 9.
41. Such a statement has been provided by me to the churchwardens with a view to publicity but it has not been returned to me yet.
42. £16 4s.
43. I keep the account in my private diary.
44. No meeting house. There are three dissenting families. Two are Methodists and, I believe, Anabaptists.
45. There is.
46. No. We are amply endowed and under terms which the present educational board of the Privy Council would not accept, viz: the church's catechism to be taught to all.
47. Boys at about 8-10, girls at 10-13.
48. Some, all the better disposed.
49. We have a night school both for males and females and the success is unquestionably good.
50. I have not.
51. Small benefices fund. Lancashire fund.
52. [Blank]

James Francis Turner

156. NORTON BAVANT   D. Wylye

1. Norton Bavant, a vicarage.
2. The Lord Chancellor, Hyde Park Gardens, London.
3. 261, of whom about 60 live some miles away from the church in isolated bits of Norton previously in other parishes.
4. Edward Eliot, instituted January 29th 1864, inducted February 1st 1864.
5. [Blank]
6. Yes, since he has been vicar, he has resided in the glebe house.
7. [Blank]
8. No.
9. No.
10. [Blank]
11. [Blank]
12. [Blank]
13. No.
14. [Blank]
15. Yes.

16. Yes.

17. Yes.

18. Not to my knowledge – except that a stained window has been put in by the parish and neighbourhood to the memory of my father who was formerly vicar of Norton Bavant.

19. [Blank]

20. [Blank]

21. Rent charge in lieu of tithes £138 per annum. Glebe about 40 acres let for £90 per annum. Chancery dividend £8 per annum. Total £236.

22. [Blank]

23. No.

24. Morning service with sermon at 10.30am. Afternoon service with sermon at 3.00pm.

25. Yes.

26. No.

27. I consider myself as reasonably hindered every morning and evening.

28. Every saints' day and Holy Day and every Wednesday in Lent. Hardly anyone attends except those over whom I have control such as schoolchildren or my own family.

29. [a] Yes [b] Yes [c] No [d] and [e] one or the other.

30. The 1st Sunday in every month.

31. Yes.

32. I can hardly tell – since I have been here 23 have communicated.

33. [Blank]

34. I cannot tell – 18 communicated on Easter Day.

35. About 12.

36. 250.

37. About 45 in the morning and about 55 in the afternoon not counting the children. The number of my congregation decidedly increases, but I have been here so short a time that possibly the increase will not be permanent but only arises from the novelty of a newly appointed vicar.

38. No.

39. 11 baptisms 2 marriages 3 burials.

40. I have no means of ascertaining. 13 persons from my parish were confirmed on March 7th 1864.

41. I make public the amount of collections. The churchwardens or others know that they may at any time see the statement of the offerings and the way they are expended.

42. £1 3s 4½d since I have been here.

43. Yes.

44. No dissenting place of worship. About 12 or 14 regular dissenters of whom one is a Plymouth Brother the rest Wesleyans.

45. Yes.

46. No.

47. Boys about 9, girls about 12.

48. I have been so short a time vicar of Norton Bavant that I cannot answer these questions. I presume that the gentleman who was <u>resident</u> curate here early in January last, duly transmitted copies of the parish register but I do not know that he did.

49. [See question 48]

50. [See question 48]

51. [See question 48]

52. [See question 48]

Edward Eliot

157. NUNTON   D. Wilton

1. Nunton.

2. See Downton.

3. 300.

4. Richard Payne.

5. At Downton.

6. At Downton.

7. Felix Buckley, living at Nunton.

8. [Blank]

9. [Blank]

10. [Blank]

11. [Blank]

12. [Blank]

13. [Blank]

14. [Blank]

15. Yes.

16. Yes.

17. Yes.

18. No.

19. [Blank]

20. [Blank]

21. See Downton.

22. See Downton.

23. Glebe house at Downton and a cottage unsuitable for residence at Nunton.

24. Two services at 11.00am and 3.30pm. During summer months an evening service at 6.00pm. Sermons at each service.

25. Yes.

26. No.

27. Morning Prayer on Friday.

28. Christmas Day, Good Friday and Ascension Day. Average attendance on such days from 20 to 25.

29. [a] Yes [b] Yes [c] Yes [d] Yes [e] No.

30. 1st Sunday in the month.

31. Yes.

32. 50.
33. None to my knowledge, but the list has only been kept since May 1863.
34. 25.
35. 20.
36. 220.
37. 100.
38. No.
39. 16 baptisms 2 marriages 4 burials.
40. In 1861 – 14; in 1862 – 2; in 1863 – 14.
41. No.
42. £8 from May 1863 to December 31st.
43. Yes.
44. One Baptist meeting house. From 20 to 40 of the above denomination.
45. Yes.
46. Yes.
47. 10 years old.
48. Yes.
49. Evening school during the winter, attendance not good.
50. Yes.
51. Diocesan fund for augmenting small benefices £5 17s.
52. [Blank]

Felix J. Buckley

158. ODSTOCK   D. Chalke

1. Odstock, a rectory.
2. Earl of Radnor, Coleshill, Berkshire.
3. About 180.
4. Charles Grove, 1817.
5. He has been resident the 275 days.
6. He has resided in the glebe house.
7. He is resident.
8. He does not.
9. He has no assistant curate.
10. [Blank]
11. [Blank]
12. [Blank]
13. It does not.
14. [Blank]
15. The church is in good order and has all things necessary for divine service.
16. The churchyard is well fenced and well kept.
17. They do.
18. No alterations have been made.
19. There is no chapel.
20. No chapel.

21. From land.

22. The benefice is not composed of any more parishes or chapelries.

23. There is only one glebe house on the benefice.

24. There are two duties performed every Sunday and a sermon alternate morning and afternoon.

25. I make no omissions.

26. I do not.

27. I do not, the parish is so small and consists of agricultural labourers who go out daily to work in the fields.

28. Ash Wednesday, Good Friday and Christmas Day. The numbers vary.

29. The Holy Communion is administered on Christmas Day, Easter Day, Whit Sunday and at Michaelmas.

30. None.

31. I do.

32. On an average 25.

33. Very few.

34. Already mentioned above.

35. Already mentioned above.

36. For about 100.

37. 80. I cannot say; sometimes the congregation is larger than at other times.

38. There is no further want of accommodation.

39. 3 baptisms 3 marriages 2 burials.

40. 4 in 1861, 3 in 1862, 3 in 1863.

41. No, but I distribute them to the sick and needy.

42. About 15s at each Holy Communion.

43. There is no book.

44. There is no dissenting chapel in the parish. There are a few Primitive Brethren and a few Roman Catholics.

45. There is.

46. I have not.

47. About 10 or 11 years of age.

48. Till they are confirmed.

49. I have not, as I have no funds or means of doing it.

50. I have.

51. Collections amounting to £7 were made for the distress of operatives in the North of England and a collection of £1 10s for the augmentation of small livings.

52. I cannot.

Charles Grove

159. OGBOURNE ST ANDREW D. Marlborough

1. The Vicarage of Ogbourne St Andrew.

2. The Dean and Canons of Windsor.

3. 518 last census.

4. George Stephen Hookey. 1858.
5. Yes.
6. Yes.
7. [Blank]
8. No.
9. No.
10. [Blank]
11. [Blank]
12. [Blank]
13. No.
14. [Blank]
15. Yes.
16. Yes.
17. Yes.
18. No.
19. [Blank]
20. [Blank]
21. Tithe commuted at £180 per annum and £20 endowment.
22. [Blank]
23. No.
24. Morning at 11.00am and Evening at 3.00pm. Sermons at each service.
25. Yes.
26. No, but every Sunday in the school.
27. No.
28. Wednesdays and Fridays during Lent. Every day in Passion Week. Ascension Day and Christmas Day. Except on Christmas Day, 30 or 40 besides the school children, and members of my own family.
29. [a] Yes [b] Yes [c] No [d] Yes [e] No.
30. On the last Sunday in the month.
31. I can recollect them all.
32. About 15.
33. They all more or less regularly communicate.
34. From 10 to 12.
35. From 8 to 10.
36. 150.
37. About 50 more or less. Increasing rather than decreasing.
38. A church is most needed at Rockley, 117 population, besides outlying cottages, 2 and 3 miles from the parish church.
39. 23 Baptisms 2 Marriages 15 Burials.
40. 11.
41. Yes.
42. £4 5s 2d.
43. Yes.
44. There is a Baptist chapel, and a room used by Primitive Methodists. Some few have been re-baptised as Baptists, but the majority say 'they are not particular

where they go', i.e. they go <u>regularly </u>no where.

45. Yes.

46. No.

47. At about 8 years.

48. Sometimes for a short, but a very short period, and that most irregularly.

49. I have wished to have an evening school, have proposed it again and again, but none will take advantage of it.

50. Yes.

51. S.P.G. £4 2s 11d. Augmentation of small benefices £1 0s 10d.

52. <u>Extreme ignorance and indifference</u> with reference to religious duties. The bulk of the lower classes go to <u>no place of worship at all.</u> The chapels are as badly, and irregularly attended as the church. The consequence is, immediately the children leave the day and Sunday schools, they soon forget all they have been taught, and when after a lapse of years, they offer themselves for confirmation, their ignorance is so great of everything bearing on that ordinance, that certificates of preparation must be refused to many of them.

George Stephen Hookey

160. OGBOURNE ST GEORGE   D. Marlborough

1. Ogbourne St George, a vicarage.

2. The Dean and Canons of Windsor.

3. 534.

4. Rev. B[enjamin] Pope, about the year 1826.

5. Non resident.

6. [Blank]

7. Robert Hinckesman[1]. Yes.

8. Nether Stowey in the Diocese of Bath and Wells.

9. [Blank]

10. [Blank]

11. [Blank]

12. [Blank]

13. No.

14. [Blank]

15. No. The church is in a most dilapidated state.

16. Yes.

17. Yes.

18. No.

19. [Blank]

20. [Blank]

21. From tithe. Gross income £260 net £230.

22. [Blank]

23. No.

24. Two Sunday services at 11.00am and 3.00pm and a sermon after each.

25. Yes.

26. No.

27. No.

28. Christmas Day and Good Friday, and one full service in the week during Lent.

29. [a] Yes [b] Yes [c] No [d] Yes [e] Yes.

30. 1st Sunday in every month.

31. A list of the number.

32. About 40.

33. I cannot say.

34. I do not know. Having held the curacy from the 14th day of last October.

35. [Blank]

36. About 210.

37. From 80 to 100. Increasing.

38. [Blank]

39. 15 Baptisms 5 Marriages 11 Burials.

40. [Blank]

41. Yes.

42. I believe about £6 a year.

43. Yes.

44. Three dissenting chapels. About 300. Primitive Methodists, Baptists and Wesleyans.

45. Yes.

46. The school is maintained by subscription and children's pence.

47. From 7 to 9 years the boys, from 10 to 12 the girls.

48. Yes.

49. I believe a night school has been tried but without success.

50. Yes.

51. For the Society for the Propagation of the Gospel £1 6s. For the aid of small benefices £1 11s 6d.

52. I believe that the damp and dilapidated state of the church hinders many from attending. Yes, the restoration of the church.

R. Hinckesman

[1] Nephew of the incumbent.

161. ORCHESTON ST GEORGE   D. Wylye

1. Orcheston St George, a rectory.

2. Wadham College Oxford.

3. 236 in 1861.

4. Gorges Paulin Lowther, 1830.

5. Yes.

6. Yes.

7. [Blank]

8. Yes – Diocese of Lichfield.

9. No.

10. [Blank]
11. [Blank]
12. [Blank]
13. No.
14. [Blank]
15. Yes.
16. Yes.
17. Yes.
18. No.
19. [Blank]
20. [Blank]
21. Rent charge and 47 acres of glebe.
22. The benefice of Orcheston St George is composed of two tythings constituting one parish.
23. Only one.
24. Two full services on Sundays at 11.00am and 6.00pm.
25. Always.
26. I devote two hours commencing at 2.00pm to catechising in my schoolroom, which I think more beneficial than catechising in church.
27. I do not.
28. On Christmas Day and Ascension Day. On Wednesdays and Fridays during Lent, and every day in the Holy Week.
29. [a] Yes [b] Yes [c] No [d] Yes [e] No.
30. On the Sunday nearest to Michaelmas Day.
31. Yes.
32. If the number of those who have ever communicated is asked for, I should state it at about 80.
33. Quite 80 have attended the Holy Communion. There were 58 present on Easter Day, and at least ten more who were lawfully hindered.
34. From 50 to 60.
35. At the Michaelmas Communion about 50.
36. About 130 exclusive of children who sit when we can place benches for them – chiefly in the chancel – they exceed 40 in number.
37. The congregation remains steady in number and attachment to the church. In the morning it is well attended by men chiefly, and in the evening it is inconveniently crowded.
38. I daresay any successor will say so. I prefer hearing it said 'if you are not early there will be no room for you'.
39. [Baptism figure not entered] 2 marriages 3 burials.[1] These two marriages are quite exceptional, none of the parties being more than sojourners in Orcheston St George.
40. I suppose this question has reference to Triennial confirmations. There were no confirmations for this parish in 1862 or 1863. [The following has been added at the bottom of the page]. In 1861 there were 17 confirmed, viz nine males and eight females. In 1864 there were only seven, all females, but five of my

confirmation class went into domestic service after the commencement of the year – two were confirmed as belonging to Maddington, and three others in different villages in the Archdeaconry of Sarum. Three young men or great lads, have been confirmed at their respective schools – Marlborough, Heytesbury and Hereford. If the catechumans which have been confirmed at the late confirmations had been confirmed at home, my number would have been 12 females and three males, keeping up my average of 7% for the last 32 years.

41. I keep an account of the distributions of the alms offered at Holy Communion, but do not make any public statement.

42. About four pounds in the year.

43. My own private memorandum.

44. No conventicle – or Beer Shop – in Orcheston St George – and two dissenters.

45. Yes.

46. No.

47. The boys come to school on Sunday till 13 or 14 and the girls stay till they go to service at 18 and 19 years of age.

48. The day school numbers about 28, but at least half of them are babies who I do not allow to come to church amongst the Sunday school which numbers always exceeding 40.

49. I have always a standing confirmation class.

50. No – but I shall before the statutable time for delivery arrives.

51. S.P.G., Lancashire claims, some local matters.

52. I have every encouragement and no impediment whatever! I feel constrained to make this awful admission.

G.P. Lowther

¹There were 6 baptisms in 1863.

162. ORCHESTON ST MARY   D. Wylye

1. Orcheston St Mary, a rectory.
2. Clare College Cambridge.
3. 155.
4. Rev John Wardale, instituted 1852.
5. Yes.
6. In the glebe house.
7. [Blank]
8. No.
9. No.
10. [Blank]
11. [Blank]
12. [Blank]
13. No.
14. [Blank]
15. Yes.

16. Yes.

17. Yes.

18. Two stained glass windows and also communion rails.

19. [Blank]

20. [Blank]

21. Tithe rent charge and glebe, value £30 per annum.

22. [Blank]

23. No.

24. [Blank]

25. Yes.

26. No.

27. No.

28. Christmas Day and Good Friday two full services. Evening service on Ascension Day and on every Wednesday and Friday in Lent. Attendance good on Christmas Day and early in Lent, but falls off towards the end.

29. [a] Yes [b] Yes [c] No [d] and [e] one or the other.

30. Quinquagesima Sunday, 8th after Trinity, 16th after Trinity and Advent.

31. Yes.

32. 65 who have been confirmed and attend church. 45 who have communicated at some time or other.

33. All of these except four have communicated at least once during 1863 of which (four) two are invalids.

34. At Easter 28, at other seasons 20 to 25.

35. [See 34]

36. 100.

37. 50 to 60 including school children. It is, I think, stationary.

38. No.

39. 4 baptisms 1 marriage 1 burial.

40. In 1861 − 8, in 1863 − 2.

41. Yes.

42. £3 in 1863.

43. Yes.

44. There are no dissenting places of worship. Baptists 32, Wesleyans four.

45. Yes.

46. No.

47. Girls at 12 or 13. Boys at 8 or 9.

48. Yes.

49. Yes: I have an evening school four times a week in winter. Average attendance about 10.

50. Not yet.

51. Salisbury Infirmary. National Society.

52. [Blank]

John Wardale

163. OVERTON cum FYFIELD   D. Avebury

1. Overton cum Fyfield with Alton Priors. The benefice is a vicarage.
2. His Grace the Duke of Marlborough is the present patron. The Palace, Blenheim.
3. Overton 790. Fyfield 150.
4. William John Browne Angell. 22nd December 1848.
5. Yes.
6. Yes.
7. [Blank]
8. No.
9. Yes.
10. 14th November 1862.
11. Revd Henry Williams, a priest.
12. No.
13. There are three churches.
14. Overton, Fyfield and Alton Priors. Dates of consecration not known.
15. Fyfield church is in good repair, also Alton Priors. Overton is very bad.
16. Yes.
17. Yes.
18. No.
19. Yes.
20. Fyfield is 1 mile from Overton, Alton Priors is 4 miles.
21. I receive £300 per annum (minus income tax) from the Duke of Marlborough.
22. I am unable to answer this question.
23. No.
24. There is one full service with sermon at 11.00am and at 3.00pm on alternate Sundays at Overton and Fyfield.
25. Yes.
26. No.
27. No.
28. There are morning prayers on Wednesdays and Fridays during Lent, and daily in Passion Week, and on Easter Monday and Tuesday.
29. [a] Yes [b] Yes [c] No [d] Yes [e] Yes.
30. On the 1st Sunday in each month.
31. Yes.
32. About 12.
33. Not one.
34. About the same number.
35. [Blank]
36. Overton 300 Fyfield 200.
37. A fair average but the congregation has decreased during the last 12 months.
38. No.
39. Overton − 15 baptisms 6 marriages 12 burials. At Fyfield − 9 baptisms 1 marriage 3 burials.
40. [Blank]

41. No, excepting through the churchwardens.

42. I have not received the account from my curate.

43. Yes.

44. A room at Fyfield is rented by the dissenters. Meetings are also held at some of the cottages called chapels.

45. Yes. There is a dame school at Overton and a room given by the Duke of Marlborough at Lockeridge where a school is kept. There is no schoolmistress at present.

46. [Blank]

47. About 10 years old.

48. A fair proportion.

49. There is a night school at Lockeridge held in the room above mentioned, which is fairly attended. Also, an evening school for the boys employed at the training stables at Fyfield.

50. Yes.

51. Two sermons were preached for the S.P.G. Society and collections made at Overton and Fyfield churches amounting to £3 5s.

52. [Blank]

W J B Angell

164. PATNEY   D. Potterne

1. Patney, a rectory.

2. The Lord Bishop of Winchester, Farnham Castle, Surrey.

3. 154.

4. Charles Maunoir McNiven, Oct 1848.

5. Yes.

6. Yes.

7. [Blank]

8. No.

9. No.

10. [Blank]

11. [Blank]

12. [Blank]

13. No.

14. [Blank]

15. Yes.

16. Yes.

17. Yes.

18. No.

19. [Blank]

20. [Blank]

21. The benefice is endowed with land in value £250 per annum.

22. [Blank]

23. No.

24. Two full services morning and afternoon at 10.30am and at 3.00pm respectively.
25. Yes.
26. No.
27. No.
28. Christmas Day, Ash Wednesday and Good Friday. More attend on Good Friday than on Christmas Day, and a very small number on Ash Wednesday.
29. The Holy Communion is administered on the first Sunday after Christmas Day, on Easter Day and on Whit Sunday and on no other day.
30. [See Q.29]
31. [Blank]
32. 13.
33. 4.
34. 8.
35. [Blank]
36. 150.
37. 30 in the morning, 45 in the afternoon.
38. No.
39. 7 baptisms 6 marriages 1 burial.
40. 10.
41. The collections are sometimes made public but not the alms at the Holy Communion.
42. [Blank]
43. [Blank]
44. None.
45. Yes.
46. [Blank]
47. The girls at about 11 or 12 years of age, the boys earlier.
48. Yes.
49. Yes. The evening school in winter was attended by 12 boys and 14 girls.
50. [Blank]
51. A collection was made on behalf of the Society for Propagation of the Gospel in Foreign Parts. Amount 17s 6d.
52. [Blank]

C.M. McNiven

165. PERTWOOD D. Wylye

1. Pertwood, a rectory.
2. Mrs Seymour, Knoyle House, near Hindon.
3. At present only 28, one cottage being empty.
4. William Reece, instituted June 26th 1863, inducted November 18th 1863.
5. He has.
6. The glebe house being now merely a labourer's cottage, he has resided at Chicklade, an adjoining parish.
7. [Blank]

8. He does not.
9. He has not.
10. [Blank]
11. [Blank]
12. [Blank]
13. It comprises only one church.
14. [Blank]
15. It is in good repair and all things duly provided, except that the bell being too large for the belfry is inside the nave, it is however soon to be placed outside.
16. The churchyard is well kept, but the fence needs repairing.
17. There is only one churchwarden, and he discharges his duties regularly.
18. No alteration has been made to my knowledge.
19. [Blank]
20. [Blank]
21. The endowment is derived from tithe, the gross value of which is £80; and there is £6 10s from Queen Anne's Bounty, making altogether £86 10s per annum (gross).
22. [Blank]
23. There is only one cottage which is said to have been the glebe house.
24. Since my institution I have had the services alternately morning and afternoon, as they were previously. The morning service at 11.00am on one Sunday, and the afternoon at 3.00pm the following Sunday. A sermon is preached at every service.
25. I do.
26. I do not catechise in the church.
27. I do not say daily the morning and evening prayers, for the whole of the small population is employed in agriculture.
28. Since my institution I have had services in the church on Christmas Day and Good Friday. The average number is 14 from my own parish, and nearly twice that number from an adjoining parish, Brixton Deverill.
29. It is administered in the church at Christmas, Easter and Whitsuntide, although not always on the very day of the festival.
30. It is administered at no other times in the church. The number of communicants, thus far, being very small, but it is more frequently administered at the house of the farmer, whose daughter is a great invalid and unable to attend church.
31. I do.
32. So far, there have been only four regular communicants.
33. Three of these have communicated regularly, the fourth being able only to receive the Holy Communion at home.
34. The average has been five.
35. The same number.
36. There is accommodation for 50 (about).
37. The average number is I believe 40. It has much increased of late.
38. There is not.
39. 1 baptism 0 marriages 1 burial.

40. I cannot learn that one was confirmed in any of those three years.

41. I have not done so hitherto, because it has not occurred to me.

42. The amount since Easter 1863 has been 13s.

43. There is.

44. There is no dissenting place of worship and all but two, I think, attend church. We have one Roman Catholic.

45. There is not.

46. I have not, there being only four children who can attend school daily. I have made arrangements for their attending school at Chicklade, which is not far distant.

47. I do not yet know, but suppose about the age of 10.

48. I believe not in time past.

49. I have not yet been able to do so at Pertwood, but hope to find some means of instruction for them.

50. I am about to do so.

51. A sermon was preached on August 2nd 1863 for the Irish Church Missions and 17s 7½d was collected. On November 29th 1863 a sermon on behalf of the fund for augmentation of small livings in this diocese, collection 6s 8d.

52. I am not aware of anything particular.

On the subject of the 28th question I wish just to add that, as the whole of the people at Pertwood are employed by the farmer, I have not thus far found it practicable to have a service in the church on any other days besides Sundays, Good Friday and Christmas Day. I am hoping, however, to succeed in inducing him to give them time to attend an afternoon service on Holy Thursday, and on Ash Wednesday (DV) of next year.

On the 37th question, the morning congregation is sometimes only five and seldom more than ten. Afternoon service being preferred by the people and the church is then often quite full.

William Reece

166. PEWSEY   D. Marlborough

1. Pewsey, St John the Baptist, a rectory.
2. The Earl of Radnor, Coleshill.
3. 2200.
4. Thomas F T Ravenshaw, 1857.
5. Yes.
6. Yes.
7. [Blank]
8. No.
9. Yes.
10. Not licensed at present, March 1864.
11. Algernon Cassan, a priest.
12. No.
13. [Blank]

14. Mortuary chapel, All Saints, Sept 1863.

15. The church is in good repair (with the exception of the roof) and is provided with the necessaries for divine service.

16. The fence is good. It is not tidily kept.

17. As far as they understand them, yes.

18. The chancel was rebuilt (except E and part of the N wall) and a south aisle added in 1861. Fitted with stalls etc for performance of divine service. Organ moved in to S aisle. Faculty. Reopened by bishop of Sarum Dec 11th 1861.

19. Burials are performed in the chapel of All Saints.

20. Half a mile.

21. Tithe rent charge £1011. 25 acres of glebe.

22. [Blank]

23. No.

24. 11.00am, 3.00pm and 6.30pm in winter. 11.00am and 6.30pm in summer. Sermon at each <u>except</u> when celebration. In summer, Evening Prayer and baptisms on the 1st Sunday in each month at 3.00pm.

25. Yes.

26. No.

27. No. I should like it personally if there were any chance of a congregation or if I had a regular choir, but even in Lent and Advent there is frequently no one at all.

28. Daily mornings in Lent and Advent. Thursday evening with sermon – this service is fairly attended. Holy Days, Wednesdays and Fridays the rest of the year. Very few. Eight is a good congregation. (This of course does not include the choir who attend on these days).

29. Yes. Ascension Day and Trinity Sunday were added in 1858.

30. 1st Sunday in each month.

31. Yes.

32. 80.

33. 6.

34. In 1863 [the figures were] Easter 46, Ascension 16, Whit Sunday 31, Trinity 21, Christmas 43.

35. Average 27.

36. The parish church would hold about 450, the mortuary chapel 40.

37. I have no means of ascertaining. Increased considerably since 1857 and certainly not decreasing now.

38. I consider that if the seats were free and not appropriated there would be room for as many as would be likely to attend at one service. As it is, the poor are almost excluded from this parish church.

39. 66 baptisms 12 marriages 42 burials.

40. 58 were confirmed in 1861, 13 of whom belonged to Manningford Bruce.

41. A statement is placed on the church door each year in January.

42. £30 0s 8½d.

43. Yes.

44. Baptist and Wesleyan chapels and a Ranters' meeting in a cottage. Perhaps a

¼ of the population. The poor and small tradesfolk are very generally dissenters. 'Particular Baptists' are most numerous.

45. Yes. A new room with master's house was built in 1862. The old room is now used as an infants' school.

46. Yes. We shall suffer considerably under the Revised Code and new byelaws. The present educational staff will have to be reduced, there being no available funds to supply the reductions made by the Committee of Council on Education.

47. 10, frequently earlier. A few, above the labouring class, stay on longer.

48. We are generally able to retain the children of church folk for a couple more years.

49. We had a night school up to the end of the winter of 1861-2, but it was so badly attended that we have not resumed it during the last two winters.

50. Yes.

51. Expenses of evening service £6 9s 1½d. Additional Curates Society £6. S.P.G. £6 8s 10¾d. Augmentation of benefices £6 6s 8d.

52. I consider the mode in which whole pues are appropriated to individuals irrespective of the number in their families, thereby rendering unavailable half the accommodation the church would afford, to be a great hindrance to one's ministry among the poor, who will not, as a rule (especially women) sit in the dark galleries which are the only free seats. It also renders an increase of services useless, as the quasi 'owners' of the pues will not allow them to be occupied in their absence. On Sunday evenings 5 or 6 pues immediately in front of the pulpit are often quite empty, while the west end of the church is inconveniently crowded. I see no prospect of any change in this respect. 'It has always been so' and the wealthy farmers are not disposed to waive their (imaginary) rights for the convenience of their less prosperous brethren. A second church has been sometimes talked of, but I should not be inclined to comment to the erection of one while the accommodation of the parish church is misappropriated.

T F Ravenshaw

167. PITTON   D. Amesbury

1. Pitton. A chapelry of the parish of Alderbury forming with Farley a separate parish for civil purposes.

2. The Lord Bishop of Salisbury.

3. 396.

4. The Revd Newton Smart. Prebendary and Rural Dean. 1843.

5. Yes.

6. In the glebe house at Alderbury.

7. [Blank]

8. No.

9. Yes.

10. September 1863.

11. Henry Barton. A deacon. (Revd J. Farnham Messenger, the resident curate of Farley is also senior curate of Pitton).

12. No.

13. Yes.

14. Alderbury church. Consecrated 1858. Dedicated by the name of St Mary. Pitton chapel. St Peter. Farley chapel – [blank]

15. Yes.

16. Yes.

17. Yes.

18. No.

19. Yes.

20. Pitton chapel is about 4½ miles from the mother church.

21. Tithe rent charge, reserved rents, glebe, Queen Anne's Bounty, Ecclesiastical Commissioners £367 4s 8d.

22. From Alderbury £216 10s. From Pitton & Farley £22 18s. Conjointly £27 16s 8d.

23. No.

24. Two full services with sermons. Morning service at 10.30 am. Afternoon service in winter at 2.30pm. Evening service in summer at 6.30pm.

25. Yes.

26. No.

27. No.

28. Evening services with sermon on all festivals and on the Wednesday in Advent and Lent. Two full services on Christmas Day and Good Friday. About 45 at the evening services.

29. [a]As a rule yes: none last year a deacon being in charge and the senior curate having H.C. at Farley. [b] Yes [c] No [d] Yes [e] Yes.

30. On the 3rd Sunday in each month.

31. Yes.

32. 70.

33. I am unable to answer this question: there having been no curate resident in Pitton during six months of last year and no record of names has been kept by the officiating minister.

34. 40.

35. 35.

36. About 250.

37. About 100 in the morning and 135 in the afternoon. Increasing since a curate became again resident in the parish.

38. No.

39. 6 baptisms 4 marriages 6 burials.

40. In 1861 – 10. None in 1862 and 1863.

41. It is proposed to do so in future.

42. I am unable to answer this question: probably about £6.

43. Yes.

44. A large Wesleyan chapel. About 100 are united members.

45. Yes.

46. Yes.

47. The girls about 12 or 13. The boys leave much younger, most of them being sent to Farley school to be under a master.

48. Yes to a considerable extent.

49. A night school was open during four months last winter, two nights a week, and was fairly successful.

50. Yes.

51. For the S.P.G. £1 3s 2d. For the fund for the augmentation of small benefices 10s.

52. No clergyman having been permanently resident in Pitton for more than two years at a time, nor in Farley since the Revd the vicar ceased to live there, dissent has become very strong and in some quarters a good deal of bitter feeling against the church has been engendered.

J. Farnham Messenger M.A.
(in the temporary absence of Rev H. Barton)

In countersigning the returns for Pitton supplied by Mr Messenger I gladly bear my testimony to the zeal and energy of Mr Barton in these early days of his ministry as a deacon.

Newton Smart, Vicar.

168. PLAITFORD   D. Amesbury

1.   West Grimstead with Plaitford chapelry.

2.   Patron Hon Mrs Fox-Strangways, Roche Court, Winterslow on behalf of her son, a minor.

3.   248.

4.   Thomas D. Morse 1855.

5.   Yes.

6.   Yes.

7.   [Blank]

8.   None.

9.   Yes – for Plaitford.

10. Not licensed.

11. Rev H.J. Morant – on the point of leaving.

12. No.

13. Two churches.

14. Grimstead and Plaitford, not known.

15. The Church at Plaitford was restored about eight years ago.

16. Yes.

17. Yes.

18. None.

19. Yes.

20. Plaitford is about 8 miles from Grimstead by the road.

21. Tithe rent charge £168 gross. Glebe let for £8. Subject to large outgoings.

22. [Blank]

23. No.

24. Two full services with sermons. 10.30am and 2.30pm.

25. Yes.

26. No.

27. No.

28. On the great fasts and festivals of the church; about half a dozen and the school children. On Good Friday – nearly as good as Sunday.

29. [a] Yes [b] Yes [c] No [d] and [e] on one or the other.

30. Once a month also at Plaitford.

31. Yes.

32. 16 at Plaitford.

33. [Blank]

34. 14 at Plaitford.

35. 16 at Plaitford.

36. [Blank]

37. Church full and increasing at Plaitford.

38. There is no further want of church accommodation but a house at Plaitford for the clergyman is greatly needed.

39. [Blank]

40. Ten in 1864 at Plaitford.

41. [Blank]

42. [Blank]

43. Yes.

44. Too many. Ranters.

45. An excellent one at Plaitford.

46. [Blank]

47. When they are old enough for work.

48. Some.

49. Last winter there was a good evening school at Plaitford. For years before there had not been such a thing.

50. Yes.

51. For augmentation of small benefices September 23rd 1863 at Plaitford – amount £1 11s 6d.

52. [Blank]

Henry Morant

169. POTTERNE   D. Potterne

1.   Potterne, a vicarage.

2.   Bishop of Salisbury.

3.   1235.

4.   Joseph Medlicott, 1837.

5.   Yes.

6.   In the glebe house.

7.   Resident.

8. No.
9. Yes.
10. 1863.
11. Thomas Walter Huthwaite, a priest.
12. No.
13. No.
14. [Blank]
15. Yes.
16. Yes.
17. Yes.
18. No.
19. No chapels.
20. [Blank]
21. Rent charge £601, glebe land 22 acres £44, surplice fees average three years £5.
22. [Blank]
23. No.
24. Two full services with sermons at 11.00am and 3.00 or 3.30pm or evening.
25. Yes.
26. No.
27. No.
28. Ash Wednesday 22, Wednesday in Passion Week 18, Good Friday 80, Ascension Day 16, Christmas Day 90, Whit Monday 120.
29. [a] Yes [b] Yes [c] No [d] Yes [e] Yes.
30. 1st Sunday in every month.
31. Yes.
32. About 65.
33. None.
34. 23.
35. 29.
36. 700 and upwards.
37. 250 to 300.
38. No.
39. 30 baptisms 6 marriages 30 burials.
40. 26 in 1861, none in 1862 or 1863.
41. All collections are made public.
42. £12 8s.
43. Yes.
44. Two Wesleyan chapels, about 30 members.
45. Yes.
46. No.
47. At 10 years of age the boys, 12 to 14 the girls.
48. The boys a very short time; somewhat longer the girls.
49. Evening school during long evenings a fair success.
50. Yes.

51. Missionary objects three sermons £14 8s 5d. Augmentation of small benefices diocese of Sarum £4 13s 6d.

52. Desecration of the sabbath. Beer and public houses.

Joseph Medlicott

170. POULSHOT   D. Potterne

1. Poulshot, a rectory.
2. Bishop of Salisbury.
3. 333.
4. William Fisher, January 1823.
5. Absent part of the year with licence.
6. Yes.
7. [Blank]
8. No.
9. Yes.
10. January 1863.
11. Spencer Fellows, a priest.
12. No.
13. No.
14. [Blank]
15. Yes.
16. Yes.
17. Yes.
18. No.
19. [Blank]
20. [Blank]
21. Glebe and rent charge.
22. [Blank]
23. No.
24. Two full services with sermons at 11.00am and 3.00pm every Sunday.
25. Yes.
26. No.
27. No.
28. Ash Wednesday, Good Friday, Ascension Day, in Lent, on Wednesdays in Easter week.
29. [a] Yes [b] Yes [c] Yes [d] Yes [e] Yes.
30. The 1st Sunday in the month.
31. No.
32. About 60.
33. Most of them.
34. 45.
35. About the same.
36. 200.
37. Nearly 200 in the summer months.

38. No.
39. 9 baptisms 0 marriages 2 burials.
40. 22.
41. No.
42. About 12s at each communion.
43. No.
44. None.
45. Yes.
46. No.
47. Boys at 9, girls at 13.
48. Yes, to some extent.
49. By night schools.
50. Yes.
51. [Blank]
52. [Blank]

William Fisher

171. PRESHUTE   D. Marlborough

1. Preshute, a vicarage.
2. The master and choristers of Salisbury Cathedral.
3. By the census of 1861 – Preshute Parish 873. Marlborough College in Preshute 269. Marlborough Union workhouse in Preshute 67.
4. Alfred George Bleeck. Instituted December 17th 1859, inducted January 21st 1860.
5. Yes.
6. There is no glebe house. He resided in the house usually occupied by the incumbent.
7. [Blank]
8. No.
9. No.
10. [Blank]
11. [Blank]
12. [Blank]
13. No.
14. The church is dedicated to St George.
15. Yes.
16. Yes.
17. Yes.
18. No.
19. [Blank]
20. [Blank]
21. The gross receipts without deductions are: from the tithes of the hamlet of Clatford £179. An augmentation grant (including income tax not deducted) from the Dean and Chapter £33 16s. Surplice fees and offerings averaging about

(per year) £8. Total £220 16s.

22. [Blank]

23. There is no glebe house at all belonging to the vicar. One belonging to the impropriator of the great tithes.

24. Morning service at 10.30am, afternoon service at 3.00pm. Sermons are preached every Sunday at both the services.

25. The morning service concludes with the sermon and the prayer for the church militant is therefore not read.

26. No.

27. No.

28. On Christmas Day, Good Friday and Ascension Day, with a service on Wednesday and Friday during Lent, with a sermon on the Wednesday evenings and on saints' days if a congregation can be got together. Christmas Day and Good Friday as on Sundays, on other occasions not more than a score besides the school children.

29. [a] Yes [b] Yes [c] No [d] and [e] alternate years.

30. On the 1st Sunday in every month.

31. Yes.

32. About 70 now living.

33. About four or five not at all, about six or seven too infirm to attend at church.

34. 26.

35. 18.

36. The church is calculated to seat 270.

37. About 200; about stationary.

38. Yes, by a district church or chapel school room in St Margaret's district, and by a conjunction with the Rockley chapel of ease for Wick and Temple districts.

39. 30 baptisms 6 marriages 25 burials.

40. In 1861 – 11 males and 4 females. In 1862 – 3 males and 9 females. In 1863 – none. Total 27.

41. Yes. A public statement of all the monies raised in the parish and the expenditure thereof is printed and distributed every year.

42. Sacramental alms £11 7s 4½d. In the poor box £1 14s 3½d. Total £13 1s 8d.

43. Yes. The distribution of every shilling is recorded and may be examined by anyone who desires to know how it is distributed.

44. There is one chapel belonging to the Primitive Methodists and one cottage meeting of Wesleyans. I cannot estimate the number of genuine dissenters, probably a little over a 100.

45. Yes, two. One in the district of Manton and another in the district of St Margaret's. Average attendance 30 to 40 in each.

46. No.

47. Boys at 9 or 10, girls at 12 to 14.

48. Yes, the boys mostly attend Sunday school till confirmation and the girls till they go out to service.

49. Yes. A night school is opened for about 14 to 18 weeks, three evenings in the week, in the winter, with an average attendance of 33. In the past season I

consider that it had a very beneficial effect.

50. Yes.

51. In January, February and March for the Lancashire relief fund £15 3s. For the Society for Propagation of the Gospel in Foreign Parts £3 7s 8d collected in May and £3 in October. Harvest thanksgiving to small livings fund £5. Harvest thanksgiving to Salisbury Infirmary 5s. For the National Society £2 6s. Total £29 1s 8d.

52. The very scattered and divided nature of the parish. The outlying hamlets are too far from any place of worship or school. The isolated character of one district – St Margaret's lying as it does the other side of the town of Marlborough with the two town parishes between, greatly weakens the influence of the incumbent therein, and necessitates the establishment of two schools (in a parish that can only bear one). The residents in St Margaret's are also more disposed to attend worship in one of the churches or chapels in the town than to come to Preshute. I don't think this evil will ever be remedied till St Margaret's is established as a district, with church and school to itself, either individually or combined with a portion of St Mary's parish Marlborough.

Alfred George Bleeck

172. RAMSBURY   D. Marlborough

1. Ramsbury, a vicarage.
2. The Crown.
3. 2800.
4. J.C.C.B.P. Hawkins, August 1840.
5. He has been resident during the whole year.
6. In the glebe house.
7. He has been resident, and the curate also.
8. He has no other benefice.
9. Yes! He has an assistant curate.
10. In June 1858.
11. Jacob Sturton, a priest.
12. He does not perform any other duty.
13. Yes! A church and a chapel.
14. Ramsbury church, date of consecration unknown, dedicated to the Holy Cross. The chapel at Axford is dedicated to St Michael.
15. Yes! Both are in good repair and duly provided.
16. Yes!
17. Yes!
18. No alterations have been made.
19. Baptisms and burials are performed in the chapel, but not marriages.
20. About 3 miles.
21. From land and rent charge. Amount is about £350 per annum.
22. The chapel is within the parish and the amount derivable from Axford of rent charge is about £36 and the rent charge from Ramsbury £89. From lands in

Ramsbury £225. Total £350.

23. The glebe house by the church and a small cottage in the village.

24. Morning, afternoon and evening at the church. Morning and afternoon alternately at Axford at 11.00am, with a sermon at 3.00pm, twice in the month with baptism, at 6.00pm with sermon.

25. Yes!

26. No!

27. Only on Wednesday and Friday mornings and on days especially appointed.

28. On Wednesdays and Fridays and festival days. Besides the schools, from 20 to 30 persons.

29. On Christmas Day at Ramsbury and on the Sunday after at Axford. On Good Friday and Easter Day at Ramsbury and on the Sunday after at Axford. Not on Ascension Day. On Whit Sunday at Ramsbury, the Feast of Trinity at Axford.

30. The 1st Sunday in every month at Ramsbury.

31. No.

32. About 110.

33. They have communicated, and frequently.

34. About 110.

35. About 60.

36. At Ramsbury 800 or 900. At Axford 160.

37. At Ramsbury on the increase, at Axford almost always full.

38. The accommodation at Axford has proved to be very successful but no other want has been stated.

39. 93 baptisms 12 marriages 53 burials.

40. Under our own care 101.

41. No! But the account is carefully kept.

42. £35 15s 5d.

43. A regular account is kept, but not in a book set apart for the purpose.

44. Independents about 70, Wesleyans 70, Primitive Methodists 90.

45. Yes.

46. No!

47. At from 12 to 14.

48. Partially!

49. There is an evening school, well attended, and the success has been considerable.

50. The copies are in progress.

51. For the S.P.G. £9 12s 7d. For increase of small benefices £7 9s 3d.

52. The parish being 7 miles long and the ministrations numerous, the infirmities of advancing age press for more help, and an additional curate would be a great blessing among the people.

J.C.C.B.P. Hawkins[1]

[1] The incumbent's full name was John Cunningham Calland Bennett Popkin Hawkins.

173. REDLYNCH   D. Wilton

1. St Mary, Redlynch. A perpetual curacy.
2. Rev R Payne, Downton.
3. 1170.
4. John Emra. May 19ᵗʰ 1838.
5. Yes.
6. In the house attached to the cure by Queen Anne's Bounty.
7. [Blank]
8. [Blank]
9. [Blank]
10. [Blank]
11. [Blank]
12. [Blank]
13. [Blank]
14. [Blank]
15. Yes.
16. Yes.
17. Yes.
18. An harmonium given to the church.
19. [Blank]
20. [Blank]
21. £100 part from Winchester College. £13 part from Downton Queen Anne's Bounty money. Total £113.
22. [Blank]
23. [Blank]
24. Two full services with sermons every Sunday at 10.30am. During the summer months an evening service at 6.00pm instead of the afternoon.
25. Yes.
26. No.
27. Prayers read on Wednesday and Friday mornings. Daily in Passion Week.
28. Good Friday. Easter Monday and Tuesday. Whit Tuesday. Ascension Day.
29. The holy communion is administered monthly. Always on Easter Day, Christmas Day and Whit Sunday but not a second time in the month in which those festivals occur.
30. [Blank]
31. [Blank]
32. [Blank]
33. [Blank]
34. About 25 the average of all the celebrations of the Lord's Day.
35. The attendance is not greater than the great festivals.
36. 400.
37. [Blank]
38. No.
39. 37 baptisms 10 marriages 15 burials.
40. In 1861 – 15; in 1862 – 12; in 1863 – 12.

41. No.
42. £5 8s 1d.
43. [Blank]
44. Baptists and Wesleyans. I cannot ascertain [the number].
45. Yes.
46. The master and mistress are not certificated.
47. About the age of 11.
48. The girls attend afterwards better than the boys.
49. There is a good evening school for boys only.
50. I send them at the end of April.
51. National Society £1 9s 4d. Church Missionary Society £2 3s 8s. Schools of Redlynch £9.
52. [Blank]

John Emra

174. ROAD HILL   D. Potterne

1. Christ Church Road Hill, a perpetual curacy.
2. The vicar of North Bradley Wilts.
3. 411.
4. Edward Peacock, 1850.
5. Yes.
6. Yes.
7. [Blank]
8. No.
9. No.
10. [Blank]
11. [Blank]
12. [Blank]
13. No.
14. [Blank]
15. In excellent repair, and all things duly provided.
16. Yes, but too small, never having been intended for a burial ground.
17. Yes.
18. No.
19. [Blank]
20. [Blank]
21. From Bounty office £134 9s 2d. Winchester College £15. Gross value £149 9s 2d.
22. [Blank]
23. No.
24. Full service and sermon at 11.00am and 6.00pm.
25. Yes always.
26. No.
27. No.

28. Ash Wednesday, Good Friday and Christmas Day.

29. [a] Yes [b] Yes [c] No [d] Yes [e] Yes.

30. Four Sundays besides days as above.

31. Yes, but not of each attendance.

32. 34.

33. [Blank]

34. 24⅓.

35. 25.

36. 700, nearly twice the population.

37. Increasing as may be seen from the statement below. Sittings let in 1851 no 19. Sittings let in 1864 no 54.

38. No.

39. 8 baptisms. 2 marriages. 6 burials.

40. In 1861 four males and five females.

41. Receipts for collections are affixed to the church door.

42. £4 7s 1d.

43. Yes.

44. None actually in the district, but several in the adjoining parish of Road in Somerset.

45. Yes.

46. Yes.

47. 11 or 12.

48. Yes.

49. No.

50. No.

51. Church Pastoral Aid Society £2 2s 3d. Collection after a meeting for the Society for the Propagation of the Gospel, but this was in the schoolroom, and therefore, perhaps, should not be inserted.

52. The district of Road Hill is so closely united, indeed so mixed up with the parish of Road in the County of Somerset with a large population and no resident clergyman, and three or four dissenting chapels, that the church's influence is hardly what it might be; the pew rents being at least four times the amount they were in 1851 shows that the church has made great progress. The churchyard is not large enough, as mentioned before: but from its position, there appears a difficulty in enlarging it, even supposing money could be raised to pay for the land and legal expenses and consecration fee. The incumbent would be glad of advice on this head.

Edward Peacock, March 25ᵗʰ 1864.

175. ROLLESTONE   D. Wylye

1. Rollestone, a rectory.

2. Lord Chancellor.

3. 52.

4. C[harles] H[enry] Ridding, 1824.

5. No.
6. No house fit for residence: at Andover.
7. J[oseph] H[olden] Johnson[1], curate; not resident.
8. Andover, diocese of Winchester.
9. [Blank]
10. [Blank]
11. [Blank]
12. [Blank]
13. No.
14. [Blank]
15. Yes.
16. Yes.
17. Yes.
18. No.
19. [Blank]
20. [Blank]
21. A small piece of glebe and tithes.
22. [Blank]
23. No house of residence.
24. In church an alternate morning service at 10.30am and afternoon at 2.30pm.
25. Yes.
26. No.
27. [Blank]
28. On the festivals.
29. [a] Yes [b] Yes [c] Yes [d] Yes [e] Yes.
30. None.
31. Yes.
32. 9.
33. None.
34. The average is 12; includes a few who do not reside in the parish.
35. [Blank]
36. 180.
37. From 50 to 140 are the number who attend according to the state of the weather – many out parishioners.
38. No.
39. No baptisms, marriages or burials.
40. None; one person in 1864.
41. No.
42. 4s.
43. No.
44. None.
45. No.
46. [Blank]
47. [Blank]
48. [Blank]

49. [Blank]
50. Not yet.
51. [Blank]
52. [Blank]

J.H. Johnson

¹ Also vicar of Tilshead

176. ROWDE   D. Avebury

1. Rowde, a vicarage.
2. John Bayntun Starky, Spye Park, Chippenham.
3. 1133.
4. The benefice is vacant by the death of Rev E. Vincent on March 28ᵗʰ last. He had held the benefice since April 1816.
5. He did reside the time prescribed by law in 1863.
6. He lived in the glebe house.
7. [Blank]
8. [Blank]
9. Yes.
10. May 9ᵗʰ 1857.
11. Henry Walter Taylor, a priest.
12. No.
13. Only one.
14. [Blank]
15. Yes.
16. Yes.
17. Yes.
18. Pulpit lowered; reading desk lowered and improved by the authority of the vicar and churchwardens.
19. [Blank]
20. [Blank]
21. Vicarial tithes – value according to commutation £339.
22. [Blank]
23. Only one.
24. Morning at 11.00am, evening at 3.00pm. During the summer months the evening service was changed from 3.00pm to 6.00pm last year. Sermons preached, except when the Holy Communion is administered.
25. Yes.
26. No.
27. No.
28. Good Friday, Ascension Day, Whit Monday, Christmas Day, Ash Wednesday. The Wednesday evenings during Lent and the Friday mornings, also Monday, Tuesday and Thursday mornings in Passion Week and on October 14ᵗʰ 1863 a thanksgiving service for the harvest at 7.00pm. Good Friday and Christmas Day the numbers are about the same as on Sunday morning. Week day service about

12. Evening service 40 to 50. Harvest thanksgiving the church was crowded.

29. [a] Yes [b] Yes [c] No [d] Yes [e] No.

30. The 1ˢᵗ Sunday in the month excepting January and those nearest Easter Day and Whit Sunday, making the total number of times 12.

31. Yes.

32. 84.

33. About 8 or 9.

34. Easter Sunday in 1861 − 49; in 1862 − 48; in 1863 − 47; average 48. Whit Sunday in 1861 − 36; in 1862 − 43; in 1863 − 34; average 37. Christmas Day in 1861 − 41; in 1862 − 31; in 1863 − 39; average 37.

35. 30 or 31.

36. According to the builder's plan 588, but this includes schoolchildren etc., so it would be difficult I think to seat 400 adults in the pews and free seating.

37. Mornings 120 or 130 to 150. Afternoons 150 to 200 or 210. Slightly increased. During the summer evenings the congregation increased decidedly.

38. A district church is much wanted for two hamlets lying within the limits of Devizes borough, the population having been increased by the militia building.

39. 27 baptisms 6 marriages 18 burials.

40. In 1861 − 29; in 1862 − 6; in 1863 − 2.

41. No, it has not been the custom here.

42. In 1861 £10 0s 9d. In 1862 £12 12s. In 1863 £14 7s 3d.

43. Yes.

44. A Wesleyan chapel. It would be difficult to distinguish them, many of those who go to chapel attending church in the morning.

45. Yes.

46. Yes.

47. Boys about 10, girls 12 or 13.

48. For a year or two.

49. By an evening school during the winter months. It has always succeeded, but especially in the last two winters.

50. The copies will be sent in June as usual.

51. Bath United Hospital £3 5s 10½d. Society for Propagation of the Gospel £2 8s 6¾d. Augmentation of small benefices fund £2 11s 4d.

52. I know of nothing beyond such impediments as are to be found in most country parishes.

Henry Walter Taylor M.A.

177. RUSHALL   D. Potterne

1. Rushall, a rectory.
2. Fellows of Merton College.
3. 220.
4. Sir Erasmus Williams Bart. I do not know.[1]
5. No.
6. No. St David's, Haverford West, S Wales.

7. William Dewdney Walker. Yes.
8. I do not know.
9. I do not know.
10. [Blank]
11. [Blank]
12. [Blank]
13. No.
14. [Blank]
15. The church wants restoration, but the present <u>repair</u> is tolerably good. Yes.
16. Yes.
17. Yes.
18. I do not know, not having been in residence so long[2].
19. [Blank]
20. [Blank]
21. I do not know.
22. [Blank]
23. No.
24. Double Sunday service (full) at 11.00am and 3.00pm. Sermons at both.
25. Yes.
26. No. The children are catechised at the Sunday school.
27. Daily prayer has been twice attempted and continued till there ceased to be a legal number of persons to form a congregation. I am sorry my services have been a failure.
28. I can only procure a congregation on Ash Wednesday and Good Friday. I intend again to make an effort for daily service.
29. [a] Yes [b] Yes [c] Yes [d] Yes [e] Yes.
30. On every 1st Sunday of the month.
31. No. They are all known to me.
32. About 12.
33. All have communicated.
34. The same number.
35. [Blank]
36. There is accommodation for the whole population.
37. 60. It has decreased since Mr Heathcote's departure. I account for this circumstance by the attraction of out parishioners by choral service, which he discontinued on the score of justice to the neighbouring priests who by this means found their congregation decreasing. He reduced the people to ordinary numbers.
38. No.
39. 12 baptisms 1 marriage 4 burials.
40. None in 1862 and 1863.
41. No.
42. £2 10s.
43. Yes.
44. One, an endowed Anabaptist chapel. About 50 Anabaptists.

45. Yes.

46. No.

47. About 9 years old.

48. Yes, up to 15 years, when they refuse to come.

49. Yes. My night schools held during the winter months are the most cheering part of my ministerial labours. Dissenters' children are glad to attend both the evening and Sunday schools and divine service also.

50. Yes.

51. Only for one purpose. For the relief of the sick and poor of my own parish.

52. I can only say that the state of the parish is a very unsatisfactory one. The interests of the principal inhabitants clash so much and there being no resident squire to reduce matters to a proper level, the divided influence has a very prejudicial effect on the spiritual welfare of the dependent poor. The farmers seek their own interests and not the people's good. I can only wish for a resident rector with an influence coextensive with his position.

William Dewdney Walker

[1] Since 1829.

[2] Replaced Mr Heathcote as curate in 1862.

178. SALISBURY ST EDMUND   D. Wilton

1. Sarum St Edmund's, a rectory.

2. The Bishop of Salisbury.

3. 4500.

4. Robert George Swayne. September 1863.

5. [Blank]

6. Yes.

7. [Blank]

8. No.

9. Yes, two.

10. On nomination of Rev T.H. Tooke[1], d December 1863.

11. H[enry] R[obert] Whelpton, J[oseph] M[ason] Austen, both priests.

12. No.

13. No, only a licensed room for Sunday evening service.

14. [Blank]

15. Not good.

16. Tolerably well.

17. Yes.

18. No.

19. [Blank]

20. [Blank]

21. Pew rents £95. Fees about £30. Endowment £59.

22. [Blank]

23. No.

24. Morning prayer 10.30am, afternoon 3.30pm, evening prayer at 6.30pm, with

sermon at each.

25. Yes.

26. No.

27. Yes.

28. Daily morning and evening. Say 10.

29. [a] Yes [b] Yes [c] Yes [d] Yes [e] Yes.

30. Every Sunday, early or late alternately.

31. I hope to do so.

32. I have no record.

33. [Blank]

34. On Easter Day 129.

35. 20 at the early, 80 or 90 at late Communion.

36. About 500 on ground floor, 100 adults in the galleries.

37. About 500, probably increasing.

38. Yes, by reseating the old and building a new church.

39. 106 baptisms 31 marriages 47 burials.

40. I have no record.

41. I intend to do so.

42. About £40.

43. Yes.

44. Three – Independent and two Wesleyan. I have no means of judging of the number of each, probably one half at least.

45. Yes.

46. Yes.

47. From 12 to 14 the boys, from 11 to 13 the girls.

48. Some few.

49. I hope to institute adult schools this coming winter.

50. Yes.

51. Schools, S.P.G., Salisbury Dispensary (£5 5s), small benefice fund, general church purposes, over all of which I have any knowledge.

52. Want of church accommodation and the systematic labours of qualified lay people, especially trained and devoted women. The profligacy encouraged by public houses, etc. Amongst the most efficient would be some wise restraint on the sale of strong drinks.

Robert Swayne

[1] Thomas Hammond Tooke, previous rector of St Edmund's

179. SALISBURY ST MARTIN   D. Wilton

1. St Martin's, Salisbury, Wilts. A rectory.

2. John Henry Campbell Wyndham Esq. The College, Salisbury.

3. 2997 by census of 1861.

4. William Wyndham Tatum. Instituted and inducted June 21st 1830.

5. Yes.

6. There is no glebe house. He has resided in a house within the limits of his

benefice.

7. [Blank]

8. No.

9. Yes.

10. August 22nd 1854.

11. Revd Lloyd Baker Walrond, a priest.

12. He is chaplain to the Wilts & Dorset female penitentiary.

13. No.

14. [Blank]

15. The church is in good general repair. The chancel is not in good repair; but is about to be repaired by the Ecclesiastical Commissioners who are the impropriators. All requisites are duly provided.

16. It is well fenced. It is in process of being levelled; burials therein having been interdicted.

17. Yes.

18. No.

19. [Blank]

20. [Blank]

21. Rent charge and Queen Anne's Bounty £193 3s 6d on an average of the last three years.

22. [Blank]

23. There is no glebe house.

24. Services with sermons at 10.30am, 3.00pm and 6.30pm.

25. Yes, excepting the Post Communion when there is a sermon or no communion.

26. No.

27. Morning Prayer daily. Evening Prayer on Christmas Day, Good Friday and Ascension Day.

28. Daily Morning Prayer. Two services with sermons on Christmas Day and Good Friday. Two services with one sermon on Ascension Day. Average attendance on daily morning prayer during the last year – on common week days nine, ordinary festivals 19.

29. [a] Yes [b] Yes, twice [c] Yes [d] Yes [e] No.

30. Twice a month including the great festivals. Three times in the month in which Easter may fall.

31. Yes, but it is only approximately correct.

32. About 180 communicate in the parish church.

33. We believe the whole of the above have communicated during the year.

34. Easter 111, Ascension 35, Whit Sunday 73, Christmas Day 63. Average of the last three years.

35. Early celebration 33, later celebration 62. Average for the year 1863.

36. Besides the school girls' seats there are 573 adults' sittings, of which 74 are occupied by 98 school boys.

37. On an average through the year, in the morning ⅚ of the adults' portion, in afternoon barely half, in the evening about ¾. I think decreasing in the afternoon,

nearly stationary at other times.

38. Not at present.

39. 68 baptisms 21 marriages 51 burials (42 in consecrated portion of the cemetery, in unconsecrated nine).

40. In 1861 − 36; in 1862 − 28; in 1863 − 33.

41. The churchwardens know the amount.

42. £35 14s 4d.

43. Yes.

44. One Roman Catholic, one Baptist and one Reformed Methodist. I am not able to state the probable number of dissenters.

45. Yes.

46. Yes.

47. This varies extremely. Probably the average would be about 11.

48. In most cases; unless they leave the parish, which is often the case.

49. No.

50. Yes.

51. Lancashire distress (third collection) £4 11s 4d; National Society £3 3s; Parish schools £8 1s; Church Missions (S.P.G.) £7 13s 4d; augmentation of small livings £8 10s 9d; Church building £5 14s 6d.

52. [Blank]

W.W. Tatum

180. SALISBURY ST THOMAS   D. Wilton

1. St Thomas, Salisbury.

2. The Dean and Chapter of Salisbury.

3. 2215.

4. William Renaud, March 1863.

5. Yes.

6. In a house in the parish, but not the house belonging to the living. With the sanction of the bishop.

7. [Blank]

8. No.

9. Yes.

10. July 1863.

11. Henry Deane, a deacon.

12. No.

13. No.

14. [Blank]

15. Yes.

16. Yes.

17. Yes.

18. No.

19. [Blank]

20. [Blank]

21. £100 per annum from the Ecclesiastical Commissioners and £40 per annum from Queen Anne's Bounty.
22. [Blank]
23. No.
24. Three full services with sermons at 10.30am, 3.00pm and 6.30pm.
25. Yes.
26. No.
27. No.
28. Every Wednesday and Friday morning, every saints' day and Holy Day, and every Thursday evening. The morning services are attended by about 10, the Thursday evening by about 50.
29. [a] Yes [b] Yes [c] Yes [d] Yes [e] Yes.
30. On the 2nd Sunday of each month after morning service and on the 4th Sunday of each month at 8.00am.
31. No.
32. About 300.
33. I consider that all have communicated.
34. At Easter 200. Whit Sunday 150. Christmas Day 90. Ascension Day 30. Trinity Sunday 70.
35. A little above 100 at the late communion, 20 at the early communion.
36. 1500.
37. Morning 900. Afternoon 350 or 400. Evening 900. There is a decrease in the summer months.
38. No.
39. 37 baptisms 19 marriages 19 burials.
40. 1861 – 26; 1862 – 30; 1863 – 22.
41. No.
42. £51 12s 10½d.
43. I keep a regular and accurate account.
44. None.
45. Yes.
46. Yes.
47. At 12 years.
48. Yes.
49. Some of them attend an evening class in the winter at my house.
50. Yes.
51. Lancashire distress (four collections) £29 8s 4½d. Church Missionary Society (two collections) £12 8s 4¾d. Expenses of evening services £8 13s 3½d. Collections for poor (Good Friday) £4 12s. Jews' Society (two collections) £9 16s 6½d. Parochial schools (two collections) £20 6s 5d. Opening of new schools £64 10s. S.P.G. (two collections) £15 5s 7¼d. Expenses of Sunday evening services £6 7s 8d. Bishop's pastoral for augmentations of poor benefices £6 12s 9d.
52. No.

William Renaud

181. SAVERNAKE   D. Marlborough

1. Savernake, a perpetual curacy.
2. The Marquess of Ailesbury, Savernake Forest, Marlborough.
3. 313.
4. John Otter Stephens M.A. 1st July 1861.
5. Yes.
6. In the house appropriated by Lord Ailesbury for the use of the clergyman.
7. [Blank]
8. No.
9. No.
10. [Blank]
11. [Blank]
12. [Blank]
13. No, but I have service on Sundays in a little school-chapel at Clench Common. I have also opened another little school-chapel at Savernake Lodge, where I have service on Friday evenings during the winter months.
14. [Blank]
15. Yes.
16. Yes.
17. Yes.
18. No.
19. I baptise on special occasions at Clench Common.
20. Clench Common distant 3 miles from the mother church. Savernake Lodge chapel about 2 miles.
21. The value of the benefice is £150 net; partly paid by the Ecclesiastical Commissioners and partly by Lord Ailesbury.
22. [Blank]
23. [Blank]
24. From October to May: Savernake at 11.00am, Clench Common 2.30pm, Savernake 4.00pm. From May to October: Savernake at 11.00am, Clench Common 3.00pm, Savernake 6.00pm. Sermons preached or lectures given at all services.
25. On Sundays when the Holy Communion is administered the sermon is sometimes omitted and the litany is said only at Clench Common, as time will not then allow of three full services between 11.00am and 4.00pm.
26. Yes, sometimes – in Lent and previous to the Rite of Confirmation being administered.
27. Daily Morning Prayer during Lent and daily Morning and Evening Prayer during Holy Week.
28. On saints' days. Also on the Wednesday evenings in Advent and Lent with sermons by special preachers, the average number of persons attending these evening services is about 75.
29. [a] Yes [b] Yes [c] No [d] Yes [e] No.
30. On the 1st Sunday in each month.
31. Yes.

32. The number that communicated last year was 223, in the year 1862 it was 176. And from June (when I took possession) to December 1861 it was 125.

33. [Blank]

34. About 25.

35. About 16.

36. About 150 in the church.

37. In the morning about 110, in the afternoon about 50, in the evening about 100.

38. No.

39. 7 baptisms 1 marriage 7 burials.

40. Mr Kingsbury held the living when the last confirmation was held in 1861.

41. Yes, all accounts are audited by the churchwardens and vestry on Easter Tuesday.

42. £11 0s 7½d (for 1863).

43. Yes.

44. There is no dissenting place of worship.

45. Yes.

46. Yes.

47. The boys between 10 and 11, the girls about 14.

48. Yes.

49. We have an evening school during the winter months.

50. Yes.

51. For the Society for the Propagation of the Gospel – sum collected £7 2s 1d. For the augmentation of small benefices – sum collected £1 13s. For the National Society – sum collected £2 3s 4d.

52. [Blank]

John Otter Stephens

182. SEDGEHILL   D. Chalke

1. Berwick St Leonard and Sedgehill, a rectory.

2. The Marquis of Westminster, Motcombe House, Shaftesbury.

3. At the last census in 1861 the population of Berwick St Leonard was 36, that of Sedgehill 193.

4. Charles Henry Grove, 4th August 1826.

5. Yes.

6. There is no glebe house. He has resided in a private house in the parish of Sedgehill.

7. [Blank]

8. No.

9. Yes.

10. He was licensed in the year 1862.

11. Joseph Holden Johnson B.A. He is a priest.

12. No.

13. The benefice comprises one church and one chapel.

14. The church of Berwick St Leonard is of a date unknown. The church was restored in 1861 by Mr Morrison of Fonthill Park. The chapel of Sedgehill was partly rebuilt and consecrated in 1844 by the name of St Mary's chapel.

15. Yes.

16. Yes.

17. The churchwarden of the parish of Sedgehill does. There is no regularly appointed churchwarden of Berwick St Leonard since the property became Mr Morrison's. His bailiff acts as churchwarden but is not officially appointed.

18. No.

19. Baptisms, marriages and burials are performed in the church and chapel respectively.

20. The chapel of Sedgehill is distant from the mother church 4½ miles.

21. A tithe rent charge and glebe.

22. The annual value of income from the parish of Berwick St Leonard is derived from 110 acres of glebe; that from the parish of Sedgehill consists of tithe rent charge and ½ acre of land adjoining the churchyard.

23. There is not any glebe house.

24. The Sunday duty in the church of Berwick St Leonard is once, either 10.30am or 2.30pm. The Sunday duty at Sedgehill chapel is twice, 10.30am and 6.30pm. Sermons are preached at these services.

25. Always.

26. Never.

27. No.

28. Ash Wednesday, Good Friday and Ascension Day. Attendance at Sedgehill on Ash Wednesday 15. On Good Friday 20 in the morning and 35 in the afternoon. On Ascension Day 15.

29. In the chapel of Sedgehill [a] Yes [b] Yes [c] No [d] Yes [e] No.

30. Once in six weeks.

31. Yes.

32. The largest number in the last three years was 34.

33. I am not aware of any professed communicants having failed to attend once at least during 1863.

34. At Easter the average of the last three years was 29. On Whit Sunday 25 and on Christmas Day 23.

35. The average number for the last three years has been 24.

36. For 60 in the church of Berwick St Leonard. For 160 in the chapel of Sedgehill.

37. The smallest congregation during the last three years has been 45, the largest 85. The congregation is nearly the same in number morning and evening. The congregation has kept nearer to the largest number more frequently during the past year. The average is I think taking good and bad weather 65.

38. No.

39. 9 baptisms 2 marriages 4 burials.

40. Four persons were confirmed of Sedgehill in 1861.

41. Yes.

42. In 1861 £6 1s 1d. In 1862 £4 17s 2d. In 1863 £5 8s 10d.

43. Yes.
44. None. There are now four families professed general Baptists.
45. Yes.
46. No.
47. Boys at 8 or 9, girls at 12 and 13.
48. Some few boys, and such of the girls as continue in the parish.
49. Our schoolmistress has a writing school in the evenings in the winter months.
50. Yes.
51. Collections were made for the Pastoral Aid Society and for the Irish church missions, but I do not recollect the sums collected at each sermon.
52. [Blank]

Charles Henry Grove

183. SEEND   D. Potterne

1. Seend, a chapelry.
2. [Blank]
3. About 1100.
4. The Rev George Hume.[1]
5. [Blank]
6. [Blank]
7. The Rev James Sanderson Serjeant. He is resident, having been duly licensed in December last.
8. [Blank]
9. [Blank]
10. [Blank]
11. [Blank]
12. [Blank]
13. No.
14. [Blank]
15. Yes.
16. Yes.
17. I have no reason to conclude otherwise.
18. No.
19. Yes – each and all.
20. [Blank]
21. [Blank]
22. [Blank]
23. [Blank]
24. There are two full services on the Sunday, viz at 10.30am and at 3.00pm. In the summer there is usually an evening service instead of an afternoon.
25. Yes.
26. I have not done so as yet.
27. No my Lord.
28. On the first day of the year. On Good Friday and during each day of Passion

Week and on Christmas Day and Ascension Day. The congregation is usually good when we have a sermon – perhaps two thirds the attendance on Sunday. Otherwise but small.

29. On Christmas Day, Easter Day, and on Whit Sunday or Trinity Sunday.

30. On the last Sunday of each month.

31. I am not aware of such a list.

32. About 50.

33. [Blank]

34. About 50.

35. Perhaps 40 or rather more.

36. About 500, inclusive of the children.

37. Perhaps 300.

38. No.

39. 20 baptisms 2 marriages 20 burials.

40. [Blank]

41. There is an annual statement usually made for the most part of such which is circulated amongst the parishioners.

42. £15 15s 11d during the last year.

43. Yes. In a book in which for many years there has been entry of the various parochial charities.

44. Two. A Wesleyan and Primitive Methodist. Perhaps 100.

45. Yes.

46. I am sorry to say we are not in receipt of this aid at present.

47. The boys from 10 to 12, the girls somewhat later.

48. Some of them – a fair proportion.

49. Not at present.

50. I am unable to say whether my predecessor transmitted them before he left but will ascertain.

51. The Society for Promoting Christianity amongst the Jews £2 19s 2d. The Church Missionary Society £5 7s 1½d. And I think also for the diocesan fund for the benefit of small livings.

52. Not anything in particular. I believe that God will own his own faithfully preached word here as elsewhere and that He does do it and am encouraged at times to believe He gives me the power to be faithful.

James Sanderson Serjeant

[1]Instituted and inducted as vicar of Melksham with Seend chapelry and Erlestoke chapelry, 1825.

184. SEMINGTON   D. Potterne

1. Semington, a chapelry attached to Steeple Ashton.

2. Magdalene College, Cambridge.

3. 460 [??][1]

4. Richard Crawley, 1828.

5. [Blank]

6. [Blank]
7. Henry Owen Crawley, resident.
8. [Blank]
9. [Blank]
10. [Blank]
11. [Blank]
12. The curate is also chaplain to the Melksham Union workhouse.
13. [Blank]
14. [Blank]
15. Yes.
16. Yes.
17. Yes.
18. No.
19. [Blank]
20. [Blank]
21. Tithe.
22. [Blank]
23. [Blank]
24. Two services, on the Sunday morning at 10.30am and in the evening at 3.00pm. A sermon at each service.
25. Yes.
26. No.
27. No.
28. On Christmas Day, Good Friday and Wednesday evenings in Advent and Lent. On the two former days, rather more than our average Sunday congregation. At the evening services, 50.
29. [a] Yes [b] Yes [c] No [d] Yes [e] No.
30. On eight other Sundays.
31. Yes.
32. 30.
33. None.
34. 24.
35. 18.
36. 160.
37. 150 including children – remains about the same.
38. No.
39. 39 baptisms 3 marriages 11 burials.
40. I have no information; none since I was licensed to the cure.
41. Yes.
42. £6 19s 4d.
43. Yes.
44. One Methodist chapel. I am unable to state the probable number of actual dissenters.
45. Yes.
46. No.

47. At 9 years of age.
48. Yes! Up to a certain age – say 15 years.
49. No.
50. No.
51. In aid of Lancashire distress £1 11s 9½d. Additional Curates Society £2 3s 2d. For augmentation of benefices 17s 4d.
52. No special impediment.

H.O. Crawley

¹ The figure is difficult to read. The curate appears to have written 450, then altered the figure to 460. *See* VCH volume IV for details relating to the census for Semington.

185. SEMLEY D. Chalke

1. Semley, a rectory.
2. Dean and Chapter of Christ Church, Oxford.
3. 700.
4. Henry Hall, February 1856.
5. Yes – more.
6. Yes.
7. [Blank]
8. No.
9. No.
10. [Blank]
11. [Blank]
12. [Blank]
13. No.
14. [Blank]
15. Yes.
16. Yes.
17. Yes.
18. No.
19. [Blank]
20. [Blank]
21. Tithe £515 glebe £100.
22. [Blank]
23. No.
24. Two full services on Sunday at 11.00am and 6.00pm or 6.30pm.
25. Of course.
26. Never.
27. No.
28. Fridays in Lent, average 50. Every day in Passion Week, average 15.
29. [a] Yes [b] Yes [c] Yes [d] Yes [e] Yes.
30. 1st Sunday in every month.
31. Only of the number at each Holy Communion.
32. 60.

33. 8.
34. 40.
35. 35.
36. 240.
37. 180.
38. [Blank]
39. 17 baptisms 8 marriages 12 burials.
40. 36.
41. No.
42. £25.
43. The amount collected at each offertory is regularly entered.
44. Baptist chapel – one third.
45. Yes.
46. My school has not yet been examined under the Revised Code.
47. Boys at 10, girls at 12.
48. Yes.
49. No.
50. Yes.
51. [Blank]
52. One of the secrets of success in dissent is the liberty given to individuals to extempore prayer. The poor weary of the sameness of a liturgy and as great prominence is given to the doctrine of conversion in all their preaching, so they are impatient of all instruction that does not encourage them in their belief that they are converted, and therefore sure of salvation. The doctrine of spiritual growth, and sanctification is not so palatable.

Henry Hall

186. SHAW & WHITLEY　D. Potterne

1. Shaw and Whitley, a perpetual curacy.
2. The Rev G. Hume, Melksham.
3. The population is somewhat under 600.
4. G. Nutt, Christmas 1848.
5. Yes.
6. Yes.
7. [Blank]
8. None.
9. None.
10. [Blank]
11. [Blank]
12. [Blank]
13. No.
14. [Blank]
15. Yes.
16. Yes.

17. Yes.

18. None.

19. No chapels.

20. [Blank]

21. The gross amount of the endowment is £100, part being made by the Ecclesiastical Commissioners and part by the vicar of Melksham.

22. [Blank]

23. [Blank]

24. There are two full services. The morning service commences at 10.30am, the evening service at 6.00pm.

25. The whole without omissions.

26. I have not catechised publicly for some years past.

27. No.

28. On Christmas Day and Good Friday and the attendance on these days is about the same as on Sunday.

29. The Holy Communion is always administered on the 1st Sunday in the month, but it has not been administered regularly on the Sundays mentioned unless these have happened on the 1st Sunday in the month. I do not remember ever to have administered it on Christmas Day.

30. [See Q 29]

31. No.

32. About 20.

33. I think they have all communicated several times during the year.

34. About 16 or 18 is the average number.

35. [See Q 34]

36. 450.

37. Somewhat under 200. There has been a slight increase during the last few years.

38. No.

39. 9 baptisms 4 marriages 5 burials.

40. No account has been kept but I think the average number is about 10.

41. No.

42. The average sum collected is 10s.

43. There is an account kept in a book of the receipts and disbursements.

44. There is a Wesleyan chapel – probably one half are dissenters - some attend chapels in the neighbouring parishes.

45. Yes.

46. Not during the last two or three years. I hope to do so next year as the mistress is preparing for the examination in order to obtain a certificate.

47. The boys leave many of them at the age of 9 or 10. The girls at the age of 11 or 12.

48. Many do attend the Sunday school after leaving the day school.

49. We have not had a night school this year but we have in former years and we hope to resume it next winter.

50. Not yet.

51. For the Church Missionary Society £17 16s 10d. For the Society for Promoting Christianity among the Jews £6 8s 8d. For the school £2 15s 3d. These amounts include the subscriptions as well as the collections at church.

52. I think that the chapel having been built in the locality many years before the church must have given dissent a very strong hold in the minds of many. The parish church is 2 miles off from many houses.

George Nutt

187. SHERRINGTON D. Wylye

1. Sherrington, a rectory.
2. The Revd A. Fane, Fulbeck, Lincolnshire.
3. 189 at the last census.
4. Mason Anderson, May 1831.
5. Yes.
6. In the glebe house.
7. [Blank]
8. No.
9. [Blank]
10. [Blank]
11. [Blank]
12. [Blank]
13. No.
14. [Blank]
15. Yes.
16. Yes.
17. Yes.
18. No.
19. [Blank]
20. [Blank]
21. Tithes commuted at £252 3s 0d. Glebe rateable value £45.
22. [Blank]
23. No.
24. Two full services on Sunday at 11.00am and 6.00pm.
25. Yes.
26. No.
27. No.
28. All the saints' days. Wednesdays and Fridays during Lent. (A sermon on Wednesday evenings, also on Good Friday). Mondays and Tuesdays after Easter. The average attendance on saints' days is between 30 and 40 including the schoolchildren.
29. On Christmas Day, Easter Day, Whit Sunday and five times besides in the year.
30. [Blank]
31. No.

32. About 40.

33. Three.

34. Easter Day 38, Whit Sunday 32, Christmas Day 38.

35. About the same number.

36. About 150.

37. About 100 in the morning and 150 in the evening. The morning congregation has increased.

38. No.

39. 7 baptisms 0 marriages 2 burials.

40. 11.

41. The receipts for collections made are put on the church door.

42. In the year 1863 the sacramental alms amounted to £5 7s 8d.

43. Yes.

44. None.

45. Yes.

46. No.

47. About 11 in the girls and 8 in the boys.

48. Yes.

49. The girls receive private instruction four hours during the week.

50. Yes.

51. June 21ˢᵗ for the Salisbury Infirmary £3 6s 7d. December 6ᵗʰ for the augmentation of small livings £1 4s 7d.

52. Nothing particular.

Mason Anderson

188. SHREWTON   D. Wylye

1. Shrewton, a vicarage.

2. The Lord Bishop of Salisbury.

3. 710.

4. Frederick Bennett, 1854.

5. No, but residing in Maddington, he has performed the duty of Shrewton for more than 275 days.

6. No, in his glebe house at Maddington.

7. [Blank]

8. Maddington, diocese of Salisbury.

9. No.

10. [Blank]

11. [Blank]

12. [Blank]

13. No.

14. [Blank]

15. Yes.

16. Yes.

17. Yes.

18. An organ has been erected in the north chancel aisle.

19. There are not any chapels.

20. [Blank]

21. Vicarial tithe rent charge £215. 28 acres of glebe, rent £40. Surplice fees about £1 10s.

22. Only one parish.

23. No.

24. Morning Prayer at 11.00am, litany communion service and sermon. Evening Prayer and sermon at 3.00pm. Evening Prayer and sermon at 6.30pm.

25. Yes.

26. No.

27. No.

28. Wednesdays, Fridays and Holy Days. Morning Prayer, litany and communion service (as the case may be) at 11.00am. About ten persons besides the schoolchildren. On Wednesday evenings during Lent and evenings during Holy Week at 7.00pm Evening Prayer and sermon. About 40 persons on the average, sometimes 60 are present.

29. [a] Yes [b] Yes [c] No [d] Yes [e] No.

30. On the 3rd Sunday in each month.

31. Yes.

32. 67.

33. 4.

34. Christmas Day 15, Easter 40, Whit Sunday 25.

35. 20.

36. 320.

37. At 11.00am − 150. At 3.00pm − about 300. At 6.30pm − 150 or more. Increasing, especially in the morning.

38. No.

39. 23 baptisms 0 marriages 8 burials.

40. In 1861 − 26. In 1862 − one. In 1863 − none.

41. Yes, by a notice in the church porch of collections in church. At the Easter vestry I always produce an account of parochial charities under my charge.

42. In 1861 - £12 7s 1d. In 1862 - £10 3s 9d. In 1863 - £12 9s 5¼d.

43. Yes.

44. A Baptist meeting house and a Wesleyan meeting house. Probably 200, about equally divided between Baptists and Wesleyans. The latter have arisen from a schism amongst the Baptists.

45. Yes.

46. Yes, united with Maddington.

47. Boys at 11, girls at 12 or 13.

48. Yes.

49. Yes, by an evening school for boys. The evening school is not so well attended as it was when we had no separate school for boys under a master and the boys left school at 8 years of age.

50. Yes.

51. For expenses of the church £5 12s. Expenses of the evening service £1 7s 3d. Salisbury Infirmary £5 3s 7d. Society for the Propagation of the Gospel £2 7s 4d. Warming the church £1 8s 6d. Total £15 18s 8d.

52. I have no more difficulties than are to be met with in most parishes, where there has been in former years great apathy on the part of the church. Till 1854 there was only one service on a Sunday. Only church room for 140 with no free seats except in a gallery. No Sunday or day school in the parish of Shrewton. Dissent was dominant. I feel very thankful for the present state of the parish. The difficulties which I have expressed in answers to former questions are less, and I am more hopeful for the future.

Frederick Bennett

189. SOUTH NEWTON   D. Wilton

1. South Newton, a vicarage.
2. Earl of Pembroke and Montgomery.
3. 717 (by census of 1861). This includes Ugford which dissevered from the parish and the Union workhouse 120 and Burdens Ball 260.
4. John Hungerford Penruddocke M.A. 1860.
5. Yes.
6. Yes.
7. [Blank]
8. [Blank]
9. [Blank]
10. [Blank]
11. [Blank]
12. [Blank]
13. [Blank]
14. [Blank]
15. Yes.
16. Yes.
17. Yes.
18. The church and chancel were rebuilt and restored within and without under the direction of T.H. Wyatt Esq by faculty and consecrated Sept 15th 1862.
19. [Blank]
20. [Blank]
21. Tithe rent charge commuted at £250.
22. [Blank]
23. No.
24. Two full services, morning at 10.30am and evening at 6.00pm. Sermons are preached at these services.
25. Always.
26. No.
27. No.
28. Christmas Day, Good Friday, Ash Wednesday, Ascension Day and during

Lent on Wednesday and Friday evenings. The morning services on these days are not well attended (about 50 or 60) evening services 100 to 150.

29. [a] Yes [b] Yes [c] Yes, until last year, as the year previous only four attended. [d] Yes [e] Yes. During the time of rebuilding the church and the services in the school room many communicants came less frequently. They are now recovering the effect of the discomfort and many new communicants have been added.

30. Every 1st Sunday in the month.

31. Yes.

32. 49 persons communicated in the church of whom 15 only did so once. Some being friends etc.

33. All these have communicated. A few who used to communicate in Rev Mr Rigden's[1] time fell away when he left (at once). A few still remain who are not steadfast.

34. Easter Day 25. Whit Sunday 18. Trinity Sunday 16. Christmas Day 16. Average 19.

35. 18½.

36. 270 sittings including the children's according to measurement.

37. Mornings about 80, evenings about 150-200. I have not counted them.

38. [Blank]

39. 17 baptisms 3 marriages 9 burials.

40. In 1861 − 20-23 (I forget the exact number); in 1862 − 0; in 1863 − 5.

41. Yes.

42. £5 17s 3½d.

43. My own private book.

44. A small room belonging to the Wesleyan Methodists. There are not very many pure dissenters, except at Burden's Ball where they chiefly attend the Wilton chapels.

45. Yes.

46. We have a certificated mistress and a pupil teacher and get a grant which has been much diminished under the new code.

47. Boys 9-10, girls 12 years.

48. The girls, but not all the boys.

49. By an evening school during the winter months which is moderately successful. The boys do not seem generally to care to go beyond a certain point.

50. Yes.

51. S.P.G. £4 16s 4d. C.M.S. £4 8s 9d. Jews £3 15s 11¼d. A.C.A.S[2]. £1 12s 8½d. Irish Church £1 0s 6d. B & F Bible Society 15s 6d. S.P.C.K. 10s 6d. Infirmary 5s.

52. I think the great impediment to the well being of my parish is the evil and godless lives of many of my farmers' sons. (There is a great improvement in the carpet factory at Wilton since I last researched on it). I think with reference to the above research, landlords should be asked as much as possible to have churchmen on their farms. I am chaplain to the Wilton Union and have services every Sunday (once with sermon) and on Friday the litany with extemporary exposition of a chapter in the New Testament. The average communicants are

about 16.

J.H. Penruddocke

[1] William Rigden, formerly curate at South Newton

[2] The abbreviations are: Society for the Propagation of the Gospel, Church Missionary Society, Additional Curates' Aid Society.

190. SOUTH WRAXALL   D. Potterne

1. Atworth with S Wraxall, a perpetual curacy.
2. The Dean and Chapter of Bristol.
3. Population of S Wraxall 341.
4. William Laxton. 1848.
5. Yes.
6. There being no glebe house, he has resided at Holt, in a house duly licensed.
7. [Blank]
8. No.
9. Answered in paper relating to Atworth.
10. Ditto.
11. Ditto.
12. Ditto.
13. Yes.
14. The Church at S Wraxall is called after St James. Date of consecration unknown. Said to be in the time of Edw III.
15. Yes.
16. Yes.
17. Yes.
18. No.
19. Yes.
20. S Wraxall is about 2 miles from Atworth.
21. Tithe rent charge and glebe.
22. The tithe rent charge of S Wraxall is commuted at £150 per annum. There is a very small portion of glebe let at 4s.
23. There is not any.
24. The Sunday duty at S Wraxall consists of morning and afternoon service on one Sunday and afternoon service only on the following Sunday. A sermon at each service.
25. Yes.
26. No.
27. No.
28. Ash Wednesday, Good Friday and Christmas Day. Attendance generally as on Sundays.
29. Christmas Day, Easter Day, Whit Sunday or the Sunday after.
30. On three other Sundays in the year.
31. No – the number.
32. Being discouragingly small I can remember them.

33. None.
34. About 16 or 18.
35. Ditto.
36. About 250.
37. Probably about 110. I think it is about stationary.
38. No.
39. 16 baptisms. 2 marriages. 4 burials.
40. [In 1861] S Wraxall 9.
41. Yes.
42. £2 16s 4d.
43. Yes.
44. There is one belonging to the Independents and some Baptists meet in a cottage.
45. Yes.
46. Yes.
47. About 11 or 12.
48. Rarely.
49. No.
50. Yes.
51. S. Wraxall. Collection for distress in Lancashire etc £4 13s 6d. Society for the Propagation of the Gospel in Foreign Parts £2 2s 9d. Small benefices augmentation fund about 15s. The exact amount I do not remember and the report I cannot, on the moment, put my hand on.
52. No.

W. Laxton

191. SOUTHBROOM   D. Avebury

1. Southbroom, a perpetual curacy.
2. Revd William Ewart, vicarage, Bishop's Cannings.
3. [Blank]
4. B[enjamin] C[harles] Dowding, May 1838.
5. He has been resident.
6. He has resided in the parsonage house.
7. [Blank]
8. He has no other benefice.
9. He has two assistant curates.
10. [Blank]
11. Revd H[enry] T[hornton] Purrier and the Revd J[ohn] K[ay] Booker, both priests.
12. [Blank]
13. It does not comprise more than one church.
14. [Blank]
15. It is in good repair and duly provided with all things necessary for the decent performance of divine service.

16. It is well fenced and as well kept as a churchyard bounded by two public roads can be.

17. They do.

18. There have been no such alterations.

19. [Blank]

20. [Blank]

21. Pew rents, surplice fees, Queen Anne's Bounty, Ecclesiastical Commissioners' grant, benefaction of Right Hon. T. Sotheron Estcourt. Total about £225 per annum.

22. [Blank]

23. [Blank]

24. Morning and evening duty at 11.00am and 3.00pm respectively. A sermon at each.

25. I do.

26. I have not been in the habit of catechising.

27. Only during Lent.

28. Litany and Holy Days. About 12 persons besides the officials and schoolchildren.

29. [a] Yes [b] Yes [c] Yes [d] Yes [e] Yes.

30. 1st Sunday in the month.

31. I have a rough list, but it is difficult where there are large houses, with many servants often changing, to keep an exact list.

32. The number of communicants is about 100. This may seem a falling off by comparison with the last return, but it arises from these being now constant. Daily service in the church or churches of the town of Devizes, which was not the case before.

33. I am afraid I cannot attempt to answer this question with accuracy.

34. Probably about 60.

35. From 30 to 40.

36. For rather more than 600.

37. About 400. I think it fluctuates but little.

38. Very great want of church accommodation by a fresh district with chapel.

39. 60 baptisms 10 marriages 46 burials.

40. In 1861 there were 15; in 1862 there were 17; in 1863 there were 3.

41. I do not.

42. Averages above £20 per annum of the last three years.

43. There is.

44. There are no dissenting places of worship.

45. There is.

46. Some of the managers are much opposed to placing the school under any degree of government control.

47. About 12 for the girls, the boys somewhat younger.

48. For a time.

49. We have tried evening schools with fluctuating success.

50. I have not yet, but am about to do so.

51. Parish schools £7 6s 3½d. Curates aid fund £2 8s 10d. Poor benefice fund £4

15s. Society for the Propagation of the Gospel in Foreign Parts £4 1s 5d.

52. The suburb of a town is I think generally deemed an unfavourable soil for the church's ministry. The population normally being the dregs of the people and often a shifting one. The chief difficulty to be met with (besides the apathy and indolence so generally complained of amongst poor workmen at the present day) is perhaps a low <u>Conventicle</u> taste, not breaking out into defined error of doctrine, but delighting in prayer meetings stimulating sermons of a style and character that would not be admissible in the church. To meet such difficulty, perhaps a lay catechist, deacon or parochial mission woman might be found the best agent. Such going out with the bishop's licence and blessing might gather in these stragglers to the fold and finally lead them to enjoy the rich services of the church. It would seem that the church of Rome allows considerable indulgence to her people in this way, always securing their <u>ultimate</u> communion with her. And it would also appear that John Wesley contemplated only this — in the commencement of his movement, e.g. always requiring his preachers to see that their hearers always received the sacraments of the church etc.

B.C. Dowding

192. STANTON ST BERNARD   D. Avebury

1. Stanton St Bernard, a vicarage.
2. The Earl of Pembroke, Wilton House.
3. 360.
4. G[eorge] T[hompson] Ward, 1842.
5. Yes.
6. In the glebe house.
7. [Blank]
8. No.
9. No.
10. [Blank]
11. [Blank]
12. [Blank]
13. Only one church, the parish church.
14. [Blank]
15. Yes in every respect.
16. Well fenced but suspect to trespassers on account of a public path through it.
17. Yes.
18. None.
19. No episcopal chapels.
20. [Blank]
21. Tithe rent commutation charge £170. Rent of glebe £70, total £240.
22. [Blank]
23. No.
24. Full morning service at 10.30am, afternoon service at 3.00pm. Sermon always.
25. Yes.

26. No. This practice has been discontinued for a great many years.

27. No. Wednesday morning prayers have been attempted several times but without success.

28. Christmas Day and Good Friday with good attendances, about 40. On Holy Thursday about six.

29. On Easter Day and Whit Sunday. The evening of Christmas Day being so much given to family meetings and parties it has been thought inexpedient to administer Holy Communion in the morning. Trinity Sunday is too close. On Whit Sunday.

30. On the 1st Sunday in the month throughout the year.

31. No.

32. 30.

33. They are all pretty regular in the attendance, about 18 in number every time. And all come in turn.

34. On Easter Day there were 25 at the table. On Whit Sunday, 18.

35. About 18.

36. 150.

37. About 100 to the best of my knowledge; the number is increasing.

38. No.

39. 12 baptisms 2 marriages 6 burials.

40. At the confirmation in 1861 there were four females and five males.

41. Generally by announcement from the pulpit on the next Sunday or immediately after meetings but not by any printed statement.

42. £5 10s 4d.

43. Yes, a private memorandum book at the vicarage.

44. One Wesleyan chapel. There are a few Wesleyans who frequently attend the church services, the Wesleyan chapel being open only in the evening. And some Baptists who attend the neighbouring parish at Allington chapel.

45. Yes.

46. No. The master, though competent, is not certificated. The school has been examined by the Bishop's Inspector and also by the Government Inspector, with approbation.

47. Boys about 8, girls about 12.

48. Only partially.

49. The evening school is well attended during the winter by boys and young men.

50. Not at present.

51. March 24th – Society for Promoting Christianity among the Jews £3 5s. Sept 23rd – Bible Society £5 16s. Dec 15th – Church Missionary Society £3 13s. Dec 27th – Church Pastoral Aid Society £2 2s 6d. Jan 22nd – Irish Church Missions to the Roman Catholics £1 10s. Collections made every Sunday for the Lancashire operatives amounting to £12 10s.

52. [Blank]

G.T. Ward

193. STAPLEFORD   D. Wylye

1. Stapleford, a vicarage.
2. The Dean and Canons of Windsor.
3. 260 at the last census.
4. George Carpenter. Instituted September 18th 1854, inducted September 23rd 1854.
5. He has.
6. In the glebe house.
7. He is resident.
8. He does not.
9. He has no curate.
10. [Blank]
11. [Blank]
12. [Blank]
13. One church only.
14. The earliest part of the church proves it to have been consecrated in the time of the Normans. It was dedicated to St Mary.
15. The nave and aisles are in good repair having been recently restored. The chancel is in a shamefully neglected condition.
16. It is well kept but not well fenced.
17. They do.
18. No alterations have been made.
19. [Blank]
20. [Blank]
21. Commuted tithes £30. Rent charge on great tithes £50. Interest on £905 4s 8d in hands of Queen Anne's Bounty £27 3s. Easter grant from the Dean and Canons of Windsor £2 10s. Easter dues 12s. Fees 10s. Gross value £110.
22. [Blank]
23. There is only one.
24. The services on Sunday are Morning Prayer at 10.30am and Evening Prayer at 6.00pm, with a sermon on each occasion. During Lent the litany is said and the children are catechised at 2.30pm.
25. The whole is said.
26. Last Lent the children were catechised as stated. The subject was the creed. The children were questioned in school by the mistress during the week previous and prepared to answer such questions as she expected might be put to them.
27. I do not.
28. There is a service with sermon on Ash Wednesday and each succeeding Wednesday during Lent. On Good Friday as on Sunday. On Ascension Day in the evening.
29. [a] Yes [b] Yes [c] No [d] Yes [e] No.
30. On other Sundays besides those named so as to make about 12 administrations in the course of the year.
31. I do.
32. 34.

33. 2.

34. 17.

35. 13.

36. 150 adults and 31 children.

37. The attendance at church is very fair for the number of inhabitants and has been about the same in number for some years past. The attendance of labourers however in the morning is below what it ought to be.

38. There is no further want.

39. 4 baptisms 2 marriages 6 burials.

40. [Blank]

41. I make the amount of every collection known in the parish.

42. The amount of sacramental alms has been about £3 yearly. Now there is a prospect of the large farms being held by resident tenants they may be expected to increase.

43. I have no such book.

44. There is one belonging to Wesleyans. There are only a few who never come to church at all.

45. There is.

46. We obtained last year £10 18s 4d.

47. Boys at 10, girls at 12.

48. Some of them.

49. I have an evening school. The average attendance at which is 12.

50. I have.

51. Two collections for the Lancashire distress fund; £3 4s 1d and £1 14s 8d. A collection to meet the expense of the introduction of new hymn book £3 11s 5½d.

52. [Blank]

George Carpenter

194. STAVERTON   D. Potterne

1. Staverton, a perpetual curacy.

2. Rev J[ohn] D[avid] Hastings, rector of Trowbridge.

3. Between 6 and 700.

4. Philip Bainbrigge Maddock, 1ˢᵗ February 1860.

5. He has.

6. In a hired house, there being no parsonage.

7. He is resident.

8. None.

9. Not any.

10. [Blank]

11. [Blank]

12. [Blank]

13. Only one.

14. [Blank]

15. Yes.

16. Well kept, but not so well fenced as could be wished.

17. Yes, I believe so.

18. No.

19. [Blank]

20. [Blank]

21. It is endowed by the Ecclesiastical Commissioners at £100 per annum.

22. [Blank]

23. [Blank]

24. Two full services, at 10.30am and 3.00pm. A sermon at each. During the winter months a lecture accompanied with prayers is given every Wednesday evening in my school room by myself.

25. Yes.

26. No. Once a month I address my afternoon sermon more particularly to the young and Sunday school children.

27. No.

28. Christmas Day, Good Friday and Ash Wednesday. Between 40 and 50 or thereabouts.

29. [a] No [b] Yes [c] No [d] Yes [e] No.

30. The 1st Sunday of every month.

31. I do.

32. 29.

33. 1.

34. 15.

35. The same.

36. 150.

37. About 60 – steady.

38. In that portion which adjoins Trowbridge I fear there is.

39. 11 baptisms 0 marriages 5 burials.

40. In 1861, 13 were confirmed.

41. No.

42. Last year £5 14s 3d.

43. Yes.

44. A Wesleyan chapel. I should think about 300, chiefly Wesleyans and Baptists.

45. There is.

46. [Blank]

47. Between 10 and 12 years of age.

48. In some cases.

49. No.

50. Not at present.

51. Church Missionary Society £2 1s. Jews Society £1 6s 3d. Also two missionary meetings in my school room after which was collected £3 4s. Total remitted this year from our parochial church missionary association including the £5 5s above stated, £10 15s.

52. [Blank]

[No signature]

195. STEEPLE ASHTON cum SEMINGTON   D. Potterne

1. Steeple Ashton cum Semington, a vicarage endowed with the great tithes of part of the parish.
2. The Master of Magdalene College Cambridge.
3. About 950.
4. Richard Crawley. Instituted June 12th 1828, inducted July 13th 1828.
5. He has.
6. In the glebe house.
7. [Blank]
8. None.
9. He has.
10. I believe he is not licensed.
11. Richard Parkinson, a priest.
12. No.
13. Yes.
14. The parish church dedicated to St Mary the Virgin. A chapel at Semington dedicated to St George.
15. They are both in good repair and the parish church is provided with necessaries for divine service. There is a separate report for Semington chapel.
16. Yes.
17. Yes.
18. None.
19. Yes.
20. 2½ miles.
21. The vicarial tithe rent charge of the whole parish and the greater part of the rectorial tithe rent charge of West Ashton.
22. The endowment of Semington is tithe rent charge commuted at £145 per annum. The whole benefice is rent charge £810 and glebe £25 per annum.
23. There is only one glebe house.
24. Two full services in the parish church at 11.00am and 3.00pm.
25. Yes, except that in giving notice of the intended celebration of the Lord's Supper, I read the whole notice only occasionally.
26. I do not catechise publicly.
27. No.
28. Christmas Day, Good Friday, Ascension Day, two full services. Prayers on festivals and a weekly full service on Fridays in Lent.
29. [a] Yes [b] Yes [c] No [d] Yes [e] Yes.
30. On the 1st Sunday in every month.
31. Yes.
32. 86.
33. 3.
34. 56.
35. 30.
36. 700.
37. It has decreased.

38. No.

39. 28 baptisms 4 marriages 19 burials.

40. 39 in 1861.

41. Yes.

42. £10 7s 5½d.

43. Yes.

44. A few Primitive Methodists, whose chapel is for sale. The Baptists from Bratton have bought a house and are fitting it up as a chapel and school. They now hold a meeting in a cottage.

45. Yes.

46. Yes.

47. About 12 years of age.

48. Yes, we have a good class of boys from 14 to 17 years of age.

49. We have an evening school for males during the winter months which Mr Parkinson superintends. The list contains 15 names, but only 12 attended regularly.

50. I have.

51. Additional Curates Society £2.

52. [Blank]

Richard Crawley

196. STEEPLE LANGFORD   D. Wylye

1. Steeple Langford, a rectory.

2. The President and Fellows of Corpus Christi College Oxford.

3. 628.

4. Michael Harrison, 6th and 7th December 1853.

5. Yes.

6. In the glebe house.

7. [Blank]

8. No.

9. No.

10. [Blank]

11. [Blank]

12. [Blank]

13. No.

14. [Blank]

15. Yes.

16. Yes.

17. Yes.

18. No.

19. [Blank]

20. [Blank]

21. Glebe and tithe rent charge.

22. [Blank]

23. No.

24. Service with sermon at 10.30am and 3.00pm.
25. Yes.
26. No.
27. No.
28. Wednesdays and Fridays in Lent. Easter Monday, Ascension Day, Christmas Day.
29. [a] Yes [b] Yes [c] No [d] Yes [e] Yes.
30. On six Sundays.
31. No.
32. [Blank]
33. [Blank]
34. 30.
35. [Blank]
36. 300.
37. 200 – stationary.
38. No.
39. 18 baptisms 5 marriages 11 burials.
40. In 1861 there were 35.
41. No.
42. £8 12s 5d.
43. No.
44. A small chapel for Primitive Methodists who are very few in number.
45. Yes.
46. Yes.
47. Boys at 9, girls at 12.
48. Yes.
49. An evening school for boys with small success.
50. Yes.
51. £8 17s 6d for Lancashire distress. £4 4s 6d for Church Missionary Society. £3 for the Society for the Propagation of the Gospel.
52. [Blank]

Michael Harrison

197. STOCKTON   D. Wylye

1. Stockton, a rectory.
2. The Lord Bishop of Winchester, Farnham Castle.
3. 288 at the last census; it has since decreased.
4. Thomas Miles M.A. 1855.
5. Yes.
6. In the rectory house.
7. [Blank]
8. He possesses no other benefice.
9. He has no curate.
10. [Blank]

11. [Blank]
12. [Blank]
13. No.
14. [Blank]
15. With some slight exceptions the church is in good repair and duly provided with what the law requires.
16. Yes. Excepting a small part of the fence.
17. With some exceptions.
18. No alterations have been made except that the chancel fabric has been in great part thoro'ly repaired.
19. [Blank]
20. [Blank]
21. A farm let for £500 a year, out of which there is an annual payment of about £23.
22. [Blank]
23. There are two houses on the glebe, one occupied by the tenant of the glebe farm. Both are near the church.
24. Morning service at 11.00am and evening service at 3.00pm, both with a sermon.
25. Yes.
26. No.
27. No.
28. Christmas Day, Ash Wednesday and Wednesdays in Lent, Good Friday and Ascension Day. The attendance in Lent is very small, the same on Ascension Day. Christmas Day about the same as on Sundays. Evening service on Good Friday is well attended.
29. [a] Yes [b] Yes [c] No [d] Yes [e] No.
30. On the first Sunday in Lent, in the month of August and about Michaelmas.
31. Yes.
32. About 64.
33. I believe all have communicated once at the least. I reckon none are communicants who have not.
34. 39 last year (42 at Easter this year).
35. 35 last year.
36. Above 200.
37. I have no means of knowing the number who attend services; they are about stationary. Evening service is well attended, morning badly.
38. No.
39. 16 baptisms 2 marriages 11 burials.
40. There were 13 in 1861; none in 1862 or 1863.
41. A statement of collections with the receipts are placed on the church door for two or three Sundays after.
42. £1 11s 4d in 1863. About that sum annually of late years.
43. There is a regular book kept.
44. There is no dissenting place of worship. There are three dissenting families

consisting of under 12 persons. Independents.

45. Yes.

46. No.

47. The boys at 8 or 9, the girls a year or two older.

48. Yes, almost without exception.

49. I have an evening school for boys through the winter months which is very well attended and I consider it of great use.

50. Yes.

51. We have seldom collections here excepting those ordered by the bishop and for the Society for the Propagation of the Gospel. The great part of the money collected at church is given by myself and the poor – my tenant and his wife giving 1s each. The collections are too unimportant to keep an account of. I think we collected 10s for the small benefices last year and £6 19s 5d for the Society for the Propagation of the Gospel. This sum includes the subscriptions to parochial association for the year. The S.P.G. is well supported here for a small parish. I remember no other collection.

52. There are unfavourable circumstances here, for which I cannot suggest a remedy.

Thomas Miles

198. STOURTON   D. Wylye

1. Stourton, a rectory.

2. Sir Henry Ainslie Hoare Bart (Stourhead).

3. 660. Of which between 90 and 100 are Roman Catholics.

4. Charles Brooke Bicknell, May 1858.

5. Yes.

6. Yes.

7. [Blank]

8. No.

9. No.

10. [Blank]

11. [Blank]

12. [Blank]

13. No.

14. [Blank]

15. Yes.

16. Yes.

17. Yes.

18. The parsonage pew has been altered.

19. [Blank]

20. [Blank]

21. Tithe rent charge, rent of glebe, a charity of the value of £12 per annum.

22. [Blank]

23. No.

24. Morning Prayer with sermon at 11.00am except on communion Sundays. Afternoon prayer with sermon at 3.00pm.

25. Yes.

26. Yes, on Wednesdays or Fridays throughout Lent I take the catechism in detail.

27. No.

28. On all Holy Days and saints' days. About eight (exclusive of children).

29. [a] Yes [b] Yes [c] No [d] Yes [e] Yes.

30. The 1st Sunday in every month.

31. Yes, a general list, not a list on each occasion.

32. 111.

33. Not keeping a list from time to time I cannot answer this with certainty.

34. In the year 1863 it was 45.

35. In the year 1863 it was 40. (There are many sick and infirm communicants with whom relatives and friends regularly communicate privately).

36. About 250 or 300.

37. It varies considerably, owing to the scattered nature of the parish and the long distance some have to come.

38. No.

39. 17 baptisms 5 marriages 8 burials.

40. 36 were confirmed (at Mere) in 1861.

41. A paper of 'parochial statistics' is affixed to the church door at the beginning of each year, giving a full statement of all these and other matters.

42. In the year 1863 it was £32 18s 5d.

43. Yes, an account of receipts and disbursements.

44. None. There is no professed dissent in the parish.

45. Yes.

46. It is entirely supported by voluntary contributions in addition to a small endowment of between £10 and £11.

47. Some few girls stay till 14 or 15. The boys generally leave at a much earlier age.

48. There is no Sunday school.

49. No.

50. Yes, on January 1st 1864.

51. Collection after a sermon for the S.P.G. 14s 1d. N.B. Most of the families in the parish are quarterly subscribers to the 'Parochial Missionary Association'.

52. [Blank]

Charles Brooke Bicknell

199. STRATFORD SUB CASTLE   D. Wilton

1.   Stratford sub Castle. A perpetual curacy.

2.   The Dean and Chapter of Salisbury Cathedral.

3.   332.

4.   Charles King. 1852.

5.   Yes.

6.   Yes.

7. [Blank]
8. No.
9. [Blank]
10. [Blank]
11. [Blank]
12. [Blank]
13. No.
14. [Blank]
15. Yes.
16. Yes.
17. Yes.
18. No.
19. [Blank]
20. [Blank]
21. £150 paid by the Dean and Chapter through the Ecclesiastical Commissioners also £10 per annum from the common fund.
22. [Blank]
23. No.
24. Two full services with two sermons.
25. Yes.
26. No.
27. Ascension Day. Every day during Passion Week and on Wednesdays during Lent, but not at other times.
28. About 10 to 14.
29. [a] Yes [b] Yes [c] No [d] Yes [e] No.
30. Michaelmas.
31. No.
32. About 40.
33. All have except a few invalids.
34. On Easter Sunday there were about 34.
35. 34.
36. 239 including the forms on which the children sit in the chancel.
37. In fine weather 80 exclusive of the school children each service. It is increasing.
38. No.
39. 8 baptisms 3 marriages 0 burials.
40. 11.
41. My accounts are always audited by Mr Edward Waters on the 1st of January. Anyone is welcome to inspect my accounts but they are not published.
42. £5 5s 10d in 1863.
43. Yes.
44. We have no regular dissenting chapel. One Baptist uses his cottage as a conventicle.
45. Yes.
46. We have an uncertificated mistress at present.
47. Boys at 10 years old, girls 14.

48. Yes.

49. Yes, we have a night school from November to February inclusive for boys. They take pleasure in coming and for the most part behave very well.

50. Yes.

51. Promoting christian knowledge among the Jews £1 5s 7½d. Propagation of the Gospel £3 0s 2d. Augmenting stipends of the poorer clergy £3 4s 10d.

52. I cannot mention anything specially but there is a bad amount of lukewarmness, if not indifference; still, the clergyman is fairly supported.

Charles King

200. STRATFORD TONY D. Chalke

1. Stratford Tony, a rectory.
2. Corpus Christi College, Oxford.
3. 107.
4. George Davies Kent, February 1848.
5. Yes.
6. Yes.
7. [Blank]
8. No.
9. No.
10. [Blank]
11. [Blank]
12. [Blank]
13. No.
14. [Blank]
15. Yes.
16. Yes.
17. Yes.
18. None.
19. Yes.
20. [Blank]
21. Tithe rent charge and glebe lands, £390.
22. [Blank]
23. No.
24. Morning and evening at 11.00am and 3.00pm, a sermon at each service.
25. Yes.
26. No.
27. No.
28. Ash Wednesday, Good Friday, Ascension Day and Christmas Day. Few attend on Ash Wednesday. My congregation always above the average on Good Friday, Ascension Day and Christmas Day.
29. [a] Yes [b] Yes [c] No [d] Yes [e] Yes.
30. The Holy Communion is administered once in six weeks.
31. Yes.

32. 24.
33. All have to the best of knowledge communicated during the year 1863.
34. 18.
35. It varies little.
36. For all my people.
37. From 60 to 70.
38. [Blank]
39. 7 baptisms 2 marriages 2 burials.
40. Three in 1862.
41. [Blank]
42. None are collected.
43. [Blank]
44. There is no dissenting place of worship.
45. Yes.
46. No.
47. At 8 years or earlier.
48. Yes, generally, till 15 years.
49. No.
50. Yes.
51. None have been made.
52. [Blank]

George D Kent

201. STUDLEY ST JOHN   D. Potterne
1. Studley St John, a perpetual curacy.
2. Rev. Prebendary Hastings, rectory, Trowbridge.
3. 335.
4. John Leech Porter, 10th July 1860.
5. Yes.
6. Yes.
7. [Blank]
8. No.
9. No.
10. [Blank]
11. [Blank]
12. [Blank]
13. No.
14. [Blank]
15. Yes.
16. Yes.
17. [Blank]
18. Yes – the addition of a wainscoting to protect those attending against the damp of the walls; the placing of a warming apparatus. Churchwardens.
19. [Blank]

20. [Blank]

21. From the Rector of Trowbridge £50 per annum; from the Ecclesiastical Commissioners £34 per annum.

22. [Blank]

23. [Blank]

24. Morning and Evening Prayer, the former at 10.30am, the latter at 3.00pm during the winter, and at 6.00pm during the summer months. During this latter portion of the year an afternoon service comprising the litany (omitted at the morning service) has been held except on the Sundays when the Holy Communion has been administered.

25. Yes, except as intimated in the previous answer 24.

26. Yes. After the afternoon service comprising the litany a portion of the catechism is made the ground work for catechistically instructing the children. A continuance of the plan is required to form a judgement, great difficulty having been as yet found in leading the children to reply.

27. [Blank]

28. Christmas Day, The Circumcision, Ash Wednesday and each following Wednesday in Lent, Good Friday and Ascension Day. 40.

29. [a] Yes [b] Yes [c] No [d] Yes [e] Yes.

30. The last Sunday in each month, when it does not coincide with or immediately follow or precede either of the foregoing (in Q29).

31. Yes.

32. Taking communicants as not extending to all confirmed but only to such as have followed up confirmation by communicating, 24.

33. 1.

34. 18.

35. 15.

36. 250.

37. 75 at Morning, 120 at Evening Prayer; neither.

38. No.

39. 2 baptisms (numbers vary, there were 26 in 1861) 0 marriages 4 burials.

40. 13 in 1861.

41. Yes.

42. £5 5s 0½d for the year ended 31st December last.

43. Yes.

44. One, Anabaptist. About one half or perhaps more (ie circa 175) chiefly Anabaptists, some Methodists.

45. Yes.

46. Yes.

47. 11 years.

48. Yes.

49. Yes.

50. Yes.

51. Missions £2 0s 9d. Church expenses £7 9s 6d.

52. The prevalence of dissent of a very ignorant and bigoted character, and the

great number of public houses in and about the parish.

John L Porter

202. SUTTON MANDEVILLE   D. Chalke

1. Sutton Mandeville, a rectory.
2. William Wyndham Esq, Dinton.
3. At the last census, 286.
4. John Wyndham[1], November 1840.
5. Yes.
6. Yes.
7. [Blank]
8. No.
9. No.
10. [Blank]
11. [Blank]
12. [Blank]
13. No.
14. [Blank]
15. In very good repair and has all things necessary.
16. Yes.
17. Yes.
18. The nave has been rebuilt and transept added in 1862, under the authority of faculty from the Bishop of Sarum. Also reseated.
19. [Blank]
20. [Blank]
21. Rent charge and glebe land.
22. [Blank]
23. No.
24. Morning and afternoon services at 11.00am and 3.00pm. Sermons alternately morning and afternoon.
25. Yes.
26. No.
27. No.
28. Ash Wednesday, Good Friday and Christmas Day.
29. Christmas Day, Easter Day, Trinity Sunday and the Sunday after the Feast of St Michael.
30. [Blank]
31. Yes.
32. [Blank]
33. [Blank]
34. 18 to 20.
35. [See 34]
36. 150, or thereabouts.
37. Always full in the afternoon. The congregation has certainly increased since

the restoration of the church.

38. The present accommodation seems sufficient.

39. 8 baptisms 2 marriages 5 burials.

40. 17 in 1861, none in the other two years.

41. I have not done so.

42. On an average, about 8 or 10s each celebration.

43. I keep a private account.

44. None.

45. There is a dame's school.

46. I have not done so.

47. About 14 or 15, boys for the most part earlier.

48. In a few cases.

49. [Blank]

50. Yes.

51. Augmentation of small benefices 15s 2d. S.P.G. £1 12s 5d.

52. I am not aware of anything.

John Wyndham

¹ Son of William Wyndham.

203. SUTTON VENY D. Wylye

1. Sutton Veny, a rectory.

2. Mr Heneage, Compton, Colerne.

3. 794.

4. George F. S. Powell, 1855.

5. Yes.

6. In the glebe house.

7. No curate.

8. No.

9. No.

10. [Blank]

11. [Blank]

12. [Blank]

13. No.

14. [Blank]

15. The church is in as good repair as the antiquity of the building admits of it being. But it must shortly be rebuilt. Duly provided.

16. Well fenced and fairly kept.

17. Yes.

18. No.

19. There are no chapels.

20. [Blank]

21. Glebe lands. £900 per annum.

22. [Blank]

23. No.

24. Full services with sermons at 10.30am and 3.00pm.

25. Yes.

26. No.

27. No.

28. Good Friday, Christmas Day, Ascension Day, Easter Monday, Whit Monday and on Wednesdays and Fridays during Lent. On Good Friday, Christmas Day and Whit Monday the congregations are usually larger than on Sundays, but on the other days the average is about 25 exclusive of the schools.

29. [a] No [b] Yes [c] No [d] No [e] Yes.

30. The Holy Communion is always administered on the Sunday after Christmas Day, Easter Day, Trinity Sunday and on five Sundays besides.

31. Yes.

32. About 80.

33. About 20.

34. About 45.

35. About 35.

36. 314 sittings besides the space allotted to the school.

37. Rather upwards of 250 and is rather increasing.

38. A new church in the place of the present one is urgently required.

39. 24 baptisms 5 marriages 14 burials.

40. In 1861 there were 40; none in 1862 or 1863.

41. I always affix to the church door the receipt from the treasurer to whom it is sent of every collection in church or otherwise, excepting the sacramental alms.

42. In 1863 £14 10s.

43. Yes.

44. There is a Baptist chapel, an Independent chapel and a ranting chapel. The Baptist chapel is in an isolated hamlet at Crockerton. The ranting chapel is at the extreme verge of the parish, within 10 yards of Tytherington and far removed from the centre of my parish. The Independent chapel is in the very middle of the parish. I cannot speak exactly as to the numbers – the Baptists are very few. The rest with few exceptions are partial churchmen, availing themselves of many of the ordinances of the church.

45. Yes.

46. Yes.

47. Girls at 11, boys at 9.

48. Yes, generally.

49. A night school during the winter attended with the most satisfactory result.

50. Yes.

51. The only collection made in church the last year was for the augmentation of small livings £5 2s 10d.

52. The urgent want of a new church in a central position.

George Powell

204. SWALLOWCLIFFE   D. Chalke

1. Swallowcliffe, a perpetual curacy.
2. Bishop of Salisbury, Palace, Salisbury.
3. At the last census, 317.
4. John Harman Samler. Licensed 14th February 1846, received in April 19th the same year.
5. Yes.
6. He has resided in the glebe house.
7. [Blank]
8. Yes, that of Ansty in the same diocese.
9. He has no assistant curate.
10. [Blank]
11. [Blank]
12. [Blank]
13. No, only one church, St Peter's.
14. [Blank]
15. Yes, with the exception of the roof of the nave, and transept, and one aisle, which owing to the plaster having been put upon the tile [?] lathes, peels off. The repair of the above is under consideration. The chancel and one of the aisles have been repaired.
16. Yes.
17. Yes.
18. No alterations have been made.
19. [Blank]
20. [Blank]
21. I have a payment made me out of the tithes, £40 less income tax and £40 from the Ecclesiastical Commissioners deducting income tax.
22. [Blank]
23. Not more than one.
24. Morning or afternoon service every Sunday at 10.30am and 2.30 or 3.00pm, according to time of year, with sermon.
25. Yes, with the exception of the church militant prayer, as I never return to the altar after the sermon, except when the communion is administered.
26. Yes, during the afternoons in the Sundays in Lent when I take some portion of the church catechism for examination.
27. No. On the Wednesdays however through the year, with the exception of time of harvest, I have morning prayers at 11.00am at which services I get about seven or eight persons, besides schoolchildren. During Lent when I have the service twice a week I get more, and a partial increase only the daily service in Holy Week, sometimes up to 15 or 20 in the evenings.
28. On Christmas Day, Ash Wednesday, Good Friday and Ascension Day when I have as many afternoons as in the mornings with the exception of Ascension Day.
29. On Christmas Day, Easter Day, Whit Sunday and Trinity Sunday if service in morning, following Sundays when in the afternoon. No Holy Communion on Ascension Day.
30. About every six or seven weeks.

31. Yes, of the number that attend each time that Holy Communion is administered and a list of the names of the confirmed who first communicate.

32. I have not a list of the total number of those who communicate, but I sh'd think I can put the average at about 50, as I generally have as many as 30 on ordinary Sundays who communicate and on festivals (as on Easter last) up to 38.

33. [See Q 32]

34. [See Q 32]

35. [See Q 32]

36. My church I should think might accommodate about 200, though said to be built for the accommodation of 268.

37. At I should think 130 or 140 including children of school. The church fills very well, especially in the afternoon.

38. No.

39. 10 baptisms 3 marriages 7 burials.

40. In the year 1861 there were 16 confirmed; none in 1862 or 1863.

41. No, I keep only a private account of the sacramental alms and the collections in church.

42. During the past year £5 15s.

43. Yes, of the collections made at the communions throughout the year.

44. I have an Irvingite chapel in the parish at which some few attend about once a month when there is a service.

45. Yes.

46. No, as I have not a certificated master I receive no benefit from the Committee of Council.

47. At about 11 or 12 when they are employed in the fields.

48. I am able to retain them in the Sunday School generally until confirmation.

49. Yes, for the last two years I have begun again my night school from October to March with pretty fair success. My master and I attend it three times a week.

50. Yes.

51. Collection for augmentation of small livings £2 16s 5d and for my S.P.G. Association from house to house £3 2s.

52. I have nothing particularly to complain of of an injurious tendency to the morals of the people, save the encouragements which the existence of two public houses in so small a parish, offers to the sea of drunkenness.

J.H. Samler

205. TEFFONT EVIAS OR TEFFONT EWYAS D. Chalke

1. Teffont Ewyas, a rectory.

2. William Fane de Salis, Teffont Manor, Salisbury.

3. 170.

4. Samuel Broomhead Ward, November 1830.

5. He has been resident 365 days.

6. In the glebe house.

7. [Blank]

8. No.
9. No curate.
10. [Blank]
11. [Blank]
12. [Blank]
13. Only one church.
14. [Blank]
15. Yes.
16. Yes.
17. Yes.
18. The roof of the private chapel renewed and the roof of the north transept renewed. This has been done at the sole expense of Mr de Salis, churchwarden.
19. [Blank]
20. [Blank]
21. Rent charge £180 and 28 acres of glebe.
22. [Blank]
23. [Blank]
24. Morning service at 11.00am prayers. Evening service at 3.00pm prayers and a sermon.
25. Yes, always.
26. Only in the school.
27. No. We should have no congregation as all are fully employed.
28. Christmas Day and Good Friday; the usual Sunday congregation.
29. [a] Yes [b] Yes [c] No [d] Yes [e] Yes.
30. On no other days.
31. Only the number.
32. From 14 to 20.
33. I believe all communicated on the following: Easter Day 14 communicated, Whit Sunday 12, Trinity Sunday 13, Christmas Day 14.
34. See above.
35. [Blank]
36. 150 or more.
37. The morning congregation probably 80 - the evening with strangers 150 or more. Congregation is increasing.
38. No.
39. 5 baptisms 1 marriage 1 burial.
40. As far as I can recollect, 1861 − 7, 1864 − 7.
41. Yes.
42. For 1863 £1 15s.
43. Yes.
44. None, I am thankful to say. Not more than six or eight.
45. Yes.
46. No. Ours is a very good school and it wishes to be kept strictly as a private school.
47. Girls at 14, the boys at 10 or 12.

48. Yes, some attend.

49. We have an evening school at the rectory twice a week which promises to be very successful.

50. Yes.

51. For the improvement of small livings only £1 collected. The family at the Manor House away.

52. I have nothing to complain of. My people attend church regularly and are a well conducted, civil, sober people.

Samuel B Ward

206. TEFFONT MAGNA   D. Chalke

1. Dinton with Teffont Magna.
2. President and Fellows of Magdalene College Oxford.
3. 291.
4. J[ames] C[harles] Stafford, June 1841.
5. Yes.
6. Yes.
7. [Blank]
8. No.
9. Yes.
10. October 1863.
11. Rev E.H. Lloyd
12. No.
13. A church and a chapel.
14. Dinton St Mary. Teffont unknown. Dates unknown.
15. Yes.
16. Yes.
17. Yes.
18. No.
19. Baptisms and marriages; burials at Dinton.
20. Under a mile and a half.
21. Nothing arises from Teffont.
22. [Blank]
23. No.
24. Twice every Sunday in the chapel a sermon and catechizing except at Morning Prayer the first Monday in the month.
25. Yes.
26. Yes, twice in the month. See Dinton. The assistant curate most generally catechises.
27. No.
28. Wednesdays, Fridays, saints' days, Ember and Rogation Days.
29. [a] Yes, early in the octave. [b] Yes, early in the octave. [c] No [d] Yes [e] No.
30. On the third Sunday in the month.
31. Yes.

32. 28. More have communicated but not very lately.

33. 6.

34. I am sorry to say that I have omitted to set down the names in my book the last twelvemonth and have mislaid some of the notes. But the number of communicants is not so great as formerly; some have left for the Ranters and the places of those who have died have not been filled up.

35. [Blank]

36. 182.

37. Not having always [been] present I cannot form an opinion, but the congregation has much fallen off. It is now I hope increasing. The Ranters are very active and successful.

38. No.

39. 10 baptisms 0 marriages, burials at Dinton.

40. 10.

41. Yes.

42. Between £30 and £40.

43. [Blank]

44. A Primitive Methodist chapel.

45. Yes, a dame school.

46. [Blank]

47. Answered on Dinton.

48. Yes.

49. I have attempted an evening school but without success.

50. Not yet for this year, but for last year yes.

51. Lancashire fund £14. Parent church building £14 10s. Small benefices £1 15s 2d. S.P.G. £1 4s.

52. The activity of the Ranters. Increased pastoral visiting. All my experience tells me that nothing will make up for it if neglected, since the church feeling has disappeared.

J.C. Stafford

207. TIDCOMBE D. Marlborough

1. St Michael's Tidcombe. A perpetual curacy.

2. The Dean and Canons of Windsor at Windsor.

3. 42 adults and 49 children, total 91.

4. Edmund Burkitt Bowman, 17th May 1862.

5. Yes.

6. Yes.

7. No curate.

8. No.

9. No curate, the incumbent is in residence.

10. [Blank]

11. [Blank]

12. [Blank]

13. No other church or chapel.

14. [Blank]

15. In good repair, just been repaired externally.

16. Yes.

17. Yes.

18. No alteration as to the fabric; a carpet, crimson long cushions at the entrance to the Holy Communion table, on the north and south sides of which are placed crimson book cushions. A little extra of crimson to the pulpit, the prayer desk and lectern, which the incumbent thought would improve the appearance.

19. There are no chapels; all such duties are performed at the church.

20. There are none.

21. C.E. Rendall Esq £22 15s. R.C.L. Bevan Esq £22 15s. Queen Anne's Bounty £26. Total £71 10s. Deduct taxes £1 16s. Net income £69 14s.

22. [Blank]

23. Only one, opposite the east end of the churchyard.

24. Two services at 10.30am and 2.45pm. Sermons at each, except on the day for the Holy Communion when there is one sermon in the afternoon.

25. Yes.

26. Not in the church, but twice on the Sunday in the schoolroom. I break up the catechism into portions, put the questions in a different form, and seek for answers sometimes in their own language.

27. No.

28. On Good Friday and Christmas Day.

29. [a] Yes [b] Yes [c] No [d] Yes [e] No.

30. At present I have increased the number of times from once a quarter to once every second month, before entering upon arrangement once per month.

31. Have the names of all in the book of offertory money.

32. 8.

33. One only, the eight is an increase over a minimum number four.

34. 8.

35. 6.

36. 120 at the church. No chapels.

37. The average number was about 15 or 17, now 35.

38. No, there is plenty of space and accommodation.

39. 11 baptisms 0 marriages 5 burials.

40. [Blank]

41. Make an entry of everything for the information of the churchwarden and family; all other parishioners are labourers.

42. Since I have been in residence from July last £1 4s 3d.

43. Yes.

44. There is a cottage where the Dissenters meet; there are eight Primitive Methodists and two Baptists in the parish, but since my cottage visitation amongst them, with only one exception, I have induced them all to attend church.

45. Yes.

46. No, we support it by private prescription.

47. At about 12. Occasionally the girls at 13 or 14.

48. Yes, they attend my scripture classes both morning and afternoon. From 26 to 30 at my Sunday school.

49. I have established night schools, which have been well attended. From 26 to 28.

50. Yes.

51. Only £1 6s has been collected at present in the parish for the poor benefice augmentation fund and £2 towards the Clothing Club.

52. I have experienced nothing to discourage, what few dissenters there are now attend the church. The extra service at the church and the night schools are appreciated and cottage visitation has a salutary effect.

E.B. Bowman

208. TILSHEAD D. Wylye

1. Tilshead, a vicarage.
2. The Lord Chancellor.
3. 500.
4. Joseph Holden Johnson, 1837.
5. Yes.
6. In the glebe house.
7. [Blank]
8. No.
9. Resident – no curate.
10. [Blank]
11. [Blank]
12. [Blank]
13. No.
14. [Blank]
15. Yes.
16. Yes.
17. Yes.
18. No.
19. [Blank]
20. [Blank]
21. Land.
22. [Blank]
23. Only one glebe house.
24. Morning at 10.30am or afternoon at 2.30pm. Evening at 6.30pm with sermons.
25. Yes.
26. No.
27. No.
28. On all the red-letter days prayers, on the festivals with sermons. Few persons attend on saints' days – never above 30. About 60 attend service and exposition

on Wednesday evenings during the winter half of the year.

29. [a] Yes [b] Yes [c] Yes [d] Yes [e] Yes.

30. No other days.

31. No.

32. The number varies, average 60.

33. To the best of my knowledge none of the above have omitted to communicate entirely during the period.

34. 60.

35. The communion is only administered on festivals.

36. In the church 306, besides children 84.

37. I do not know the average number; there is no alteration.

38. No.

39. 14 baptisms 4 marriages 5 burials.

40. 18 persons were confirmed in 1861; 29 in 1864.

41. Only collections.

42. They vary from 14s to 20s.

43. Yes.

44. There is no regular meeting house for dissenters. There is preaching in a cottage, but there are only two professed dissenters.

45. Yes.

46. No.

47. Boys at 8 or 9, girls at 12.

48. The greater part of them, yes.

49. Not by evening schools, for want of funds.

50. Not yet – they wait the churchwarden's signature.

51. The schools and Clothing Club, about £16. Lights £3.

52. I know of nothing to impede my ministry.

J.H. Johnson

209. TISBURY   D. Chalke

1. Tisbury, a vicarage.

2. Rt Hon Lord Arundel, Wardour Castle.

3. 2368.

4. F[rancis] E[dmund] Hutchinson, 10th March 1858.

5. Yes.

6. Glebe house.

7. [Blank]

8. [Blank]

9. Yes.

10. October 1861.

11. Revd J[ohn] H[enry] K[irwan] Ward, a priest.

12. No.

13. No; a licensed school room.

14. [Blank]

15. Yes. In temporary, not permanent, repair.
16. Yes.
17. Yes.
18. No, except some trifling additions, such as stools, lamps, and various small things, alms boxes for example.
19. Yes.
20. [Blank]
21. Tithe rent charge £365 net. Less curate's salary £40 and payments to Queen Anne's Bounty £63, leaving about £260.
22. [Blank]
23. No.
24. Morning 10.30am, afternoon 3.00pm, evening 6.00pm. Newtown school room in the afternoon at 3.00pm.
25. Yes.
26. Children in Lent. They are prepared generally, without knowing the particular questions to be put. Being only on week days, there is not much opportunity of judging of the effect, but the congregation seem much interested. If congregations will bear it, it conveys more instruction than any sermons can possibly convey.
27. No.
28. Wednesdays – average 40. Christmas Day – 150. Ash Wednesday – 90. Good Friday – 120. Ascension Day – 100.
29. [a] Yes [b] Yes [c] No [d] Yes [e] Yes.
30. Twice a month at Tisbury, once at Newtown.
31. No.
32. About 150.
33. None.
34. 40.
35. 32.
36. 500.
37. 250 to 270 in the evening. 150 in the afternoon. 200 in the morning. The congregation is slightly increasing and has, I believe, continued to increase steadily for some years.
38. A chapel at Newtown. A school chapel at Chicksgrove.
39. 51 baptisms (an increase on previous years) 5 marriages (less than average, which is about 8) 43 burials (double the number last year).
40. In 1863 there were 42 (21 males and 22 females).
41. Yes. Receipts are placed on the church door. A printed circular is to be issued this year.
42. £11 18s 4¼.
43. Yes.
44. Roman Catholic 600. Independent 400. Wesleyans 150. Each has a chapel.
45. Yes.
46. Yes.
47. Boys at 9 or 10. Girls at 13 to 15, with the exceptions of artisans etc who stay longer.

48. Yes, almost all.

49. Yes. They are well attended and maintain the education of the children, keep them in communication with the clergyman and attendance on Sunday school. And, if they do not succeed in establishing any strong religious feeling, promote at any rate that self respect and carefulness of conduct which keep them out of scrapes. If any get into mischief, they are sure to absent themselves. They have nearly all passed the examination of the Committee of Council, and some that of the Society of Arts. Most are members of the library and Reading Room. All the church members are regular at church, and many of dissenting families nevertheless attend church pretty regularly. The influence obtained over them, although a very rough set (as is the case with all the lower class in Tisbury) is so great that they would do almost anything I asked them. The greater number are young men, who have joined in the school irrespective of the day school, and they ought if possible after 15 years to be kept separate from the regular night school under the master, into which I am convinced that in every rural parish the boys in the day school ought to be <u>regularly drafted,</u> at least as early as 9 or 10, otherwise they will <u>never take to work.</u>

50. No.

51. S.P.G £11 8s 4¼d (including subscriptions). Choir £1 10s 5d (besides subscriptions). Schools £3 11s 6½d. Additional Curates Society £3 19s 0¼d (besides subscriptions). Bishop's letter for small benefices £4 12s 7½d. Total £25 1s 11½d.

52. The existence of a Non Conformist body of more than half of the parish, which almost precludes the possibility of enforcing salutary discipline in schools and parish, for fear of driving doubtful members into the open mouths of so many lions. The greatest need is that of resident gentry to support the clergyman. The next: good education to enable the people to judge better for themselves between Protestant dissent, Romanism and the church. Education is wanted even more among the middle than the lower classes; and for this reason, I purpose, with the patronage of the clergy and Bishop if it can be obtained, to establish middle schools, on church principles, for the district. I intend at once advertising to take a limited number of borders, and if the plan works well, to develop it into regular middle schools with an efficient staff of teachers and ecclesiastical supervision, as at Shoreham[1] on a smaller scale.

F.E. Hutchinson

[1]New Shoreham Protestant Grammar School, in Shoreham (Sussex) was established in 1852 to counteract Anglo-Catholic teaching.

210. TOCKENHAM WEEK   D. Avebury

1. Tockenham. A rectory.
2. The Lord Chancellor.
3. About 160.
4. Thomas Hyde Ripley. Instituted A.D. 1828 (according to clergy list)[1].
5. [See 6]

6. At Wootton Bassett vicarage house.

7. P.C. West – resident.

8. A perpetual curacy in diocese of Durham.

9. [Blank]

10. [Blank]

11. [Blank]

12. [Blank]

13. No.

14. [Blank]

15. The church is kept in a state of repair and provided with all things needful.

16. The churchyard is well kept and the due repair of the fences shall not be lost sight of.

17. Yes.

18. No.

19. [Blank]

20. [Blank]

21. [Blank]

22. [Blank]

23. No.

24. Sunday duty in the church at 11.00am and 3.00pm (the latter service transferred to 6.00pm during the summer months).

25. Not invariably – but never omit for my own ease or pleasure.

26. The state of the parish does not allow of it which I deeply regret.

27. No – nor would it be expedient to make the attempt.

28. Ash Wednesday, Good Friday and Christmas Day. Perhaps 50 on an average, besides school children.

29. Only four times a year, viz Christmas Day, Easter Sunday, the Sunday next to Michaelmas and one intermediate Sunday.

30. [See 29]

31. Yes.

32. 15.

33. All are quite regular.

34. The same as above.

35. The same as above.

36. About 130.

37. About 60 – nearly stationary.

38. No.

39. 5 baptisms 1 marriage 3 burials.

40. Nine persons in 1861.

41. That does not seem necessary.

42. £1 14s 7d.

43. Yes.

44. During last year, a dissenting place of worship has been opened very near the church, though not in the parish. I cannot state the number of dissenters in the parish. The dissenting influence is felt in every part, except the farm houses. The

dissenters are called Ranters or Primitive Methodists.

45. Yes.

46. No.

47. Boys at 10, girls 11 or 12.

48. Yes, at present.

49. Evening school during winter. Success is apparent first in the progress of the boys and young men, second, their personal acquaintance with their clergyman, third, their attendance at church.

50. Yes.

51. Collection for the Society of the Propagation of the Gospel £0 19s 4d. Collection for clergy fund £1 0s 9d.

52. My ministry is certainly hindered by the prevalence of dissent in the parish and neighbourhood. This state of things can only be met, in my opinion, by more faithful diligence on the part of the minister – in holding fast and setting forth, publicly and privately, the church's form of sacred words, to guide definitely our principles, faith and practice.

P Cornelius West

¹ The year given by the curate is correct.

211. TOLLARD ROYAL   D. Chalke

1. Tollard Royal, a rectory.

2. John H. Austen, Tollard Royal.

3. 594, viz Tollard Royal 374, Tollard Farnham¹ 220.

4. John H. Austen, 1860.

5. Yes.

6. In the glebe.

7. [Blank]

8. No.

9. No.

10. [Blank]

11. [Blank]

12. No.

13. No.

14. [Blank]

15. Yes.

16. Yes.

17. Yes.

18 No.

19. [Blank]

20. [Blank]

21. [Blank]

22. [Blank]

23. No.

24. Two full services (viz. prayers and sermon at each) at 11.00am and 3.00pm.

25. Yes.
26. No.
27. No.
28. Mornings of all Wednesdays during the season of Lent and each day in Passion Week. Congregation about 12 besides the school. Evenings of each Wednesday during Lent, congregation good, maybe 60-80. Good Friday, Ascension Day, Christmas Day, Ash Wednesday.
29. [a] Yes [b] Yes [c] No [d] No [e] No.
30. The 1st Sunday of every month, except that nearest to Easter Day.
31. Yes.
32. 114. This number applies to Tollard Royal, including the private administrations of Tollard Farnham. Those who attend at Farnham church will doubtless be returned in the list of that parish.
33. [Blank]
34. 40.
35. 20 to 27.
36. The church accommodates 154 adults. The school seats are overcrowded.
37. The church is usually fairly filled in the mornings and <u>overfilled </u>in the evenings. Impossible for the congregation to increase because the church is too small and hence <u>excludes </u>very many who desire to attend more regularly than they now do and very many who doubtless would otherwise do so occasionally, and perhaps habitually if they could find seats.
38. The church might well be enlarged by the erection of a side aisle at a cost not exceeding £400.
39. 3 baptisms 26 marriages 12 burials.
40. In 1861 – 11; in 1862 – 10.
41. Not in regard to the offerings at the Holy Communion which I consider to be inexpedient. The amount and receipt for all other collections I post in the church porch. I would here mention that the Wilts and Dorset Bank (into which I am directed to pay collections) object to give a written acknowledgement of this receipt.
42. [Blank]
43. I keep a regular account.
44. No dissenting place of worship. In Tollard Royal no absolute dissenters.
45. Yes.
46. No.
47. Boys at 12 and 14, girls at 14.
48. Yes, boys to 16 and girls to 17.
49. An adult evening school is held during the winter months with considerable success.
50. Yes.
51. Propagation of the gospel society, augmentation of benefices.
52. I am conscious of no requirement besides an extension of church accommodation, as above stated.

John H. Austen

¹ A tithing to the north of Farnham village in Dorset, which was owned by the de Tollard family of Tollard Royal until 1885, when it was joined with Farnham.

212. TROWBRIDGE HOLY TRINITY   D. Potterne

1. Holy Trinity. District parish church, Trowbridge, a perpetual curacy.
2. The Rev J.D. Hastings, Trowbridge.
3. 2357.
4. Digby Walsh, August 1858.
5. Yes.
6. Yes.
7. [Blank]
8. No.
9. Resident, with a curate.
10. September 1862.
11. Rev F Bromley. In priest's orders.
12. No.
13. Only one church.
14. [Blank]
15. Yes.
16. Yes.
17. Yes.
18. No.
19. [Blank]
20. [Blank]
21. £50 per annum from the rector. £80 per annum from the Ecclesiastical Commission. £100 per annum from fees and pew rents.
22. [Blank]
23. One only.
24. Two services, at 11.00am and 6.30pm. A sermon at each.
25. The entire service.
26. No.
27. There is not daily service.
28. Morning prayers on saints' days and Holy Days. Wednesdays and Fridays in Lent, and the whole of Holy Week, when there is also evening service with a sermon. Two services on Ash Wednesday with a sermon in the evening. Two services on Ascension Day with a sermon at both.
29. [a] Yes [b] Yes [c] Yes [d] Yes [e] Yes.
30. The second and last Sunday in every month.
31. No.
32. About 30.
33. All have done so.
34. Between 25 and 30.
35. Between 12 and 20.
36. 1300.

37. About 500. Increasing.

38. If all the population were churchmen there would not be room for them in the church. As it is, it is large enough for those who wish to attend the church.

39. 6 marriages 62 burials.[1]

40. 25 in 1862.

41. No.

42. £4 19s.

43. No.

44. None. More than half the population are dissenters belonging to every kind of denomination.

45. Yes.

46. Yes.

47. About 15.

48. Yes.

49. There is an evening school at the mother parish.

50. Yes.

51. Expenses of the church collections on first Sunday of every month £36 in the year past. S.P.G. £5 Schools £7. To pay debt on restoration of the church £16.

52. [Blank]

Digby Walsh

[1] The baptism figure is missing. The numbers for 1863 were 31 baptisms, 6 marriages, 62 burials.

213. TROWBRIDGE ST JAMES   D. Potterne

1. Trowbridge, a rectory.

2. This parish is now being transferred to Trustees by the patron Revd John D. Hastings.

3. 7200.

4. John D. Hastings, July 1841.

5. Yes.

6. Yes.

7. [Blank]

8. No, except a prebendal stall.

9. Yes, two.

10. One last November, the other some years back.[1]

11. Revd William Warren, priest and Revd R[ichard] K[ing] Bedingfield.

12. Mr Bedingfield is assistant master in the grammar school in this town.

13. One church and one chapel.

14. The name of the mother is reputed to be St James, but there is no certainty on this point. The name of the chapel is St Stephen's, consecrated 1863.

15. Both churches in good repair and all things necessary provided for the performance of divine service.

16. Yes.

17. Yes.

18. No alterations.

19. Yes, baptisms and marriages.

20. About three or at most five minutes' walk from the mother church.

21. Tithes, land and Easter offerings. Gross amount £838, net £390.

22. One moiety of £17 from West Ashton parish and £25 modus from Staverton.

23. Only one glebe house.

24. Morning 10.30am, afternoon 3.00pm and evening 6.15pm. Sermons at each service except on baptism days - then catechising children.

25. Yes.

26. Once in the month, generally on the subject of baptism. I believe this to be a useful plan.

27. No daily service.

28. Saints' days service at 8.00am. Attendance very small, sometimes but eight persons. A week evening service attendance about 300.

29. [a] Yes [b] Yes [c] No [d] Yes [e] Yes.

30. The 1st Sunday in the month.

31. Yes.

32. About 300.

33. None.

34. Between 80 and 100.

35. 120.

36. 1000 in the mother church and nearly 700 in the chapel of ease.

37. Between 7 and 800.

38. I should be glad to have another church for about 500 sittings.

39. 56 baptisms in the parish church and 74 in the chapel of ease. 25 marriages in the parish church. 95 burials in consecrated ground.

40. In 1861, 60 persons were confirmed.

41. Yes.

42. £32 7s 10d.

43. Yes.

44. Seven – one Wesleyan, two Independents, three Baptist and one Socinian. The congregations reputed small.

45. Yes.

46. Yes.

47. About 12 or at most 13 years of age.

48. Yes.

49. Both by adult and evening schools or rather classes, with good success.

50. Not yet, the clerk is preparing them.

51. Wiltshire Missionary Students' Association £15 15s 7d. Irish Church Missions £7 15s. Jews Society £6 1s. National School Society £4 7s 4d. Church Missionary Society £9 12s 6d. Church Restoration Holywell £5. Thanksgiving for harvest – this sum was applied to the alms houses £23 5s. S.P.G Society £7 11s 4d.

52. [Blank]

John D Hastings

¹ Bedingfield was priested in 1834.

214. TYTHERINGTON   D. Wylye

1. Tytherington is a prebend in Heytesbury church and a hamlet of Heytesbury parish, I have therefore answered for it in the Heytesbury return.

2.

3.

4. John Knight, 1836.

5.

6.

7.

8.

9.

10.

11.

12.

13.

14.

15. Moderately so.

16. No burials.

17.

18.

19. Baptisms only.

20. One and a quarter miles.

See the Heytesbury return for answers.

John Knight

215. UPAVON   D. Potterne

1. Upavon, a vicarage.

2. The Lord Chancellor is at present the patron.

3. 508 according to the census of 1861.

4. Henry Simon Charles Crook, June 1840.

5. Yes.

6. Yes.

7. [Blank]

8. No.

9. No.

10. [Blank]

11. [Blank]

12. [Blank]

13. No.

14. [Blank]

15. The leaden roof of the church ought to be removed. The church itself is in substantial repair as regards the pews, but the north wall of the nave is in a bad state.

16. The churchyard will never, I fear, be kept in good order on account of a right of way through it.

17. They discharge their duties as far as the law compels them.

18. The two unsightly square pews have been removed by order of the impropriators (King's College) and two carved oak stall seats have been placed there. The chancel rails have been restored at the cost of the vicar. The appearance of the chancel is greatly improved.

19. [Blank]

20. [Blank]

21. Tithe rent charge and the rent of two acres of glebe gross amount £150, net income £130.

22. [Blank]

23. No.

24. Two full services with two sermons every Sunday at 11.00am and 3.00pm. The same on Christmas Day and Good Friday; morning prayers on Ash Wednesday and Holy Thursday, and during Passion Week.

25. Yes.

26. No.

27. No.

28. As stated above, on Christmas Day and Good Friday when the attendance is about the same as on Sunday. On Ash Wednesday and Holy Thursday the attendance is very small.

29. [a] Yes [b] Yes [c] No [d] Yes [e] No.

30. Once every quarter.

31. No, only the numbers.

32. About 40.

33. None, except in cases of sickness.

34. About 40.

35. 30.

36. 250.

37. About 200 (there is an increase in both at each service).

38. No.

39. 11 baptisms 2 marriages 5 burials.

40. In 1861 − 26.

41. No.

42. For the year 1863 £5 9s 6d.

43. Yes.

44. One dissenting meeting house. The probable number of dissenters is about 70. Particular Baptists.

45. Yes.

46. No.

47. The boys at 9. The girls generally leave at 12.

48. Yes, for the most part.
49. Many of the boys attend an evening school from November to March. There is some apparent success.
50. Yes.
51. Thanksgiving for the harvest, applied to the support of the night school, 1863, £2 12s. Collection for the distressed cotton operatives in Lancashire £15.
52. [Blank]

Henry Simon Charles Crook

216. UPTON LOVELL D. Wylye

1. Upton Lovell, a rectory.
2. The Lord Chancellor.
3. 210.
4. William Gray, May 1842.
5. Yes.
6. Yes.
7. [Blank]
8. No.
9. No.
10. [Blank]
11. [Blank]
12. [Blank]
13. No.
14. [Blank]
15. Yes. Very good repair and duly provided.
16. Yes.
17. Yes.
18. None in the chancel; but in the church, the pulpit has been removed to a much more convenient place, by which also additional accommodation has been gained, and the church will now hold 200 persons. The alteration was made by the churchwardens with the consent of the parishes and the knowledge of the Rural Dean.
19. [Blank]
20. [Blank]
21. The tithes commuted at £320 a year and glebe land let at present at £70 a year.
22. [Blank]
23. Only one.
24. Two full services, with a sermon at each. The morning service is always at 11.00am, but the evening service in the <u>winter</u> is at 6.00pm; when it is at Boyton at 3.00pm. In the summer it is at 3.00pm, when it is at Boyton 6.00pm.
25. Yes.
26. No.
27. No.

28. The 1ˢᵗ day of Lent, every day during Passion Week and Christmas Day.

29. [a] No [b] Yes [c] No [d] Yes [e] No.

30. The 1ˢᵗ Sunday <u>after Christmas Day</u> and the 1ˢᵗ Sunday in October.

31. No.

32. 32.

33. Only one.

34. From 22 to 28.

35. About the same.

36. 200.

37. From 70 to 80 in the morning and from 170 to 200 in the evening.

38. No.

39. 8 baptisms 1 marriage 2 burials.

40. None.

41. No.

42. £2 8s.

43. No.

44. None.

45. Yes.

46. No.

47. From 8 to 10.

48. Yes, always.

49. There has been an evening school both for boys and girls for several years and it has been attended with great success.

50. Not yet.

51. To defray the expense of the lights for the evening service, the collection amounted to £1 19s 2½d, leaving a balance of £1 17s 4½d to be paid by the rector.

52. No. Since the last visitation, a chancel organ (built by Messrs Bevington and Sons) has been erected and the services are now choral and the Salisbury hymn book is used, and it is to this that I principally attribute the great increase to the congregation.

William Gray

217. UPTON SCUDAMORE   D. Wylye

1.   Upton Scudamore, a rectory.

2.   Provost and Fellows of Queens College, Oxford and the Visitors of the Michel Foundation.

3.   407.

4.   John Baron, instituted 26ᵗʰ September, inducted 28ᵗʰ September in the year 1850.

5.   Yes.

6.   He has resided in the glebe house.

7.   [Blank]

8.   No.

9. Yes, Rev F[rederick] A[ugustus] Alley.
10. 28th December 1861.
11. Rev F.A. Alley, priest.
12. No.
13. No.
14. [Blank]
15. Yes.
16. Yes.
17. Yes.
18. No alterations have been made.
19. [Blank]
20. [Blank]
21. Rent charge, gross amount £490. Glebe about £30. Rectory house and garden and small fields.
22. [Blank]
23. There is only one.
24. Morning service with sermon at 10.30am. Evening service with sermon at 3.00pm.
25. Yes.
26. No.
27. No.
28. On Ash Wednesday and Good Friday. The congregations are not counted; very few on Ash Wednesday.
29. [a] Yes [b] Yes [c] No [d] Yes [e] No.
30. On the 1st Sunday in each month.
31. No.
32. About 25.
33. I have not observed.
34. 25.
35. 20.
36. 158.
37. The congregation is not counted but appears to remain about the same.
38. Thoulston and Chapmanslade which are partly in the parish of Upton Scudamore are more than two miles distant from the parish church. By building a small, cheap church and endowing it by redeeming if possible the tithes of the extinct chapelries of Norridge and Thoulston.
39. 10 baptisms 4 marriages 9 burials.
40. I have not preserved any record.
41. No.
42. For the year ending 31st December 1863 £15 0s 11d.
43. Yes.
44. A Baptist meeting house. Many of the dissenters come to church. I have not ascertained the number of dissenters.
45. Yes.
46. No.

47. [Blank]

48. I am able to retain the girls in a Sunday school.

49. I have an evening school for lads, from Michaelmas to Lady Day, two nights in the week, Mondays and Thursdays. The numbers have been kept up to nearly 20. There has been success in teaching the lads to write and cipher, but not much in Christianising or civilising them.

50. Not as yet.

51. For Missions only, in consequence of the debt still remaining for the restoration of the church. Amount about £3. All the receipts for collections are kept, but I should not be able to answer this very accurately without delay.

52. The want of a quiet library or study, but this want is in the course of being supplied by the munificence of a relative.

John Baron

218. URCHFONT or ERCHFONT   D. Potterne

1. Erchfont, a vicarage.

2. The Dean and Chapter of Windsor.

3. [Blank][1]

4. S[kinner] C[hart] Mason, January 1860.

5. Yes.

6. Yes.

7. [Blank]

8. The parish of Stert.

9. The help of the Rev H.T. Purrier, a curate of Devizes.

10. [Blank]

11. The Rev H.T. Purrier is a priest.

12. He is Mr Dowding's curate, St James' parish.

13. Two churches.

14. St Mary's and St James the Less at Stert.

15. I think that much is required to be done outside of Erchfont church. At Stert the church is in good repair.

16. Yes.

17. Yes.

18. The interior of Erchfont church is being restored and reseated, under the authority of a faculty. The chancel is also being entirely changed in its arrangements and much beautified. The old gallery is taken down and the poor will be much better accommodated.

19. Yes.

20. 3 miles.

21. Tithes. Erchfont £304, Stert £80.

22. [Blank]

23. No.

24. Morning and afternoon at Erchfont, and morning and afternoon at Stert alternately, at 10.30am and 3.00pm. Sermons are preached at the services, except

when the Holy Communion is administered.

25. Yes.

26. No.

27. No.

28. During Lent on Wednesdays and Fridays and every day in Passion Week in Erchfont. Also at Stert a service with lecture on Friday evenings in Lent.

29. [a] Yes [b] Yes [c] No [d] Yes [e] Yes.

30. The 1st Sunday in every month at Erchfont.

31. I keep the numbers.

32. Between 70 and 80 at Erchfont, 15 at Stert.

33. I think that all at one time or another have communicated.

34. 65. 14 at Stert.

35. 50.

36. Church between 5 and 600. Stert church about 150.

37. The church having been closed for some time it is difficult to say.

38. The increased want is being supplied.

39. 35 baptisms 7 marriages 26 burials.

40. 45.

41. Yes, to those concerned.

42. £8 3s 3d.

43. Yes.

44. A small chapel[2], and about a dozen dissenting families.

45. Yes.

46. Yes.

47. About 12.

48. Yes, most of them.

49. We have a night school in winter for young men which is tolerably successful.

50. Yes.

51. The Diocesan Ch Bd Soc[3] The S.P.G. The schools, thanksgiving for harvest. £3 8s 9d. £2 3s. £2 3s.

52. The public house and beer shop, together with the weakness of human nature.

S.C. Mason

[1] 1459 in 1861.

[2] Built by Independents, but in 1851 it was being shared with Baptists.

[3] Diocesan Church Building Society.

219. WARMINSTER CHRIST CHURCH   D. Wylye

1. Christ Church, Warminster, a perpetual curacy.

2. Rev J.E. Philipps, vicarage, Warminster.

3. 2170.

4. Robert Rosseter Hutton, March 1860.

5. Yes.

6. Yes.

7. [Blank]

8. No.
9. No.
10. [Blank]
11. [Blank]
12. [Blank]
13. No.
14. [Blank]
15. Yes.
16. Yes.
17. Yes.
18. The position of the pulpit and reading desk has been changed under the sanction of the Archdeacon and some of the free seats altered so as to give accommodation to the choir increasing the number of free seats.
19. [Blank]
20. [Blank]
21. Ecclesiastical Commissioners £21, Queen Anne's Bounty £66 4s 2d, pew rents about £44, fees about £15, Easter offerings about £4, total £150 4s 2d.
22. [Blank]
23. No.
24. Morning 10.30am, afternoon 3.00pm only during the winter months, evening 6.30pm, a sermon at every service.
25. Yes.
26. No.
27. Yes.
28. Every Wednesday evening during Lent. Wednesday and Friday morning. Holy Week daily morning and evening. Good Friday as on Sunday. Christmas Day morning and afternoon. Ascension Day morning. On a wet morning I have had no one; on a fine morning (Good Friday) 600; on a fine evening (Good Friday) 400.
29. [a] Yes [b] Yes [c] No [d] Yes [e] Yes.
30. On the 1st and 3rd Sundays in every month and on the Harvest Festival.
31. Yes, but I cannot keep it accurately.
32. About 200.
33. All.
34. Last year Easter 156, Whit Sunday 74, Trinity 44, Harvest Festival 127, Christmas 72.
35. About 110 each month.
36. 822.
37. Morning 800, afternoon 130, evening 600 – increasing.
38. No.
39. 55 baptisms 14 marriages 32 burials.
40. None. Belonging to this parish there were confirmed elsewhere in 1861 – 33, in 1862 – 44, in 1863 – 8.
41. Yes.
42. In 1861 - £26 15s 6d. In 1862 £32 9s. In 1863 £31 5s 2d.

43. Yes.

44. A Methodist chapel. About 1000, principally Methodists, Independents and Socinians.

45. Yes.

46. Yes.

47. About 10.

48. Yes.

49. No.

50. No.

51. Lancashire relief £10 10s, organ repairs £7 5s 6d, Church Missionary Society £5 8s 8d, lighting and warming fund £10 18s, Sunday school £14 17s 10d, Society for the Propagation of the Gospel £4 8s 10d.

52. [Blank]

R.R Hutton

220. WARMINSTER ST DENYS   D. Wylye

1. Warminster, a vicarage.

2. The Lord Bishop of Salisbury, The Palace, Salisbury.

3. 3829.

4. James Erasmus Philipps, August 5th 1859.

5. Yes.

6. Yes.

7. [Blank]

8. No.

9. Yes.

10. Charles David Crawley, priest September 24th 1860. Walter Hill, priest March 16th 1862. Florence Thomas Wethered, priest March 1st 1863. John Rule, deacon September 20th 1863.

11. [See Q 10]

12. Walter Hill is Tutor at the Mission House.

13. A chapel in the hands of Feoffees. St Lawrence.

14. Parish church of St Denis. Chapel of St Lawrence.

15. Yes.

16. Yes.

17. Most faithfully.

18. A new west window has replaced a very dilapidated one. Three new seats in the chancel aisle.

19. Baptisms are occasionally performed in the chapel of St Lawrence but neither marriages nor burials.

20. ½ mile.

21. £450. 120 acres of land, cottages, £52 13s 6d rent charge, Easter dues, surplice fees.

22. [Blank]

23. No.

24. At the parish church at 10.30am, 3.00pm and 7.00pm, a sermon at each service. Exception on the 1st Sunday in the month in the morning. St Lawrence at 10.30am with sermon.

25. Yes.

26. No.

27. Yes.

28. Every day twice either in the church or the chapel. About 30 in the morning and 20 in the afternoon. On Friday evening when a sermon is preached 120.

29. [a] Yes [b] Yes [c] Yes [d] Yes [e] Yes. There is no celebration in the chapel on these days but two celebrations on Christmas Day and Easter Day at the church.

30. Every Sunday and the Feast of the Circumcision.

31. Yes, but it is yet imperfect.

32. About 400.

33. [Blank]

34. Christmas Day 177. Easter Day 245. Ascension Day 27. Whit Sunday 122. Trinity Sunday 49.

35. 1st Sunday in the month 120. 3rd Sunday in the month 50. Other Sundays at 8.30 a.m. 20-30.

36. 1400 in the parish church, 100 in the chapel of St Lawrence.

37. 1000-1200 in the morning, 400-600 in the afternoon, 1400 in the evening. Not decreasing. The congregations on some days increasing. Better this year than usual on Good Friday.

38. Yes. A chapel of ease on the Boreham Rd.

39. 84 baptisms 18 marriages 68 burials.

40. In 1861 – 57, in 1862 – 77, in 1863 – 37, in 1864 – 66.

41. Yes – yearly.

42. At the parish church £96 3s 7¼d. At St Lawrence £16 10s 10d. Total £112 14s 5¼d.

43. Yes, in the book of the services.

44. Chapel of the Independents, large number; Baptists, not very many; Wesleyans, a small number; Unitarians, a very small number. The probable number of dissenters is about a third of the population. The church is gaining ground and there is a growing disposition to return to her.

45. Yes.

46. Yes.

47. 10½ years in the boys' school, 11½ in the girls' school.

48. Yes.

49. Yes. A night school for men and lads, three nights in the week for six months. We have had 136 present at one time. The average has been 96, being above that of the year before, which was 91. Taught by male and female voluntary teachers.

50. They shall be sent in as soon as possible.

51. For the poor £53 8s 1d. Towards maintenance of curates £14 4s 4d. Expenses of choir £13 8s 6½d. Total Thanksgiving Harvest collection £32 10s, propagating the gospel society £16, Salisbury Infirmary £5 10s, Bath Hospital £5 10s, Charmouth Hospital £5 10s. Poor benefices of the diocese £15 12s 11¾d. Total

£129 3s 11¼d. Collected at the Chapel of St Lawrence £18 3s 1d. [Grand] total £147 7s 0¼d. This £147 7s 0¼d <u>includes</u> the sacramental alms.
52. [Blank]

James Erasmus Philipps

221. WEST ASHTON   D. Potterne

1.   West Ashton, a perpetual curacy.
2.   Walter Long Esq, M.P.
3.   [Blank]
4.   Marlborough Sterling Berry, June 1861.
5.   Yes.
6.   In the glebe house.
7.   [Blank]
8.   [Blank]
9.   [Blank]
10. [Blank]
11. [Blank]
12. [Blank]
13. [Blank]
14. [Blank]
15. Yes.
16. Yes.
17. Yes.
18. [Blank]
19. [Blank]
20. [Blank]
21. £100 tithe and £100 endowment by patron.
22. [Blank]
23. [Blank]
24. Morning and afternoon or evening service (according to time of year) every Sunday, a sermon at each.
25. Yes.
26. I have not done so.
27. I have not daily service.
28. Christmas Day, Ash Wednesday, Good Friday, Ascension Day. Full congregation at Christmas, half on Good Friday, one third on Ascension Day and Ash Wednesday.
29. [a] Yes [b] Yes [c] No [d] Yes [e] No.
30. On the 2nd Sunday in every month as a rule.
31. Yes.
32. 34.
33. 2.
34. The same as at other times.
35. 27.

36. 210.

37. 110. Some decrease latterly owing to temporary causes.

38. No want.

39. 11 baptisms 1 marriage 6 burials.

40. 20 in 1861, none since.

41. The collections for societies are stated at the annual meetings.

42. £9 10s 5½d.

43. Yes.

44. [Blank]

45. Yes.

46. It is not needed.

47. At 12 in the case of girls, 9 or 10 in the case of boys.

48. Yes.

49. Evening school for boys, well attended.

50. Yes.

51. Pastoral Aid Society £1 11s 6d. Jews Society £3 17s 4d. Irish Church Missions £6 0s 6d. Church Missionary Society £5 5s 1½d.

52. Nothing special.

M.S. Berry

222. WEST DEAN   D. Amesbury

1. West Dean with East Grimstead annexed; a rectory.

2. Rev. Henry Glossop, Isleworth, Middlesex.

3. 450.

4. G[eorge] G[oodwin] P[ownall] Glossop[1], 1861. Inducted 10th June.

5. Yes.

6. In the rectory.

7. [Blank]

8. No other benefice.

9. No curate.

10. [Blank]

11. Rev. T[homas] Morse helps out on Sunday by taking one service.

12. Yes, he is rector of West Grimstead.

13. Yes, two.

14. West Dean – St Mary's; part of it 1250. East Grimstead – Holy Trinity; about 1856.

15. At West Dean no, at East Grimstead yes.

16. Yes.

17. Yes.

18. No.

19. At East Grimstead baptisms only.

20. 2½ miles.

21. Rent charges and glebe lands.

22. West Dean rent charge £410 plus glebe £100 plus a house. East Grimstead

rent charge £215 plus glebe £37. Total value £762 plus the rectory.

23. No, only one.

24. For East Grimstead see other paper. For Dean – Sundays at 10.30am and 2.30pm with a sermon at each time. Holy Communion once a month and then no sermon. On saints' days at 7.00pm with sermon. N.B. only one such service in one week – never more.

25. I omit the prayer for the church militant except at Holy Communion.

26. Not as a rule, but at East Grimstead I used the church as a place for the catechumens to meet in. This place I found convenient.

27. No.

28. Christmas Day, Good Friday and Ascension Day. Also see above no 24.

29. At West Dean [a] Yes [b] Yes [c] No [d] Yes [e] Yes. At East Grimstead [a] Yes [b] Yes [c] Yes [d] No [e] No.

30. 1st Sunday in each month.

31. No.

32. About 12 and 30.

33. None that I know of.

34. 10 and 25.

35. 9 and 20.

36. Dean holds 160 with much discomfort. E.G. holds 80 well.

37. Dean 100–120. E.G. 60–65.

38. Dean church must be rebuilt so as to hold more and to 'accommodate' all in it.

39. 8 baptisms 2 marriages 3 burials.

40. None.

41. No.

42. In 1862 £5 4s 4d. In 1863 £7 1s.

43. No, not separate.

44. A chapel for Wesleyans at each end of my parish.

45. Yes.

46. Yes at Dean, not at E.G.

47. Girls go at 13, boys at 9.

48. Not much.

49. Night schools at each place. Great success at Dean as long as I went to it frequently myself, but only then.

50. Yes.

51. From January 1863 to January 1864 at Dean church, not counting meetings in the school. S.P.G. sermon 21st April £1 15s 7d. Poor benefices sermon October £1 14s 7¼d. Additional curates sermon October 14s 3d.

52. I find the best of my people are dissenters and so all (or nearly all) the fervour and zeal are on their side and I get no 'teachers' on that account. I have determined to try to get a resident curate at East Grimstead but I find unmarried men do not like to 'keep house' and married men want a larger house than I can get for them. I should like to see a parsonage built on the glebe there but I cannot afford yet to build one; could I borrow the money on security of the rent charge??

G.G.P. Glossop
[1] Son of Henry, who was Rector of West Dean with East Grimstead 1811-1821.

223. WEST GRIMSTEAD   D. Amesbury
1. West Grimstead with Plaitford chapelry.
2. Patron Hon Mrs Fox Strangways, Roche Court, Winterslow on behalf of her son, a minor.
3. 251.
4. Thomas D. Morse, 1855.
5. Yes.
6. Yes.
7. [Blank]
8. No.
9. For Plaitford.
10. Unlicensed.
11. Rev H[enry] J[ohn] Morant, a priest.
12. No.
13. Two churches.
14. Grimstead and Plaitford; not known.
15. Yes.
16. Tolerably well.
17. Yes.
18. A <u>very</u> slight alteration has just been made in the chancel – doing away with two seats.
19. Yes.
20. About 8 miles.
21. Tithe rent charge and glebe.
22. Grimstead tithe £260, glebe £19 15s. Total £279 15s gross. Subject to large outgoings.
23. No.
24. Two full services at 10.30am and 6.00pm.
25. Yes.
26. No.
27. No.
28. Ash Wednesday and once a week in Lent, Good Friday, Christmas Day and Ascension Day.
29. [a] Yes [b] Yes [c] No [d] and [e] one of these.
30. Once a month.
31. There are so few that no list is required.
32. The average number 9 or 10, total 20.
33. 4 or 5.
34. 9 or 10 – occasionally 14 or 15.
35. About the same.
36. Here, the church is large enough to hold 150 or 160.

37. About 60; slightly improving.

38. No.

39. 9 baptisms 1 marriage 0 burials.

40. 5.

41. No.

42. In 1863 £2 16s 6d.

43. Yes – but not in a separate book.

44. A Wesleyan chapel and about 100 Methodists.

45. Yes.

46. Not at present, but I hope shortly to do so.

47. Boys between 9 and 10, girls about 11.

48. Yes, but not over 14 or 15 years of age.

49. I had a very good night school last winter.

50. Not yet.

51. June 8th missionary meeting £1 16s 4d. December 6th missionary sermon 13s 9d. October 18th for small benefices 11s. Total £3 1s 1d.

52. Dissent. The Wesleyans are very aggressive; but I am happy to say, their numbers do not increase. This parish has been for years, as is well known, one of the strongholds of Methodism. [The following is crossed out, due to the school re-opening] A Methodist school which has been in existence for many years has been recently given up, and the children are coming over to the church school. This is the most hopeful event that has occurred during my incumbency. It is now simply a question of time. I look upon it as certain that the character of the parish will slowly but surely alter, and the church will make way in the place. Hitherto one has worked with no apparent encouragement and with great weariness of spirit.

Tuesday April 5th. I am sorry to say that the school above referred to was most unexpectedly – to all parties, Methodists and churchmen – re-opened yesterday.

Thomas D. Morse

224. WEST HARNHAM D. Chalke

1. [Blank]

2. [Blank]

3. 285.

4. [Blank]

5. [Blank]

6. [Blank]

7. Rev D[uncombe] H[Erbert] Sawyer, resident as Salisbury.

8. [Blank]

9. [Blank]

10. [Blank]

11. [Blank]

12. [Blank]

13. No.

14. [Blank]
15. Yes.
16. Yes.
17. Yes.
18. No.
19. [Blank]
20. [Blank]
21. [Blank]
22. [Blank]
23. [Blank]
24. There is divine service at 10.30am and 3.00pm. On alternate Sundays only at 3.00pm. Sermons at all services except when the Holy Communion is administered.
25. Yes.
26. No.
27. No.
28. On Christmas Day, Ash Wednesday, Good Friday and Ascension Day about 13 adults, and on Wednesdays in Lent about 12.
29. Yes, on Christmas Day. [The other four occasions] if there is morning service.
30. 1st Sunday in every month.
31. Yes.
32. 20.
33. Five, and two sick persons who communicated privately.
34. 10.
35. 8.
36. About 120.
37. About 30 adults, besides children; no difference.
38. No.
39. 8 baptisms 1 marriage 2 burials.
40. In 1863 − 4.
41. Yes.
42. £4 10s 11½d for the last 18 months.
43. Yes.
44. None. 15 families of Congregationalists, Wesleyan Reformed Methodists, Primitive Methodists.
45. Yes.
46. Yes.
47. Boys at about 8 years of age, girls about 13.
48. Yes in most instances.
49. Yes. About 25 young men and boys attended last winter.
50. Not yet.
51. £1 2s 2½d was collected for the Society for the Propagation of the Gospel.
52. Dissent and a great coldness to religion among the poor generally.

D.H. Sawyer

225. WEST KNOYLE D. Chalke

1. West Knoyle, a vicarage.
2. Earl of Pembroke.
3. 180.
4. J[ames] W[alter] Cardew, 1842.
5. Yes.
6. [Blank]
7. [Blank]
8. [Blank]
9. [Blank]
10. [Blank]
11. [Blank]
12. [Blank]
13. [Blank]
14. [Blank]
15. No. The evil to be complained of in small parishes of this kind (where there are not two parties) is that, whilst the tenant farmers receive a deduction from their rents, on account of church rates, the sum so allowed by the landlord is never expended – but the outlay on the church is confined to the most niggardly limits. I fear that this may be a reason why the tenants are so zealous for the maintenance of church rates; and I have no hope that there will be any remedy for the penuriousness of the tenants, until the landlords cease to allow deduction in the rents for rates, and keep the supervision of the church expenditure for the church in their own hands.
16. Yes.
17. [Blank]
18. [Blank]
19. [Blank]
20. [Blank]
21. Vicarial tithes commuted at £152.
22. [Blank]
23. [Blank]
24. Two full services with sermons.
25. [Blank]
26. No.
27. No. the obvious reason, is that 'the people' would not 'come to hear God's word, and pray with him'.
28. Christmas Day and Good Friday.
29. Holy Communion administered once in six weeks throughout the year, of which Easter is one.
30. [Blank]
31. [Blank]
32. 7 or 8.
33. [Blank]
34. [Blank]

35. [Blank]
36. Accommodation for the population.
37. 30.
38. [Blank]
39. [Blank]
40. [Blank]
41. The receipt of collection received is posted on the church door.
42. £0 0s 0d.
43. [Blank]
44. Preachings are held in a cottage: they call themselves 'Meetingers'. As baptised into the church and buried in the churchyard, all the population are church people. As using the licence of attending cottage or camp meeting they may be claimed to be dissenters.
45. There is a daily school.
46. [Blank]
47. 11 or 12 years of age.
48. No, as a general rule.
49. No.
50. The parish register copies are always taken by the churchwardens to the annual visitation.
51. For the Infirmary – the collection was £3 or £4, but the usual collection is about 15s or 16s.
52. That which impedes improvement, is traditionary <u>habit</u> of limiting their public worship to occasional attendance at church, which habit appears not to be changed. The only thing which may help to break through the established custom of neutrality towards the church maybe further teaching on the Prayer Book, when they have left the day school which leaves them so ignorant.

J.W. Cardew

226. WEST LAVINGTON or BISHOP'S LAVINGTON   D. Potterne

1. Bishop's Lavington, a vicarage.
2. The Lord Bishop of Salisbury.
3. 1589.
4. Matthew Wilkinson, June 29th and July 8th 1852.
5. Yes.
6. Yes.
7. [Blank]
8. No.
9. No.
10. [Blank]
11. [Blank]
12. [Blank]
13. No.
14. [Blank]

15. Yes.

16. Yes.

17. Yes, all duties usually discharged.

18. Only by introduction of stained glass, and the alteration of a screen window, all approved by the Bishop.

19. [Blank]

20. [Blank]

21. Tithe £356 8s 6d. Glebe rents £44.

22. Only one parish.

23. No.

24. [Blank]

25. Yes.

26. Usually in Lent, but not last Lent or the year before.

27. Daily Morning Prayer.

28. Average number at daily prayer 10 or 12. On Good Friday and Christmas Day probably 100 to 150.

29. [a] Yes [b] Yes [c] No [d] Yes [e] No.

30. On the 1st Sunday of every month.

31. Yes, but probably not complete.

32. About 80.

33. Between 65 and 75.

34. 32.

35. 23.

36. 500.

37. About 150 to 200 in the morning, from 400 to 500 in the afternoon according to the weather, stationary.

38. The tything of Fiddington is far from the church. Littleton is also a place where a chapel would be useful.

39. 47 baptisms 10 marriages 24 burials.

40. In 1861 – 71, in 1862 –2, in 1863 –3.

41. Only known to the churchwardens and collectors.

42. £9 15s 1d (1861). £8 19s 2d (1862). £8 8s (1863).

43. Yes.

44. Two chapels, one belonging to 'Baptists' the other to Independents. I cannot estimate the number of each; it is not large.

45. Yes.

46. No.

47. Girls about 12. Boys go to an endowed school very early.

48. Yes, in some cases, but many go to the dissenters Sunday school.

49. The evening school does not prevent, as yet, the going away to the dissenters' school.

50. Yes.

51. For S.P.G., for augmentation of poor benefice fund, for Salisbury Infirmary. Amounts mislaid.

52. There is more than ordinary difficulty in this parish in influencing young

men, from the circumstance of our endowed school educating gratuitously all boys. The difficulties of the Sunday school are the most perplexing to my mind of all parochial questions.

M. Wilkinson

227. WESTBURY   D. Wylye

1. Westbury with Dilton, a vicarage.
2. The Lord Bishop of Salisbury.
3. At the last census, 3674.
4. Henry Hinxman Duke. Collated October 10th 1850. Inducted October 19th 1850.
5. Yes.
6. In the glebe house.
7. [Blank]
8. No.
9. Yes.
10. After the ordination on the second Sunday in Lent, in this present year.
11. Albert Moore, a deacon.
12. No.
13. Yes.
14. The parish church of Westbury. Date of consecration unknown. Dedicated by the name of the church of All Saints. The church or chapel of Dilton. Date of consecration unknown. Dedicated by the name of St James.
15. As regards the parish church of Westbury – yes. As regards the chapel at Dilton – some slight repairs are needed, to which attention has been called by the Rural Dean.
16. Yes.
17. Yes.
18. The chancel of the parish church has been rebuilt by faculty from the Bishop's Court. No alterations have been made in the chapel at Dilton.
19. Yes, in the church or chapel of Dilton.
20. The chapel at Dilton is about 2 miles distant. There is also a schoolroom in Westbury Leigh, licensed for divine worship about 1¼ miles distant.
21. Tithes commuted at £235 0s 6d. Rents of glebe lands and tenements £116 11s. Grant (reserved rent) of Ecclesiastical Commissioners £56.
22. The chapelry of Dilton is considered as included <u>within</u> the parish of Westbury, having no separate endowment.
23. No.
24. At the parish church, 10.30am, 3.00pm and 6.00pm. At St James's Dilton 3.00pm (on Sundays for Holy Communion at 10.30am). There are sermons preached at each of these services.
25. Yes.
26. No – the custom has been discontinued since the rebuilding of the chancel was commenced.

27. Yes, morning and evening daily in the parish church.

28. On the principal festivals there are services in the chapel at Dilton. From 20 to 30 only attend them.

29. Yes, on each of these days in the parish church. On Christmas Day, Easter Day and Whit Sunday at Dilton chapel.

30. Every Sunday.

31. Yes.

32. About 145 persons communicated in the parish last year.

33. There are a few, in addition to those above mentioned, who have formerly been communicants but were not so last year.

34. In the entire parish rather over 100.

35. From 50 to 60.

36. The parish church contains 1111 seats (including 205 for children). The chapel of St James Dilton about 120. The schoolroom at Westbury Leigh about 100.

37. I have no means of answering this question. Much room is lost in the church through the operation of the 'pew system' which works as injuriously here as in any parish that I have known.

38. It would be very expedient if the licensed schoolroom at Westbury Leigh were exchanged for a small chapel of ease.

39. At the parish church: 91 baptisms 15 marriages 38 burials. At St James's church Dilton: 7 baptisms 0 marriages 6 burials.

40. The memorandum has been mislaid or inadvertently destroyed, and I am unable to give the exact number.

41. The churchwardens and some of the principal parishioners are always acquainted with the sums collected.

42. £44 16s 1d (making, with the sum of the collections noted below, a total of £71 10s 3¾d).

43. Yes.

44. Two for Independents, two for Baptists and one for Wesleyans, comprising a great part of the population, and nearly all in those parts which are distant from the church.

45. Yes – separate schools for boys, girls and infants.

46. Yes.

47. Few are remaining over 13 years; a large proportion are removed at a very early age.

48. Yes – the larger portion remain to 21 or 22 years of age.

49. An evening school for boys every night in the week, with fair and increasing success. An evening school for girls (at the house of Mrs Stafford Brown) with very considerable success.

50. They are transcribed, and are awaiting the signature of the churchwardens.

51. For the parochial schools £9 5s ¾d. For the Society for the Propagation of the Gospel £9 8s 7¼d. For the augmentation of small benefices £8 0s 8d.

52. [Blank]

Henry H Duke

228. WESTWOOD   D. Potterne

1. Westwood, a rectory. Forming part of the benefice of Bradford.
2. Dean and Chapter of Bristol.
3. 360.
4. W[illiam] H[enry] Jones, 1851.
5. Yes.
6. Yes, at Bradford.
7. [Blank]
8. No.
9. See the returns under 'Bradford'.
10. [Blank]
11. [Blank]
12. [Blank]
13. Two.
14. Both are my own churches. The 'dedication' of Westwood is not actually known.
15. Yes.
16. Fairly.
17. Yes.
18. No.
19. Yes.
20. See the returns under 'Bradford'.
21. See the returns under 'Bradford'.
22. See the returns under 'Bradford'.
23. No.
24. Full service morning and afternoon with sermons.
25. Yes.
26. No.
27. Not at Westwood, but at Bradford.
28. Christmas Day and Good Friday. The usual congregation about 80 in the morning and 100 in the afternoon.
29. [a] Yes [b] Yes [c] No [d] Yes [e] No.
30. It is administered every other month at Westwood now (since last July).
31. I know them all.
32. About 20.
33. None, except two aged sick people to whom Holy Communion has been privately administered.
34. About 15.
35. About 15.
36. 130.
37. Mornings about 80, afternoons 90-100.
38. No.
39. 10 baptisms 1 marriage 6 burials.
40. 67 in 1861.
41. No. The churchwardens have a statement given to them by me.

42. £2 15s 9d.

43. I keep an exact account myself.

44. One Wesleyan chapel. One room used as a Baptist meeting house. Wesleyans about 120, Baptists about 30.

45. Yes.

46. They have given building grants but that is all.

47. 10.

48. Yes.

49. I have had a class of young pupils for confirmation etc and think good has been done by keeping up the same after the confirmation has taken place. About 12 still attended the class up to about a month ago.

50. They will be sent immediately.

51. [Blank]

52. The great want of Westwood is a clergyman actually resident among the people. If the Ecclesiastical Commissioners in whom much property in this neighbourhood is now vested, would build a house at Westwood now, good might result from my being able to get a curate to reside there, though I feel there would be even then difficulties in the arrangement. I know not that there are any special difficulties, beyond those which we all have to lament.

W.H. Jones

229. WHITEPARISH   D. Amesbury

1. Whiteparish, a vicarage.

2. The Trustees of R Bristow Esq, Broxmore Park, Romsey.

3. 1250.

4. William R. Tomlinson, 1837.

5. No.

6. No – he has resided at Brighton and Nice.

7. William John Swayne – he resides in the glebe house.

8. Yes. The rectory of Sherfield English in the diocese of Winchester.

9. [Blank]

10. [Blank]

11. [Blank]

12. [Blank]

13. No.

14. [Blank]

15. Yes.

16. Yes.

17. Yes.

18. No.

19. [Blank]

20. [Blank]

21. £150 per annum derived from vicarial rent charge.

22. [Blank]

23. No.

24. Morning service with sermon at 11.00am. Evening service with sermon at 3.00pm in the winter and 6.00pm during the summer.

25. Yes.

26. No.

27. No.

28. The festivals and saints' days, Wednesdays and Fridays during Lent. Average on festivals 200 on other days 150. (Including the children of the school).

29. [a] Yes [b] Yes [c] Yes [d] Yes [e] Yes.

30. On the 1ˢᵗ Sunday in every month.

31. Yes.

32. About 70 or 80.

33. About 20.

34. 40 or 50.

35. 30.

36. 300 probably. But it is difficult to be certain in consequence of the irregularity of the pews.

37. 200. About stationary.

38. There is, owing to the straggling nature of the parish and the distance of many houses from the church, also owing to the bad arrangement of the pews. This might be remedied by reseating the church.

39. 32 baptisms 6 marriages 23 burials.

40. My predecessor left no record in 1861. There were no confirmations in 1862 and 1863.

41. A statement is distributed at the Easter vestry.

42. £17 last year. Average £20.

43. Yes.

44. Two. Probably 3 or 400. Wesleyan and Primitive Methodists.

45. There are three daily schools.

46. Yes.

47. 11 and 12.

48. Yes.

49. Yes. There is a night school during the winter months which has been well attended.

50. Yes.

51. The Salisbury Infirmary £4 10s 1d. The Society for the Propagation of the Gospel £1 2s 8d.

52. The bad arrangement of the pewing of the church tends to drive away the poor. The parish is also too large to be properly superintended by a curate alone – a thorough restoration of the parish church would be most beneficial. I see no remedy for the second evil under the peculiar circumstances of the case, combined with the poverty of the benefice. Lastly the crowded state and bad condition of the labourers' cottages.

William John Swayne

230. WILCOT or WILCOTT with OARE   D. Marlborough

1. Wilcott with Oare, a vicarage.
2. Col. W. Wroughton, Stowell Lodge.
3. About 600.
4. H[enry] Smelt. March 1856.
5. He has.
6. He resided in the glebe house.
7. He resided himself.
8. He possesses no other benefice.
9. He has an assistant curate.
10. May 1863.
11. Rev Arthur Llewellyn, a priest.
12. He is, I believe, still curate to Rev D Llewellyn at Easton.
13. There are two churches, one at Wilcott and the other at Oare.
14. The church at Oare is dedicated to the Holy Trinity.
15. Yes.
16. Yes.
17. Yes.
18. No alterations have been made.
19. Baptisms and burials are performed at Oare but no marriages.
20. The church at Oare is about 2 miles from that at Wilcott.
21. About £190 from tithes and 15 acres of land at Stert.
22. About £70 of rent charge arises from Oare.
23. There is only one glebe house.
24. One full duty in the church at Oare, 11.00am and 3.00pm on alternate Sundays. 11.00am and 3.00pm every Sunday at Wilcott. These are full duties.
25. Yes.
26. No.
27. I do not.
28. On Good Friday, the usual congregation. On Ash Wednesday about 10.
29. [a] Yes [b] Yes [c] Yes [d] Yes [e] alternate with the previous[?]
30. Generally on the Sundays after at Oare.
31. No. I know them all.
32. 40.
33. They have.
34. The above.
35. [Blank]
36. About 500. 300 at Wilcott and 200 at Oare.
37. I do not know, for while I read and preach I cannot count.
38. [Blank]
39. [Blank]
40. 26.
41. I generally state to the churchwardens the amount of any collection that may be made.
42. £3 10s 4d.

43. A regular account is kept.

44. There is a Wesleyan chapel at Oare.

45. Two.

46. I have not.

47. Between the ages of 8 and 12.

48. Yes.

49. There are evening schools both at Wilcott and Oare.

50. They await the churchwarden's signature.

51. The schools at Wilcott and Oare. The Church Pastoral Aid Society. For the distress in Lancashire.

52. [Blank]

H. Smelt

231. WILSFORD cum LAKE   D. Amesbury

1. Wilsford cum Lake, a vicarage conjoined with Woodford.

2. The Lord Bishop of the diocese.

3. 140.

4. Robert Money Chatfield, August 5th 1830.

5. Yes, in Woodford.

6. Yes, in Woodford.

7. I am acting as officiating minister without stipend, with the concurrence of the vicar, and of your Lordship.

8. No.

9. [Blank]

10. [Blank]

11. [Blank]

12. [Blank]

13. [Blank]

14. [Blank]

15. It is so.

16. It is so.

17. They do.

18. No alterations have been made.

19. [Blank]

20. [Blank]

21. Rent charge in lieu of tithe value £52 10s gross.

22. Answered in the Woodford paper.

23. No.

24. Two full services – in the morning at 10.30am and in the afternoon at 2.30pm in the winter and 3.00pm in the summer. A sermon is preached at each of these services.

25. I do.

26. I have never done so. I am inclined to think if _well done_ it would be useful in a rural population.

27. No.

28. On Christmas Day, Good Friday and Ash Wednesday. The average number who attend on the two former days, is, I think, about 80. On Ash Wednesday about 40.

29. [a] On the Sunday after [b] Yes [c] No [d] and [e] Either.

30. On the 1st Sunday in every month.

31. I have not hitherto done so but I keep an amount of the number who attend each Holy Communion.

32. [Blank]

33. [Blank]

34. 38.

35. 35.

36. 123 including children.

37. About 90 – increasing.

38. It is at present sufficient.

39. 5 baptisms 0 marriages 6 burials.

40. I think 8.

41. I have not done so.

42. In 1861 – £23 14s 9d. In 1862 – £24 12s 3d. In 1863 – £23 8s 3d.

43. Yes.

44. We have not a single dissenter in the parish.

45. Yes.

46. It is too small. The school is supported by Mr Loder and myself.

47. The boys about 7 or 8. The girls about 10 to 12.

48. We are usually able to do so for several years.

49. I have had an evening school for 4 months in the winter, attended and taught chiefly by myself. I hope with some considerable success.

50. Yes.

51. Society for the Propagation of the Gospel (I have mislaid the amount of this collection). Church Missionary Society £3 0s 6d. Jews' Society £3 1s 6d. Harvest thanksgiving £2 5s 2d.

52. [Blank]

Edward Duke[1]

[1] Curate of Wilsford

232. WILSFORD cum MANNINGFORD BOHUNE   D. Potterne

1. Wilsford or Willesford. The benefice is a vicarage.

2. George Ernest Howman, rector of Barnsley. Address is Barnsley Rectory, Cirencester, Gloucestershire.

3. 267 in Wilsford, according to the last return.

4. William Francis Raymond. Instituted and Inducted in the year 1835.

5. He is non-resident.

6. He resides at Stockton in Worcestershire.

7. George D'Urban John Hough. He is resident.

8. He is rector of Stockton in the Diocese of Hereford.

9. He is non-resident.

10. He is non-resident.

11. [Blank]

12. [Blank]

13. The parish comprises one church with a chapel of ease.

14. There are no documents to show either the date of consecration or the name by which Wilsford was dedicated to God. Manningford Bohune chapel of ease was consecrated in 1859 and dedicated to God by the name of 'All Saints'.

15. The Church of Wilsford is in bad repair. A meeting will be shortly held on the subject. We are well provided with all things necessary for the due performance of divine service.

16. Yes.

17. Yes.

18. No.

19. Burials and baptisms are performed at the chapel of ease.

20. 2 miles across the fields, 2½ miles round the road.

21. From a tithe rent charge and a small corn rent on the rectory. There is also an endowment of £700 in the hands of the Governors of Queen Anne's Bounty given by the Revd G.E. Howman to the vicar of Wilsford in 1859 in aid of the chapel of ease of Manningford Bohune but the interest of money arising from the endowment has never been received as yet by the vicar of Wilsford.

22. The parish is composed of two tythings, viz Wilsford and Manningford Bohune. Gross annual value of Wilsford about £135. Ditto Manningford Bohune £140 10s.

23. There is only one glebe house, commonly called the vicarage.

24. Two full services. In summer at 11.00am and 6.00pm. During the remainder of the year at 11.00am and 4.30pm. A sermon is preached at each service.

25. Yes.

26. No.

27. No.

28. Ash Wednesday, Good Friday and Christmas Day.

29. [a] Yes [b] Yes [c] No [d] Yes [e] Yes.

30. On four other Sundays.

31. No, not in this parish. Those who do attend are so regular that I can trust to my memory.

32. All professing with the exception of 15 or 20.

33. None with the exception of the 17 or 18 usually regular ones.

34. 17 or 18.

35. About the same.

36. I have seen the Benefit Club, consisting of about 140 men, pretty well fill the building as full as it would hold.

37. Not more than 35 or 40 in the morning. Of an evening about 120. The attendance of an evening is better than when I came, but there is little or no improvement of a morning. The women are the most irregular. NB These

numbers do not include the schoolchildren.

38. No.

39. 7 baptisms 1 marriage 13 burials.

40. There was a confirmation in 1861 (just before I came here). I have never heard the <u>exact</u> number, but I should say about 12 or 15. In 1862 none were confirmed; nor were there any in 1863.

41. Not of the offertory, but I do of collections.

42. About £2 10s.

43. Not in a book set apart for that special purpose by the parish; but I do keep an account in a private book of my own.

44. There is no dissenting place of worship in the parish, but I have 15 or 20 who go to a neighbouring parish where there is a chapel.

45. Yes, and very fairly attended.

46. No.

47. Boys at 8 or 9, girls at 12 or 13.

48. Yes, I have no difficulty in this respect.

49. Yes. I have in the winter an adult evening school for men and lads twice a week; and one for girls once a week. They are both capitally attended, and all the scholars, without a single exception, made good progress. In several instances I was quite surprised. These schools are quite self-supporting, and I only give my time. This last winter was the third year. A portion of the pence paid in goes to the schoolmistress who always attends and assists me.

50. Yes.

51. The past year has been a dreadful one for sickness; and having been obliged, almost weekly, to call upon the parish for local charities – such as linen for the sick, clothes, bedding, coal, wine, meat and very many other things, I did not make any collection for foreign objects. It cost my two farmers, <u>besides</u> a dreadfully heavy poor rate bill, upwards of £50 <u>each</u> to support the people when suffering from the fever, to say nothing about what loss they sustained by the shortness of labour. Even now they are short of hands, and have a number of men who cannot do more, in real labour, than half a day's work, though receiving full pay.

52. I beg to state that I have to contend against a great decrease in the annual subscriptions towards my school owing to the embarrassed state of the affairs of a large, landed proprietor. I fear at times that I shall be obliged to close my school in consequence; but of course, this will not be done if I can possibly avoid it. I have only three other persons to apply to – viz the Vicar and two tenant farmers.

George D'Urban John Hough

233. WILTON cum NETHERHAMPTON.   D. Wilton.

1. Wilton, a rectory.

2. Earl of Pembroke.

3. 2000.

4. Revd Richard Seymour Conway Chermside.[1]

5. Yes.
6. Yes.
7. [Blank]
8. [Blank]
9. Yes, two.
10. One in 1860, one in 1863.
11. Revd Dacres Olivier and Revd Adam Fairbairn, both in full orders.
12. No.
13. Yes, one also at Netherhampton.
14. St Catherine's Netherhampton, date of consecration unknown.
15. Yes.
16. Yes.
17. Yes.
18. None.
19. [Blank]
20. [Blank]
21. Commuted tithe rent charge circa £500 glebe £17 2s 6d total £517 2s 6d.
22. [Blank]
23. No.
24. 10.30am, 3.30pm, 6.30pm. Sermons morning and evening.
25. Yes.
26. Yes.
27. Yes.
28. Every day – twice – and in Lent, Advent and occasional services in the old chancel.
29. [a] Yes [b] Yes [c] Yes [d] Yes [e] Yes.
30. 1st and 3rd Sunday in every month.
31. No. I did once, but the shifting of the population and occasional influx of communicants from Wilton House render such a list practically useless.
32. [Blank]
33. [Blank]
34. From 90 to 110.
35. From 60 to 70.
36. About 700, children included.
37. Impossible to give with accuracy.
38. The churchwardens are unable to assign seats satisfactorily to all applicants, yet I can hardly say a new church is wanted.
39. 62 baptisms 9 marriages 32 burials.
40. In 1861 – 50. The lists for 1862 and 1863 are imperfect.
41. Yes.
42. For the year 1863, £39 2s 1½d.
43. Yes.
44. One Independent Chapel, one Wesleyan, one Wesleyan Seceders and one Primitive Methodist.
45. Yes.

46. Yes.

47. Peculiar circumstances make it difficult to fix a real average.

48. Yes.

49. Yes. Very fair success with a regular night school and classes in connection with the Literary Institute.

50. Yes.

51. Lent Ember collection £6 11s 8d towards new hymn books for the church. Trinity Ember collection £6 1s 4d for the Society for the Propagation of the Gospel. Michaelmas Ember collection £6 14s 7d towards Parochial Curate Aid Fund. Christmas Ember collection £5 3s 2¾d for diocesan society for augmenting small livings.

52. The organisation and variety of dissenting bodies, which however offer no special characteristics in this parish.

Richard Chermside

¹Chermside arrived at Wilton in 1848.

234. WINKFIELD or WINGFIELD   D. Potterne

1. Winkfield, a rectory.

2. The trustees are Canon Hall, Clifton; Dean Goode, Ripon; Rev James Cooper and Rev J.H. Gurney – both of London; and Rev H Houghton, Cheltenham.

3. Nearly 350.

4. Edward Meade M.A. Oxon. Instituted 1ˢᵗ July 1842, inducted 9ᵗʰ July 1842.

5. Yes.

6. Yes, in the glebe house.

7. [Blank]

8. No other.

9. Not during the last year.

10. [Blank]

11. [Blank]

12. [Blank]

13. No.

14. [Blank]

15. In very good repair, except a little settling of the south porch, which will be attended to at once. It is duly provided with all things necessary etc.

16. Yes.

17. Yes.

18. A small transept has been added on the north side, to use as a baptistry, and for the better accommodation of the Sunday school and also to provide additional sittings for 12 persons. For this addition a faculty was duly obtained.

19. No chapels.

20. [Blank]

21. Tithe rent charge £260 per annum, and glebe land 18 acres let at 35s per acre.

22. [Blank]

23. Only one.

24. Two full services, with sermon at each. Morning service, from September to April, beginning at 10.30am, and afternoon service at 3.00pm. From April to September, service at 11.00am and at 6.00pm and 6.30pm (in the longest days).

25. Yes.

26. There is no public catechising.

27. There are not morning and evening prayers daily in the parish church.

28. On Christmas Day and Good Friday, two full services, and the attendance at the morning service numbers the same as on Sundays. On Ash Wednesday, in Passion Week, Easter Monday and Tuesday, Ascension Day, Whit Monday and Trinity. On Ash Wednesday the attendance is good, on the other days named, the average is about 15, besides school children.

29. [a] Yes [b] Yes [c] No [d] Yes [e] No.

30. Not on fixed Sundays, but so as to be administered about twice in three months.

31. Yes.

32. 56.

33. Two; one through indisposition and domestic hindrances, the other through a prolonged absence from this parish.

34. 37. But the average, last year, was reduced by the absence of two families, for some months, in consequence of alterations in their houses.

35. 35.

36. For 165 in the church, chancel and transept, besides accommodation for Sunday school children.

37. Average congregation, children included, 150. Some increase, attributable to the presence of larger households.

38. The accommodation is sufficient.

39. 8 baptisms, 0 marriages 11 burials. There was unusual mortality among the children, through the prevalence of scarlet fever.

40. In the year 1861 there were 14.

41. Yes, at the Easter vestry.

42. £9 0s 8d, for the year ending December 31st 1863.

43. A regular entry is made, but not in a book kept solely for that purpose.

44. There is no dissenting place of worship. The number of dissenters is about 12, but few of these at all decided in their separation. They belong to the denomination mostly known as Baptists.

45. Yes.

46. No application has been made for aid to the Committee of Council in Education.

47. The boys at the age of about 10 years. The girls are sometimes kept to the age of 13 or 14 but they usually leave, or become irregular in attendance at the age of 12 years.

48. As many as 13 boys are now attending the Sunday school, who have left the day school, and the same is the case with three girls.

49. There having been no assistant curate during the last year, the evening

school has somewhat languished, but there has been an attendance of 10 youths, instructed two evenings a week by the incumbent's wife.

50. Yes.

51. For Church Missions to the Jews £2 17s. For Church Missions to the Heathen £4 19s 10d. For augmenting of small benefices £3 10s.

52. Since the last triennial visitation no new circumstances of impediment to ministerial success have arisen, worthy of special mention. The experience of the last three years has, however, served to confirm the remarks made under this heading on previous occasions.

Edward Meade

235. WINSLEY D. Potterne

1. Winsley, a perpetual curacy.
2. The Dean and Chapter of Bristol.
3. 655.
4. Francis Stephen Forss. Instituted October 11th 1862, inducted October 18th 1862.
5. Yes.
6. No glebe house – resided in the parish.
7. [Blank]
8. No.
9. Yes.
10. April 8th 1863.
11. Charles L. Hardman, a priest.
12. No.
13. Two churches.
14. A Church at Winsley and one at Limpley Stoke; dates and names not known.
15. Yes.
16. Yes.
17. Yes.
18. No.
19. [Blank]
20. [Blank]
21. £147 per annum from tithe rent charge and surplice fees.
22. £117 per annum from Winsley and £30 per annum from Limpley Stoke.
23. No glebe house.
24. Two full services with sermons at 11.00am and 6.15pm.
25. Yes.
26. No.
27. No.
28. Christmas Day, Ash Wednesday, Good Friday and Ascension Day, and on every Wednesday evening during Lent. 100 about the average.
29. [a] Yes [b] Yes [c] Yes [d] Yes [e] Yes.
30. Every 6th Sunday.

31. Yes.
32. 40.
33. They have all.
34. 17.
35. 18. Many more communicants since Christmas.
36. 434.
37. 161. Very much increasing.
38. No.
39. 18 baptisms 6 marriages 17 burials.
40. [Blank]
41. Yes.
42. £4 12s 11d.
43. Yes.
44. A Wesleyan and a Baptist chapel.
45. No – one greatly needed.[1]
46. No.
47. [Blank]
48. [Blank]
49. [Blank]
50. Yes.
51. For augmenting of small benefices £1 16s. For the S.P.G. Society £2 11s 10d.
52. The want of a parsonage greatly hinders my usefulness and the need of a schoolroom is much felt. We are obliged to hold the Sunday school in the church and during the week the children of the parish are under no moral training. A schoolroom would be very useful for giving lectures and readings during the winter evenings and by these and other means I believe I should be able to gain a greater influence for good over the people.

F.S. Forss

[1] A National School opened in 1869

236. WINTERBOURNE BASSETT   D. Avebury

1. Winterbourne Bassett, a rectory.
2. The President and Fellows of Magdalen College Oxford.
3. 248.
4. Henry Harris. Instituted Mar 10th & Inducted Mar 20th 1858.
5. Yes.
6. In the glebe house.
7. [Blank]
8. No.
9. No.
10. [Blank]
11. [Blank]
12. [Blank]
13. No.

14. [Blank]
15. Yes.
16. Yes.
17. Yes.
18. No.
19. [Blank]
20. [Blank]
21. Tithe rent charge <u>gross</u> annual value £674 15s 6d. 40 acres of glebe at £61 12s tithe barn let at £1. Total £737 7s 6d.
22. [Blank]
23. No.
24. On Sundays at 11.00am and 3.00pm (except during the summer). In the summer the evening service is at 6.00pm. There is a sermon after each service.
25. Yes.
26. No.
27. No.
28. On Christmas Day and Good Friday the service is the same as on Sundays. On Ascension Day and on Ash Wednesday and on every Wednesday in Lent there is evening service with sermon at 6.30pm. The attendance on Christmas Day is good with an average attendance of about 80. On Good Friday it is larger than on any other day in the year sometimes over 100. On Ash Wednesday tolerably large an average about 60 or 70. On the remaining days from 20 to 40.
29. [a] Yes [b] Yes [c] No [d] Yes [e] No.
30. On the 1ˢᵗ Sunday in Lent and the 1ˢᵗ Sunday in Advent, twice between Whit Sunday and Advent Sunday.
31. No.
32. 40.
33. 12.
34. About 16.
35. About 16.
36. For somewhat about 140 I believe.
37. 70 or thereabouts. I do not perceive either an increase or decrease in it.
38. No.
39. 4 Baptisms 0 marriages 5 Burials.
40. In 1861 14 persons. In 1862 and 1863 none.
41. No.
42. In 1863 it was £3 16s 3d.
43. Yes.
44. A cottage is used as a meeting house for Primitive Methodists. Several of the parishioners attend it and there are about 20 of these who do not come to church except on Good Friday. Most however of those who attend the meeting also come to church.
45. Yes.
46. No.
47. The girls generally leave at about 10 years old and the boys still earlier. Few

boys remain after 5.

48. Yes for several years.

49. There is an evening school during the winter months for boys which is tolerably successful.

50. I have given them to the churchwarden for transmission.

51. There was only one collection made <u>in the church</u> in 1863 viz Oct 18th for the society for the augmentation of benefices. £1 13s 4d. (But in January of the same year £4 6s was collected through the parish for the Lancashire operatives. And on March 5th a collection of £1 6s 2d was made for the S.P.G after a meeting in the school room).

52. [Blank]

Henry Harris

237. WINTERBOURNE DAUNTSEY　D. Amesbury

1. Winterbourne Dauntsey.
2. The Bishop of Salisbury.
3. 171.
4. John H Cartwright, 1844.
5. Resident in Winterbourne Earls.
6. No glebe house.
7. [Blank]
8. Incumbent of Winterbourne Earls, diocese of Salisbury.
9. None.
10. [Blank]
11. [Blank]
12. [Blank]
13. No.
14. [Blank]
15. Fairly so.
16. Fairly so.
17. Yes.
18. No.
19. [Blank]
20. [Blank]
21. Bounty Office and grant of Ecclesiastical Commissioners.
22. [Blank]
23. [Blank]
24. Morning service at 10.30am and sermon. Evening service at 2.30pm and sermon.
25. Yes.
26. No.
27. No.
28. Christmas Day, Good Friday and Ascension Day; attendance few.
29. [a] Yes [b] Yes [c] Yes [d] and [e] on one of these.

30. Four or five other times.
31. No.
32. [Blank]
33. [Blank]
34. Total number of communicants in 1863, 62.
35. [See 34]
36. Between 100 and 150.
37. Average not known – attendance as usual.
38. No.
39. 3 baptisms 1 marriage 1 burial.
40. Eight in 1861.
41. Sometimes receipts affixed at church door.
42. £2 0s 5d in 1863.
43. Yes.
44. A chapel used by reformed Methodists.
45. In Winterbourne Earls.
46. No.
47. Boys at 7, 8 or 9 years old. Girls at 10 or 11.
48. Some attend at Sunday school.
49. No.
50. Yes.
51. Church Missionary £2 6s 2d. Propagation of the gospel 16s 4d. Total £3 2s 6d.
52. [Blank]

John H Cartwright

238. WINTERBOURNE EARLS   D. Amesbury
1. Winterbourne Earls.
2. Bishop of Salisbury.
3. 276.
4. John H Cartwright, 1851.
5. Yes.
6. No glebe house.
7. [Blank]
8. Winterbourne Dauntsey.
9. No.
10. [Blank]
11. [Blank]
12. [Blank]
13. No.
14. [Blank]
15. In such a state as renders divine service impracticable.[1]
16. No.
17. [Blank]

18. No.
19. Marriages and burials. Baptisms in Winterbourne Dauntsey church.
20. [Blank]
21. Bounty Office and portion of rent charge of tithes.
22. One parish.
23. No glebe house.
24. No services.
25. [Blank]
26. [Blank]
27. [Blank]
28. [Blank]
29. Answered in paper of Winterbourne Dauntsey.
30. [Blank]
31. [Blank]
32. [Blank]
33. [Blank]
34. [Blank]
35. [Blank]
36. [Blank]
37. [Blank]
38. [Blank]
39. 3 baptisms 0 marriages 2 burials.
40. Eight persons.
41. [Blank]
42. [Blank]
43. [Blank]
44. Conference Methodists have a chapel in Hurdcott.
45. Yes.
46. No.
47. As in Winterbourne Dauntsey.
48. Some.
49. No.
50. Yes.
51. None.
52. [Blank]

John H Cartwright

[1] In 1867 the decision was taken to demolish the two existing churches at Winterbourne Earls and Winterbourne Dauntsey, and to replace them with one new parish church in Winterbourne Earls.

239. WINTERBOURNE GUNNER   D. Amesbury

1. Winterbourne Gunner or Cherborough, a rectory.
2. Present patron, the Lord Chancellor.

3. About 170.

4. Edward George Griffith, Easter 1853.

5. Yes.

6. In the glebe house.

7. [Blank]

8. No.

9. No.

10. [Blank]

11. [Blank]

12. [Blank]

13. No.

14. [Blank]

15. No, very far from it, as far as repair is concerned.

16. By no means.

17. No, but one attends church constantly.

18. A slight alteration has been made in the church sittings; one seat has been divided into two; and a front or stand constructed in respect of another seat.

19. [Blank]

20. [Blank]

21. Tithe commutation £219 6s 6d. Glebe 9 acres £13 10s. Total £232 16s 6d.

22. [Blank]

23. No.

24. Two services with sermons; in the winter season at 10.30am and 2.30 or 3.00pm. In the summer at 10.30am and 6.00pm.

25. I omit the offertory sentences and the prayers for the church militant; I omit nothing else.

26. No.

27. No.

28. Christmas Day, Ash Wednesday, Ascension Day and Good Friday. The attendance much the same as a Sunday on Christmas Day and Good Friday, but very small on Ash Wednesday and Ascension Day.

29. [a] Yes [b] Yes [c] No [d] and [e] one or the other.

30. The 1ˢᵗ Sunday in Lent; the last Sunday in August and October respectively.

31. I keep a memorandum to that effect.

32. 21 belonging to this parish.

33. All have communicated, and with two exceptions repeatedly.

34. During the past year, 11 was the smallest number, 23 the largest, 14 the average.

35. [See 34]

36. About 70 with comfort.

37. It is not possible to strike an average, so much depending on the season of the year, the weather, the name of the Minister for the day at the meeting house, and other circumstances. The attendance may I think be said to vary from 12 to 50.

38. No want of further church accommodation in the sense of enlarged or increased church accommodation, but great want of improved church accommodation.

39. 5 baptisms 2 marriages 2 burials.

40. 11.

41. I affix a statement of the sum on the church door, and I publish the same on the cover of a localised parish magazine.

42. £3 3s 11d during the past year.

43. I keep a private memorandum.

44. A Wesleyan meeting house. Nearly all in my parish attend the meeting house more or less, when the church is not open, i.e. the winter evenings.

45. There is one in Winterbourne Earls, for the three Winterbournes.

46. [Blank]

47. 13 or 14.

48. Not to any extent.

49. Not with any great success.

50. I propose doing so immediately.

51. During the year 1863 no collections were made, owing to local circumstances. Two sermons, one for the S.P.G. (which has been preached) and the other in obedience to your Lordship's pastoral, were postponed to the present year.

52. I might (as your Lordship is privately aware) make a lengthened reply to this question. I can however, add nothing further to the painful circumstances already within your Lordship's cognizance, than to express my deep regret, that the feelings entertained towards me by my immediate neighbour and sole acting churchwarden (and which must necessarily impede my own ministry, and the welfare of the church around here) seems to be more bitter than ever. The only remedies I can suggest, are either (1) the resignation, or (2) the exchange of my living. 1. In justice to my family, as well as myself, I cannot contemplate this further alternative. 2. If your Lordship can in any way assist me with respect to this latter, I shall be truly grateful, But I beg it to be distinctly understood that my own only motive in so desiring an exchange, has reference to this painful matter.

Edward G Griffith

240. WINTERBOURNE STOKE D. Wylye

1. Winterbourne Stoke, a vicarage.

2. Lord Ashburton, Bath House, Piccadilly.

3. 365.

4. Charles Lawford, 1847.

5. Yes.

6. Yes.

7. [Blank]

8. Berwick St James, Sarum.

9. No.

10. [Blank]

11. [Blank]

12. [Blank]

13. No.

14. [Blank]
15. Yes.
16. Yes.
17. Yes.
18. [Blank]
19. [Blank]
20. [Blank]
21. Rent charge commuted at £240.
22. [Blank]
23. No.
24. Services at 11.00am and 6.00pm. Sermon at each.
25. Yes.
26. No.
27. No.
28. Wednesdays in Lent, Good Friday, Ascension Day and Christmas Day.
29. [a] Yes [b] Yes [c] No [d] Yes [e] Yes.
30. The 1st Sunday in October.
31. Yes.
32. 36.
33. None.
34. 25.
35. The same.
36. About 200.
37. I never counted. There is a very fair congregation in the morning and very large in the evening.
38. No.
39. 15 baptisms 5 marriages 7 burials.
40. 20.
41. No.
42. £3 15s.
43. Yes.
44. No place of worship; about a dozen Baptists and as many Wesleyans.
45. Yes.
46. Yes.
47. Boys at 8, girls at 10 or 11.
48. The girls come, but not many boys.
49. Evening school in the winter well attended by the boys from 12 to 17 years of age.
50. Not yet.
51. I have not kept a record.
52. No.

Charles Lawford

241. WINTERSLOW   D. Amesbury

1. Winterslow, a rectory.
2. The President and Fellows of St John the Baptist's College, Oxford.
3. 950.
4. Edward Luard. Instituted and inducted December 1846.
5. Yes.
6. Yes.
7. [Blank]
8. No.
9. Yes.
10. August 1854.
11. George Noel Freeling, a priest.
12. No.
13. No, but there is a proprietary chapel licensed in which service is performed.
14. [Blank]
15. Yes.
16. Yes.
17. Yes.
18. None.
19. Yes.
20. The proprietary chapel is distant 1½ miles.
21. Rent charge apportion at £887; glebe land 53 acres value £82.
22. [Blank]
23. No.
24. Two services at the church at 11.00am and 3.00pm. One service at the proprietary chapel at 6.30pm.
25. Yes.
26. Not in the church but at the school.
27. No.
28. Every Wednesday evening in the chapel. On Christmas Day, Ash Wednesday, Good Friday, every Friday in Lent, Ascension Day and the Monday in Whitsun week. The number of persons is small except on Christmas Day and Good Friday.
29. On Christmas Day, Good Friday, Easter Day and either Whit Sunday or Trinity Sunday.
30. The 1st Sunday in every month in the church. Four times a year in the chapel.
31. Yes.
32. 115.
33. Four.
34. Easter with Good Friday – 61. Whit Sunday or Trinity – 32. Christmas – 26. These are the average during the last three years.
35. 28.
36. In the church 400, the chapel 100.
37. 200; much the same average for some years.
38. No.
39. 28 baptisms 4 marriages 8 burials.

40. 38.

41. Yes.

42. £22 6s a year is the average during the last three years.

43. Yes.

44. No means of ascertaining the number of dissenters.

45. Yes.

46. Yes.

47. 10.

48. Not many.

49. At evening school with moderate success.

50. Yes.

51. Expenses of the chapel £2 3s. Schools £4 9s 6d. Infirmary and Charmouth Convalescent Home £5 16s. Augmentation of small benefices £5 15s. Total £18 3s 6d.

52. [Blank]

Edward Luard

242. WOODBOROUGH D. Avebury

1. Woodborough, a rectory.

2. William Thomas Wyld, Woodborough.

3. 400.

4. William Thomas Wyld, 1835.

5. I was at home 294 days.

6. In the glebe house.

7. [Blank]

8. Yes. Blunsdon St Andrew in the diocese of Gloucester and Bristol.

9. As assistant curate.

10. In 1862.

11. Rev Douglas Gawn, a priest.

12. That of Alton Priors as curate.

13. One church.

14. [Blank]

15. Yes.

16. Yes.

17. Yes.

18. The church was rebuilt in the year 1861, a faculty being obtained and was consecrated by your Lordship January 28th 1862. The church holds 280 persons.

19. [Blank]

20. [Blank]

21. Rent charge commuted at £315 and glebe land about £100 per annum.

22. [Blank]

23. No.

24. Two full services, morning at 10.30am and evening at 2.30pm.

25. Yes, always allow no omission at all.

26. No.

27. No.

28. Ash Wednesday and Good Friday. One evening during Lent and four days in Passion week. In Lent about 40 on the average and Passion week about 15 besides school children.

29. [a] Yes [b] Yes [c] Yes, but only an evening congregation [d] Yes [e] No.

30. 1st Sunday in Lent and at Michaelmas.

31. Yes.

32. 45.

33. About six.

34. From 25 to 30 and upwards.

35. About 23.

36. About 280.

37. About 75 in the morning besides 50 or 60 schoolchildren, about 95 adults in the afternoon, sometimes 115.

38. No.

39. 7 baptisms 3 marriages 5 burials.

40. In 1861 there were 8 males and 13 females, total 21.

41. No.

42. About £4.

43. I keep my own private account.

44. One Wesleyan. I cannot say the number exactly. All Honey Street are dissenters and there are three preachers there. There are only six regular dissenters in the village and only four families not dissenters in Honey Street I should say.

45. Yes.

46. No.

47. Boys at 7, girls about 8.

49. Adult evening school for males from October to March.

50. Yes.

51. Propagation of the Gospel in Foreign Parts, poor benefices and church building.

52. I have nobody to support me in church matters. The farmers take no interest in the church and do not care whether their servants and boys observe the Sabbath or not. The system of cattle feeding is so great on one farm that the servants declare they have no time to go to church. I have now only one communicant among my farmers and owing to the chief people not being communicants I can trace the absence of many others. We have also a wretched public house over which I have now no control. As to remedies, I see none so long as the parish is under the present landlords. I have one landlord (tenant in one) who drinks with his own labourers.

William Thomas Wyld

243. WOODFORD   D. Amesbury

1.   Woodford, a vicarage.

2. The Lord Bishop of the diocese.

3. 500.

4. Robert Money Chatfield, 1830.

5. Yes.

6. In the glebe house.

7. [Blank]

8. No.

9. No.

10. [Blank]

11. [Blank]

12. [Blank]

13. Yes – Wilsford.

14. Woodford All Saints and Wilsford St Michael.

15. Yes.

16. Yes.

17. Yes.

18. No.

19. [Blank]

20. [Blank]

21. Vicarial tithe and augmentation by the Ecclesiastical Commissioners.

22. Woodford £180, Wilsford £52 10s, augmentation by Ecclesiastical Commissioners £17, ditto £70. All rent charge per annum.

23. No.

24. Two full services on Sunday, morning and evening, 10.30am and 6.00pm. Sermons always preached at the same time.

25. Yes.

26. No.

27. No.

28. During Lent on Wednesday evenings, Christmas Day and Good Friday. About 50 or 60 during Lent. On Christmas Day and Good Friday, full congregations.

29. [a] Yes [b] Yes [c] No [d] Yes [e] No.

30. On the 1st Sunday in each month.

31. Yes.

32. 140.

33. 18.

34. 40 or 50.

35. The same.

36. In Woodford there is accommodation for 312 including children.

37. I never counted them, but there is always a good congregation. The appropriated seats being occupied and the free sittings well filled in the morning and in the evening crowded, so as to require room in the appropriated part.

38. No, it is sufficient for the wants of my own parishioners. Sometimes on Sunday evenings there is not room enough in the free seats.

39. 18 baptisms 3 marriages 15 burials.

40. 29.

41. Yes.

42. £11 13s 11¼d. Less than former years in consequence of some gentry having left the parish.

43. Yes.

44. None. A few Wesleyans, but most of them come to church also.

45. Yes.

46. No. The schoolroom does not come up to the regulations of the Privy Council on Education.

47. Boys on average at 8. Girls till they go to service.

48. Yes. Many become teachers when confirmed.

49. Yes, but I do not find it prospers unless I attend it myself, which with a large family to attend to is not practicable.

50. Yes.

51. S.P.G., C.M.S., Jews' Society, schools of the parish, Irish Church Missions, augmentation fund for poor clergy, and cotton manufacturers besides the monthly sacramental alms. C.M.S. £2 12s. S.P.G. collection made at a meeting in the schoolroom. Jews £3 19s 3s. Schools £4 17s 9d. Augmentation fund £1 16s 8½d. Irish church missions £3 18s 6d. Cotton manufacturers £3 0s 1d. Total £20 4s 3d.

52. [Blank]

R.M. Chatfield

244. WOOTTON BASSETT   D. Avebury

1. Wootton Bassett, a vicarage.

2. The Earl of Clarendon.

3. 2000.

4. Thomas Hyde Ripley. Instituted Oct 13th and inducted Dec 24th 1813.

5. Yes.

6. Resident in glebe house.

7. [Blank]

8. Tockenham Wick, the adjoining parish to Wootton Bassett.

9. Yes.

10. 16th May 1863.

11. John Curgenven, a priest.

12. No.

13. No.

14. [Blank]

15. Yes.

16. Yes.

17. Yes.

18. No.

19. [Blank]

20. [Blank]

21. Tithe commutation and glebe land. Gross amount about £570 net about £450.

22. [Blank]

23. No.

24. Three services with sermon on Sundays at 11.00am, 3.00pm and 6.30pm.

25. Yes.

26. No.

27. No.

28. Christmas Day, Good Friday, Ash Wednesday, Wednesdays in Lent, Passion week, Monday and Tuesdays in Easter week. Monday and Tuesday in Whitsun week and Ascension Day. Attendance uncertain.

29. [a] Yes [b] Yes [c] No [d] No [e] Yes.

30. Eight times a year in all.

31. No.

32. [Blank]

33. [Blank]

34. 60.

35. 40.

36. About 500.

37. [Blank]

38. [Blank]

39. 46 baptisms 11 marriages 53 burials.

40. In 1861 over 70.

41. No.

42. £11 10s.

43. Yes.

44. The Independents, the Wesleyan Methodists and Primitive Methodists have each a place of worship. Numbers uncertain.

45. Yes.

46. Yes.

47. From 10 to 12.

48. Many of them.

49. By a night school during the winter months.

50. Yes.

51. Society for the Propagation of the Gospel, National Schools, augmentation of small livings.

52. No.

Thomas Hyde Ripley

245. WOOTTON RIVERS D. Marlborough

1. Wootton Rivers, a rectory.

2. St John's College, Cambridge and Brasenose College, Oxford present alternately.

3. 435 by the last census.

4. William Jackson Brodribb. Date of institution April 1860.

5. Yes.

6. Yes.
7. [Blank]
8. No.
9. No.
10. [Blank]
11. [Blank]
12. [Blank]
13. No.
14. [Blank]
15. Yes.
16. The fences are not in good order. It will be necessary before long to enlarge the churchyard and fresh fencing will then be put.
17. Yes.
18. The church and chancel were completely restored in the year 1862.
19. [Blank]
20. [Blank]
21. Tithe rent charge.
22. [Blank]
23. No.
24. Two services every Sunday, at 10.30 am and 3.00pm in winter, and at 10.30am and 6.00pm in summer. A sermon is preached at each service.
25. Yes.
26. No.
27. No. In a small agricultural parish I do not think it would be possible to collect a congregation.
28. On Christmas Day, Ash Wednesday, Good Friday and Ascension Day. On Christmas Day and on Good Friday the church is well attended, but not on the other two days.
29. [a] Yes [b] Yes [c] No [d] Yes [e] Yes.
30. Usually on the 1st Sunday of every month.
31. Yes.
32. 20 (of them five or six are very rare communicants).
33. 6 or 7, I believe.
34. 10.
35. 7.
36. For about 175.
37. About 130. It is considerably larger in the summer evenings. The congregation, I think, remains almost stationary in respect of numbers.
38. No.
39. 19 baptisms 1 marriage 13 burials.
40. 11 persons were confirmed in this parish in 1861.
41. Yes.
42. £2 8s during the last year.
43. Yes.
44. There are none.

45. Yes.

46. No, because the present building is unfit for the purpose. New schools are on the point of being erected.

47. At about 10 years of age.

48. Yes, to a considerable extent.

49. There is a night school during four months in winter. The average attendance has been 15 or 16.

50. They will be transmitted early in April.

51. For the Society for the Propagation of the Gospel and for the Augmentation of Small Benefices.

52. I think the chief difficulty with which a clergyman has to contend in an agricultural parish is the early age at which children are removed from school, and the consequent ignorance in which they grow up. Also I regard the employment of women for work in the fields as hurtful to their moral and spiritual interests. But I am unable to suggest a remedy for an evil which arises from the low wages of our agricultural labourers.

William J Brodribb M.A.

246. WORTON   D. Potterne

1. Worton and Marston, a perpetual curacy.
2. Revd Joseph Medlicott.[1]
3. Between 500 and 600.
4. Augustus Edward Aldridge, September 1853.
5. Yes.
6. Yes, in my own house.
7. [Blank]
8. No.
9. No.
10. [Blank]
11. [Blank]
12. [Blank]
13. No.
14. [Blank]
15. Yes.
16. Yes.
17. Yes.
18. No.
19. [Blank]
20. [Blank]
21. Tithe and augmentations, gross £180 3s 5d.
22. [Blank]
23. [Blank]
24. 10.45am and 6.15pm, sermons at both.
25. Yes.
26. No.

27. No.

28. Christmas Day and Good Friday, near a Sunday's congregation.

29. Twelve times a year on the last Sunday in each month; exceptions Easter Day, Whit Sunday or Trinity in place of more (?) normal time.

30. None.

31. No.

32. Varies.

33. Do not know.

34. Same as at others.

35. [Blank]

36. 260.

37. Without children about 150.

38. No.

39. Specified in forms sent. 1 or 2 marriages.[2]

40. One.

41. All amounts annually given.

42. £6.

43. No.

44. Two, Wesleyans and Primitives.

45. Yes.

46. No, not in need of it.

47. Cannot say anything definitely.

48. Yes in some cases.

49. Yes successfully.

50. Yes.

51. Jews, Church Missionary Trust, Church Society, Hospital Bath, Lancashire distress and other local objects, poor benefices.

52. [Blank]

A.E. Aldridge

[1] Vicar of Potterne.

[2] The parish registers recorded 16 baptisms, 2 marriages and 10 burials.

247. WYLYE D. Wylye

1. Wylye, a rectory.

2. Trustees of the Earl of Pembroke.

3. 489.

4. Joseph Samuel Stockwell, institution 21st December 1840.

5. I have.

6. In the glebe house.

7. [Blank]

8. No.

9. I have no curate.

10. [Blank]

11. [Blank]

12. [Blank]

13. One church.
14. [Blank]
15. It is.
16. It is.
17. They do.
18. None in particular.
19. [Blank]
20. [Blank]
21. £492.
22. [Blank]
23. One.
24. Prayers and sermon at 10.30am. Prayers at 3.00pm. The litany and sermon at 6.00pm.
25. In the morning and afternoon.
26. I do not.
27. I do not.
28. Good Friday, Ash Wednesday, Ascension Day, Wednesdays and Fridays during Lent.
29. [a] Yes [b] Yes [c] No [d] and [e] one or the other.
30. The 1st Sunday in every month.
31. I do.
32. 75.
33. 11.
34. 35 to 40.
35. 25 to 30.
36. 312.
37. 250 to 300.
38. There is no want of further accommodation.
39. 7 baptisms 2 marriages 10 burials.
40. In 1861 there were 18.
41. I do not – but I keep an account.
42. £7 16s 1½d.
43. I have.
44. One – Congregational of all denominations.
45. There is.
46. I have not.
47. 10 or 11.
48. Some few only.
49. I have an evening school through the winter months – success very satisfactory.
50. I have.
51. Church Missionary £4 12s 1d. Harvest thanksgiving £5 16s 7d (Charmouth Hospital). Society for the Propagation of the Gospel £6 15s 0¼d. Total £17 3s 0¼d.
52. [Blank]

J.S. Stockwell

248. YATESBURY   D. Avebury

1. Yatesbury, a rectory.
2. [Blank]
3. 230.
4. Alfred Charles Smith.[1]
5. Yes.
6. In the glebe house.
7. [Blank]
8. No.
9. [Blank]
10. [Blank]
11. [Blank]
12. [Blank]
13. No.
14. [Blank]
15. Yes.
16. Yes.
17. Yes.
18. [Blank]
19. [Blank]
20. [Blank]
21. [Blank]
22. [Blank]
23. No.
24. Sunday morning at 11.00am, afternoon at 3.00pm. Sermons at both services.
25. Yes.
26. [Blank]
27. [Blank]
28. On Holy Days. Wednesdays and Fridays during Lent.
29. [a] Yes [b] Yes [c] Yes [d] Yes [e] No.
30. [Blank]
31. [Blank]
32. [Blank]
33. [Blank]
34. [Blank]
35. [Blank]
36. [Blank]
37. [Blank]
38. [Blank]
39. 6 Baptisms 3 Marriages 6 Burials.
40. [Blank]
41. [Blank]
42. [Blank]
43. [Blank]
44. Baptist chapel.

45. Yes.
46. [Blank]
47. [Blank]
48. Yes.
49. Night school during the winter months.
50. [Blank]
51. [Blank]
52. [Blank]

R. L. Wild, locum tenens for A.C. Smith

¹Smith presented himself to the living in 1852

249. ZEALS GREEN D. Wylye

1. Zeals Green, a perpetual curacy.
2. Revd C.H. Townsend as vicar of Mere.
3. About 650.
4. William Byard Dalby. Date of licence September 17ᵗʰ 1863 reading in September 27ᵗʰ 1863.
5. Since date of licence he has been constantly resident, with the exception of three weeks.
6. In a house in the adjoining parish (there being no glebe house).
7. [Blank]
8. No.
9. Yes.
10. He has not yet been licensed.
11. Revd Edward Inman – a priest.
12. No.
13. No: the district has only one church, consecrated in 1846 and dedicated as St Martin.
14. [Blank]
15. Yes.
16. Yes.
17. Yes.
18. None.
19. [Blank]
20. [Blank]
21. £65 per annum from the Ecclesiastical Commissioners. £30 per annum from the same (Salisbury Deanery Estate). £3 per annum from the Royal Bounty Fund. Total £98.
22. [Blank]
23. There is no glebe house.
24. Morning and afternoon service at 10.30am and 3.00pm on Sundays, with sermons at each.
25. Yes; except that the offertory prayer for the church militant is not ordinarily used after the sermon.

26. During the short time since my appointment I have not catechised.

27. No, such never having been the practice, I have not yet attempted to commence it.

28. On Christmas Day, New Year's Day, the first day of Lent, Good Friday and Ascension Day. On Christmas Day from 100 to 150 attend – on the other occasions less than 30, exclusive of school children.

29. [a] Yes [b] Yes [c] No [d] and [e] one or the other.

30. At intermediate periods between these festivals, the Holy Communion is administered on Sundays at intervals varying from a month to six weeks.

31. I have not yet been enabled to obtain an exact list.

32. I estimate the number of communicants at about 50.

33. From the late date of my appointment I am unable to answer this.

34. Last Christmas Day 42. Easter Day 15.

35. About 20 to 25.

36. The church has sittings for 296.

37. About 200, with considerable fluctuations, on account of the large number of dissenters in the parish, but on the whole, not decreasing.

38. There seems at present ample accommodation.

39. 15 baptisms 0 marriages 13 burials.

40. I can find no record of any candidates in these years.

41. I have not hitherto done so except by informing the churchwardens.

42. Varying from 9s to 16s each occasion and amounting to about £5 a year.

43. Yes.

44. There is a chapel belonging to Independents and one belonging to Primitive Methodists. The former may number 150, the latter 50, and there are besides about 20 Roman Catholics.

45. Yes.

46. No; the mistress is not certificated.

47. About 9 years old.

48. In one or two instances, but not as a rule.

49. No such attempt has yet been made.

50. Yes.

51. [Part of the page is missing]

52. The prevalence of dissent, long in possession of the field, and uncounteracted of late years by any actually resident minister of the church, is a great obstacle, at present scarcely more than attempted to be met, by the curates lodging amongst the people, or within a few minutes' walk. I should fear that nothing really effectual or permanent can be done until a house be built, to form a centre for the operations of the church socially in the district. The parishioners are well disposed, but from long habits acquiesce in the partition of the parish between the church and dissent.

William Byard Dalby

INDEX OF PERSONS AND PLACES

References are to page numbers. Parish entries, as arranged alphabetically through the document, are printed in bold, followed by the entry number assigned to them in this edition. Places are (or were in 1864) in Wiltshire unless otherwise stated.

Abbott, – (Mrs) 232
Abingdon, Berks 69
Ailesbury, George
  Brudenell-Bruce, 2nd
  Marquess of xvii, 95,
  127, 135, 136, 161, 186,
  199, 278
Aldbourne (1) xxii, 1-2;
  see also Woodsend
Alderbury (2) 2-4, 51,
  143, 144, 25, 257; see
  also Whaddon
  Union Workhouse 51,
  130, 131
Aldridge, Augustus Edward
  377, 378
All Cannings (3) 5-6,
  141; see also Allington
Alley, Frederick Augustus
  333
Allington (4) 6-8, 11
Allington, in All Cannings
  5-6, 296
Alresford, Hants 5, 141
Alt, Just Henry 140, 141
Alton Barnes (5) 8-10;
  see also Honey Street
Alton Priors, in Overton
  250, 371
Alvediston (6) 10-11
Amesbury (7) 11-13
  Deanery 2, 6, 11, 38, 46,
  62, 88, 123, 124, 128,
  143, 147, 188, 194, 196,
  204, 226, 233, 238, 256,
  258, 340, 342, 351, 354,
  364, 365, 366, 370, 372
Anderson, Mason 287, 288
Andover, Hants 269
Angell, Wiiliam John
  Browne 250, 251
Ansty (8) xv, xx, 13–15,
  313

Antrobus, Sir Edmund 12,
  141
Antrobus, Lady Anne 141
Archer, William 185
Armstrong, Robert L 173,
  174
Arundell, John, 12th Baron
  xx, 13, 117, 320
Ashburton, Francis Baring,
  3rd Baron 5, 27, 141,
  368
Ashdown Park, Berks 6
Ashe a Court-Holmes,
  William Henry, 2nd
  Baron Heytesbury 172
Ashton, Rood, in West
  Ashton 179
Ashton, Steeple 282, 300-1
Ashton, West 328, 339-40
Astley, Sir Francis Dugdale
  35, 142, 210
Atkinson, Robert Moulton
  165
Atwood, Thomas G P 159,
  160
Atworth (9) xx, 15–16,
  164, 292; see also
  Cottles
Austen, John H 324, 325
Austen, Joseph Mason 273
Avebury (10) 16-18
  Deanery 5, 8, 16, 17, 24.
  25, 32, 37, 49, 55, 57,
  59, 70, 71, 76, 87, 91,
  100, 109, 132, 141, 169,
  174, 177, 206, 236, 250,
  270, 293, 295, 322, 362,
  371, 374, 380
Avon, River (Bristol) 50
Awdry, William Henry
  205, 206
Axford, in Ramsbury 264,
  265

Badger, William Collins
  132, 133
Barford St Martin (11)
  xxiv, 18-21; see also
  Grovely
Baring, Francis, 3rd Baron
  Ashburton 5, 27, 141,
  368
Barnsley, Glos 55, 355
Baron, John 332, 334
Barrington, Shute xi, xxiii
Bartlett, Symeon Taylor
  142, 143
Barton, Henry 3, 144, 256,
  258
Bath, Som 87, 148, 165
  Mineral Water Hospital
  139, 229
  (United) Hospital xxv,
  9, 45, 88, 110, 141, 171,
  192, 210, 223, 271, 338,
  378
Bath and Wells, Diocese
  245
Bath, John Alexander
  Thynne, 4th Marquess
  of 78, 103, 105, 145,
  146, 185, 190, 192,193,
  203, 229
Baverstock (12) 21-2
Baydon (13) 22–4
Baynham, Arthur 75, 76
Bedingfield, Richard King
  327, 329
Bedwyn, Great 127, 161-3
Bedwyn, Little 159, 199-
  200
Beechingstoke (14) 24–5;
  see also Broad Street
Bemerton 157, 160-1
Bennett, Frederick 207,
  209, 288, 290

Bennett, John Cunningham Calland 265

Berkshire xi, *see also* Abingdon, Ashdown Park, Chieveley, Coleshill, Hungerford, Lambourn, Reading Hospitals, Windsor

Berry, Marlborough Sterling 339. 340

Berwick Bassett (15) 25-7

Berwick St James (16) xx, 27-8, 368

Berwick St John (17) xvi, xx, 28-30

Berwick St Leonard (18) xvi, xx, 30–2, 279, 280

Bevan, R C L 155, 318

Bevan, S 155

Bevington, Messrs and Sons 332

Bicknell, Charles Brooke 304, 305

Birdbush, in Donhead St Mary 118

Birmingham Canal Company 156

Bishop's Cannings (19) 32-3, 87, 293; *see also* Coate, Horton

Bishopstone (South Wilts) (20) xxv, 19, 34-5

Bishopstrow (21) 35-7

Blackland (22) xx, 37–8, 71, 72; *see also* Theobald's Green

Blackmore, Richard White 118, 120

Blandy, Francis Jackson 232, 233

Bleeck, Alfred George 262, 264

Bleeck, William 186, 188

Blenheim Palace, Oxon 250

Bligh, Henry 160

Blunsdon St Andrew 371

Boreham, in Warminster 176, 338

Boscombe (23) 38-40

Bouchier, Barton 153, 154

Boulay, Francis H Du 169, 171

Bourne, Robert Burr 116, 118

Bouverie, Edward Pleydell- 200

Bouverie, William Pleydell-, 3rd Earl of Radnor 200, 242, 254

Bowerchalke (24) xix, 40-1, 53, 54

Bowman, Edmund Burkitt 317, 319

Bowood Bowood House 109

Boyton (25) 41–3, 331; *see also* Corton Lambert Chapel 42

Bradford on Avon (26, 27) 43–6, 350 Union Workhouse 43, 44

Bradford, Charles William 91, 92

Bradley, Maiden 177, 209-10

Bradley, North xvii, xxii, 235-6, 267

Bramshaw (28) 46–7; *see also* Fritham, Nomansland

Bratton (29) xxii, 47-9, 301

Bremhill (30) 49–50, 110, 174, 175; *see also* Foxham, Spirt Hill

Bridges, C 148

Brighton, Sussex xv, 176, 351

Brigmerston, in Milston Brigmerston House 226

Bristol xvi Dean and Chapter 15, 44, 182, 197, 213, 292, 350, 361 Gloucester and, Diocese xii, 5, 141, 371

Bristow, Robert 351

Britford (31) 51-2, 130

British and Foreign Bible Society 221

Brixton Deverill (32) 52-3, 253

Brixton, West, Surrey 121

Broad Chalke (33) xvi, xvii, xx, 10, 40, 53-5

Broad Hinton (34) 55-7

Broad Street, in Beechingstoke 25

Broad Town (35) xxvi, 56, 57-9

Brodribb, William Jackson 375, 377

Brodrick, Alan 46, 47

Bromham (36) 59-60; *see also* Spye Park

Bromley, F 326

Broughton Gifford (37) 60-2

Brown, Meredith 87, 88

Brown, Mrs Stafford 349

Broxmore Park, in Whiteparish 351

Brudenell-Bruce, George, 2nd Marquess of Ailesbury xvii, 95, 127, 135, 136, 161, 186, 199, 278

Bryan, Reginald Guy 155, 157

Buchanan, Thomas Boughton 166, 168

Buckerfield, Francis Henchman 95, 97

Buckinghamshire, *see* Eton College

Buckley, Felix J 241, 242

Bulford (38) xxi, 62–4

Bulkington (39) xix, 64–5, 191

Buntingford, Herts Coles Park 225

Burbage (40) 65–7; *see also* Ram Alley

Burbidge, Edward 1

Burcombe (41) xxiv, 67–8; *see also* Ugford

Burden's Ball, in South Newton 290, 291

Burder, Charles Sumner 168, 169

Burderop Park, in
Chisledon 84
Burgess, Thomas xxv
Burkitt, William Esdaile
73, 74
Burrard, Lady Mary
Standley Allen 164
Buttermere (42) xx,
68-70

Calley, Henry 84
Calne (43) xvi, 24, 37,
38, 70-1, 72, 109, 169,
206; *see also* Sandy
Lane
Union Workhouse 70
**Calstone Wellington
(44)** xx, 37, 38, 71-3
Cambridge xv-xvi
Clare College 248
King's College 53, 330
Magdalene College 282,
300
Queens' College 233
St John's College 375
Cannings, All 5-6, 141
Cannings, Bishop's 32-3,
87, 293
Canterbury Province, New
Zealand 40
Cape Town, South Africa
104
Cardew, James Walter 345,
346
Carey, Tupper 131, 137,
138, 146, 147
Carlisle 20
Bishop of 20, 148
Carpenter, George 297,
298
Cartwright, John H 364,
365, 366
Cassan, Algernon 254
Caswall, Henry 147, 148
Caswall, Robert Clarke
162
Cavan, S 70
Chalfield, Great xx, 15,
164-5
Chalke Deanery 10, 13,
18, 21, 28, 30, 34, 40,
51, 53, 78, 79, 99, 102,

106, 115, 116, 118, 130,
133, 137, 145, 152, 154,
157, 181, 183, 220, 242,
279, 284, 307, 310, 312,
314, 316, 320, 324, 343,
345
Chalke, Bower 40-1, 53, 54
Chalke, Broad xvi, xvii,
xx, 10, 40, 53, 54
Chamberlain, Samuel 208
Chapmanslade, in Corsley
and Dilton 104, 114,
333
Charlcutt, in Bremhill 50,
175
Charlton, in Donhead St
Mary 118, 119
Charlton All Saints (45)
73-4
Charlton St Peter (46)
75-6
Charmouth, Dorset
Convalescent Home
(Hospital) 20, 21, 338,
371, 379
Chatfield, Robert Money
354, 373, 374
Cheltenham, Glos 359
Cherhill (47) 76-7
Chermside, Richard
Seymour Conway xvii,
357, 359
Cheverell, Great 165-6
Cheverell, Little 200-1
Chichester, Henry Pelham,
3rd Earl of 106
Chicklade (48) xx, 78-9,
252, 254
Chicksgrove, in Tisbury
321
Chieveley, Berks 132
Child, Alfred 6, 8, 11
Chilmark (49) xx, xxi,
79-81; *see also* Ridge
Chilton Foliat (50) xx,
81-2
Chippenham 270
Chirton (51) xxv, 82-4;
see also Conock
Chisenbury and Chute,
Prebend 6
Chisledon (52) 22,

84-5, 121-2; *see also*
Burderop Park, Coate
Chitterne (53) xvi, 86-7
Chittoe (54) 32, 87-8; *see
also* Nonsuch
Cholderton (55) 88-90
Chretien, Charles Peter
88, 90
Chute (56) 6, 90-1
Chute, Chisenbury and,
Prebend 6
Cirencester, Glos 55, 355
Clack, in Lyneham 206,
207
Clarendon 3
Clarendon, George
William Frederick
Villiers, 4th Earl of 374
Clarke, John William 100,
102
Clatford, in Preshute 262
Cleather, George Ellis
82, 84
Cleather, George Parker
1, 2
Clench Common, in
Milton Lilborne 278
Clerk, David Malcolm
192, 194
Clifford, Caroline 175
Clifton, Glos 359
Clyffe Pypard (57) 57,
91-2
Coate (Cote), in Bishop's
Cannings 33
Coate, in Chisledon 85
Codford St Mary (58)
92-4
Codford St Peter (59)
94-5
Colerne 311
Coles Park, Buntingford,
Herts 225
Coleshill, Berks 242, 254
**Collingbourne Ducis
(60)** 95-7
**Collingbourne Kingston
(61)** 97-9
Collis, G 70
Colton St Andrew,
Norfolk 195
Compton Bassett (63)

24, 100–2, 206, 311
**Compton
  Chamberlayne (64)**
102–3
Connaught, Ireland 180
Conock, in Chirton 83
Coombe Abbey, Warwicks
  6
Coombe Bissett (62) 51,
  99–100, 183, 184
Coombs, Lower, Middle
  and Upper, in
  Donhead St Mary 118
Cooper, James 359
Corkson, William 55
Corsley (65) 103–5; *see
  also* Chapmanslade
Corton, in Boyton 42
Cosway, Samuel 90, 91
Cote (Coate), in Bishop's
  Cannings 33
Cottles, in Atworth 15
Coulston, East 125-7
Craven, William 2nd Earl
  of 6
Crawley, Charles David
  337
Crawley, Henry Owen
  283, 284,
Crawley, Richard 282, 300,
  301
Cricklade Deanery xii
Crockerton (66) 105–6,
  203, 204, 229, 230, 312
Crofton, in Great Bedwyn
  163
Croix, Henry C de St 105,
  203, 229
Crook, Henry Simon
  Charles 213, 329, 331
Crook-ites 213
Cumberland, *see* Carlisle
Curgenven, John 374

Dalby, William Byard 381,
  382
Damerham (67) xxiv,
  106–9
Daniell, George Warwick
  Bampfylde 220, 221
Darland, Revd Mr 53
Davenport, George 70

Davis, Thomas John 150,
  151
de St Croix, Henry C 105,
  203, 229
Deacon, John 148
Dean, West 129, 340-2
Deane, Henry 276
Denison, Edward xii, xvii,
  xxiii, xxv
Deptford, Surrey 125
Derry Hill (68) 109–10
Desprez, Philip S 10, 11
Deverill, Brixton 52, 253
Deverill, Hill 176-7
Deverill, Kingston 192-4
Deverill, Longbridge 105,
  106, 177, 192, 203-4,
  229, 230, 253
Deverill, Monkton 105,
  106, 203, 204, 229-30
Devizes (69, 70) 110–13,
  138, 191, 271, 294, 334;
  see also Southbroom
  Grammar School xix
Dilton (71) 113, 348, 349;
  see also Chapmanslade
Dilton Marsh (72) xx,
  113-15
Dingley, Samuel Richard
  34
Dinton (73) 80, 115–16,
  310, 316, 317
Dishon, Henry C 126, 127
Dixon, J H 69, 70
Dodson, N 69
Donhead (not specified) 29
**Donhead St Andrew
  (74)** 116-18, 120
Donhead St Mary (75)
  xvi, 118–20; *see also*
  Birdbush, Charlton,
  Coombs, Ludlow
Dorset xi, *see also*
  Charmouth,
  Farnham, Motcombe,
  Shaftesbury
Dowding, Benjamin
  Charles 293, 295, 334
Dowding, Townley
  William 218, 220
Dowding, William 188,
  189

Downton (76) xxii,
  120–1, 241, 266
Draycot Foliat (77)
  121-2
Du Boulay, Francis H 169,
  171
Dublin, Ireland xvi
Duke, Henry Hinxman
  113, 348, 349
Duncan, John 206, 207
Durham, Diocese of 323
Durnford (78) 123-4
Durrington (79) 124-5
Dyer, William xvii, 190,
  191

Earle, Alfred 230, 232
East Coulston (80) 125-7
East Grafton (81) 127-8,
  161; *see also* Wilton
  West Grafton 128
East Grimstead (82) xx,
  128-30, 340, 341, 342
East Harnham (83) 51,
  130-2
East Kennett (84) 132-3
East Knoyle (85) xxii, 31,
  133-5
  Knoyle House 252
East (Market) Lavington
  215-16
Easterton, in Market
  Lavington 216
Eastman, George 121, 122
Easton (Royal) (86) xvii,
  135-6, 353
Ebbesbourne Wake (87)
  xx, xxiii, 137-8, 146
Edgell, Edward Betenson
  59, 60
Edington (88) 138-9; *see
  also* Tinhead
Elers, Edward Henry 157
Eltham, Kent ? 89
Eliot, Edward 239, 241
Elliott, E B 176
Emra, John 266-7
Enford (89) 139-41
Erchfont (Urchfont) 334-5
Erlestoke 221, 222, 282
  Erlestoke Park 138
Essex, *see* Loughton

Estcourt, T Sotheron 294
Etchilhampton (90) 5, 141-2
Eton College, Bucks xii
Everett, Edward 210, 211
Everleigh (91) 142-3
Everleigh House 35
Ewart, William 32, 33, 293
Eyre, G 47

Faber, John Cooke 78, 79
Fairbairn, Adam 358
Fane, Arthur 42, 287
Farley (92) xxvi, 2, 3, 143–5, 256, 257, 258
Farnham Castle, Surrey 133, 251, 302
Farnham (Tollard Farnham), Dorset 325, 326
Farthing, George Lax 15, 164, 165
Feltham, William 49, 175
Fennell, George Keith 140
Ffinch, Matthew Mortimer 118
Fiddington, in West Lavington 347
Fifield Bavant (93) xx, xxiii, 137, 145-7
Figheldean (94) xxvi, 147-8
Fisher, Cecil Edward 49
Fisher, William 261, 262
Fisherton Anger (95) 53, 148-50
Fisherton De La Mere (96) 150-1
Fishlake, John Roles 200, 201
Fittleton (97) 151-2
Fitzmaurice Henry Petty-, 4th Marquess of Lansdowne 26, 71
Fletcher, Henry Mordaunt 109. 110
Folkestone, Kent 142, 210
Folkestone, Jacob Pleydell-Bouverie, Viscount 74
Fonthill Bishop (98) 152-4
Fonthill Gifford (99)

154-5
Fonthill House 280
Ford, in Laverstock 197
Forss, Francis Stephen 197, 199, 361, 362
Fosbury (100) 70, 155-7
Fovant (101) 157-8, 160
Fowle, Edmund 8
Fowle, Fulwar William 6, 8, 11, 13
Fox, Sir Stephen 4
Fox-Strangways, – (Mrs) 258, 342
Foxham, in Bremhill 49, 50, 175
France, see Nice
Freeling, George Noel 370
Fritham, in Bramshaw 46, 47
Froxfield (102) 158-60
Froxfield College 186
Duchess of Somerset's Hospital 159-60
Fugglestone St Peter (103) 160-1
Fulbeck, Lincs 287
Fyfield 250, 251

Gale, John Henry 227, 228, 229
Garsdon 5, 141
Gawn, Douglas 371
Girdlestone, Francis Gurney 194
Girdlestone, Henry 194, 196
Glossop, George Goodwin Pownall 128, 130, 340, 342
Glossop, Henry 128, 130, 340
Gloucester, Dean of 148
Gloucester and Bristol, Diocese of xii, 5, 141, 371
Gloucestershire, see Barnsley, Cheltenham, Cirencester, Clifton
Goatacre, in Hilmarton 175, 178
Goddard, Francis 177, 179
Goddard, Horatio Nelson

91
Goode, William 359
Gore, Mr 33
Grafton, East 127-8, 161
Grafton, West, in East Grafton 128
Grant, Alexander 212, 213
Gray, William 331, 332
Great Bedwyn (104) 127, 161-3; see also Crofton
Great Chalfield (105) xx, 15, 164-5
Great Cheverell (106) 165-6
Great Wishford (107) 166-8; see also Grovely
Greenly, John Prosser 197
Griffith, Charles Arthur 28, 30
Griffith, Edward George 367, 368
Grimstead, East xx, 128-30, 340, 341, 342
Grimstead, West xxiv, 129, 258, 340, 342-3
Grosvenor, Richard, 2nd Marquis of Westminster 154, 279
Grove, Charles 242, 243
Grove, Charles Henry 30, 31, 279, 281
Grovely, in Barford St Martin and Great Wishford 20
Guernsey 205
Gurney, J H 359
Guthrie, John xvi, 70, 71

Hackleston (Haxton) 151
Ham (108) 168-9
Hamilton, Anthony xii
Hamilton, Isabel xiii
Hamilton, Walter Kerr xii-xiii, xvi, xvii, xix, xxi, xxiii, xxv, 133
Hammond, John William 93, 94
Hammond, Mr 30
Hampshire, see Alresford, Andover, Bramshaw, Fritham, Romsey, Sherfield English,

Winchester
Handley, Augustus Bernard
   148
Hardman, Charles L 198,
   361
Harnham, East 51, 130-2
Harnham, West 99, 183,
   184, 343-4
Harris, Charles Amyand
   49, 50, 174, 176
Harris, Henry 362, 364
Harrison, Michael 301, 302
Hastings, John David 298,
   308, 326, 327, 328
Haverford West, Pembs 271
Hawaii 213
Hawkins, John
   Cunningham Calland
   Bennett Popkin 264,
   265
Haxton (Hackleston) 151
Heathcote, Gilbert Vyvyan
   272, 273
Heaven, William Henry
   232
Heddington (109) xxiv-
   xxv, 169-71
Heneage, George H
   Walker 24, 206, 311
Herbert, George xx, 114
Herbert, George Robert
   Charles, Earl of
   Pembroke and
   Montgomery 34, 79,
   157, 160, 166, 201, 290,
   295, 345, 357, 378
Hereford 248
   Diocese 356
Hertfordshire, see
   Buntingford,
   Knebworth
Hewish (Huish) 186-8
Heytesbury (110) 171-3,
   194, 236, 248, 329
Heytesbury, William
   Henry Ashe a Court-
   Holmes, 2nd Baron 172
Heywood (111) 173-4
Highway (112) xx, 49,
   174-6
Hill Deverill (113) 176-7
Hill, Richard Humphrey

51, 52
Hill, Edward 202, 203
Hill, Walter 337
Hills, Thomas 133
Hilmarton (114) 177-9;
   see also Goatacre
Hilperton (115) 179-81
Hinckesman, R 246
Hindon (116) 181-2, 252
Hinton, Broad 55-7
Hinxman, Charles 21
Hinxman, John Newton
   123, 124
Hoare, Sir Henry Ainslie
   304
Hodgson, John Dryden
   161, 163
Holt (117) 15, 182-3, 292
Holywell, Flints 328
Homington (118) xxiii,
   51, 99, 183-5
Honey Street, in Alton
   Barnes 372
Hony, William Edward
   21, 22
Hook, Walter 111, 112
Hookey, George Stephen
   244, 245
Hornby, Charles Edward
   223
Horningsham (119) 177,
   185-6; see also Longleat
Horton, in Bishop's
   Cannings 33
Hough, George D'Urban
   John 355, 357
Houghton, H 359
Howman, George Ernest
   55, 355, 356
Huish (Hewish) (120)
   186-8
Hume, George 221, 223,
   281, 285
Hungerford, Berks 12, 55,
   81, 155
Hurdcott, in
   Winterbourne
   Dauntsey 366
Hutchinson, Francis
   Edmund xviii, xxiv,
   320, 322
Huthwaite, Thomas Walter

260
Hutton, Robert Rossiter
   335, 337
Hyde, Charles Frederick
   113, 115

Idmiston (121) 188-9; see
   also Porton
Imber (122) xvii-xviii,
   190-1
Indian Mission 13
Inman, Edward 381
Ireland, see Connaught,
   Dublin
Irish Church Missions 37,
   53, 103, 127, 154, 254,
   281, 291, 296, 328,
   340, 374
Isleworth, Middlesex 128,
   340
   Silver Hall 128

Jackson, John Edward xviii
Jacob, James John 185, 186
Jersey 55
Johnson, Joseph Holden
   xvi, 31, 32, 270, 279,
   319, 320
Jones, William Henry 44,
   46, 350, 351
Jupe, Charles xxii, 135, 225

Keble, John xii
Keevil (123) 64, 191-2
Kellaways 50
Kemp, Edward A Welch-
   121
Kennett, East 132-3
Kent, see Eltham,
   Folkestone
Kent, George Davies 307,
   308
King, Bryan 16, 18
King, Charles 305, 307
Kingsbury, Thomas Luck
   279
Kingston Deverill (124)
   192-4
Kinnaird, Arthur 155
Knebworth, Herts 67
Knight, John 171, 173, 194,
   329

Knook (125) 171, 172, 194

Knoyle, East xxii, 31, 133-5
Knoyle House 252
Knoyle, West 345-6

Lake, in Wilsford cum Lake 354
Lambert, Richard Umfraville 182, 183
Lambourn, Berks 6
Lancashire xvi
Lancashire Relief (Distress) Fund xxv, 13, 24, 33, 35, 43, 49, 52, 53, 60, 61, 68, 74, 79, 82, 103, 108, 113, 116, 154, 160, 192, 207, 220, 239, 248, 264, 276, 277, 284, 293, 296, 298, 302, 317, 331, 337, 354, 364, 378
Landford (126) 194–6
Langford, Little 201-3
Langford, Steeple 301-2
Lansdowne, Henry Petty-Fitzmaurice 4th Marquess 26, 71
family 109
Laud, William 55
Laverstock (127) 196–7; *see also* Ford
Lavington, Market (East) 215-16
Lavington, West (Bishop's) 346-8
Lawford, Charles 27, 28, 368, 369
Laxton, William 15, 16, 292, 293
Lear, Francis 34, 35
Lee, Harry xvii, 235, 236
Lichfield xii
Diocese 246
Limpley Stoke (128) 197–9, 361
Lincolnshire, *see* Fulbeck
Little Bedwyn (129) 159, 199-200
Little Cheverell (130) 200-1
Little Langford (131) 201-3

Littlecote, in Ramsbury 81
Littleton Pannell, in West Lavington 347
Littlewood, Samuel 138, 139
Llewellyn, Arthur J C 135, 136, 353
Llewellyn, David xvii, 135, 136, 353
Lloyd, E H 115, 316
Lockeridge, in Overton 251
Loder, Mr 355
London 80, 239, 359
Piccadilly 27, 368
London Jews Society 157
Long, Walter 179, 339
Longbridge Deverill (132) 105, 106, 177, 192, 203-4, 229, 230, 253
Longleat, in Horningsham 78, 103, 190, 192
Loughton, Essex xii, xiii
Lowther, Gorges Paulin 246, 248
Luard, Edward 370, 371
Ludgershall (133) 204-6
Ludlow, Henry Gaisford Gibbs 173
Ludwell, in Donhead St Mary 118, 119
Lyneham (134) 206–7; *see also* Clack

Macdonald, William Maurice 37, 71
M'Dowell, John Ramsay 149, 150
McNiven, Charles Maunoir 251-2
Maddington (135) 207-9, 248, 288, 289
Maddock, Philip Bainbrigge 298
Maiden Bradley (136) 177, 209-10
Malmesbury 5, 141
Deanery xii
Manchester Relief Fund 30, 196, 213
Manningford Abbots

(137) 210-11
Manningford Bohune, in Wilsford xv, 355, 356
Manningford Bruce (138) 212-13, 255
Manton, in Preshute 263
Marden (139) 213-15
Market (East) Lavington (140) 215-16; *see also* Easterton
Marlborough (141, 142) xxv, 1, 22, 65, 68, 81, 84, 90, 95, 97, 121, 127, 135, 142, 155, 158, 161, 168, 186, 199, 210, 212, 217–20, 225, 227, 243, 245, 248, 250, 251, 254, 262, 264, 278, 317, 339, 353, 375
Union Workhouse 132, 262
Marston 377
Marston, South 23
Martin (143) xxiii, 106, 107, 220-1
Martin, Edward B 2, 3, 4
Mason, Skinner Chart 334, 335
Mathews, John 132
Maton, L P 207
Maund, W 205
Mayo, J 37
Mead, Richard Gawler 171
Meade, Edward 359, 361
Medlicott, Joseph 259, 261, 377
Melksham (144) 221–3, 282, 285, 286
Union Workhouse 283
Mere (145) xxii, 135, 223-5, 305, 381
Messenger, J Farnham 2, 3, 144, 145, 256, 258
Methuen, Francis Paul 5
Methuen, Henry Hoare 141
Methuen, Thomas 142
Methuen, Thomas Anthony 5, 6, 141, 142
Meyrick, Edwin 22, 84, 85, 121
Michel Foundation 332

Middle Winterslow, in
    Winterslow 189
Middlesex, *see* Isleworth
Mildenhall (146) 225-6
Miles, Thomas 302, 304
Miller, J R C 44
Millner (Milner), Thomas
    Darnton 62, 63
Milston (147) 63, 226-7;
    see also Brigmerston
Milton Lilbourne (148)
    227-9; *see also* Clench
    Common
Monkton Deverill (149)
    105, 106, 203, 204,
    229-30
Monkton Farleigh (150)
    230-2
Montgomery, Earl of, *see*
    Pembroke, Earl of
Moore, Albert 348
Morant, Henry John 258,
    259, 342
Morgell, Crosbie 133
Morres, Arthur Philip 130,
    132
Morrice, William David
    105, 106, 203, 204, 229,
    230
Morrison, Alexander J W
    57, 59
Morrison, Alfred 280
Morse, Thomas D 129,
    258, 340, 342, 343
Motcombe, Dorset 154,
    279
Mullins, George 164

Nelson, Frances Elizabeth,
    Dowager Countess 194
Nether Stowey, Som xv,
    245
Netheravon (151) 232-3
Netherhampton 357, 358
Newman, John Henry xii
Newnton, North xxv-
    xxvi, 236-8
Newton Tony (152)
    xxiii, 233-5
Newton, South 68, 233,
    290-2
Newtown, in Tisbury 321

Nice, France xv, 351
Nomansland, in Bramshaw
    46, 47
Nonsuch, in Chittoe 87
Norfolk, *see* Colton St
    Andrew, Norwich
Norridge, in Upton
    Scudamore 333
North Bradley (153)
    xvii, xxii, 235-6, 267
North Newnton (154)
    xxv-xxvi, 236-8
North Tidworth (155)
    xx, 238-9
Norton Bavant (156)
    xxi, 239-41
Norwich, Norfolk 195
Nunton (157) 51, 120,
    241-2
Nutt, George 285, 287

Oare, in Wilcot 135, 187,
    353, 354
Oates, Titus 55
Odstock (158) 242-3
**Ogbourne St Andrew
    (159)** xxiv, 243-5; *see
    also* Rockley
**Ogbourne St George
    (160)** xv, 245-6
Olivier, Dacres 358
**Orcheston St George
    (161)** xxvi, 246-8
**Orcheston St Mary
    (162)** 248-9
Overton (163) 250-1;
    see also Alton Priors,
    Lockeridge
Owen, John 40, 41
Owen, William 106, 109,
    220
Oxford xv-xvi, 164
    All Souls College 18
    Bishop of 82
    Brasenose College 375
    Christ Church 75, 209,
        215, 284
    Corpus Christi College
        301, 307
    Diocese 55, 69
    Exeter College 21, 62
    Magdalen College 41,

115, 151, 316, 362
    Merton College 271
    New College 8, 28, 118
    Oriel College 88
    Pembroke College 94
    Queen's College 332
    St John's College 92, 370
    St Peter's-in-the-East xii
    Wadham College 246
Oxfordshire, *see* Blenheim
    Palace, Oxford

Pannel, John 205
Parkinson, Richard 300,
    301
Patagonian Mission 223
Patney (164) 251-2
Paulett, Lord Charles 99
Payne, Richard xxii, 73,
    120, 121, 241, 266
Peacock, Edward 267, 268
Pearse, Thomas 151, 152
Pearson, C B 67
Pearon, Thomas 215, 216
Peill, John Newton 233,
    235
Pelham, Henry, 3rd Earl of
    Chichester 106
Pembroke and
    Montgomery, George
    Robert Charles
    Herbert, Earl of xiii-
    xiv, 34, 79, 157, 160,
    166, 201, 290, 295, 345,
    357, 378
Penruddocke, Charles 102
Penruddocke, John
    Hungerford 290, 292
Penruddocke, T A 95
Penruddocke family 102
Perrott, Octavius George
    Dalhousie 217
Pertwood (165) xx, 252-4
Petty-Fitzmaurice Henry,
    4th Marquess of
    Lansdowne 26, 71
Pewsey (166) xv, xxii, 8,
    227, 254-6
    Union Workhouse 135
Phelps, Arthur Whitmarsh
    102, 103
Philipps, James Erasmus

335, 337, 339
Pigott, Wellesley Pole 157, 158, 160, 161
Pitton (167) xxvi, 2, 3, 143, 144, 145, 256–8
Plaitford (168) 258–9, 342
Plenderleath, W Charles 76, 77
Pleydell-Bouverie, Edward 200
Pleydell-Bouverie, Jacob, Viscount Folkestone 74
Pleydell-Bouverie, William, 3rd Earl of Radnor 200, 242, 254
Pollard, Henry Smith 99, 100, 183, 185
Pongas Mission 148, 163, 220
Pooke, William Henry 65, 191, 192
Poore, Charles Harwood 97, 99
Pope, Benjamin xv, 245
Popham, E W L 81
Popham, John Leybourne 81, 82
Popham, William 43, 44
Porter, John Leech 308, 310
Porter, William Carmichael 120
Porton, in Idmiston 188, 189
Potterne (169) 259-61
    Deanery 15, 43, 44, 60, 64, 75, 82, 110, 112, 125, 138, 139, 151, 164, 165, 179, 182, 190, 191, 197, 200, 213, 215, 221, 230, 232, 235, 251, 259, 261, 267, 271, 281, 282, 285, 292, 298, 300, 308, 326, 327, 329, 334, 339, 346, 350, 355, 359, 361, 377, 378
Poulshot (170) 261-2
Powell, George F S 311, 312
Powell, John 176, 177
Preshute (171) 262-4; see

also Clatford, Manton, Temple, Wick
Preston, George Henry 116
Purrier, Henry Thornton 293, 334
Purvis, Fortescue Richard 37, 38, 72, 73
Pyper, Richard 47, 49

Radcliffe, Alston William 236, 238
Radcliffe, Frederick Adolphus 226, 227
Radcliffe, William Coxe 154, 155
Radnor, William Pleydell-Bouverie, 3rd Earl of 200, 242, 254
Ram Alley, in Burbage 66
Ramsbury (172) 264–5; see also Axford, Littlecote
Ravenshaw, Thomas F T 254, 256
Raymond, William Francis xv, 355
Reading Hospitals, Berks 82
Redlynch (173) 266–7
Reece, William 252, 254
Renaud, William 276, 277
Rendall, Charles Edward 226, 318
Richards, George 86, 87
Richmond, William Alexander 87
Ridding, Charles Henry 268
Ridge, in Chilmark 80
Rigden, William 292
Ripley, Thomas Hyde 322, 374, 375
Ripon, Yorks 359
Road Hill (174) xxii, 267-8
Robinson, Henry Mowld 200
Roche Court, in Winterslow 258, 342
Rockley, in Ogbourne St Andrew 244, 263
Rollestone (175) xx,

268-70
Romsey, Hants 351
Rood Ashton, in West Ashton 179
Rowde (176) 270-1
Rowley, Richard 209, 210
Ruddle, Charles Snelling 124, 125
Rugby School, Warwickshire xii
Rushall (177) xv, xxi, xxiv, 271-3

St Croix, Henry C de 105, 203, 229
St Davids, Pembs xv
Salis, William Fane de 314, 315
Salisbury (178, 179, 180) xiii, xviii, xxi, 273-7
    Bishop's Palace 1, 52, 90, 313, 337
    Cathedral xiii, 80, 196, 262
    Dispensary 274
    Infirmary xxv, 21, 25, 55, 87, 152, 155, 191, 194, 206, 209, 221, 233, 249, 264, 288, 290, 338, 347, 352
    Theological College xiii
    Training College xxiii-xxiv
Salisbury, Bishop of xiv, 2, 25, 38, 49, 52, 65, 70, 76, 87, 90, 100, 143, 147, 174, 230, 232, 256, 259, 261, 273, 288, 313, 337, 346, 348, 364, 365
Salisbury, Dean and Chapter of 51, 109, 183, 276, 305, 381
Salusbury, C T 84
Samler, John Harman 13, 15, 313, 314
Samuels, Geoffrey 235
Sandy Lane, in Calne 88
Sarum Church Union Society 74
Savernake (181) 278-9
Savernake Forest 135, 161, 162, 278

Savernake Park 95
Sawyer, Duncombe
    Herbert 99, 184, 343,
    344
Schwabe, W H 165, 166,
    169
Scott, John James 62, 63
Sedgehill (182) xx, 31,
    279–81
Seend (183) 221, 222,
    281–2
Semington (184) 282–4,
    300
Semley (185) 120, 284–5
Serjeant, James Sanderson
    281, 282
Seymour, Edward
    Adolphus, 12ᵗʰ Duke of
    Somerset 176, 209
Seymour, Jane 252
Shaftesbury, Dorset 30, 279
Shalbourne 155
Shaw and Whitley (186)
    285–7
Shaw House 164
Sherfield English, Hants
    xv, 351
Sherrington (187) 287–8
Shoreham, Sussex 322
    New Shoreham
    Protestant Grammar
    School 322
Shrewton (188) 208, 209,
    288–90
Shripple, in Winterslow
    189
Skipper, John Benson 213,
    215
Sladen, Edward Henry
    Mainwaring 8, 10
Slatter, William 105, 203,
    229
Smart, Newton 2, 4, 144,
    145, 256, 258
Smelt, Henry 353, 354
Smith, Alfred Charles xviii,
    380, 381
Smith, William 23, 24
Soames, Charles 225, 226
Somerset 105, 176, 186,
    203, 229, 268; *see also*
    Bath, Nether Stowey,

Somerton, Taunton,
    Wells Cathedral
Somerset, Edward
    Adolphus Seymour,
    12ᵗʰ Duke of 176, 209
Somerton, Som 209
South Africa 104
South Marston 23
South Newton (189)
    68, 233, 290–2; *see also*
    Burdens Ball
    Wilton Union
    Workhouse 290, 291
South Wraxall (190) 15,
    292–3
Southbroom (191) 32,
    293–5
Southby, Anthony 62, 63
Southby, Ellen 64
Spirt Hill, in Bremhill 50
Spye Park, in Bromham
    87, 270
Stafford, James Charles 115,
    116, 316, 317
Stallard, George 127, 128
Stannmer (Stanmore) Park,
    Sussex 106
**Stanton St Bernard
    (192)** 295–6
Stanton, Thomas 65, 67
Stapleford (193) 297–8
Starky, John Bayntun 270
Staverton (194) 298–9,
    328
Steeple Ashton (195)
    282, 300–1
Steeple Langford (196)
    301–2
Stephens, John Otter 278,
    279
Stert 334, 335, 353
Stockton (197) 302–4
Stockton-on-Teme, Worcs
    xv, 355, 356
Stockwell, Joseph Samuel
    236, 378, 379
Stourton (198) 186,
    304–5
Stourhead 304
Stowell, Hugh 65
Stowell Lodge, in Wilcot
    353

Stowey, Nether, Som xv,
    245
Strangways, *see* Fox-
    Strangways
**Stratford sub Castle
    (199)** 305–7
Stratford Tony (200)
    307–8
Strickland, Emmanuel
    52, 53
Studley (201) xx, 308–10
Sturton, Jacob 264
Surrey, *see* Deptford,
    Farnham Castle, West
    Brixton
Sussex, *see* Brighton,
    Shoreham, Stanmer
    Park
Sutton Mandeville (202)
    xxi, 310–11
Sutton Veny (203) 311–12
Swallowcliffe (204) xx,
    13, 14, 312–14
Swayne, Robert George
    273, 274
Swayne, William John xvi,
    351, 352
Swindon 84

Tait, Thomas Henry 179,
    181
Tandy, John Mortimer xix,
    64, 191
Tatum, William Wyndham
    274, 276
Taunton, Som xii
Taylor, Thomas 38, 40
Taylor, Simon Watson, 138
Taylor, Henry Walter 270,
    271
Teale, William Henry 110,
    112, 113
**Teffont Evias (Ewyas)
    (205)** xxvi, 314–16
Teffont Magna (206) 115,
    116, 316–17
Temple, in Preshute 263
Terence (Latin author) 118
Theobald's Green, in
    Blackland 38
Thistlewaite, Alexander
    102

Thomas, Edward Thomas
Watson 221
Thomson, John 55, 57
Thorowgood, M A 121
Thoulston, in Upton
Scudamore 333
Thynne, John Alexander,
4th Marquess of Bath
78, 103, 105, 145, 146,
185, 190, 192,193, 203,
229
Thynne, Thomas, Viscount
Weymouth 185
Tidcombe (207) 155,
317-19
Tidworth, North xx, 238-9
Tilshead (208) xvi, 270,
319-20
Tinhead, in Edington 139
Tisbury (209) xviii,
xix, xxiv, 102, 320-2;
see also Chicksgrove,
Newtown, Wardour
**Tockenham (Week)
(210)** 207, 322-4, 374
Tockenham Wick 374
Tollard Farnham, Dorset
325, 326
Tollard Royal (211)
324-6
Tomlinson, William R
xv, 351
Tooke, Thomas Hammond
274
Tower, Charles 79, 81
Tower, – (Mrs) 80
Tower, T G 40
Townsend, Charles Henry
223, 225, 381
Trotman, Edward Fiennes
67, 68
Trowbridge (212, 213)
xxi, xxii, 179, 298,
299, 308, 309, 326-9;
see also Studley
Turner, Charles 182
Turner, James Francis 238,
239
Tytherington (214) 171,
172, 312, 329
Tytherton, West 50

Ugford, in Burcombe 67,
68, 290
Upavon (215) 213, 329-31
Upton Lovell (216) xxi,
331-2
**Upton Scudamore
(217)** 332-4; *see also*
Norridge, Thoulston
Urchfont (218) 334-5

Vicary, Edward John 26, 27
Villiers, George William
Frederick, 4th Earl of
Clarendon 374
Vincent, E 270

Wales, *see* Haverford West,
Holywell, St David's
Walker, Richard Zouche
41, 43
Walker, Robert Graves
181, 182
Walker, William Dewdney
272, 273
Walrond, Lloyd Baker 275
Walsh, Digby 326, 327
Walsh, John Henry Arnold
35, 37
Warburton, William 38
Ward, George Thompson
295, 296
Ward, John Henry Kirwan
320
Ward, Samuel Broomhead
xxvi, 314, 316
Wardale, John 248, 249
Wardour, in Tisbury 13,
118, 320
Warminster (219, 220)
xxi, xxiv, 36, 176, 190,
335-9; *see also* Boreham
Boreham Road 338
Warren, Edward B 217, 218
Warren, William 327
Warwickshire, *see* Coombe
Abbey, Rugby School
Waterfall, George Howard
29
Waters, Edward 306
Waugh, James Hay 103,
104, 105

Waugh, – (Mrs) 104
Welch-Kemp, Edward A
121
Wells Cathedral, Som 193
Wells, Bath and, Diocese
245
West Ashton (221) 300,
328, 339-40; *see also*
Rood Ashton
West Brixton, Surrey 121
West Dean (222) 129,
340-2
West Grafton, in East
Grafton 128
West Grimstead (223)
xxiv, 129, 258, 340,
342-3
West Harnham (224) 99,
183, 184, 343-4
West Knoyle (225) 345-6
**West (Bishop's)
Lavington (226)** 346-
8; *see also* Fiddington,
Littleton Pannell
West Tytherton 50
West, P Cornelius 323, 324
Westbury (227) xxii, 47,
113, 348-9
Westminster, Richard
Grosvenor, 2nd Marquis
of 154, 279
Westwood (228) 44,
350-1
Wethered, Florence
Thomas 337
Weymouth, Thomas
Thynne, Viscount 185
Whaddon, in Alderbury 4
Whaddon, near Hilperton
179, 180
Whelpton, Henry Robert
273
Whiteparish (229) xv,
xvi, 351-2; *see also*
Broxmore Park
Whitley, Shaw and (186)
285-7
Wick, in Preshute 263
Wight, Isle of 164
Wightwick, Henry 94, 95
Wilcot (230) 353-4; *see
also* Oare, Stowell

Lodge

Wild, R L 381

Wilkinson, John 60, 62

Wilkinson, Matthew 346, 348

Williams, David 8

Williams, Sir Erasmus xv, 271

Williams, Henry 250

Williams, Rowland xvi-xvii, 10, 40, 53, 55

Wilsford (232) xv, 355-7

Wilsford cum Lake (231) 354-5, 373; *see also* Lake

Wilson, George Leroux 53

Wilton (233) xvii, 20, 161, 291, 357-9, 361

Deanery 67, 73, 120, 148, 160, 241, 266, 273, 274, 276, 290, 305, 357, 358, 361

Wilton House 79, 157, 166, 201, 295, 358

Wilton, in East Grafton 128

Wilton Union Workhouse, in South Newton 291

Wiltshire Archaeological & Natural History Society xviii

Winchester, Hants xvii

College 73, 120, 235, 266, 267

Training College xxiii

Winchester, Bishop of xiv, 69, 133, 152, 168, 251, 302

Winchester, Dean and

Chapter of 97, 124, 191

Winchester, Diocese, 269, 351

Windsor, Berks 317

Dean and Canons (Chapter) xv, 11, 12, 158, 243, 245, 297, 317, 334

Wingfield (Winkfield) (234) 359-61

Winsley (235) 197, 198, 361-2

Winterbourne Bassett (236) xxiii, 362-4

Winterbourne Dauntsey (237) 364-5, 366, 368; *see also* Hurdcott

Winterbourne Earls (238) 364, 365-6, 367, 368

Winterbourne Gunner (239) 366-8

Winterbourne Monkton 17

Winterbourne Stoke (240) xvi, xx, 27, 368-9

Winterslow (241) 189, 258, 342, 370-1; *see also* Roche Court, Shripple Middle Winterslow 189

Wishford, Great 166-8

Woodborough (242) 25, 371-2

Woodford (243) 354, 372-4

Woodsend, in Aldbourne 1

Wootton Bassett (244) 91, 323, 374-5

Wootton Rivers (245) 375-7

Worcestershire, *see* Stockton-on-Teme

Worthington, John 199, 200

Worton (246) 377-8

Wraxall, South 15, 292-3

Wroughton, George W 353

Wyatt, Thomas Henry 290

Wyld, Calcraft Neeld 81

Wyld, William Thomas 371, 372

Wylye (247) 236, 378-9

Deanery 27, 35, 41, 47, 52, 86, 92, 94, 103, 105, 113, 150, 166, 171, 173, 176, 185, 192, 194, 201, 203, 207, 209, 223, 229, 239, 246, 248, 252, 268, 287, 288, 297, 301, 302, 304, 311, 319, 329, 331, 332, 335, 337, 348, 368, 378, 381

Wyndham, John, 310, 311

Wyndham, John Henry Campbell 274

Wyndham, William, 310, 311

Yarmouth, Isle of Wight 164

Yatesbury (248) xviii, 380

Yorkshire, *see* Ripon

Zealand, New 40

Zeals Green (249) 381-2

WILTSHIRE RECORD SOCIETY
(AS AT NOVEMBER 2023)

President: DR NEGLEY HARTE
Honorary Treasurer: IAN HICKS
Honorary Secretary: MISS HELEN TAYLOR
General Editor: DR TOM PLANT

Committee:
DR J. CHANDLER
DR J. HARE
S.D. HOBBS
MS A. MCCONNELL
MRS S. THOMSON
S. RAYMOND
I. SLOCOMBE

Honorary Independent Examiner: MISS S BROWN

PRIVATE MEMBERS

Note that because of recent legislation the Society no longer publishes members' addresses in its volumes, as it had done since 1953.

Honorary Members
OGBURN, SENR JUDGE R W
SHARMAN-CRAWFORD, MR T

ADAMS, MS S
ARKELL, MR R
BAINBRIDGE, DR V
BATHE, MR G,
BAYLIFFE, MR B G
BENNETT, DR N
BERRETT, MR A M
BERRY, MR C
BLAKE, MR P A
BRAND, DR P A
BROCK, MRS C
BROWN, MR D A
BROWN, MR G R
BROWNING, MR E
BRYSON, DR A
CAWTHORNE, MRS N
CHANDLER, DR J H
CLARK, MR G A
COOPER, MR S
COUZENS, MR T

CRAVEN, DR A
CROOK, MR P H
CROUCH, MR J W
CROWLEY, DR D A
CUNNINGTON, MS J
DAKERS, PROF C
D'ARCY, MR J N
DODD, MR D
EDE, DR M E
ELLIOTT, DR J
ENGLISH, MS K
FORREST, DR M
GAISFORD, MR J
GALE, MRS J
GHEY, MR J G
GODDARD, MR R G H
GRIFFIN, DR C
GRIST, MR M
HARE, DR J N
HARTE, DR N
HEATON, MR R J
HELMHOLZ, PROF R W
HENLY, MR C
HERRON, MRS Pamela M

HICKMAN, MR M R
HICKS, MR I
HICKS, PROF M A
HILLMAN, MR R B
HOBBS, MR S
HOWELLS, DR Jane
INGRAM, DR M J
JOHNSTON, MRS J M
KENT, MR T A
KITE, MR P J
KNEEBONE, MR W J R
KNOWLES, MRS V A
LANSDOWNE, MARQUIS OF
LAWES, MRS G
MARSHMAN, MR M J
MOLES, MRS M I
MORLAND, MRS N
NAPPER, MR L R
NEWBURY, MR C COLES
NEWMAN, MRS R
NICOLSON, MR A
NOKES, MR P M A
OGBOURNE, MR J M V
OGBURN, MR D A

PATIENCE, MR D C
PERRY, MR W A
PLANT, DR T
POWELL, MRS N
PRICE, MR A J R
RAILTON, MS A
RAYMOND, MR S
ROBERTS, MS M
ROGERS, MR K H
SHELDRAKE, MR B

SHEWRING, MR P
SKINNER, MS C
SLOCOMBE, MR I
SMITH, MR P J
SPAETH, DR D A
STONE, MR M J
SUTER, MRS C
SUTTON, MR A E
TATTON-BROWN, MR T
TAYLOR, MISS H

THOMSON, MRS S M
WADSWORTH, MRS S
WILLIAMSON, MR B
WILTSHIRE, MR J
WILTSHIRE, MRS P E
WOODCOCK, LADY L
WOODFORD, MR A
WOODWARD, MR A S,
YOUNGER, MR C

UNITED KINGDOM INSTITUTIONS

Aberystwyth
  National Library of
    Wales
  University College of
    Wales
Birmingham. University
  Library
Bristol
  University of Bristol
    Library
Cambridge. University
  Library
Cheltenham. Bristol
  and Gloucestershire
  Archaeological Society
Chippenham
  Museum & Heritage
    Centre
  Wiltshire and Swindon
    History Centre
Coventry. University of
  Warwick Library
Devizes
  Wiltshire Archaeological
    & Natural History
    Society
  Wiltshire Family History
    Society

Durham. University
  Library
Edinburgh
  National Library of
    Scotland
  University Library
Exeter. University Library
Glasgow. University
  Library
Liverpool. University
  Library
London
  British Library
  College of Arms
  Guildhall Library
  Inner Temple Library
  Institute of Historical
    Research
  London Library
  The National Archives
  Royal Historical Society
  Society of Antiquaries
  Society of Genealogists
Manchester. John Rylands
  Library
Norwich. University of
  East Anglia Library

Nottingham. University
  Library
Oxford
  Bodleian Library
  Exeter College Library
St Andrews. University
  Library
Salisbury
  Bourne Valley Historical
    Society
  Cathedral Library
  Salisbury and South
    Wilts Museum
Swansea. University
  College Library
Swindon
  Historic England
  Swindon Borough
    Council
Taunton. Somerset
  Archaeological and
    Natural History
    Society
Wetherby. British Library
  Document Supply
  Centre
York. University Library

INSTITUTIONS OVERSEAS

AUSTRALIA
Adelaide. University
  Library
Crawley. Reid Library,
  University of Western
  Australia

CANADA
Toronto, Ont

University of Toronto
  Library
Victoria, B.C. McPherson
  Library, University of
  Victoria

UNITED STATES OF
AMERICA
Ann Arbor, Mich. Hatcher

Library, University of
  Michigan
Athens, Ga. University of
  Georgia Libraries
Atlanta, Ga. The Robert
  W Woodruff Library,
  Emory University
Bloomington, Ind. Indiana
  University Library

Boston, Mass. New England Historic and Genealogical Society

Boulder, Colo. University of Colorado Library

Cambridge, Mass. Harvard College Library

Chicago
Newberry Library
University of Chicago Library

Davis, Calif. University Library

East Lansing, Mich.

Michigan State University Library

Fort Wayne, Ind. Allen County Public Library

Houston, Texas. M.D. Anderson Library, University of Houston

Ithaca, NY. Cornell University Library

Los Angeles
Young Research Library, University of California

Minneapolis, Minn.

Wilson Library, University of Minnesota

San Marino, Calif. Henry E. Huntington Library

Urbana, Ill. University of Illinois Library

Washington. The Folger Shakespeare Library

Winston-Salem, N.C. Z.Smith Reynolds Library, Wake Forest University

LIST OF PUBLICATIONS

The Wiltshire Record Society was founded in 1937, as the Records Branch of the Wiltshire Archaeological and Natural History Society, to promote the publication of the documentary sources for the history of Wiltshire. The annual subscription is £15 for private and institutional members. In return, a member receives a volume each year. Prospective members should apply to the Hon. Secretary, c/o Wiltshire and Swindon History Centre, Cocklebury Road, Chippenham SN15 3QN. Many more members are needed.

The following volumes have been published. Price to members £15, and to non-members £20, postage extra. Most volumes up to 51 are still available from the Wiltshire and Swindon History Centre, Cocklebury Road, Chippenham SN15 3QN. Volumes 52-71 are available from Hobnob Press, c/o 8 Lock Warehouse, Severn Road, Gloucester GL1 2GA. Volumes 1-55 are available online, at www.wiltshirerecordsociety.org.uk.

1. *Abstracts of feet of fines relating to Wiltshire for the reigns of Edward I and Edward II*, ed. R.B. Pugh, 1939
2. *Accounts of the parliamentary garrisons of Great Chalfield and Malmesbury, 1645–1646*, ed. J.H.P. Pafford, 1940
3. *Calendar of Antrobus deeds before 1625*, ed. R.B. Pugh, 1947
4. *Wiltshire county records: minutes of proceedings in sessions, 1563 and 1574 to 1592*, ed. H.C. Johnson, 1949
5. *List of Wiltshire boroughs records earlier in date than 1836*, ed. M.G. Rathbone, 1951
6. *The Trowbridge woollen industry as illustrated by the stock books of John and Thomas Clark, 1804–1824*, ed. R.P. Beckinsale, 1951
7. *Guild stewards' book of the borough of Calne, 1561–1688*, ed. A.W. Mabbs, 1953
8. *Andrews' and Dury's map of Wiltshire, 1773: a reduced facsimile*, ed. Elizabeth Crittall, 1952
9. *Surveys of the manors of Philip, earl of Pembroke and Montgomery, 1631–2*, ed. E. Kerridge, 1953
10. *Two sixteenth century taxations lists, 1545 and 1576*, ed. G.D. Ramsay, 1954
11. *Wiltshire quarter sessions and assizes, 1736*, ed. J.P.M. Fowle, 1955
12. *Collectanea*, ed. N.J. Williams, 1956
13. *Progress notes of Warden Woodward for the Wiltshire estates of New College, Oxford, 1659–1675*, ed. R.L. Rickard, 1957
14. *Accounts and surveys of the Wiltshire lands of Adam de Stratton*, ed. M.W. Farr, 1959
15. *Tradesmen in early-Stuart Wiltshire: a miscellany*, ed. N.J. Williams, 1960
16. *Crown pleas of the Wiltshire eyre, 1249*, ed. C.A.F. Meekings, 1961
17. *Wiltshire apprentices and their masters, 1710–1760*, ed. Christabel Dale, 1961
18. *Hemingby's register*, ed. Helena M. Chew, 1963
19. *Documents illustrating the Wiltshire textile trades in the eighteenth century*, ed. Julia de L. Mann, 1964
20. *The diary of Thomas Naish*, ed. Doreen Slatter, 1965
21–2. *The rolls of Highworth hundred, 1275–1287*, 2 parts, ed. Brenda Farr, 1966, 1968
23. *The earl of Hertford's lieutenancy papers, 1603–1612*, ed. W.P.D. Murphy, 1969
24. *Court rolls of the Wiltshire manors of Adam de Stratton*, ed. R.B. Pugh, 1970
25. *Abstracts of Wiltshire inclosure awards and agreements*, ed. R.E. Sandell, 1971
26. *Civil pleas of the Wiltshire eyre, 1249*, ed. M.T. Clanchy, 1971
27. *Wiltshire returns to the bishop's visitation queries, 1783*, ed. Mary Ransome, 1972
28. *Wiltshire extents for debts, Edward I – Elizabeth I*, ed. Angela Conyers, 1973
29. *Abstracts of feet of fines relating to Wiltshire for the reign of Edward III*, ed. C.R. Elrington, 1974

30. *Abstracts of Wiltshire tithe apportionments*, ed. R.E. Sandell, 1975
31. *Poverty in early-Stuart Salisbury*, ed. Paul Slack, 1975
32. *The subscription book of Bishops Tounson and Davenant, 1620–40*, ed. B. Williams, 1977
33. *Wiltshire gaol delivery and trailbaston trials, 1275–1306*, ed. R.B. Pugh, 1978
34. *Lacock abbey charters*, ed. K.H. Rogers, 1979
35. *The cartulary of Bradenstoke priory*, ed. Vera C.M. London, 1979
36. *Wiltshire coroners' bills, 1752–1796*, ed. R.F. Hunnisett, 1981
37. *The justicing notebook of William Hunt, 1744–1749*, ed. Elizabeth Crittall, 1982
38. *Two Elizabethan women: correspondence of Joan and Maria Thynne, 1575–1611*, ed. Alison D. Wall, 1983
39. *The register of John Chandler, dean of Salisbury, 1404–17*, ed. T.C.B. Timmins, 1984
40. *Wiltshire dissenters' meeting house certificates and registrations, 1689–1852*, ed. J.H. Chandler, 1985
41. *Abstracts of feet of fines relating to Wiltshire, 1377–1509*, ed. J.L. Kirby, 1986
42. *The Edington cartulary*, ed. Janet H. Stevenson, 1987
43. *The commonplace book of Sir Edward Bayntun of Bromham*, ed. Jane Freeman, 1988
44. *The diaries of Jeffery Whitaker, schoolmaster of Bratton, 1739–1741*, ed. Marjorie Reeves and Jean Morrison, 1989
45. *The Wiltshire tax list of 1332*, ed. D.A. Crowley, 1989
46. *Calendar of Bradford-on-Avon settlement examinations and removal orders, 1725–98*, ed. Phyllis Hembry, 1990
47. *Early trade directories of Wiltshire*, ed. K.H. Rogers and indexed by J.H. Chandler, 1992
48. *Star chamber suits of John and Thomas Warneford*, ed. F.E. Warneford, 1993
49. *The Hungerford Cartulary: a calendar of the earl of Radnor's cartulary of the Hungerford family*, ed. J.L. Kirby, 1994
50. *The Letters of John Peniston, Salisbury architect, Catholic, and Yeomanry Officer, 1823–1830*, ed. M. Cowan, 1996
51. *The Apprentice Registers of the Wiltshire Society, 1817– 1922*, ed. H. R. Henly, 1997
52. *Printed Maps of Wiltshire 1787–1844: a selection of topographical, road and canal maps in facsimile*, ed. John Chandler, 1998
53. *Monumental Inscriptions of Wiltshire: an edition, in facsimile, of Monumental Inscriptions in the County of Wilton, by Sir Thomas Phillipps*, ed. Peter Sherlock, 2000
54. *The First General Entry Book of the City of Salisbury, 1387–1452*, ed. David R. Carr, 2001
55. *Devizes Division income tax assessments, 1842–1860*, ed. Robert Colley, 2002
56. *Wiltshire Glebe Terriers, 1588–1827*, ed. Steven Hobbs, 2003
57. *Wiltshire Farming in the Seventeenth Century*, ed. Joseph Bettey, 2005
58. *Early Motor Vehicle Registration in Wiltshire, 1903–1914*, ed. Ian Hicks, 2006
59. *Marlborough Probate Inventories, 1591–1775*, ed. Lorelei Williams and Sally Thomson, 2007
60. *The Hungerford Cartulary, part 2: a calendar of the Hobhouse cartulary of the Hungerford family*, ed. J.L. Kirby, 2007
61. *The Court Records of Brinkworth and Charlton*, ed. Douglas Crowley, 2009
62. *The Diary of William Henry Tucker, 1825–1850*, ed. Helen Rogers, 2009
63. *Gleanings from Wiltshire Parish Registers*, ed. Steven Hobbs, 2010
64. *William Small's Cherished Memories and Associations*, ed. Jane Howells and Ruth Newman, 2011
65. *Crown Pleas of the Wiltshire Eyre, 1268,* ed. Brenda Farr and Christopher Elrington, rev. Henry Summerson, 2012
66. *The Minute Books of Froxfield Almshouse, 1714–1866*, ed. Douglas Crowley, 2013

67. *Wiltshire Quarter Sessions Order Book, 1642–1654,* ed. Ivor Slocombe, 2014

68. *The Register of John Blyth, Bishop of Salisbury, 1493–1499,* ed. David Wright, 2015

69 *The Churchwardens' Accounts of St Mary's, Devizes, 1633–1689,* ed. Alex Craven, 2016

70 *The Account Books and Papers of Everard and Ann Arundell of Ashcombe and Salisbury, 1745–1798,* ed. Barry Williamson, 2017

71 *Letters of Henry Hoare of Stourhead, 1760–81,* ed. Dudley Dodd, 2018

72 *Braydon Forest and the Forest Law,* ed. Douglas Crowley, 2019

73 *The Parish Registers of Thomas Crockford, 1561–1633* ed. John Chandler, 2020

74 *The Farming Diaries of Thomas Pinniger, 1813-1847,* ed. Alan Wadsworth, 2021

75 *Salisbury Domesday Books, 1317–1413,* ed. John Chandler and Douglas Crowley, 2022

Further details about the Society, its activities and publications, will be found on its website, www.wiltshirerecordsociety.org.uk.

1864 VISITATION RETURN QUESTIONS

1. What is the name of your parish, and is the benefice a rectory, vicarage or perpetual curacy?
2. State the name and address of the patron or patrons.
3. What is the amount of the population of your parish?
4. What is the name of the incumbent, and the date of his institution and induction.
5. Has he during the last year been resident the time prescribed by law, viz, 275 days?
6. Has he resided in the glebe-house, or where else?
7. If not resident, who is the curate? And is he resident?
8. Does the incumbent possess any other benefice? If so, state in what Diocese or Dioceses?
9. If resident, has he any assistant curate.
10. If he has an assistant curate, when was he licensed?
11. What is his name, is he a priest or deacon.
12. Does the assistant curate perform any other duty as incumbent, curate, lecturer, chaplain, master, or assistant in any school; and where?
13. Does the benefice comprise more than one church or chapel?
14. If so, enumerate them, and give the date of consecration, and the name by which each was called when it was dedicated to God
15. Is your church or chapel in good repair, and duly provided with all things necessary for the decent performance of divine service according to law?
16. Is your churchyard well fenced and well kept?
17. Do your churchwardens regularly discharge their duties?
18. Have any alterations been made in the church or chancel, either as to the fabric or in the manner of fitting up, since my last visitation, and if so, under what authority? Specify what they are.
19. Are baptisms, marriages and burials performed in the chapels (if any) respectively?
20. What is the distance of each chapel from the mother church?
21. What are the sources and amount of the endowments of the benefice?
22. If the benefice is composed of two or more parishes or chapelries, state how much of the annual value, whether from glebe, tithe, rent charge or otherwise arises from each.
23. Is there more than one glebe house of residence on the benefice? If so, where are they respectively situated?
24. What is the Sunday duty in the church and chapels (if any) respectively? Mention the hours appointed for the different services, and whether sermons are preached or lectures given at those services.
25. Do you always say the whole service without omissions?
26. Do you ever catechise publicly in your church? If so, be good enough to state shortly what method you pursue, and what your opinion is as to its advantage.
27. Do you when at home and not otherwise reasonably hindered, say daily the

Morning and Evening Prayers in the parish church or chapel?

28. On what days of the year besides Sundays is there service in the church and chapels (if any) respectively. And what average number of persons attend on those days?

29. Is the Holy Communion administered in your Church and Chapels (if any) on Christmas Day, Easter Day, Ascension Day, Whit Sunday, the Feast of Trinity?

30. On what other days is the Holy Communion administered?

31. Do you keep a list of communicants?

32. What is the number of communicants in your parish?

33. How many of these have not to the best of your knowledge communicated in your church or chapel (if any) during the year ending 31ˢᵗ December 1863?

34. What is the average number of communicants at the great festivals?

35. What is the average number at other seasons?

36. For what number of worshippers at one time is there accommodation in your church or chapels (if any) respectively?

37. What is the average number of your congregation; is it increasing or decreasing?

38. Is there any want of further church accommodation in your parish? If so, in what manner do you think it desirable that this want should be supplied?

39. What number have been baptised, married, buried in the past year?

40. What number of persons have been confirmed in your parish in the years 1861, 1862, 1863.

41. Do you make public for the information of your parishioners any statement of the offerings and collections in your church and chapels (if any)?

42. What has been the amount of the sacramental alms?

43. Is any regular account kept of them in a book set apart for that purpose?

44. What dissenting places of worship are there, and what is the probable number of dissenters in your parish or chapelry, and of what denomination?

45. Is there a daily school in your parish?

46. Have you been able to take advantage of the aid offered by the Committee of Council on Education for the improvement of your school?

47. At what age do the children in your parish ordinarily cease to attend the daily school?

48. Are you able to retain them in your Sunday school after they have ceased to attend the daily school?

49. Have you adopted any other mode of retaining them under instruction by adult or evening schools? And if so, what success have you found to attend such schools?

50. Have you transmitted copies of the parish register for the last year ending the 31st December to the office of the Registrar of the Diocese, at Salisbury?

51. State the different objects for which collections have been made at your church and chapels (if any) during the last year and the sums collected.

52. Can you mention anything which specially impedes your own ministry or the welfare of the church around you? Can you also suggest any remedies?

Signature.

www.ingramcontent.com/pod-product-compliance
Lightning Source LLC
Chambersburg PA
CBHW060755100426
42813CB00004B/823